PSYCHIATRY AND THE LEGACIES OF EUGENICS

PSYCHIATRY AND THE LEGACIES OF EUGENICS

HISTORICAL STUDIES OF ALBERTA AND BEYOND

EDITED BY FRANK W. STAHNISCH AND ERNA KURBEGOVIĆ

AU PRESS

Published by AU Press, Athabasca University
1200, 10011 – 109 Street, Edmonton, AB T5J 3S8

https://doi.org/10.15215/aupress/9781771992657.01

Cover design by Marvin Harder
Interior design by Sergiy Kozakov
Printed and bound in Canada

Library and Archives Canada Cataloguing in Publication
Title: Psychiatry and the legacies of eugenics : historical studies of Alberta and beyond / edited by Frank W. Stahnisch and Erna Kurbegović.
Names: Stahnisch, Frank, editor. | Kurbegović, Erna, 1984- editor.
Description: Includes bibliographical references and index.
Identifiers: Canadiana (print) 20200213202 | Canadiana (ebook) 20200213210
ISBN 9781771992657 (softcover) | ISBN 9781771992664 (pdf)
ISBN 9781771992671 (epub) | ISBN 9781771992688 (Kindle)
Subjects: LCSH: Eugenics—History—20th century—Case studies. | LCSH: Eugenics—Canada, Western—History—20th century—Case studies. | LCSH: Eugenics—History—20th century. | LCSH: Eugenics—Canada, Western—History—20th century. | LCSH: Psychiatry—History—20th century. | LCSH: Psychiatry—Canada, Western—History—20th century. | LCGFT: Case studies.
Classification: LCC HQ751 .P79 2020 | DDC 363.9/2—dc23

This book has been published with the help of a grant from the Federation for the Humanities and Social Sciences, through the Awards to Scholarly Publications Program, using funds provided by the Social Sciences and Humanities Research Council of Canada.

We acknowledge the financial support of the Government of Canada through the Canada Book Fund (CBF) for our publishing activities and the assistance provided by the Government of Alberta through the Alberta Media Fund.

Canada Alberta Government

"Eugenics Society Exhibit," 1930, Photographs and Plans of Eugenics Society Exhibits, Eugenics Society Archive, London, SAEUG/G/30/40, Wellcome Library. Photograph courtesy of Wellcome Library.

CONTENTS

FOREWORD

Guel A. Russell

At the International Summit on Human Gene Editing in Washington, DC, held December 1–3, 2015, scientists advocated caution, declaring that the clinical implementation of gene editing would be "irresponsible" at present. They recommended proceeding with thoughtfulness and care "to assess the many scientific, ethical, and social issues associated with human gene editing" until there would be a broad societal consensus about the appropriateness of any proposed change.[1] This was not surprising with such formidable editing tools of "unprecedented ease and precision" as CRISPR-Cas9 (Clustered Regularly Interspaced Short Palindromic Repeats), which could alter human heredity and affect the germ line. Of particular note was a reference to being "part of a historical process that dates from Darwin and Mendel's work in the 19th century" and the question that motivated the meeting: "How, if at all, do we as a society want to use this capability?"[2]

That historical process gave rise to "eugenics"—the devastating social movement of the first half of the twentieth century that emerged in the wake of the rediscovery in 1905 of Bohemian monk and naturalist Gregor Mendel's (1822–84) genetic discoveries.[3] How society manipulated that knowledge to create a pseudo-science sanctioned by medicine and the law embodies cautionary lessons. The present volume, *Psychiatry and the Legacies of Eugenics: Historical Studies of Alberta and Beyond*, provides a critical analysis of the consequences that resulted when genetics, psychiatry, and deeply embedded societal biases and institutional self-interests converged. This approach contributes to a greater understanding of not only the historical complexity of the mechanisms that underlie eugenics but also the contemporary social issues that may arise from genetics. In the narrative process, the questions raised in the individual chapters and the continuous threads brought out in the introductory overview and conclusions by the editors are most timely. Eugenics is not a closed book of past history. It casts a long shadow over both science and society in the Western world and, in fact, also globally.

Historically, the eugenics movement found in the emerging science of classical Mendelian genetics supportive evidence for the utopian theory of the Victorian polymath Francis Galton (1822–1911) of improving society through "selective breeding" of "hereditary genius."[4] In the United States, however, under the influence of Charles Davenport (1866–1944), the first director of the Eugenics Record Office at Cold Spring Harbor, New York, positive eugenics became negative "dysgenics." The emphasis shifted to prevention of the breeding of those perceived as genetically "defective." These were not only the inmates of institutions and the physically disabled, but the socially and mentally inadequate, as well as the economically disadvantaged, consisting largely of women and children. Categorized by psychologists and psychiatrists as "unfit" or "degenerate," ranked on the basis of intelligence quotient (IQ) tests,[5] and diagnosed by neurologists and psychiatrists as "feeble-minded," they were perceived as a parasitic burden on society and seen to pose a threat to the germ plasm (gene pool) as a whole.[6] With heredity as the root cause, systematic control of reproduction through compulsory sterilization became a convenient solution to economic, social, moral, and behavioural problems, yet ignored their complexity.

An important aim of the studies assembled in this book is to draw attention to the key role of psychiatrists and clinical psychologists in the interests of spurious societal and institutional benefit. Historically, they provided the ranking, the labels, and the justification to influence the law as to who would be segregated in institutions, involuntarily sterilized, or prevented entry, in the case of immigrants from eastern and southern Europe. Although the primary focus here is on the application of eugenic ideals to the mental health systems and psychiatric institutions in western Canada, the treatment of the subject balances individual experiences, specific cases, and comprehensive critical analyses place eugenics within a broader context of international links. The studies highlight how German-speaking psychiatrists and neurologists during the Nazi period in Europe developed their eugenics programs based on preceding theories from Victorian Britain and methodologies from North America. The contributors to this edited collection demonstrate how the basic eugenics assumptions, arguments, and forms of implementation (e.g., stigmatizing labels, sexual segregation, compulsory sterilization) were continuous despite geographical, political, and cultural differences.

It is highly significant that geneticists, and even ardent progressive eugenicists like Henry J. Muller (1890–1976), despite their enthusiasm for its utopian ideal, had quickly identified the eugenic fallacy in attributing social behaviour, economic, class, and gender differences to inborn causes and heritability, to the exclusion of environmental influences (such as economic depression), as well as its dependence on the subjective, unreliable evidence of "pedigree charts."[7]

The increasing criticisms of eugenics views by geneticists and biologists for lack of scientific evidence did not halt the tragic consequences of, first, legalized compulsory sterilization in North America and, then, the elimination of those deemed "unworthy of life" in the euthanasia program of Nazi Germany.[8] What gave rise to bioethics as a discipline was the need to safeguard against such violations of individual rights, whether those of patients or of experimental subjects, in vulnerable segments of society. The editors did not limit contributions to the first half of the twentieth century, however; chapters cover the postwar period too, when eugenics was discredited and genetics separated itself from this precursor "pathological science."[9]

This volume leaves no doubt that a view of eugenics as a purely historical phenomenon would miss the insights into its powerful legacy and minimize its fundamental relevance to current parallel problems. The potential danger is not the science of genomics, or gene editing on its own, any more than was the scientific introduction of Mendelian genetics into the fields of agriculture and biology. It is the possible resurgence of a form of "biological determinism,"[10] a societal consensus whereby individuals are reduced to the sum of their genes alone, the complex connectome of genetics and environment is disregarded, and this reduction is extended to similarly account for differences in social groups or populations.[11] The focus here is on the relation of eugenics to psychiatry, what Stephen Jay Gould diagnosed in his book *The Mismeasure of Man* as the intrinsic problem: the "pervasive propensity in society" to "use numbers to rank people in a single series of worthiness, invariably to find that oppressed and disadvantaged groups—races, classes, sexes—are innately inferior and deserve their status."[12]

In the encounter of genomic science and society, the most important safeguard is a critical account and detailed analysis of what occurred with eugenics. This book goes a long way toward bending the moral arc towards justice.[13]

ACKNOWLEDGMENTS

We are truly indebted to the wonderful contributors to this edited collection. Thank you for submitting your valuable scholarship and for your patience throughout the editorial process of this book. We have very much enjoyed your input, discussions, and collaboration on this project.

During the research period for this book, we have been further inspired, constructively motivated, and supported by various colleagues, students, friends, and to a significant extent by the members of the "Living Archives on Eugenics in Western Canada" group. We are extremely grateful and pleased to have the opportunity here to express our sincere gratitude to all of them, even if many will no longer recollect our earlier exchanges, draft discussions, and exciting conversations that we shared during our workshops and continuous research group meetings. We mention most of them here by name, as an expression of our deep gratitude to them: Erika Dyck (team leader, Archives and Collections), Department of History, University of Saskatchewan, Bruce Uditsky (team leader, Reproductive Choice in an Ableist World), CEO Emeritus, Alberta Inclusion; Anne Hughson, Community Rehabilitation and Disability Studies, University of Calgary; John Dossetor, Health Ethics Centre, University of Alberta; Judy Lytton; Amy Kaler, Department of Sociology, University of Alberta; Christine Ferguson, English Studies, University of Glasgow; Nick Supina III, community visual artist; Dick Sobsey (ret.), Department of Educational Psychology and director of John Dossetor Health Ethics Centre, University of Alberta; Gregor Wolbring (team leader, Post-Eugenics Futures), International Centre for Bioethics, Culture, and Disability, University of Calgary; Geoffrey Reaume, Faculty of Health, York University; Doug Wahlsten (ret.), Department of Psychology, University of Alberta; Natasha Nunn (team leader, Technical Team); Michael Billinger; Glenn Griener, Department of Philosophy, University of Alberta; Kathryn Harvey; Kyle Whitfield, Faculty of Extension, University of Alberta; Raymond Frogner; Colette Leung; Rob Wilson (team leader, Eugenics Frames); Alexandra

Minna Stern, Department of Medicine, University of Michigan; Molly Ladd-Taylor, History Department, York University; Paul Weindling, Oxford Brookes University; Lene Koch, Department of Health Services, University of Copenhagen; Paul Lombardo, Faculty of Law, Georgetown University; Heidi Janz; Joanne Faulker, ARC Future Fellow, Macquarie University; John Sutton; Wendy Kline, Department of History, University of Cincinnati; Karen Stote, Women and Gender Studies, Wilfrid Laurier University; Allan Garber, Parlee McLaws LLP; Leilani Muir, sterilization survivor, activist, member of the Living Archives on Eugenics Governing Board; and, certainly, Moyra Lang, who as Living Archives on Eugenics project coordinator facilitated and supported the many steps that have finally led to the publication of this volume.

A substantial part of the book was compiled and written when Frank W. Stahnisch held a visiting scholarship at the Centre for the History of Science, Technology, Medicine, and Society at the University of California at Berkeley. There, some of his colleagues read earlier drafts and graciously supported ongoing research steps toward this volume. The Office for History of Science and Technology at Stephens Hall provided a stimulating working milieu, which has thus far been incomparable. At the University of Calgary, our colleagues—especially in the Hotchkiss Brain Institute, the O'Brien Institute for Public Health, the History and Philosophy of Science program, and the Science, Technology, Environment, and Medicine Studies laboratory—have provided a fertile and enriching context in which to complete this project. It has been our pleasure to work with Donna Weich, Beth Cusitar, Mikkel Dack, Brenan Smith, and Keith Hann, whose editorial advice and meticulous correction of the English in this manuscript fostered the writing process. We are furthermore indebted to the gracious support of a community-based research grant entitled "Living Archives on Eugenics in Western Canada – CURA," from the Social Sciences and Humanities Research Council of Canada, with Professor Robert A. Wilson at the University of Western Australia (formerly at the University of Alberta), as the principal investigator and project director. This financial support helped greatly at all stages of the research and publication process.

The archivists, librarians, and assistants at many libraries and archives provided crucial aid in collecting historical materials (see also the section Archival Sources and Library Collections). We are grateful for their professionalism and have benefitted from their knowledge in finding people, sources, and contextual information. As they are so many, we cannot mention them here by name yet would like to acknowledge the institutions to which we are extremely grateful for the help we received: the Mackie Family Collection in the History of Neuroscience and Taylor Family Digital Library at the University of Calgary; University Library of the University of Alberta; Provincial Archives of Alberta; Provincial Archives of Manitoba; Zweigbibliothek fuer Medizingeschichte of the Humboldt University of Berlin; the Medizinische Zentralbibliothek and the Library of the Humboldt University; the Staatsbibliothek Preussischer Kulturbesitz; the Deutsches Bundesarchiv in Koblenz, Germany; the Aussenarchiv of the Max Planck Institute for Psychiatry; the Archives of the Max Planck Society in Berlin; the Library of the Max Planck Institute for Brain Research in Frankfurt am Main; the German National Library in Frankfurt am Main; the Archives of the Institute for the History of Medicine and Medical Museum at the University of Zurich; Library and Archives Canada in Ottawa; the Rockefeller Foundation Archives in Sleepy Hollow, NY; and the Library of Congress and National Archives and Records Administration in Washington, DC.

We also thank Athabasca University Press in Edmonton for encouraging this project and for making this volume on the history of eugenics and its intricate connections with the history of psychiatry and neurology possible. In particular, we wish to include Megan Hall, Pamela Holway, Alison Jacques, Connor Houlihan, Marvin Harder, and Sergiy Kozakov along with two anonymous reviewers who commented thoroughly on our earlier manuscript.

Finally, we wish to extend special thanks to our colleagues in the University of Calgary's History of Neuroscience Interest Group, who gave us frequent and highly constructive feedback during the planning and writing phases of this book. We would also like to thank the Awards to Scholarly Publications Program of the Canadian Federation for the Humanities and Social Sciences for their support.

Frank W. Stahnisch and Erna Kurbegović

PROLOGUE

Eugenics and Its Study

Robert A. Wilson

As the current volume attests, contemporary academic and public interest in the history of eugenics and its contemporary significance continues to grow. The volume's focus on the role of psychiatry in the eugenics movement in Canada and internationally and the relationship between eugenics and psychiatry more generally allows a multidirectional start to be made on raising and addressing difficult questions that have remained unasked. The Living Archives on Eugenics in Western Canada project is pleased to have been able to offer support both for the workshop at which many of the papers here were first presented and for the publication of this book.

My comments are organized around three chief thematic tasks. First, I will provide some idea of the trajectory of the scholarship on eugenics over the past thirty-five years that set the context for the contributions to the current volume. Second, I will articulate a view of the relationships between eugenics and disability, on the one hand, and eugenics past and eugenics present, on the other. This should make it clear that eugenics and eugenic thinking are of more than historical interest. And third, I will make some remarks more directly relevant to the book's specific focus on the connections between eugenics and psychiatry—connections that have been underexplored in the literature to date, to which this collection makes a significant contribution. The second of these themes is the focus of the admirable commentaries by Marc Workman (chapter 9) and by

Gregor Wolbring (chapter 10), while the editors' introduction and their concluding chapter both articulate a detailed view on the third of these themes. My own general views on eugenics have been developed in a number of publications in the past few years.[1]

FROM ARCHIVES TO ACTIVISM

Between the appearance of historian Daniel Kevles's *In the Name of Eugenics*, with its focus on the relationship between biological science and eugenics, and legal scholar Paul Lombardo's *Three Generations, No Imbeciles*, on the famous *Buck v. Bell* case, interest spread steadily among scholars in articulating the broader relevance of the history of eugenics for a cluster of contemporary issues.[2] This cluster ranged from issues of reproductive autonomy to science and scientism, biological (particularly genetic) determinism, and disability and human variation. Since 2010, the contemporary resonances of eugenics have spiked, not only in concert with ongoing concerns about emerging biotechnologies (such as CRISPR), but also as there has been further reflection on broader social policies, such as forced child removal and immigration restriction, as means of achieving eugenic ends.

Accordingly, the ways in which eugenics has been taken up by scholars have diversified during this time and the resulting scholarship has increasingly connected with issues of ongoing significance for people marginalized in our societies by eugenic ideas, practices, and policies. For example, recent years have seen the publication of a major handbook on the history of eugenics, several journals that have dedicated special issues to eugenics, books exploring eugenics in North America in more detail, as well as those focused particularly on eugenics in Alberta, and the appearance of eugenic survivor testimony and memoirs.[3] The present volume continues and extends this trend into the domain of psychiatry, though the task of integrating this extension with emerging work within the Mad Pride movement headed by psychiatric survivors remains one for future scholarship.[4]

Recognition of the need for public engagement around eugenics can be understood against two dissonant social contexts that are especially poignant in North America. First, in the early 2000s, official apologies were made by the governments of four of the thirty-one American states to have passed eugenic sterilization laws: Virginia, Oregon, and North Carolina, in 2002, and California, in 2003. These apologies followed in the wake of over eight hundred settled legal actions in Alberta, Canada, brought by sterilization survivors against the Government of Alberta for wrongful confinement and sterilization under the province's Sexual Sterilization Act (1928–72), as well as revelations of the relative recency of eugenic sterilization in the Scandinavian countries.[5] Second, in the past ten years it has been revealed that sexual sterilization continues to be practised in several disparate circumstances: for example, on women and girls with intellectual disabilities in Australia, and on women in the California prison system.[6] While the settlements and apologies were intended to make it clear that eugenics was a matter of a regrettable past, that view is undermined by ongoing sterilization of just the sorts of people who were the target of past eugenics policies and laws. The dissonance here, in turn, raises questions about the forms that eugenic policy takes beyond sterilization, and the manifestations of "newgenic" thought and practice that exist now, well beyond the explicit, self-conscious eugenics era of the past.

UNDERSTANDING DISABILITY AND NEWGENICS

Disability has never been far beneath the surface in the trading zone between eugenics past and newgenics present.[7] Perceived and ascribed disabilities of body and mind were one of the core traits that provided the basis for institutionalization and sterilization on eugenic grounds for the first seventy-five years of the twentieth century. This is so even though, as Douglas Wahlsten shows in chapter 2, the basis for policies of sexual segregation and sterilization reflected ignorance and confusion about the basics of genetics and the nature of inheritance of what elsewhere I call "eugenic traits."[8] Since that time, the eugenic preoccupation with the character of future generations has seeped into what have become everyday practices in the realm of reproductive choice. As Marsha Saxton and Adrienne Asch have forcefully argued, the use of prenatal screening technologies to facilitate the selective abortion of fetuses with features that signify disabling traits—the paradigm here being trisomy 21 in a fetus indicating Down Syndrome in the child—expresses a negative view of such disabilities sufficient to warrant terminating an otherwise wanted pregnancy.[9] The eliminative structure of what disability theorist Rosemary

Garland-Thomson has called *eugenic logic* persists in contemporary practices governing reproductive choice, social inclusion, and democratic participation and their relationship to disability.[10]

The assumption that it would be better if disability simply did not exist, which underlies eugenic logic, runs deep in contemporary social thought and practice, deep enough to pass as common sense. That those who would make the same assumption about dark-skinned people would be critiqued as harbouring racism serves as a marker of how distinctively disability is presently conceptualized as something negative: misfortunate, regrettable, limiting, disease-like, in need of elimination. This tie between eugenics and contemporary disability studies, however, also suggests (less depressingly) that eugenics and reflection on its history can also play a more positive role in disability politics. Survivor testimony of what it was like to be housed in the training schools for the feeble-minded and subjected to dehumanization beyond strictly eugenic policies constitutes a major source of knowledge about eugenics in Alberta. Revelations of the lackadaisical application of intelligence tests, of the use of those deemed to be "morons" to care for so-called "low-grade" children, and of the effects of extensive psychotropic experimentation by the medical superintendent at the Provincial Training School for Mental Defectives (PTS), Dr. Leonard J. Le Vann (1915–87), are just three examples.[11]

As we move to articulate a more complex and complete collective memory of the explicitly eugenic era, I suspect that such survivor knowledge will increasingly reinforce and support the view that the disability activism slogan "nothing about us without us" has epistemic as well as political resonance.[12] Together with the standpoint of those surviving newgenics, this insider witnessing of eugenics opens up a role for oral history in reflecting on the question, What sorts of people should there be? Like other neutral-sounding questions, surface appearances here mask the fact that this one sits very differently with those on either side of eugenic logic.

EUGENICS AND PSYCHIATRY

The most prominent cluster of traits that featured as the basis for eugenic sterilization policies in North American and Europe were mental or psychological, falling into two traditional categories: the first—including so-called mental deficiency, mental defectiveness, feeble-mindedness, idiocy, and imbecility—concerned people with or deemed to have subnormal levels of intelligence, typically from birth and often ascribed from early in childhood; the second was the paradigmatic concern of psychiatry and psychiatrists: insanity, lunacy, psychosis, madness.[13] Even though psychologists—the non-medical competitor to psychiatrists—were in effect the gatekeepers to feeble-mindedness through their development and adoption of intelligence testing and their special connection to childhood research and education, psychiatrists played an active role in the administration and enforcement of eugenic policies, especially in Europe, as documented in a number of the contributions to the current volume.[14]

Psychologists used intelligence quotient (IQ) tests as their major diagnostic technological weapon in the eugenic "war against the weak," and their role in the eugenic past has a long history of having been well discussed by scholars.[15] The contribution of psychiatrists, by contrast, is lesser known and is sometimes thought to be more contingently related to the profession of psychiatry and more idiosyncratic. Again, the present volume challenges this view and constitutes the beginnings of a more systematic consideration of psychiatry, alongside psychology and genetics, as forming one of the many disciplinary branches in the eugenic tree. Together with neurologists, psychiatrists are clinicians of the brain and of the presumed departures from its normal function that lead to failures in the nervous system and psychiatric symptoms.[16] German psychiatrist Emil Kraepelin's (1856–1926) views of nervous degeneration and the psychiatric genetics of Ernst Ruedin (1874–1952)—both discussed in several of the chapters herein—and, more generally, hereditary views of psychiatric traits represent major ways in which psychiatry influenced the trajectory of eugenics.[17] The scientific authority that psychiatry inherited from its medical standing, however, gave the discipline a much broader role in diagnosis, treatment, and recommendation than it would otherwise have had.

In Canada, perhaps as elsewhere, what could pass for scientific authority was sometimes surprising. Dr. John MacEachran (1877–1971), chair of the Alberta Eugenics Board for most of its forty-three-year history—and the subject of chapter 1, by Henderikus J. Stam and Ashley Barlow—occupied that role not only by virtue of his position as the long-standing provost of the University of Alberta (1911–45), but also as the founding chair of what was to become its Department of Philosophy, Psychology, and Education. MacEachran's scientific authority rested at least in part in his being perceived as a psychologist, despite the fact that his two doctoral dissertations were both squarely within the discipline of philosophy. Moreover, MacEachran never, so far as I can determine, published a single paper in psychology in his long career and life. Likewise, Dr. Le Vann, medical superintendent of the PTS from 1949 until 1974, passed himself off as a psychiatrist when he in fact had no such accreditation in Canada, as was revealed in the 1995 lawsuit that eugenics survivor Leilani Muir brought against the province of Alberta for wrongful confinement and sterilization.[18] Le Vann's authority as a putative psychiatrist likely made it easier for him to engage in psychotropic drug experimentation on children at the PTS and may even have been partially responsible for his initial appointment as the medical superintendent there.

What this says about the strength of eugenic ideology, about the seriousness of confining and sterilizing those deemed feeble-minded, and about the tangled relationships between eugenics, institutionalization, and clinical sciences, including psychiatry, will be informed by the kind of work that the present volume undertakes as well as that in the field of philosophical psychiatry.[19]

LIST OF FIGURES AND TABLES

FIGURES

LIST OF TABLES

PSYCHIATRY AND THE LEGACIES OF EUGENICS

INTRODUCTION

This volume examines an important historical problem, namely, how governments, progressive groups, and professional associations were co-opted by the ideologies and fashionable scientific claims of contemporary eugenicists. It links the troubled eugenics history in western Canada to further developments on the international stage and examines the manifold legacies of eugenics—for example, its inhumane diagnostic and treatment thrust in psychiatry and medicine, the widespread and enduring conceptual undertones in official legal texts and government policies, and the detrimental consequences for patients and asylum inmates, who had been forcefully sterilized or whose partnerships and marriages were prohibited by professional caregivers and sometimes even family members—through more recent movements for compensation by its victims in Canada and abroad. This book represents an important and essential endeavour that examines several related topics in the history of eugenics together with the history of mental health and psychiatric developments in an international format that allows for comparisons between detailed case studies from several Canadian provinces, US states, and European countries spanning the first half of the twentieth century. Methodologically, it represents a collection of international case studies on eugenics that in themselves consider the social discourses, government policies, and long-term consequences of eugenics, as well as its ensuing cultural influences and profound legacies. This book thereby aims at providing a historical and likewise critical analysis of eugenics in western Canada through the assembled detailed case studies. These allow for the comparison of scientific and social trends as well as an understanding of the variations in decision-making processes on both the governmental and professional level, and further cultural and discourse contextualization of such developments with similar processes in Germany, Europe, and the United States. The book also examines the ways in which eugenics discourses were themselves influenced by legal and political discussions, as well as scientific and media representations, and the eugenic and often racist effects on both official policy and prevailing social attitudes through a variety of policy and institutional case studies. These include examinations of, among others, sterilization, public health nursing, sexual and reproductive health, neuropsychiatric and medical research practices, police searches and legal trials, official compensation programs, and media representations in contemporary newspapers, broadcast speeches, and films. The historical case studies are followed by two comparative commentaries, from a community activism and a disability studies angle, and finally a contextualizing conclusion.

This volume is based largely on the papers presented and discussed at the first joint conference of the International Society for the History of the Neurosciences (ISHN) and Cheiron (the International Society for the Behavioural and Social Sciences).[1] This volume results from previous research pursued by a group of Canadian and international historians and interdisciplinary scholars assembled in the Living Archives on Eugenics in Western Canada, a Community-University Research Alliance initiative, which has been supported by the Social Sciences and Humanities Research Council of Canada.[2] The workshop at this conference was entitled "Eugenics and Psychiatry—Analyzing the Origin, Application, and Perception of Early Forced Sterilization Programs from a Medical History Viewpoint," with Robert A. Wilson and Frank W. Stahnisch acting as the convenors. The workshop, held at the Banff Centre for the Arts in Banff, Alberta, brought together historians, philosophers, psychologists, sociologists, and disability scholars to discuss the knowledge basis and sociocultural background in the public mental health sector spanning from the late 1880s to the early 1970s.

In order to analyze this problem field in a more comprehensive fashion, scholars working on Canada's eugenics situation, as well as its international counterparts, were invited to contribute to this volume to discuss the effect of brain psychiatry and developments in the neurological sciences within the socioeconomic contexts of the time.[3] These contextualizing chapters round out the professional perspectives (from nurses and eugenics board members) and the disability studies and media analysis angles, as well as the consequences of coerced sterilization and experimentation, which had not been addressed or discussed at the conference workshop itself.

This book can thereby offer new insights through a decidedly comparative approach and through its focus on psychiatry and its role in the "eugenics movement." The volume focuses primarily on the history of eugenics developments in western Canada as a whole, yet with a specific concentration on Alberta and its far-reaching forced sterilization program. Where applicable, chapters also include discussions of the sterilization program and legal context of the province of British Columbia as well as the indirect, medicine-, and public health–driven eugenics activities in Saskatchewan (see, for example, chapters 2, 3, and 5 and the conclusion). Chapter 5, for instance, entitled "Eugenics in Manitoba and the Sterilization Controversy of 1933," offers intriguing insights on the differences between Manitoba and the rest of western Canada in terms of political, religious, social, and feminist discourses, thus providing an important comparative perspective. These historical developments are then related to their international contexts, particularly regarding the dimension of psychiatry, neuroscience, and medicine.

During the twentieth century, Canada participated in two devastating world wars and experienced the economic catastrophe of the Great Depression,[4] which led to the introduction of controversial public health and psychiatric measures. This book seeks to cast new light on the practice of eugenics through the lenses of psychiatry and clinical neurology. It argues that these medical discourses contributed in important ways to the development and adoption of eugenics policies and practices for solving perceived societal problems associated with "nervous degeneration" and "bad genetic stock," as becomes quite visible in chapter 7 ("The "Eugenics Paradox": Core Beliefs of Progressivism versus Relics of Medical Traditionalism—The Example of Kurt Goldstein").

The book's focus is hence on the role of psychiatry in the eugenics movement; further, it argues that the relationship between eugenics and psychiatry more generally allows a multi-directional beginning to be made on raising and answering intricate questions. These include, for instance, the presentation of psychologists and psychiatrists in their research programs, publications, and academic lectures (see chapters 2 and 7), struggles with the social and political effects of "modernity" in public discourse (in chapter 6), and promulgation and defences of particular "degenerative views" in psychiatry that underpinned widespread cultural beliefs about "the age of nervousness"[5] in Europe and in the United States (chapters 6, 7, and 8). About one-fourth of the patients in psychiatric hospitals during the 1920s and 1930s were patients with physical forms of illnesses,[6] and nurses and psychiatrists alike sought to promote new epidemiological research and care models for "nervous degeneration" (such as alcoholism, feeble-mindedness, epilepsy, neurasthenia), including answers to these social conditions being phrased in decidedly eugenic language: patient segregation, marriage counselling, and early ideas about forced sterilization (see chapters 3, 4, and 5). Many prominent psychiatrists now began to focus on "nervous degeneration" as a rhetorical means by which to promote their own eugenics agendas, particularly within debates about the consequences of urbanization. Hence, they acted as scientific under-labourers and as a new breed of medical experts in an increasingly politicized health-care field.

Taken together the chapters highlight how contemporary psychiatric and neurological views influenced the forms in which eugenics discourses influenced social and health policy along with public attitudes (particularly visible in chapters 4 and 8).

The works comprising this volume thus raise questions as to the motives of provincial and national governments in Canada as well as overseas in introducing pieces of eugenics legislation and forced sterilizations, health counselling programs, and so on. In this respect, how different were the medical communities in other countries in their reception of eugenics views, and to what extent did the medical profession become active in influencing eugenics legislation in different jurisdictions? What factors prompted psychologists, psychiatrists, and other physicians to collaborate in mutual research programs for policy initiatives and political programs? What were the intrinsic conceptual assumptions that fostered the bioscientific and genetic approaches in psychiatry and mental health, followed by the brain psychiatry of leading figures such as German clinical researcher Emil Kraepelin (1856–1926), his North American pupils, and counterparts like Adolph Meyer (1866–1950)? In what ways was the Canadian health-care system, especially in the western provinces, affected by widened international discussions in the United States, Britain, and central and northern Europe?[7]

In particular, a substantial connection between the chapters concerning Alberta, western Canada, Germany, and other parts of Europe is revealed in the international eugenic, psychiatric, and anthropological trends in existence during the same period under investigation. Strong links can be seen between specific chapters, eliciting the interlinking of different themes and conceptual topics such as Victorian sensibilities and public mental health concerns; scientific ideologies as drivers of contemporary sterilization and counselling programs; the involvement of nurses, legal scholars, physicians, and superintendents in eugenic debates; public and media perceptions of eugenic principles and goals; the political, economic, and legal ambivalences between traditionalists and progressivists; and explicitly anti-modern attitudes and stances. The contributors' antithetical reasoning vis-à-vis established scholarly norms and previous findings asserts a methodological approach that helps to bring out both similarities and comparative contrasts between North American, German, and European applications of eugenic thinking. The methodological approach used in this book makes visible the background of eugenics in German psychological science and psychiatry, particularly how eugenic programs were abetted by the conceptualizations of the brain and mental structure emerging in the historical period and intellectual milieu under consideration. Some of these models and theories promised and alluded to deeper understandings of psychological, intellectual, and cognitive factors in mental and public health. These theories however stood in a problematic context of racist ideologies and anthropological perspectives that focused primarily on the biological causes of degeneration in psychiatry and neurology, while neglecting the important social contexts at the time. With the breakthrough of Charles Darwin's (1809–82) evolutionary concepts, many Victorians envisaged an active world of commerce and progress. The discourse of degeneration appeared to match up excellently with the contemporary thinking in Britain, and later other parts of Europe, of being at the cutting edge of an industrialized and affluent modern world. Nevertheless, by the end of the nineteenth century, evolutionary theories nurtured new fears of social, cultural, and racial decline and complete degeneration.[8] Degeneration became an influential concept and well-entrenched trope for literary writers and philosophers as well. Derivative notions of degeneration, as in the fields of psychiatry and mental health, developed in line with other evolutionary ideas and became part of the astonishing imaginative resource that Darwin's theory of the survival of the fittest had introduced.[9]

From this perspective, the book addresses an interdisciplinary readership of currently active psychiatrists, neuroscientists, mental health nurses, psychologists, and public health workers that will extend beyond the scholarly communities of historians, humanists, and mental health researchers. We are confident that this edited collection will interest a professional health-care and medical readership by offering new and complementary perspectives to the existing body of general literature on eugenics in North America.

CANADIAN EUGENICS

At the turn of the twentieth century, scientific and social discourses about eugenics, biological anthropology, and racial hygiene received increasing attention not only from psychiatrists, medical doctors, and social scientists but also from the general public.[10] The early notions of eugenics had largely been developed and formed by the natural philosopher Francis Galton.[11] His views on the importance of the inheritance of biological, psychological, and sociological human traits greatly influenced British upper and middle classes, who by the end of the nineteenth century had begun to fear widespread societal degeneration. Low birth rates among the upper classes—and elevated rates among the lower classes—along with the considerable army casualties of the Boer Wars (1880–81; 1899–1902) and the poor health of the working class caused many British subjects to fear a "racial suicide" and thereby created a space for the eugenics movement to emerge.[12] Following Galton's ideas, a considerable number of British eugenicists advocated for selective breeding by encouraging the "fit" to reproduce (positive eugenics) and limiting reproduction among the "unfit" (negative eugenics).[13] This situation was not unique to Britain; eugenics began to spread in many parts of the Western world, including Canada. Eugenic programs worked to redefine human morality and social behaviours, as well as acceptable qualities of mental health and biological fitness.[14] Concerns as to what would happen to society if the "unfit" were allowed to reproduce led to collective anxieties, which many Canadians of higher social standing shared. This concern was captured in a 1933 article by a prominent Manitoba physician, Byron M. Unkauf (1905–83), which helps to explain why so many middle-class Canadians eagerly accepted the "science" of eugenics: "Fifty years ago there were 64 mental defectives confined to institutions per 100,000 population, to-day there are 236. As a result . . . if the rate of increase of insanity continues for 75 years, half the population will be in asylums living off the other half."[15] This prospect also accounted for the fact that medical doctors and, particularly, alienists, psychiatrists, and neurologists were attracted to the specific answers that inheritance-oriented eugenic thought offered for problems of diagnosis and psychiatric treatment in medicine.[16] The individual cases explored in this volume (see especially chapters 1 through 5) nevertheless present a rather common perception of eugenics as a late nineteenth- and early twentieth-century phenomenon.[17]

The widespread appeal of Social Darwinian political philosophies and the hereditary sciences in biology also led many regional governments in Canada and the United States to enact eugenics legislation, including sterilization laws, particularly in the first decades of the twentieth century.[18] As is visible from the proceedings of the Select Standing Committee on Law Amendments, in the Canadian context, a large number of provincial governments voiced concerns over the effect of feeble-mindedness and mental deficiency on society.[19] Often, these governments viewed individuals with inherited conditions as economic burdens. Owing to the economic downturn of the late 1920s and early 1930s, government officials were often quick to think that the cost of running mental institutions needed to be reduced. They frequently held that such individuals would threaten the health and well-being of the other residents of their provinces, an assumption based primarily on the Mental Hygiene surveys conducted in many Canadian provinces in the 1920s by the founder of the Canadian National Committee for Mental Hygiene (CNCMH), Dr. Clarence M. Hincks (1889–1966)—who, interestingly enough, had suffered from clinical depression himself.[20] These surveys, which had been commissioned by the provincial governments to assess the mental health status in the Canadian provinces, revealed that the extent of feeble-mindedness was high and that it was associated with many of the provinces' prevailing social problems.[21]

While Canadian eugenics had originated in the late nineteenth century, similar to the United States it reached its peak in the 1920s and 1930s.[22] The effects of the First World War, the Great Depression, and increasing immigration to Canada caused many middle-class Canadians to fear national degeneration, as such concerns about social degeneration had previously influenced British and American societies as well.[23] In the late nineteenth and early twentieth centuries, a significant number of new non-British immigrants settled in Canada. As historian Angus McLaren has previously shown, native-born Canadians were frightened not so much by the quantity of immigrants as by their biological and social "quality," many having arrived from non–Anglo Saxon countries.[24] The influence of eugenic thought is likewise evident in Canadian immigration policies.[25] By 1900, such policies tended toward tighter immigration restrictions, and amendments to the Immigration Act following this period were laced with eugenic language.[26] With high numbers of immigrants entering Canada at this time, eugenicists believed that the country's national character was under threat. High losses of life in the First World War similarly heightened fears of "race suicide" among middle-class Canadians. Many believed that the "best" men were losing their lives in the war, while the "unfit" remained at home and continued to reproduce.[27] The early years of the twentieth century also witnessed the ever-increasing power of the medical profession. In the years that followed, individuals such as Helen MacMurchy (1862–1953), a prominent women's health activist, social reformer, and Toronto-trained physician, as well as Dr. Hincks, the aforementioned Ottawa mental health activist, greatly influenced public health reforms and eugenic policies in western Canada (see chapters 3, 4, and 5). Throughout the 1920s and early 1930s, fears of the unfit and feeble-minded had swept the country and many eugenicists, including MacMurchy and Hincks, called for sexual segregation and, eventually, the sterilization of the targeted populations.

By tracing this infamous history, the assembled contributions in this collection make a valuable research contribution to the ongoing scholarship about eugenics in the Canadian provinces. Historians and scholars such as Angus McLaren, Ian Dowbiggin, and Erika Dyck have previously given important overview accounts of the earlier development of eugenics, particularly in the western provinces.[28] With regard to the connection between the "old eugenics movement," between the 1920s and the 1970s, and the new reproductive technologies in late twentieth-century medicine, one of the most influential works on eugenics in Canada remains *Our Own Master Race: Eugenics in Canada 1885–1945*.[29] In this book, McLaren explores the motives behind "race betterment" campaigns, supported by many Canadian social and medical eugenicists, and he shows that many prominent Canadians (including famous feminists, politicians, and social democrats, among others) had been fascinated by eugenic ideas. More recent studies have looked at the longevity of sterilization legislation in Alberta, arguing that by the time negative eugenics science had been discredited internationally, Alberta's sterilization legislation had moved beyond the purview of the general public, allowing for the quiet continuation of such practices.[30] In recent years, McLaren and Dowbiggin have added new monographs on the foundations of reproductive health, including Dowbiggin's *The Sterilization Movement and Global Fertility in the Twentieth Century* and McLaren's *Reproduction by Design: Sex, Robots, Trees, and Test-Tube Babies in Interwar Britain*.[31] The explanation of Alberta's predominance in eugenics in Canada rests with the well-established scholarly arguments that eugenics was so robust as public policy in Alberta that it could counter the social and scientific decline elsewhere, thanks to immigration fears, an uninformed public, and a lack of broad knowledge about Nazi eugenics and the Holocaust, along with economic arguments.

Since McLaren's landmark study, other works have emerged using archival resources such as institutional records and patient files to offer important insights into the living conditions within contemporary institutions. Jana Grekul's article "Sterilization in Alberta, 1928 to 1972: Gender Matters," for example, explores the gendered treatment that eventually led to the sterilization of many individuals, primarily women.[32] Other scholars, such as nursing historian Geertje Boschma, are concerned with the relationship families had with mental institutions after their family members had been admitted.[33] In recent years, historians have also focused on the complex relationship between the Catholic church and eugenics in Canada.[34] For example, Sebastien Normandin's "Eugenics, McGill and the Catholic Church in Montréal and Québec, 1890–1942" maps out the groups that supported eugenics—particularly academics—and those that did not, especially the Roman Catholic church.[35] Normandin shows that while French Catholics criticized eugenic means, such as sterilization and birth control, they did not object to the goal of encouraging the "fit" to reproduce. Normandin's discussion of the Catholic response to eugenics shows that religious opinion was also, historically, an important driving force for the social support or rejection of eugenics programs in North America and elsewhere.[36]

With respect to socially progressive political programs and thought in the western Canadian province of Saskatchewan, historians such as Alex Deighton have recently worked out that, in contrast to its neighbouring provinces to the west—Alberta and British Columbia—Saskatchewan never enacted laws that legitimized negative eugenics measures.[37] These scholars have shown that despite the fact that Saskatchewan never implemented a centralized eugenics program, there was still enthusiasm for eugenics in the province during the 1920s and 1930s. An absence of legislation does not mean that eugenics would not have been popular—quite the contrary with respect to laws and practices that regarded marriage counselling and segregation practices of people perceived as "mentally unfit." In the early twentieth century, such eugenic ideas played out in provincial institutions, where individuals deemed "mentally defective" were segregated.[38] Protagonists advocated for the relocation of those seen to be mentally defective to the "Home for Defectives" in Regina or, later (after 1914), to Saskatchewan's first mental hospital, in North Battleford, not too far west of Saskatoon. Shortly after the end of the First World War, in 1921, the province in fact started to institutionalize the "mentally defective" at a newly constructed mental hospital outside the city of Weyburn.[39] The period from the 1920s to the 1930s proved to be the high point of eugenic thinking in Saskatchewan, stirred and fostered by what was seen as the recent success of Alberta's Sexual Sterilization Act in 1928.[40] The two provinces had close agricultural, economic, and human resource connections, so that not a few inhabitants of Saskatchewan came to argue that their province should develop similar sterilization legislation as well.[41]

Politically, in 1929, the Conservative and Progressive coalition Co-operative Government came into power and championed the project of eugenics in Saskatchewan. Partially driven by technocratic thinking, it sought a greater role for state politics in public health, psychiatry, and medicine-related topics. As part of the government's social medical agenda, the topic of "the sterilization of mental defectives" was included among an array of public health measures, including plans for state health insurance and free consultative medical (poly)clinics.[42] Eugenic ideology was successively employed by hospital administrators who associated "mental deficiency" and "feeble-mindedness" with a host of social problems including crime and alcoholism.[43]

Throughout the 1930s, eugenics legislation was perceived as a serious public health–related option for dealing with increasing mental health problems, alcohol addiction, social deviance, and insufficient institutional hospital support for psychiatric patients in the province. A sterilization bill was first developed in 1930 and did in fact pass the early stages required to be made into law, with just one vote against the parliamentary motion.

Shortly before this statute could be legally formalized, however, the government was abolished and replaced by the Co-operative Commonwealth Federation (CCF), which withdrew the eugenics bill—a move that has been attributed to rising religious Catholic opposition.[44] Yet, as in other Canadian provinces that instituted not centralized eugenics programs "from above" but rather individual projects "from below" (as Erna Kurbegović also argues in chapter 5), Saskatchewan followed through with eugenic activities and endeavours by using institutionalization, counselling, and sexual segregation measures. Also in 1930, the province passed the so-called Mental Defectives Act, which became effective on February 1, 1931.[45] It allowed inhabitants of Saskatchewan to name individuals to a Justice of the Peace, who was to evaluate if they should be sent to a provincial training school. However, such a training school was never built, and the "mental defectives" were sent to the Weyburn Mental Hospital instead.[46] This led to an almost exponential increase of the patient population and hence extended social pressure to conceptualize other eugenic measures and forms of medical counselling in a decentralized form throughout the province. This development was only aggravated three years later, when new prevention legislation was established that mandated that all men who intended to marry were to receive a physical and mental exam by psychiatrists or family physicians, in order to prohibit the marriage of "imbeciles" and "idiots." Later legislation, established in 1936 under the CCF government, further constrained "mentally defective" individuals and the "mentally ill" from marrying. Catholics in Saskatchewan had opposed the province's "top-down" eugenics legislation in 1930 as conflicting with their religious convictions, yet often enough they endorsed such eugenics measures "from below" as counselling, sexual segregation, and anti-marriage legislation.[47] By the late 1930s, however, support for eugenics had declined in the province, and with the election of the CCF under Tommy Douglas (1904–86) in 1944, the new government promoted greater care and training for those deemed mentally defective.[48] More recently, there has been a renewed focus on the history of sexual sterilization in Saskatchewan, and Canada broadly, as a result of revelations from Indigenous women who were coerced to undergo tubal ligations at Saskatoon Health Region hospitals between 2005 and 2010.[49]

While the works of the above scholars offer instructive new insights into the history of eugenics, the "checkered history" of eugenics of western

Canada still remains to be added to—an undertaking that this volume embarks on by drawing scholarly attention particularly to the place of psychiatry, public mental health, and eugenically motivated research in the brain sciences.[50] For this endeavour, it is also necessary to understand past medical, social, and political processes. In the history of intellectual culture, these exchanges have been characterized in the existing scholarship as forming part of the political and social climate of the 1920s.[51] However, in revising the narrative of the quiet longevity of sterilization practices in Alberta after the Second World War, the particular medical and mental health implications of the eugenics movement still have to be mapped and explored. Together, the chapters assembled here detail the ways in which medical, social, political, and religious factors overlapped when shaping the eugenics movements in western Canada and beyond. In Alberta, for instance, the pro-eugenics United Farmers Association was elected to office in 1921, while, in contrast, liberal-progressives formed the Manitoba government in 1927 and were rather critical and disapproving of the eugenics-related policy decisions made farther west.[52]

The rural province of Alberta particularly stood out from the Canadian context, with its enactment of the Sexual Sterilization Act of 1928.[53] Such eugenics legislation was rare in Canada in the 1920s, though a number of state governments south of the border had passed similar laws.[54] Alberta's legislation was rather exemplary in terms of the sociopolitical and legal discussions taking place at that time in other Canadian provinces, such as Manitoba and Saskatchewan, as discussed above,[55] the exchanges with international experts (from the United States, Britain, and Germany), and its long-standing existence (forty-four years!). Since the inception of the eugenics sterilization program, the Department of Public Health in the province of Alberta was particularly interested in and closely monitored the progress of the eugenics sterilization program, especially in the main hospitals of Edmonton (University Hospital), Calgary (Calgary General Hospital), and Ponoka (Provincial Mental Hospital).[56] The provincial sterilization program was only revoked in 1972, by the government headed by Premier Peter Lougheed (1928–2012), following wider political, social, and legal protest that questioned the juridical and moral grounds of the prevailing laws.[57] In the time of its existence, the Sexual Sterilization Act led to the forced sterilization of at least 2,835 Albertans who were deemed "mentally defective" or "unfit."[58] Within Alberta's eugenics program, many of the men, women, and children subjected to such negative eugenics methods came from socially vulnerable populations, including psychiatric patients, asylum inmates, prisoners, and Indigenous people. It is striking to note that even among these groups more women than men were sterilized, and many who were sterilized had been unemployed.[59] From the vast dimensions of the eugenics program in the province of Alberta, it becomes obvious that the Sexual Sterilization Act changed the lives of many; indeed, it affected the social and psychological situation of a large number of victims well beyond its repeal in the early 1970s.

During a time when the great majority of provincial and state governments were either decommissioning or disregarding their sterilization laws—whether because of insufficient public finances, an increase in public scrutiny, or the discrediting of hereditary science (as Douglas Wahlsten describes in chapter 2)—Alberta's expanding legislation appears to have been socially uncontested.[60] However, the study of eugenics in Canada has focused primarily on the political, social, and economic conditions that made eugenics laws possible (particularly in Alberta and British Columbia).[61] Historians and scholars of eugenics have given several reasons as to why the forced measures were mostly given up in North American after 1945. First, eugenics policies became increasingly discredited in the postwar period because of their association with the murderous euthanasia programs that targeted psychiatric patients, handicapped individuals, and other "racially inferior" populations in Nazi Germany (see also chapter 8).[62] Second, while Alberta took much longer to repeal its eugenics legislation, the support for such ideas had already declined in other Canadian provinces, such as Saskatchewan, by 1940.[63] Many Canadians stopped calling themselves eugenicists, even though eugenic thought did not disappear completely from their minds, and this is particularly so in medical fields such as psychiatry and clinically oriented human genetics.[64] Some of the chapters here, on the prevalence of eugenics in Canada in the postwar period, trace these developments. Third, the Eugenics Society of Canada that had formed in Ontario lost much of its financial support in the early 1940s and began to decline shortly after.[65] Family allowances were implemented in 1945, and the welfare state in Canada emerged shortly after the end of the Second World War.[66] The main purpose of such social welfare programs was twofold: to help families and to prevent another economic depression. Eugenicists opposed this type of state intervention because, supposedly, it benefitted those whom they deemed irresponsible, defective, and unfit.[67]

Following these narratives, it is a main argument of this book that neuropsychiatrists' concerns about pathologies and diseases—intrinsically linked to inheritable and genetic conditions—made these professionals and mental health administrators particularly prone to siding with the new science of eugenics in order to build their academic and social reputation. This book offers new insights based on its explicit focus on psychiatry and the field's role in the eugenics movement especially in western Canada.

THE ISSUE OF PSYCHIATRY

In the early twentieth century, psychiatrists and doctors of nervous diseases were especially prone to accept the scientific and social offers of the eugenic tradition, first in Germany and the United States, then in Canada, and increasingly in other European countries.[68] Particularly influential in the emerging field of interdisciplinary psychiatry and neuroscience was Swiss-French psychiatrist Bénédict Augustin Morel (1809–73), whose *Traité des dégénérescences physiques, intellectuelles et morales de l'espèce humaine et de ces causes qui produisent ces variétiés maladives* (Treatise on degeneration) was fully dedicated to the social problems of the time, and Morel's medical conceptualizations were taken up by many psychiatrists, alienists, and neurologists at the turn of the century.[69] Clinical psychiatrist Auguste Forel (1848–1931) and neuroanatomist and neurologist Constantin von Monakow (1853–1930) in Zurich, for example, integrated Morel's approach and searched for morphological alterations in the human brain[70]—an aspect of research that psychiatric epidemiologist and geneticist Ernst Ruedin (1874–1952) in Munich further prolonged into a thorough analysis of hereditary influences on mental health.[71] These developments in psychiatry and mental health occurred in a profound cultural context of bourgeois fears about "nervous degeneration"—fears that were exacerbated after World War I when discourses about the "neurology of disaster" and brain psychiatry's return to conditions of "nervousness," "war neurotics," psychiatric trauma, and hereditary disease loomed large in many Western countries.[72] The cultural discourse of bourgeois fears led to an overall medicalization of the cultural discourse, as historian Joachim Radkau's *Das Zeitalter der Nervositaet* (Age of nervousness) suggests.[73]

The 1880s and 1890s can be seen as watershed years in the disciplinary formation of modern psychiatry and neurology, a period in which both fields were still seen as either belonging to one and the same discipline or as remaining parts of internal medicine.[74] As a number of medical and social historians point out, the cultural diagnosis of "growing nervousness" and "nervous degeneration" must be understood as a popular cultural leitmotif of the late nineteenth century.[75] Although this is now a fairly accepted view, it is valuable to note that "nervousness" was normally associated more with the mental health field. It therefore does not come as a surprise that Wilhelm Erb (1840–1929), one of the foremost neurologists, used the following terms to discuss the question:

> There can be no doubt that the political, social and cultural circumstances, and anything else that may here be included, have an extraordinary influence on the human nervous system. Nervousness has indeed increased to an enormous degree.... Its causes can easily be found in the spirit of our day, in the modern way of life, in the progress and the sophistication of our culture, in the new creations of modern being, and indeed in social intercourse.[76]

When Erb gave this academic lecture as the principal of the University of Heidelberg, he addressed the issue of "nervous degeneration" at the height of cultural restoration in the Wilhelminian Empire in Germany.[77] This is not surprising, although the audience listened to Professor Erb as the director of the Clinic for Internal Medicine and not as the kind of faculty member whom contemporaries had easily associated with the psychiatrists of their day. In his own scientific work, Erb (similar to Alois Alzheimer [1864–1915] in Germany and Forel in Switzerland at the same time)[78] had introduced a number of clinical signs and symptoms into medical diagnostics and psychosomatic medicine. Erb's statement can thereby serve as an orientation through many of the contributions in this volume, which examine—from different biographical, institutional, and cultural perspectives—the material changes that contemporary psychiatric and neurological discourse associated with "nervous degeneration" and "bad genetic stock" brought about.[79] It must be noted, however, that this view reflected not only psychiatrists' professional assumptions but also opinions, prevalent among middle- and upper-class populations on both sides of the Atlantic, that "cultural degeneration" had rapidly ensued.[80]

A stronger concern for the individual body resulted in widespread medical reconfigurations, programs to sustain public health, and new cultural conceptions of psychiatric illness (often referred to as "inherited feeble-mindedness").[81] Irrespective of the somatic or psychic poles of this spectrum, the specific medical reconfigurations took place in a general framework of eugenic theorizing.[82] Physicians concerned with the wider treatment of nervous diseases, as well as psychiatrists, were particularly likely to endorse the scientific ideas and social programs of the eugenic tradition that gained traction in Europe and in North America, so that when taking a closer look at psychiatry and neurology as new scientific disciplines toward the end of the nineteenth century, the "culturization" of medical discourses becomes more perceptible.

THE INTERNATIONAL EUGENICS MOVEMENT

Canadian and North American eugenics history can hardly be examined without taking the international trajectories of the modern eugenics movement into account. As noted above, this movement emerged at the turn of the nineteenth century, based largely on the anthropological work of Galton, who promoted "healthy living" and "social purity" through the implementation of both positive and negative eugenics practices.[83] The later nineteenth century witnessed the broad reception of Galton's ideas regarding the heredity of human traits such as intelligence, feeble-mindedness, and criminality.[84] In 1910, in Cold Spring Harbor, New York, Charles B. Davenport (1866–1944) established the Eugenics Record Office (ERO), which soon became a major hub for biological and statistical research in eugenics for North America at large.[85] By 1917, fifteen US states had enacted sterilization laws; by 1937, that number was thirty-one.[86] Based on positivistic thinking and trust in hereditary science, as well as the social aspirations of the Progressive Era, the United States became the unrivalled international leader of the eugenics movement in the interwar period.[87]

Although eugenics—as both a social and a scientific movement—had existed in Germany since 1905 (when the Munich Society for Racial Anthropology was formed with a deliberate eugenics mandate), and the politically changing governments of the Weimar Republic had applied eugenics-oriented policies to their health and social programs, it was only with the commencement of the Nazi period that Germany enacted racial and eugenics laws quantitatively and qualitatively more drastic than those in the United States.[88] On a national level, it was the Law for the Prevention of Offspring with Hereditary Diseases—passed in 1933—that permitted the sterilization of citizens all over Germany who were medically diagnosed as "feeble-minded," "schizophrenic," "epileptic," or afflicted with other "incurable diseases." These medical categorizations followed the theories of Freiburg psychiatrist Alfred Erich Hoche (1865–1943), as he had conceptualized them in 1920, shortly after the First World War.[89] The situation was exacerbated by the enactment in 1935 of the Nuremberg Race Laws, which detailed strict racial classifications—on the basis of previously accepted agricultural breeding protocols—and forbade both sexual and marital relations between Jewish and Aryan German citizens.[90]

On many levels, Nazi Germany attempted to surpass the amount and breadth of American eugenics programs, by instituting the Division for Inheritance Statistics at the German Research Institute for Psychiatry (which assembled data on all Germans diagnosed with eugenically relevant psychiatric and neurological conditions), as well as multiple large-scale research programs at the Berlin Kaiser Wilhelm Institute for Anthropology and Human Genetics and the Kaiser Wilhelm Institute for Brain Research.[91] Following a visit by eugenic scientists and legislators in Germany in 1934, the head of the American Eugenics Society, Leon Fradley Whitney (1894–1973), even described the eugenics initiatives in the United States as "something very like what Hitler has now made compulsory" and brought to widespread application.[92]

The intensity of the transnational exchanges and collaboration was also visible within the community of contemporary psychiatrists and neurologists, as addressed by, for example, clinical psychiatrist Oswald Bumke (1877–1950). Bumke, trained at the Leipzig school of brain psychiatry, succeeded Kraepelin in the chair of psychiatry at the University of Munich in 1924. Bumke regarded it as the duty of any patient groups to guarantee their further existence through their own means, not to rely continuously on the support of nurses, wardens, or physicians. This claim had already been made before the First World War—as promoted by Bumke's influential treatise *Ueber Nervoese Entartung* (On nervous degeneration)[93]—but with the political conditions of the interwar period, it became much more widespread and accepted.[94] Right-wing and left-wing psychiatrists similarly focused on "nervous degeneration" as a rhetorical means to strengthen their individual claims as under-labourers of an increasingly politicized health-care field and emphasized the cost effectiveness of state-run mental health programs (see chapter 7).[95]

These conceptual changes and discipline-building developments occurred in a period of increasing academic exchanges and international relations, especially between young North American medical doctors and European psychiatrists.[96] These exchanges significantly modified research and health-care landscapes on either side of the Atlantic.[97] Between the establishment of the German Research Institute for Psychiatry in 1917 and the declaration of war with the United States in 1941, nearly two hundred junior researchers and visiting professors from North America travelled to Munich to work in the institute's laboratories and clinical wards.[98]

A noteworthy protagonist deeply enmeshed in transatlantic relations was the Swiss-born psychiatrist Adolph Meyer, who already possessed well-established contacts with North American colleagues from an earlier research visit in 1891 and later became a full professor of psychiatry at Johns Hopkins University in Baltimore as well as a leading figure in US psychiatry.[99] Meyer represented a "central node" of the North American neuroscientific network and was an important mediator and referee to the Rockefeller Foundation as the major funding institution of biomedical research and public health before the Second World War.[100] His engagement and the Rockefeller Foundation's subsequent decision-making processes essentially fostered a pre-existing and now tightening network of well-respected medical scientists between basic researchers, public health workers, and clinically active psychiatrists.[101] Financial support from North America was considerable: from the 1920s onward, the Rockefeller Foundation was one of the first foreign institutions to react to the devastating effects of the war on German medical research and higher learning institutions.[102] In fact, the advent and recovery of many major scientific endeavours in interwar Germany would be inconceivable without taking the American financial contributions into account.[103] Specifically, this support resulted in increased and sustained funding of the eugenics-related Kaiser Wilhelm Institute for Brain Research in Berlin-Buch, Kaiser Wilhelm Institute for Anthropology in Berlin-Dahlem, and the German Research Institute for Psychiatry in Munich.[104]

McLaren argues that "mentally deficient" patients institutionalized in hospitals and psychiatric wards were often seen as an economic burden in Canada and North America as well—a sentiment that increased during the hardships of the Great Depression in the early 1930s.[105] Grekul shows that the future aims of the CNCMH included a campaign against "crime, prostitution, and unemployment," conditions that the committee related to the social circumstances of the "feeble-minded" in Canadian society.[106] In fact, eugenic tendencies similar to those in Alberta, with its "top-down" legalistic approach, can also be seen in the neighbouring province of Saskatchewan and its psychiatric and mental health past. Individual chapters in this book refer to the localized and regional "bottom-up" approaches to eugenics in Saskatchewan in passing, yet the historical situation there was very different from those in Alberta, many American states, and European countries. No full-fledged "program of eugenics" existed in Saskatchewan after the withdrawal in 1930 of its proposed Mental Defectives Act.[107]

While the ideas of the CNCMH influenced many Canadians, a watershed moment in the history of Canada's eugenics movement occurred when Tommy Douglas, the future premier of Saskatchewan, admitted to the press that he had been "turned away from eugenics" following a trip to Germany in 1936.[108] Increasingly informed through newspaper reports and radio programs about the Nazi race laws and the resulting forced emigration to North America of tens of thousands of non-Aryan or politically oppositional individuals, Canadians became more and more suspicious about the racially grounded social and health programs in Nazi Germany.[109] Following the end of the Second World War, when the realities of patient euthanasia in asylums and hospitals and the atrocities in concentration camps became widely known, eugenics policies were increasingly discredited.[110]

However, despite the growing public knowledge in both the United States and Canada, which also challenged the scientific underpinnings of existent North American eugenics programs, Alberta's sterilization program saw a second peak in numbers at the end of the 1940s.[111] One explanation for the anomaly of the Alberta eugenics program has been the observation that, immediately following the Second World War, a baby boom ensued and the overall population in western Canada began to surge.[112] The influx of patients into institutions such as the Provincial Training School in Red Deer—which became the primary "feeder institution" for the eugenics program from the 1950s onward—may have motivated the Alberta Eugenics Board (AEB) to increase the number of patients considered for sterilization.[113] In fact, many similar complexities, local histories, and international exchanges of the Canadian and North American eugenics landscape have only begun to emerge and to be tackled in the scholarship.

INDIVIDUAL CONTRIBUTIONS TO THIS VOLUME

Reflecting several recent trends in the history of eugenics, psychiatry, and mental health as a whole, the chapters included in this volume reveal a continuing interest in the interrelationship of public health and psychiatric perspectives in the scholarship on Canadian and international eugenic developments. For example, these contributions show both the social and political appeal that the eugenics movement has had for psychiatrists, alienists, and neurologists, as well as other medical experts, in the first half of the twentieth century—in particular, when relating ready biological answers to complex and pressing social issues since the First World War, the Great Depression, and the emergence of Fascism and Nazism in central Europe. Of course, this can hardly be achieved without considering the philosophical and theoretical trends of the time—trends that extended between North America and Europe and gave rise to active and robust transatlantic eugenics networks—when comparing the scientific assumptions in contemporary genetics, anthropology, and psychology with the sociopolitical theories and aspirations. Most of the chapters in the first part of the book thereby deal with individual case examples of Canadian history, particularly in the western Prairie provinces.[114] As a collection of international case studies on eugenics, this volume examines eugenics in western Canada through an international lens that considers the discourses, policies, and consequences of eugenics along with its legacies. The points drawn out in chapters 9 and 10, by the two commentators, relate these historical contributions largely to contemporary policy and human rights debates by drawing on more recent developments such as gene editing, experiments with the artificial womb, parenting by people with disabilities, and immigration legislation related to people with disabilities.

International networks and relationships within psychiatry and mental health in relation to eugenics movements are taken into account in the second part of the book (chapters 6 to 8), which places them in a wider cultural, political, and public health context. This volume thereby offers an authentic overview of the existing breadth and depth of current eugenics scholarship in Canada, the United States, and Europe, while adding to the closure of a research lacuna pertaining to the specific psychiatric and mental health implications of eugenics approaches in their legal, sociopolitical, and health-care settings between 1905 and 1972. Although focused specifically on the western Canadian context, it places the analysis in a wider international context, providing more general appeal to any reader with interests in eugenics, disability, scientific expertise, public authority, and the historical and current relationships between them.

In her foreword, Guel A. Russell focuses on the International Summit on Human Gene Editing held in Washington, DC, in 2015, which saw a scientific debate about the opportunities and ethical concerns around the clinical implementation of gene editing in human populations. As Russell importantly emphasizes, new methodological precision technologies in gene editing, such as CRISPR-Cas9 (Clustered Regularly Interspaced Short Palindromic Repeats), also offer essential "newgenics" opportunities for physical and mental trait selection, genetic repair, and enhancement choices on the horizon of human bioengineering. She places the research directions, historical case studies, and contemporary disability studies commentaries in this volume in a wider context of the critical analysis of "eugenics futures" and "newgenics tendencies," in which similar social and progressivist tendencies of today meet with stunningly augmented biotechnological opportunities and prospects, thus causing prevalent bioethics concerns.

In his prologue, Robert A. Wilson—the former principal investigator of the multi-centre research group Living Archives on Eugenics in Western Canada—highlights a recent interest among philosophers, historians, disability activists, and other scholars in exploring the historical, political, and economic conditions of the Sexual Sterilization Act of Alberta (1928–72) and its implementation. Four themes have emerged as being of particular interest in this research endeavour: first, the analysis of recently accessible historical source material in Canada and elsewhere; second, the exploration of collective memories of eugenics that have entered into the collective consciousness of almost three generations of Canadians, Americans, and Europeans; third, the often neglected perspective of mental and physical disability in the self-acclaimed or externally designated eugenics experts of the prewar and postwar periods; and fourth, the implications that historical and philosophical developments still have today on matters of the social inclusion of different "sorts of people" in education, health, and general social participation in Western industrialized societies such as Canada. Such historical and philosophical developments still influence the so-called post-eugenics period, in which modern genetic diagnostic technologies, reproductive methodologies, and medically therapeutic approaches emerge and often perpetuate social clichés and pejorative views about mental illness and physical disability as socially "unwanted" or in need for medicalization. Related assumptions too often circulate around the idea that key eugenic practices are continuously conceptualized as forms of wrongful accusations, which helps to make sense of the functioning of those practices and their distinctive features. This may seem like a peculiar and indirect acceptance of eugenic practices, such as through the classification of people as "feeble-minded" or "morons" who were thereby rendered vulnerable to sterilization or criminalization.[115] However, it could also appear as a very direct expression of what Anglo-Irish essayist Jonathan Swift (1667–1745) had in mind with "A Modest Proposal," namely, an intellectual blueprint for eugenics to be taken seriously in its own right. According to Wilson, the scientific plausibility of eugenics was further enhanced by newspaper coverage in editorials and articles as well as contemporary radio programs. He further provides insights into the mechanisms through which both historical eugenic and recent "newgenic" practices have operated, both inside the minds of the individuals involved in those practices and through their group interactions.

In the introduction, Frank W. Stahnisch and Erna Kurbegović map and contextualize the relationship of eugenics to the field of psychiatry and mental health (see Appendix, table A2), while highlighting the specific Canadian and transatlantic perspectives under scrutiny. Western Canada is of special interest to the scholars assembled herein. The experience of two world wars and the Great Depression during the first half of the twentieth century exacerbated existing societal problems in Canada that related to minority populations, including the mentally ill and new immigrants. At the same time, this period also witnessed influential social reform movements related to medically oriented areas such as public health and psychiatry, one of which—eugenics—categorized abnormal populations from the normal ones and led to controversial public mental health measures (see Appendix). The book's historiographical focus concerns eugenics in Canada and beyond from the late 1920s to the 1970s.

Henderikus J. Stam and Ashley Barlow in their chapter, "John M. MacEachran and Eugenics in Alberta: Victorian Sensibilities, Idealist Philosophy, and Detached Efficiency," scrutinize the intentions and motives of the former head of the Department of Philosophy and Psychology at the University of Alberta. MacEachran was in fact the only Canadian academic psychologist who trained with the German doyen of experimental psychology, Wilhelm Wundt (1832–1920), in 1907 at the University of Leipzig. With the joint aim of improving society, as Stam and Barlow argue, it was not entirely surprising that both the new science of experimental psychology and the application of the latest findings in human genetics and inheritance became inextricably linked during their inceptions. The scientific and social eugenics movement frequently intersected, while contemporary psychologists became deeply involved in the eugenics movement at the beginning of the twentieth century.[116] While focusing on the ideals of the so-called exact sciences, and their application to the new humanistic knowledge fields, the pioneers of experimental psychology and mental hygiene applied what they saw as a progressivist impulse to answer to the latest social problems, such as "social deprivation," "alcoholism," and "feeblemindedness." Chapter 1 shows how, in their attempt to reform the social and health-care conditions in the province of Alberta, MacEachran and other members of the provincial eugenics board came to patronize the autonomy and self-interest of the forced-sterilized, violate their physical and mental integrity, and disregard their humanity. Stam and Barlow identify MacEachran's psychology-psychiatry background as well as the academic and social world he inhabited, concluding that his training left him entirely ill-suited to the sort of work he infamously became known for.

As Stam and Barlow demonstrate, understanding the role that experimental psychology played with respect to eugenic thinking, legislation, and medical application requires in-depth consideration and analysis of the significance of the ideology of scientific progressivism, along with the connections between this ideology and mental health concerns. Indeed, sterilization was part of a general set of practices intended to alleviate mental and physical disease, social ills, and poverty in the early twentieth century. As other historians of eugenics have also noted in recent years, it is important that the history of sterilization practices be carefully delineated at the local level to prevent the erroneous assumption that there was a single historical event.[117] Stam and Barlow's contribution explores particularly problematic details of eugenics history in western Canada and factors that influenced the fusion between scientific psychology and applications of forced sterilization programs.

In chapter 2, entitled "The Consequences of Eugenic Sterilization in Alberta," Douglas Wahlsten describes in detail how the genetic science of eugenics—even at the time of its emergence, in the late nineteenth century—was known to be inaccurate and did not support the bold biological and social claims of eugenicists around Charles Davenport in the United States and elsewhere. Historically, various international eugenic programs since the 1910s set out to reduce the frequency of some well-defined disorders of the nervous system, as caused by an assumed defect in their germ plasm inherited from the parents; these eugenicists claimed to have found good scientific principles in the 1920s and 1930s that could explain such defects in the general population. Yet even at the beginning of the twentieth century it was clear to physicians and biologists that the more severe defects are generally very rare. Whether such a program should be voluntary and implemented through education and counselling or forcible by edict of the government was a question of ethics and politics at the time, however, and not one of biological science.[118] Many other important human traits such as intelligence, personality, and emotions were known scientifically to be highly complex and could not be traced to simple pathways of inheritance. Chapter 2 concludes that the AEB had no understanding of the science of genetics and, further, that most real geneticists had long abandoned eugenics as a legitimate field by the 1930s at the latest. On the other hand, there appeared to be plenty of evidence supporting environmental factors in the development of traits like intelligence, which makes for an intriguing and interesting scholarly contrast.

Early in the twentieth century, eugenic programs emerged internationally that were intended to alter physical and mental defects in the population, their scientific and genetic principles based on selective breeding that improved strains of farm animals. These principles were well known and publicly accepted by the 1930s and 1940s and were widely taught in agricultural colleges until the 1950s. However, even though critical scientific discussions about the fundamentals and the (limited) breadth of genetic understanding in agricultural science were prevalent at the time, there is no evidence that the AEB was ever aware of these discussions or even cared about such scientific principles. Rather, the practices of the AEB appear to have been based only on social prejudice, not on genuine genetic knowledge. The board members' scientific or medical "expertise" was evidently determined by allegiance to a pseudo-scientific creed—one that allowed the government of the time and the eugenics movement at large to deny the fundamental humanity of their victims, who suffered not only from loss of their sexual reproductive rights and violation of their self-identity and private sphere, but also from inflicted physical and mental harm (see Appendix, table A3). Human rights were disregarded and the forced sterilization methods often had severe health consequences—such as major hemorrhaging, infections, and scarring—beyond the annihilation of the reproductive rights and choices among the victims. As such, without doubt, the eugenics activities turned out to also be crimes under contemporary Canadian law.

The participation of the nursing community in Canadian eugenics initiatives is one example of the strong role played by a specific professional group in the pursuit and application of both positive and negative eugenics measures among the mentally ill and physically handicapped at the time. In chapter 3, "The Involvement of Nurses in the Eugenics Program in Alberta, 1920–1940," Diana Mansell investigates the first decades of the twentieth century as years in which the Canadian government actively recruited immigrants from Britain, Europe, and the United States in order to support the settlements in the newly founded provinces of western Canada.[119] As McLaren and other scholars have shown, the resulting immigration movement included fairly large numbers of non-English-speaking individuals arriving from eastern European countries. With increasing numbers of eastern European immigrants arriving (from the Ukraine, Russia, and Poland), the white Anglo-Saxon classes in Canada became increasingly concerned about what they saw as a process of the "multiplication of inferior populations."[120]

As is well known from the literature and further expanded upon by Mansell, the newly founded province of Alberta saw a ready solution in the enactment of its Sexual Sterilization Act, which remained in existence until 1972. The act was supported by many prominent first-wave feminists, such as Nellie McClung (1873–1951) and Emily Murphy (1868–1933), who argued that it would be harmful to those targeted by this act to be subjected to the rigours of parenthood, as well as harmful to their offspring, and that these "idiots" were a burden to society at large.[121] Nurses too supported Alberta's new eugenics program and the philosophical ideology behind sterilization, yet their role in promoting eugenics in the western Canadian provinces has not been studied very extensively. Chapter 3 explores their contribution to mental health nursing and the promotion of birth control measures in an overtly eugenics context. The involvement of public health nurses is taken into account here, since much of their work was directed at the health and psychiatric surveillance in the integration process of new immigrants to Canada. The period between the 1920s and the 1940s represents a time in nursing history when nurses' duty to care was increasingly influenced by the attitudes and values of those societies in which they worked, so that these cannot be artificially separated from the health-care and research perspectives undertaken in the medical and health-care fields.

Chapter 4, titled "The Alberta Eugenics Movement and the 1937 Amendment to the Sexual Sterilization Act," by Mikkel Dack, introduces another important Alberta development that attracted national and international attention. The scholarly study of eugenics legislation in Alberta has appeared rather over-focused on matters regarding the province's original Sexual Sterilization Act, passed in March 1928, along with the political, social, and economic conditions of the 1920s. Although the 1928 act was of great significance, being the first sterilization law passed in Canada, it was its 1937 amendment and the allowance of involuntary sterilization measures that made Alberta's eugenics movement truly distinct both in Canada and in comparison to many American state laws. His chapter intriguingly shows that at a time when many other regional governments were revising their sterilization laws and regulations, Alberta still expanded its own legislation. Although similar laws were met with fierce opposition in other provinces and states, this new amendment of 1937 remained virtually unopposed in Alberta. As a result of such limitations in research, historical explanations have often proved to be exaggerated, inaccurate, and misleading. By dismissing the preconceived notions and arguments of the past, as Dack argues, we lose and important intellectual residue from which to derive important insights, critical depths, and bases for comparisons when dealing with more recent forms of eugenics in social and criminal law, reproductive medicine, and biomedical experimentation in Canada and beyond.

Erna Kurbegović, in chapter 5, "Eugenics in Manitoba and the Sterilization Controversy of 1933," provides an insightful counterpoint to the scholarly discussion of the existent eugenics programs in Alberta and British Columbia. The debate in Manitoba focused on the sterilization clause within the Mental Deficiency Act of 1933. The clause called for sterilization of those deemed to be "mentally defective," if the provincial psychiatrists deemed it necessary and the patient provided consent (see Appendix). Based on the often superficial understanding of human genetics at the time, many in the medical profession presumed that "mental deficiency" was hereditary and thus would be passed on to future generations if the respective individuals were allowed to reproduce. A profound debate occurred not only within the Manitoba legislature between designated career politicians but also within communities across the province. Clearly, as Kurbegović shows, there was much opposition to the bill in this province, primarily from Roman Catholics. However, a significant amount of support also emanated from within the province's medical profession. In mid-1933 the Mental Deficiency Act passed but without the controversial sterilization section, which was defeated by one vote. Chapter 5 provides an analysis of the debate in Manitoba by investigating both sides of the political controversy in order to understand how different segments of society viewed eugenics and sexual sterilization during the interwar period. Kurbegović's findings pertaining to Manitoba can be seen as a fruitful countering foil that allows the political eugenics developments in other western Canadian provinces, particularly Alberta and British Columbia, to be placed in a more adequate historical perspective.

Chapter 6, by Celeste Tường Vy Sharpe, entitled "'New Fashioned with Respect to the Human Race': American Eugenics in the Media at the Turn of the Twentieth Century," analyzes the public and media construction of the notion of a better race for human beings in early twentieth-century North America. Ever since the term "eugenics" entered the realm of public discourse in 1883 with Francis Galton's publication—defined as "the science which deals with all influences that improve the inborn qualities of a race; also with those that develop them to the utmost advantage"—it had intrigued not only medical doctors, psychiatrists, and scientific experts but also politicians, social reformers, and activists, as well as Western societies at large.[122] At the turn of the twentieth century, the United States grappled with social pressures resulting from two decades of intense industrialization and urbanization.[123] Subsequently, eugenics achieved its greatest level of success and support in the 1920s and 1930s, following the establishment of the ERO in 1910 and the 1927 Supreme Court decision in *Buck v. Bell*, which upheld the constitutionality of forced sterilization vis-à-vis patients' claims against physicians and their institutions. Also, increased fear of the fecundity of immigrants created a panic about "race suicide." In the convergence of competing ideologies and global pressures, eugenics emerged in the United States as a proposed solution to the perceived ills of society. Chapter 6 analyzes how eugenics was discussed in US print media between 1900 and 1909 and how this discourse thereby reflected social values and perceptions. Newspaper articles consistently blended established nineteenth-century conceptions of scientists as vessels of progress, racial hierarchies, and marriage with messages that emphasized the collective over the individual and, more significantly, the need to reform society through scientific means. These frameworks sought to present eugenics in an ideologically familiar manner to gain public support for sterilization programs and legislation.

In chapter 7, Frank W. Stahnisch addresses the issue of social progressivism as a philosophical and democratic ideal among many eugenics experts in the interwar period and the stark contrast with the denigrating theoretical and anthropological assumptions as well as demeaning medical actions that contemporary nerve doctors and psychiatrists took with their involvement in the eugenics programs of the time. His example is the German-American neurologist Kurt Goldstein (1878–1965), regarded by many as an impressive interdisciplinary scholar who made numerous and lasting contributions to the fields of clinical neurology, brain psychiatry, experimental psychology, medical rehabilitation, and philosophical anthropology. Goldstein tried to combine the analytical approach of classical neurology with a holistic theory of brain function while likewise integrating the insights of contemporary "Gestalt theory" into psychology. In the clinical departments that he chaired at the Universities of Frankfurt am Main and Berlin in Germany, Goldstein not only educated medical students and residents in basic brain research and neuropathology but also trained them in broader psychoanalytic and clinicopathological approaches that emphasized the distinct need for a more humanistic attitude among future medical doctors.[124]

Rarely, however, has the fact been explored that Goldstein also ardently embraced eugenicist and racial-anthropological ideals—ideals that may be found in his concise 1913 book *On Eugenics* (*Ueber Rassenhygiene*). In this early work, Goldstein discusses, for example, the interdependencies of structural brain anomalies that have clinical neurological symptoms. With respect to this publication, the argumentation becomes somewhat interwoven with elements from the "degeneration" and "exhaustion" discourse that display major cultural characters of Weimar medicine and science. Among some of his other claims, Goldstein stated that "the relationship of hereditary conditions" does not point at specific characteristics but aspires to ameliorate the human race by eliminating unfit individuals. With similar biologistic formal rhetoric, Goldstein sided with many ardent contemporary racial anthropologists. In particular, his language invokes that of the psychiatrist Alfred Erich Hoche (1865–1943), who later—and along with Heidelberg law professor Karl Binding (1841–1920)—coined the disturbing term "life not worth living." In fact, *On Eugenics* was published out of Hoche's psychiatric department in the medical faculty of the University of Freiburg, where Goldstein had served as a clinical research associate. Though Stahnisch does not intend to exempt Goldstein from his early views on eugenics, he emphasizes the latter's social progressivist inclinations that motivated his eugenic theorizing in the 1910s, by combining these assumptions with relics of traditionalism in medicine. This "paradox of eugenics" has haunted many social progressivists of that period. Many of these individualists shared eugenics ideals; however, individuals such as Goldstein—after his emigration to America—and Tommy Douglas, the respected Canadian health-care politician, eventually discarded them. Nevertheless, several psychiatrists and biomedical researchers carried the promotion of eugenics forward in time, such as the Swiss-German psychiatrist Ruedin, while thus laying the basis for the inhumane health care system in the National Socialist period in Germany. In considering Goldstein's *On Eugenics* in its wider social and cultural contexts, chapter 7 untangles some philosophical trends and eugenics convictions that emerged from the context of modernity and its many antagonisms.[125]

In chapter 8, "Too Little, Too Late: Compensation for Victims of Coerced Sterilization," Paul Weindling—a long-standing international specialist on eugenics and medical interventions in human subjects—takes the important transatlantic dimension of knowledge exchanges in the eugenics and medico-psychiatric fields masterfully into account. Whereas European sterilization has been seen as a direct transfer of North American (notably Californian) sterilization programs in the later 1920s, this chapter outlines a far more complex and diverse forms of sterilization policies. Weindling emphasizes the dynamic interplay of state welfare and mental health policies, politics, religion, and public attitudes, which determined both the forms that sterilization took and (a matter of further complexity) its incidence. The chapter accordingly examines the following forms of sterilization: segregation of mental defectives in the United Kingdom; legislation at a provincial level, notably in Vaud, Switzerland; "voluntary" legislation at a national level from Denmark (1929) onward, notably in Scandinavia; professional sterilization, with the examples of Finland and German-speaking Swiss cantons; coercive sterilization in Nazi Germany on a legislative basis; X-ray sterilization, notably in the Nazi concentration camp of Auschwitz; sterilization on the recommendation of professionals and guardians, such as in Canada and in the United States; and vasectomy for personal contraception later in the postwar period.

These various types of sterilization policies had a complex take-up, with an uneven incidence over time and place and a changing pattern of rationales and target groups in such contexts as Nazi Germany and Scandinavia. After the Second World War, sterilization presented complex problems of legality, particularly in Germany under its Allied occupation and in Austria. Moreover, a range of issues surrounds the demand for, practice of, and denial of re-fertilization, as well as the compensation procedures for sterilization victims. This dense and exhaustive contribution highlights the immense diversity of the incidence of sterilization within Europe, particularly when neglected contexts such as Switzerland and eastern Europe are figured in. It also points to possible North American as well as specifically Canadian comparisons and links as relevant to the early twentieth-century discourse of eugenics and psychiatry. Finally, this chapter on compensation, along with the first of the two commentaries, connects the historical studies herein with more recent discussions regarding disability and human rights.

This collection involves several intriguing themes about the wider relationship of eugenics, psychiatry, and mental health, which are connected by distinctly Canadian and transatlantic perspectives. The consequences and legacy of the eugenics movement are taken up in a commentary section at the end of the book, which links the historical insights with current issues such as "ableism" and "dis-ableism" and "newgenics," thus demonstrating the value of a deeper historical understanding in present-day debates. Furthermore, the two commentaries emphasize the interdisciplinary and transnational ambitions of this volume. In Commentary One (chapter 9), Marc Workman looks at the disability rights movement in Canada and considers the ways in which the beliefs that motivated eugenicists continue to influence the treatment of people with disabilities. In particular, he explores the issues of immigration and disability and parenting with disability from a disability rights perspective. Workman's interpretation is that the disability rights movement in Canada has brought about significant legal protections for people with disabilities. However, despite these major legislative victories, Canadians with disabilities still face greater challenges from a socioeconomic perspective than do their non-disabled counterparts. The chapters in this book describe a number of violations of the rights of people with disabilities: compulsory sterilization, scientific experimentation, institutionalization, and euthanasia. Based on these insights, Workman points out that in Canada the most deplorable of these actions took place primarily before the emergence of the disability rights movement in the 1970s. His commentary not only highlights the importance of collective action for those living with disabilities; it also illuminates some of the attitudes about disability that were behind past eugenic initiatives and that persist today.

In Commentary Two (chapter 10), Gregor Wolbring goes one step further in unearthing the philosophical constructions that lay at the centre of the eugenics discourse since its beginnings. In particular, he analyzes the language used, pointing out that the categories of "mentally/physically unfit," "feeble-minded," "morons," and so on were always construed from an angle of binary opposition that contrasted the "unable" with the "able" and the "abnormal" with the "normal," similar to the analysis of French philosopher and historian of medicine George Canguilhem (1904–95) in his well-known book *On the Normal and the Pathological*.[126] Wolbring interprets the recent concept of "ableism" in contrast to the socially pejorative and medicalizing concepts of the eugenics discourse in psychiatry and mental hygiene since the beginning of the last century. By commenting on the historical examples presented in this volume, he reveals that the uses of "ableism" and "dis-ableism" are and have been limited in both content and scope. Ableism values certain abilities, which leads to dis-ableism, or discrimination against the "less able." Ableism often confuses the valuing of or obsession with ability with the term "dis-ableism." However, besides confusing ableism with dis-ableism, speaking about ableism only in connection with the so-called "disabled people" or the "handicapped" is also problematic, as these chapters show from psychiatric, mental health and nursing care, scientific and legal, and public media and policy perspectives.

In their concluding chapter, Stahnisch and Kurbegović emphasize the ways in which the history of eugenics can help us to understand ongoing debates over control of social participation and reproductive rights in modern industrialized societies. The historical eugenics perspective can lead us to question new technological practices, especially those that screen for the "abnormal" development of a fetus, thus giving parents the technical option of abortion rather than fostering a societal debate about support of the "dis-abled" or differently "en-abled" in our modern societies, as Wilson and Wolbring argue.[127] Lastly, technological advances allow individuals in modern societies to be selective; for example, in vitro fertilization provides the option to choose the "best" embryos and discard the "unfit." Therefore, the history of eugenics remains important because it offers insights into current scientific research and medical ethics as well as recent reproductive policies and practices. This volume provides an excellent perspective on bridging historical analysis in the first section, in which chapters 1 to 5 focus mainly on issues in western Canada, while chapters 6 through 8 provide valuable case studies from Europe and the United States, thus introducing transatlantic and transnational perspectives into considerations of contemporary policy and human rights issues. Individually, the chapters are significant in several fields and can be seen as important contributions in various different areas. The editors, Stahnisch and Kurbegović, anticipate that the book will be of particular interest to researchers and teachers in the fields of the histories of eugenics, public mental health, medicine, nursing, and psychiatry. Yet it can also be a productive read for scholars and workers in disability studies, human rights, medical ethics, legal and compensation studies, and public affairs, particularly in Canada. The two commentaries, together with the introduction and conclusion, build a bridge toward open and urgent issues of our time when dealing with disability, the future prospects of the new genetics field, and their wider social and public interest and response.

1

John M. MacEachran and Eugenics in Alberta

Victorian Sensibilities, Idealist Philosophy, and Detached Efficiency

Henderikus J. Stam and Ashley Barlow

John M. MacEachran (1877–1971) was initially one of the more enigmatic, and eventually one of the more disreputable, characters in the history of Alberta's long-running eugenics program.[1] The fact that he was also the only Canadian student of German experimental psychologist Wilhelm Wundt (1832–1920), as well as the founder of the Philosophy and Psychology Department at the University of Alberta, makes him of more than passing interest. Yet officially there is very little that we know about him save for the outward details of his life.[2] MacEachran was very careful, purposely or otherwise, to leave little behind and it has only been in the last few years that we have come to know more, albeit just a little more, about this seemingly paradoxical yet important figure at the centre of Alberta's eugenics program.[3] He drafted the founding constitution for the Canadian Psychological Association, in 1940, and he remained as head of the University of Alberta's Department of Psychology until the end of World War II. His reputation as a successful university administrator was nevertheless severely tested after a very public re-examination of his work as the chair of the Alberta Eugenics Board (AEB) from 1929 to 1964. Although MacEachran died in 1971, a lawsuit brought by Leilani Muir against the Government of Alberta in 1995 raised the issue of her involuntary sterilization along with that of almost three thousand others.[4]

In this chapter, we review those details and evaluate the discontinuity between MacEachran's public role as AEB chair and his place as the founding professor of philosophy and psychology at the University of Alberta. However, we will argue that the discontinuity is not quite as perplexing as it appears on the surface, if we consider MacEachran's career and philosophy as an outgrowth of a nineteenth-century, Victorian-style world view married to a progressive notion of social engineering. What is truly perplexing is the way in which MacEachran remained resistant to change.

After his death, MacEachran's role as a pioneer in Alberta's first university would be overshadowed by his role as the chair of the province's eugenics board. His portrait (see Figure 1.1) would be removed from the Department of Psychology, and his name removed from a seminar room, and discussions would ensue in both the philosophy and psychology departments (finally separated in the 1950s) at the University of Alberta as to how to re-evaluate his place in the history of the university and province.[5] This even led to the revocation of the honours associated with MacEachran's legacy.[6]

MACEACHRAN'S LIFE

The basic outlines of MacEachran's life are generally well known,[7] but somewhat more can be gleaned from the transcripts of an interview that MacEachran gave toward the end of his life.[8] John Malcolm MacEachran was born into a farming family on January 15, 1877, near Glencoe, Ontario. His father, David MacEachran (b. 1850?) had emigrated from Scotland and married Christina MacAlpine (b. 1855?). John MacEachran had two sisters and five brothers, most of whom became farmers, yet he chose to become a teacher after attending what probably was the Model School in Strathroy until the age of eighteen in 1895 (he received what was known then as a first-class certificate). After taking up a teaching post at Ivan, Ontario (just northwest of London) for an unspecified period of time (though likely no more than a year or two), he decided to study at university. Salaries for teachers, especially rural teachers, were relatively low in Canada during the latter years of the nineteenth century and the first decade of the twentieth century.[9] MacEachran had decided to go to the University of Toronto but was dissuaded from doing so by a local clergyman, who suggested he should instead study with philosopher John Watson (1847–1939) at Queen's

Figure 1.1 Portrait of John M. MacEachran, ca. 1944, from the University of Alberta's Department of Psychology. It was removed from the now-renamed MacEachran Conference Room. Likewise, his name was removed from a seminar room at the University of Alberta. Photograph courtesy of the University of Alberta Archives. Accession Number: 1971-217-4-001.

University.[10] Oddly, MacEachran claimed in a 1970 interview with Roger Myers that he had avoided the University of Toronto and gone to Queen's because he was "not keen" on Presbyterian doctrine; Queen's was in fact still dependent on the Presbyterian Church, at least until 1912, whereas the University of Toronto was by this time an openly secular institution.

At Queen's, MacEachran appeared to thrive under Watson's tutelage, claiming later in life that he did not agree with Watson's idealism—a peculiar claim given the few writings on philosophy MacEachran left behind.[11] Watson was a Scottish philosopher who had received his MA from the University of Glasgow in 1872 and then been appointed to Queen's University, in Kingston, Ontario, on the basis of his reputation among the idealist Caird brothers—John (1820–98) and Edward (1835–1908), both professors in Glasgow.[12] As philosophers Leslie Armour and Elizabeth Trott note, Watson was recognized as the major proponent of Canadian idealism and a renowned metaphysician.[13] Furthermore, he was instrumental in the creation of the United Church of Canada in 1925. MacEachran claimed that Watson received the second PhD that Queen's had ever awarded, a claim that we could not substantiate and that was unknown to the archivists at Queen's. MacEachran notes he spent four years with Watson, although this could simply be a reference to the former's PhD studies.

MacEachran arrived at Queen's in 1897 and received a master's degree in 1902. He was appointed a fellow and tutor that year as an assistant to Watson; he received his PhD in 1906. Presumably his doctorate concerned idealist philosophy, particularly the philosophy of Immanuel Kant (1724–1804) and Georg Wilhelm Friedrich Hegel (1770–1831) in Germany, although his dissertation appears to be lost.[14] In his paper "Twenty-Five Years of Philosophical Speculation" (1932), MacEachran professed his deep respect for Watson's style of critique and argument. He compared Watson's critique of hedonist philosophies to David's victory over Goliath. MacEachran was, in his own words, awed by the way that Watson managed "to dissect and negate each position of these philosophers by using their own arguments against them." Watson's style of argument, as well as the ideas he discussed in his textbooks, influenced MacEachran's own opinions on education. Throughout much of his later writing, MacEachran espoused the value of education, and the power that educators had over society. In a speech entitled "A Dream of Olympus" presented to the Faculty Club at the University of Alberta, in which MacEachran compared professors and teachers to Greek gods, Watson's influence on his own opinions and philosophical perspectives was evident.[15] Watson advocated the virtues of self-discipline in his writings and MacEachran appeared to have carried these virtues forward into his own writing on education. Publicly at least, MacEachran showed nothing but respect for Watson and emulated his rather formal and grandiloquent style of writing.

After graduating from Queens, MacEachran wished to take up the study of psychology in Germany.[16] In 1906, he left for Berlin (later he would recall this to be 1902, but that was clearly another mistake). He does not say with whom he wished to study but it is likely that he would have wanted to either meet or study with Carl Stumpf (1848–1936), the renowned philosopher and psychologist who founded the Institute of Psychology at the University of Berlin in 1900. According to Thomas Nelson, based on an interview with MacEachran, the latter and Stumpf were unable to establish an amiable research relationship and MacEachran remained in Berlin for only nine months.[17] In his 1970 interview with Myers, MacEachran refers to an unnamed professor in Berlin (likely Stumpf) who had asked him, "What training have you had?," presumably referring to his training in psychology. MacEachran said that he replied, "I have had none." However, in his dissertation—published in Leipzig in 1910—he mentions that he attended lectures with Friedrich Paulsen (1846–1908), Otto Pfleiderer (1839–1908), Alois Riehl (1844–1924), Erich Schmidt (1853–1913), Ulrich von Wilamowitz-Moellendorff (1848–1931), and Heinrich Woelfflin (1864–1945), in addition to Stumpf. These were important figures in early twentieth-century German intellectual life: Paulsen was one of the most notable students of experimental psychologist Gustav Theodor Fechner (1801–87); Pfleiderer was an influential liberal theologian; Riehl was a neo-Kantian philosopher who succeeded Wilhelm Dilthey (1833–1911) in his university professorship in 1905; Schmidt had the chair of German language and literature in Berlin; Wilamowitz-Moellendorff was a renowned classicist; and Woelfflin was an art historian and critic.

In 1907, MacEachran went to Leipzig to study with Wilhelm Wundt at the University of Leipzig. The elder Wundt was by this time already seventy-five years old. Between 1876 and 1919, Wundt supervised a total of 186 dissertations at Leipzig, of which 33 were American.[18] Although his recollections are sparse, MacEachran completed a thesis with Wundt on pragmatism in German (*Pragmatismus*).[19] We know very little of his time in Leipzig, other than the odd anecdote he repeated from time to time about Wundt (for example, about Wundt's poor hearing). It does appear that MacEachran spent at most two years in Leipzig, leaving in 1909, but some of this time was taken up travelling to other cities in Europe.

When he approached Wundt to determine whether he could study with him, MacEachran wanted Wundt to give him "an *Arbeit* in psychology." Yet according to MacEachran, Wundt then said, "No, you are not a psychologist. You are a philosopher. You had better take something on philosophy."[20] Although recalled more than sixty years after the fact, it was true that Wundt was writing his ten-volume *Voelkerpsychologie* at the time and was no longer actively engaged in experimental psychology research. Furthermore, MacEachran indeed had no training in psychology. Apparently, MacEachran himself suggested the topic of pragmatism and Wundt finally agreed—"because they didn't know anything about pragmatism in Germany."[21] In 1907, while MacEachran was writing his thesis on pragmatism, American philosopher William James (1842–1910) coincidentally published his own book on the subject, of which MacEachran was quite critical.[22] In 1910, MacEachran finished his thesis. It was published by Leipzig University under the title *Pragmatismus: Inaugural-dissertation zur Erlangung der Doktorwuerde der hohen philosophischen Fakultaet* (Pragmatism: Inaugural dissertation for the completion of the doctorate for the higher philosophical faculty). At Leipzig, MacEachran also later thanked Karl Gotthard Lamprecht (1856–1915), Johannes Volkelt (1848–1930), and Wilhelm Wirth (1876–1952) as his professors in his dissertation. This was not irrelevant to his dissertation nor presumably to his development as a scholar. Lamprecht had founded the *Institut fuer Kultur- und Universalgeschichte* at the University of Leipzig and thus was supportive of Wundt's new work on the *Voelkerpsychologie*. Volkelt was an anti-positivist philosopher, and Wirth was one of Wundt's assistants.

A number of commentators on MacEachran, including Nelson and Myers, have referred subsequently to MacEachran as a "pragmatist," presumably both in its colloquial sense, as someone who is practical and reasonable, as well as in its philosophical sense.[23] However, MacEachran's thesis was in fact a critique of pragmatism, not a sympathetic appraisal. Although he claimed that he had thought of going to study with William James, and he used James's shorter version (the 1892 *Briefer Course*) of the *Principles of Psychology* in his early teaching career, MacEachran concludes his thesis by noting that pragmatism may have been seen as "a new humanism" and a "new Renaissance in the philosophy,"[24] but much of the pragmatist principles were already to be found in the philosophies of the Greek philosophers Protagoras (481–411 BC) and Socrates (ca. 470–399 BC), as well as in the German idealists Kant, Johann Gottlieb Fichte (1762–1814), and even Johann Wolfgang von Goethe (1749–1832). MacEachran was particularly critical of pragmatism's conception of truth.[25] He later described James's writing as flippant and opportunistic.[26] Nevertheless, MacEachran provided a complete account of the pragmatic perspective. His conclusion was that while the "Pragmatists had affirmed that there was no one truth . . . so it turned out that there was no one Pragmatism."[27] According to MacEachran, Wundt was very pleased with the thesis and the examination was quick and successful. MacEachran had succeeded in completing his second PhD. However, instead of remaining in Europe (MacEachran was fluent in German, and likely French as well) or taking up a position at an established American university where psychology's reputation and growth was now ascendant, MacEachran chose to go to Edmonton, Alberta, a very small Prairie city with a population then of approximately twenty-three thousand people.[28] He remained there for the rest of his life, save for a brief foray as paymaster of the 196th (Western Universities) Battalion serving in France during World War I.[29] Apparently, Henry Marshall Tory (1864–1947), mathematics professor and inaugural president of the University of Alberta, had already hired MacEachran in 1908 but then wired him not to come since they did not need a philosopher that year (the first year that classes were offered at the University of Alberta). One account of this change was that Tory was allowed to hire only four professors in the university's first year. However, in order to secure MacEachran's place at the new university, Tory deliberately travelled to Paris to make amends and persuade MacEachran to come to Alberta (see Figure 1.2).[30] MacEachran agreed, cancelled the remainder of his planned European tour, and arrived in 1909 to teach philosophy and psychology.

Why MacEachran chose the University of Alberta as his first and only professorship remains unclear. As Nelson noted, MacEachran's reasons were always vague but certainly influenced heavily by Tory.[31] According to the classicist Walter Hugh Johns (1908–85), Tory's first and most important duty was to recruit high-ranking professors from other schools in order to create a prestigious faculty for the university's first semester.[32] Tory

Figure 1.2 Portrait photograph of John M. MacEachran, ca. 1920, at about the time he began his career at the University of Alberta. Photograph courtesy of the University of Alberta Archives. Accession Number: 1971-217-003.

decided not to hire any professor studying or working in Alberta, in order to promote the high educational standards of the University of Alberta. He thus embarked on his ambitious attempt to recruit only the best scholars from Canada and the United States. In staffing the Department of Philosophy and Psychology he must have logically turned to Germany, where the foundations of psychology were firm, and discovered MacEachran, a Canadian student of both philosophy and psychology possessing two distinct doctoral degrees. It is unclear how Tory persuaded MacEachran to travel to the new province of Alberta—founded just three years before the opening of the university in Edmonton—to teach at a university that had not yet been fully built. However, it is likely that MacEachran was intrigued by the opportunity to create a department tailored entirely to his own educational interests. MacEachran was to be the only professor in the Psychology and Philosophy department and would have the freedom to teach whatever he saw fit.[33] Furthermore, Nelson speculates that the challenge of creating a department that would meet Tory's expectations intrigued MacEachran, and he thus accepted Tory's offer. Despite the remoteness of the new province of Alberta and the daunting task of creating an entire department on his own, MacEachran likely saw this as a promising opportunity. It was not a fast-growing department; by 1938 it still only had three faculty members. When asked why he decided to stay in Edmonton for his entire career, MacEachran replied that "a man should stick to what he starts to do"—not a very forthcoming statement.[34]

MacEachran did not appear to do any original research during his entire career at the university. Not that this mattered a great deal—the new university needed instructors and administrators to create the foundations of a modern institution of higher learning and teaching, which was a priority. In addition to a few short articles, MacEachran also left a seemingly unfinished book-length manuscript entitled *An Outline of Modern Philosophy* in the archives. This would likely have served as a textbook for undergraduate classes, and typed and copied chapters may very well have been passed out to students; indeed, it may have been created not as a text for publication but rather as simply his notes to students.[35] The University of Alberta provided MacEachran with multiple teaching and administrative duties over the length of his career. He was appointed the first provost, in 1914 (apparently because he was the only bachelor among the faculty), and was given the duties of handling student affairs and discipline.[36] He held multiple administrative appointments at the university over his career but none so important or controversial as the one he held outside the university: chairmanship of the Alberta Eugenics Board (AEB).[37]

EUGENICS IN ALBERTA

The broad history of Alberta's eugenics program is now widely known. It has been discussed at length in contemporary historical accounts, and elements of this program are also considered in chapters 2, 3, and 4.[38] In short, the United Farmers of Alberta government passed the Sexual Sterilization Act in 1928, enabling the creation of a eugenics board responsible for approving cases brought before it for sterilization. The original members of the AEB were Dr. Edgerton Pope (1874–1949), Dr. Edward G. Mason (1874–1947), MacEachran, and the secretary, Mrs. Jean H. Field (d. 1974?). The University of Alberta and the Council of the College of Physicians appointed Pope from Edmonton and Mason from Calgary. MacEachran and Field were appointed by the province's Lieutenant Governor, William Legh Walsh (1857–1938).[39] The board, when presented with an inmate of a mental hospital, was tasked with examining and interviewing the patient. Sterilization would be recommended if board members unanimously agreed that the inmate could be safely "discharged if the danger of procreation with its attendant risk of multiplication of the evil by transmission of the disability to progeny were eliminated."[40] The Sexual Sterilization Act required consent of the patient or, if in the board's opinion the patient was incapable of giving consent, the spouse or parents of the inmate were permitted to consent on the inmate's behalf before the board authorized the sterilization. In 1937, the legislation was amended to widen the definition of "mentally defective person" and thus increase the scope of potential sterilization candidates (see chapter 4). This amendment stated that a mentally defective person was any person "in whom there is a condition of arrested or incomplete development of mind existing before the age of eighteen years, whether arising from inherent causes or induced disease or injury."[41]

A further revision of the act, in 1942, included new sections for those suffering from the neurological conditions of epilepsy and Huntington's chorea. In the case of individuals suffering from Huntington's chorea, if consent was not obtained, the AEB was still able to recommend sterilization of the individual. This occurred in such cases where the board believed such a procedure was in the best interest of a patient. The 1942 revision also removed the requirement of consent in the cases of mental defectives, while still requiring the consent of "psychotics" before sterilization would be approved.

Chief psychiatry social worker E. Mary Frost (b. 1918?) noted in 1942 that in its first year of operation the board recommended the sterilization of only four individuals, and sterilization of three of these individuals was completed. By 1936 (the year before the Sexual Sterilization Act was modified) the number of recommended operations had increased to 191, with 78 actually performed. In 1937, 202 sterilizations were recommended and 105 were performed.[42] Although the number of sterilizations performed in 1937 seems to be much higher than in previous years, this number was actually equal to the 105 sterilizations performed in 1934, when the original act was still in effect. It would appear that changes to the legislation in 1937 did not have a direct and immediate effect on the number of sterilizations performed. Frost's research indicated that the number of mental defective cases passed and subsequently sterilized remained similar to that of cases before 1937. Between 1932 and 1936 the number of recommended sterilizations was 779; between 1937 and 1941 the number of recommended sterilizations was also 779. After 1941, however, the number of sterilizations recommended by the AEB increased steadily until 1969, when only 63 operations were performed. It is also remarkable that the board spent less and less time reviewing cases brought before it. As members of the AEB grew more comfortable in their position, they would often spend only five to ten minutes reviewing cases, and more often than not, the board would recommend sterilization. AEB records from 1959 indicate that 95 cases were presented to the board that year and 94 of these were passed.[43] On June 2, 1972, the newly elected Progressive Conservative government of Premier Peter Lougheed (1928–2012) repealed the Sexual Sterilization Act.[44] By this time 2,822 individuals had been sterilized, with 4,725 cases actually passed by the AEB.[45]

It is important to note that the Alberta government used three arguments to repeal the act. The first was that it was based on outdated medical knowledge and was ambiguous as well, allowing too much latitude in its interpretation. The second was that the act did not protect those involved in the sterilization program from civil liability. Most important, however, was the argument voiced by David King (b. 1946), then legislative secretary to Premier Lougheed and the sponsor of the motion to repeal the act:

> That is, simply, that the act violates fundamental human rights. We are provided with an act, the basis of which is a presumption that society, or at least the government, knows what kinds of people can be allowed children and what kinds of people cannot.
>
> In support of this position the act provides the opportunity—which, admittedly, has not recently been used but which exists in the act—for the government to order the sterilization of certain people without consent. It is our view that this is a reprehensible and intolerable philosophy and program for this province and this government.[46]

Although there was some resistance from certain groups to the repeal of the Sexual Sterilization Act, it did not come from the AEB.[47] The Women of Unifarm, a rural women's organization, actually met with members of cabinet to persuade the government to reintroduce eugenics legislation. They argued that "because we believe the unborn child has the basic right to begin life with as few handicaps as possible, we affirm that people certified to be mentally unfit to become parents should have their reproductive capabilities curtailed."[48] However, given the newly elected Lougheed government's proclaimed dedication to introducing a provincial bill of rights (which was done in March 1972), the Sexual Sterilization Act was widely seen as a clear obstacle to those rights.[49]

A lawsuit brought against the Government of Alberta in 1995 by Leilani Muir, a survivor of sterilization, generated a great deal of publicity about a chapter of Alberta history that had up to then been relatively little known to those outside of medical or legal circles.[50] Muir's successful challenge led to an apology from the government and a subsequent payment of $740,780 plus costs.[51] It was this case that led to a range of academic works on eugenics in Alberta by historians and sociologists.[52]

MACEACHRAN AND EUGENICS

Despite the large number of articles and books now published about the Alberta eugenics program, MacEachran's influence beyond chairing the committee remains vague. He was, by all accounts, an intensely private man who was circumspect with others. As noted, Roger Myers, a historian of psychology from the University of Toronto, interviewed MacEachran in 1970 for an oral history project, the transcripts of which are now located in the Canadian Psychological Association archives at Library and Archives Canada. The interview contains virtually no comment on the nature of MacEachran's work with the AEB. However, Myers reported later to a former faculty member of the University of Alberta that MacEachran had spoken at length about his experience with the board over a glass of Scotch whiskey after Myers had turned off the tape recorder.[53]

Given the paucity of records left by MacEachran, speculation about his motivations for remaining on the AEB is largely groundless. He retired from the University of Alberta in 1945, at the age of sixty-eight. Nonetheless, he maintained his position as AEB chair until he was eighty-eight. The last meeting he attended—meeting no. 327—was on May 28, 1965. Heather Pringle, writing in *Saturday Night* magazine in 1997, noted that MacEachran "clung to the chairmanship like a bull terrier for nearly forty years."[54] It was not for compensation—in Smith's survey of the psychology department's salary distribution in 1928, the year the AEB was established, MacEachran's salary would have been $5,500 per year.[55] In contrast, his salary for chairing the board was only $375.[56] The AEB met only a few times per year, at different mental hospitals around the province. Chairing the board was neither physically taxing nor financially rewarding. MacEachran likely did the work because he believed it to be important; that is, he believed the generally held conception that sterilizing "mental defectives" was a genuine contribution to society. However, it also likely enhanced his stature among other professionals, and meetings were infrequent enough that he could continue such work after his university retirement without excessive strain.

The AEB files are remarkably absent of personal notes and indications of the life of the committee. The board went about its business quietly and efficiently, with little change in personnel over the years. Only twenty directing members constituted the board over the years of its operation, from 1929 to 1972.[57] And like MacEachran himself, the AEB itself was a model of bureaucratic efficiency. With remarkably little oversight, and with the overt assistance of the medical profession, the AEB operated out of the public eye. Occasional notes in the board meeting minutes indicate a nagging concern about legal issues. For example, in 1935, between meetings 72

(September 19) and 73 (December 18), an excerpt from the *British Medical Journal* was typed out and circulated among AEB members. The excerpt was part of a report on a meeting by the Section of Obstetrics and Gynaecology of the Royal Society of Medicine with the Eugenics Society, held on February 15, 1935, "for a discussion on sterilization of women, including indications—medical and eugenic—technique, and the legal position."[58] The excerpt focused on the report by a Mr. Cecil Binney (1897–1966), barrister-at-law, who argued that "the sterilization operation might come within the Offences against the Person Act (1861), and it ha[s] long been held that the person's consent was not a defence in a charge of maiming." Furthermore, "with regard to lunatics and mental defectives, if the sterilization of normal persons was a crime, the sterilization of persons who could not give consent and did not properly understand what was proposed would be so much more a crime.... [Sterilization] in the case of lunatics and mentally deficient persons [was] always unlawful unless undertaken for health reasons."[59] The excerpt was circulated within the AEB but there are no comments in the minutes about this or any acknowledgment that the members discussed it. Despite such lack of evidence regarding reception and discussion of the excerpt, its attachment to the minutes ensured that it must have come to the attention of the board.

No other Canadian province had a system in place like the province of Alberta, as is well known.[60] Further, numerous commentators have mentioned the speed at which the board's work was done.[61] By examining the number of cases discussed at the meetings, Jana Grekul estimates that the AEB spent an average of thirteen minutes per case across the decades of its existence.[62] The amount of time varied per case, of course, but during the 1940s the average was about eight minutes.[63]

Anomalous cases would take longer—and we present one here as an illustration of the kinds of discussions that were taken up by the board. This example is the case of a woman who requested a reversal of her operation, which led to some considerable discussion during the meeting of June 14, 1945.[64] The young woman had written to Dr. David L. McCullough (life dates unknown), the superintendent of the Provincial Training School for Mental Defectives in Red Deer, on January 23, 1945:

> Being as I have been under your care since I was 11 1/2 yrs old I naturally feel that no Dr. could help me as much as you can doctor. My first important question is: Is it possible for me to have my sterile [*sic*]

> fixed, so that I can have children of my own? [My husband] is willing to pay for the operation if it must be done & I am willing with the help of God & my husband[']s help to take the chance or risk what ever it maybe [*sic*] & I am counting on you doctor as my doctor & friend, to help me find the happiness that I am striving for.

Apparently there was no answer from McCullough; a subsequent letter was written on March 23, 1945:

> I hope that you or Miss ____ will find time to answer the questions that I asked you in my last letter to you Doctor McCullough for as you know that I am over 25 years old now & to my idea if I can get fixed up now, while I am still young & I still have my health & strength, I think that I'd have an easier time & it would maybe heal up a lot better too, don't you think so Doctor? I sure would like to have some children of my own if I possibly can, for I get pretty lonesome at times, especially when [my husband] is away & I am by myself nearly all the time & I hardly get away from here at all & I sure get lonesome & fed up at times. There are times when I feel & think that married life isn't so wonderful at all, especially when its a childless marriage & I wonder at times how a Doctor could ever think of such a thing as sterilization? For life certainly is no good without children that is, as far as I am concerned.

McCullough finally answered these letters, providing a chatty rendition of life at the school. In the middle of the letter, in the fourth paragraph, he wrote, "So far as I know, your operation cannot be undone. Remember always . . . that it was done for your own good. You would not want children who might have to come here and spend many years or perhaps their whole life in an Institution."

The board's discussion resulted in the following notes in the minutes:

> This letter had already been answered satisfactorily by Dr. D. L. McCullough of the Provincial Training School, Red Deer, so it was not felt that the Board need take any further action in the matter. . . . During the discussion regarding the above letter, a question was raised as to whether or not it would be illegal to undo an operation which had been ordered according to law. It was felt that this question be discussed with a legal advisor such as Mr. W. S. Gray, at a later date.

Thus, while efficient, the AEB took time to address some concerns raised by former patients, even if it was only to keep liability at bay.[65] However, it is clear that many cases must have been accepted and moved through in a matter of a few minutes if time was also taken for this kind of discussion.

MACEACHRAN'S PHILOSOPHY AND EUGENICS

Except for clearly being an ardent supporter of the work of the AEB, MacEachran made little public mention of his thinking on the matter of eugenics save for a brief period in the early 1930s. Several items remain in the record, including an article in the journal *Mental Hygiene* in 1932 and a talk given to the United Farm Women's Association the same year, later published in full in what was then called the *Press Bulletin*, a University of Alberta publication. The talk broadly addressed the "cure and prevention of crime," and MacEachran argued in favour of the eugenics program:

> We should endeavour to get away from a very costly form of sentiment and give more attention to raising and safeguarding the purity of the race. We allow men and women of defective intelligence or of these criminal tendencies to have children. There is one remedy for such eventualities and we fortunately have begun to make use of it in Alberta—although not yet nearly extensively enough. This is the Alberta Sterilization Act. Since the state must assume most of the load of responsibility in connection with its defective children, it surely is justified in adopting reasonable measures to protect itself against their multiplication.[66]

Although the rhetoric of "safeguarding the purity of the race" was in fact widely adopted by those in favour of the eugenics program,[67] especially among the United Farm Women's Association, MacEachran argues in favour of sterilizing those with "criminal tendencies" as well.[68] This was echoed in several other talks and papers in 1931 and 1932. Critical of the justice and prison system for its inability to reform inmates, MacEachran also argued that offenders were usually those with low intelligence. Ultimately, it was people like him, the philosophers and psychologists, who should take their "rightful" position as administrators of punishment.[69]

Remarkably, he was silent after the mid-1930s, at least as far as any public pronouncements were concerned—no more articles, presentations, or public comments on eugenics. MacEachran was by then in his mid-fifties and had reached the zenith of his career. He was a successful academic and a government official with an important function. He would no longer draw attention to the latter, whether by design, through a personal commitment to privacy, or through a realization that the work was in some ways controversial.

This was also true for any further publications on philosophy. His unpublished lecture notes with textbook character, on philosophy, were framed around an eclectic collection of traditional philosophers, heavily favouring idealist philosophers from Plato (428/27–348/47 BC) forward. His thesis, as noted above—written in 1908 and defended in 1909—was on pragmatism. In 1933, he published an article in a local, edited work composed of lectures commemorating the twenty-fifth anniversary of the founding of the University of Alberta. MacEachran's contribution was a lengthy disputation on the nature of what he termed "speculative philosophy" in the nineteenth and twentieth centuries. His emphasis in this publication was a defence of idealist philosophy. He contrasted the great age of German idealism (Kant, Hegel) with British idealism of the late nineteenth century. Francis Herbert Bradley (1846–1924) appears to be the key philosopher for MacEachran and was treated to special mention: "Bradley's *Appearance and Reality* has sometimes appeared to me like a magnificent sonata in which a minor and a major chord are woven into a melody that is repeated in a multitude of variations, representing the transforming power of philosophic contemplation which persists in viewing all aspects of life in the totality of their significance."[70] French philosopher Henri Bergson (1859–1941) also received special praise for his philosophy of time and his *élan vital*: "Bergson was a genuine prophet of the spiritual life in the most elevated and less conventional sense of that term, as indicating a delicate sensitivity to the refinement and beauty of the inner life of imaginative spontaneity and contemplative creativeness in which man rises to his highest."[71] Having critiqued William James in 1909, MacEachran now found in James's notion of "pure experience"—originally published in 1904 but apparently not known to MacEachran until 1912—something that resonated with idealism. Thus he concluded his essay with a paean to the unity of knowledge, an all-encompassing metaphysical vision of the universe, "only that deeper understanding which is born of knowledge and of love will enable us to penetrate the inner secrets of life, to illuminate its true spiritual values and to give direction in the world of practical affairs."[72]

The only time MacEachran's philosophy and his work in mental health came together in a published form was in his 1932 article in *Mental Hygiene.* The editor's note accompanying this paper states, "This article by Professor MacEachran indicates something of the debt that mental hygiene owes to Greek culture. This is the first of a series of articles to be contributed to MENTAL HYGIENE by various men of distinction."[73] The article is a meditation on the relevance of ancient Greek philosophy for mental hygiene, in particular the philosophy of Plato and the use of *katharsis* in Greek thought. It is a fairly standard account relying largely on the *Charmides* and *Republic* as sources. Katharsis was for Plato a cleansing of the body that in the *Charmides* is expanded to include a cleansing of the soul. The physician must treat the whole, not merely one part or the other, Socrates is made to say.[74]

MacEachran then appealed to Plato's dialogues the *Laws* and the *Republic* for their focus on restricted marriage and childbearing as a form of ensuring that only the mentally and physically fit reproduce, reading into Plato a standard nineteenth-century version of eugenics. MacEachran argued, "We may not, perhaps, be prepared to go as far as Plato recommends in the way of restricting marriage and the procreation of children; but it is well to recognize that about twenty-five hundred years ago the greatest thinker in the western world was giving the most careful consideration to problems that we, in spite of our much vaunted progress and efficiency, have scarcely attacked or even seriously ventured to discuss in public."[75] His concluding comments reiterate the importance of the Greek ideal of *katharsis* and how it "grew into a great purifying philosophy of life."[76] Although MacEachran addresses neither the problem of eugenics directly nor the genuine problems of mental hygiene as these were present in the early years of the Great Depression, he does make a case for human perfection through philosophy. Yet his article is a contribution neither to philosophy nor to mental hygiene but instead rehearses a theme present elsewhere in MacEachran's philosophical writings: namely, the perfectibility of humankind and the regulation of the social realm.

What to contemporary sensibilities will seem like a great chasm, or at the very least a contradiction, between the fine language of philosophy and the dark work of sterilizing the "mentally unfit" was not so for MacEachran. His work on the AEB was of a piece with his philosophical outlook: it was left to those who were capable and willing to move society forward to make the necessary decisions for those who were not.

That MacEachran was able to continue to work on the AEB until 1965 was all the more remarkable for the deeply disturbing accounts of the Nazi regime that would have been widely disseminated after World War II. The Nazis sterilized somewhere between three hundred and four hundred thousand people following the introduction of a sterilization law in 1934.[77] More than two hundred "hereditary health courts" were established to facilitate this work, not unlike the eugenics board. Not only the presence of the death camps but also the sterilization and murder of those deemed inferior prior to the war were already well known following the Nuremberg trials.[78] We have no idea how this news may or may not have affected MacEachran or other members of the board. Yet perhaps his public silence after the early 1930s is not so difficult to interpret. Regardless, his continued and enthusiastic work for the board can only be seen as an endorsement of the principles of eugenics and the rightness of sterilizing those deemed unfit to reproduce.[79]

In this respect, MacEachran's philosophical preferences suited his work on the AEB. His ability to carry on was facilitated by the board's lack of accountability, the remoteness of Edmonton and Alberta in the contemporary Canadian context, and the province's conservative orientation to family and society. The confluence of progressivism and eugenics, forged in the early twentieth century, had long before begun to unravel, while the board continued its work.[80] Yet that work was protected by statute. We surmise that MacEachran's personal ethics were protected by an idiosyncratic and highly idealized philosophical world view that supported his understanding of himself as a good public servant, furthering the work of providing the "good life" for a majority of citizens. He was, in effect, doing the work of creating a new society. However, his wilful ignorance of the consequences of Nazi eugenics as well as his insistence on remaining chair of the eugenics board long past retirement age suggest that he had little concern for the people he was charged to protect. Instead, his status as a government and medical insider appear to have governed his actions. His isolation from changing academic norms and developments in science and philosophy, in addition to his inability to read the signs of the times, made him an anachronism on the Prairies in the second half of the twentieth century. This would have been harmless were it not for his indifferent adherence to a practice of sterilization that was based on what a later generation would clearly see as a violation of human rights.

2

The Consequences of Eugenic Sterilization in Alberta

Douglas Wahlsten

It is widely, although perhaps not universally, held today that eugenic sterilization in Alberta was morally, legally, and politically wrong. The judge in the case of *Muir v. Alberta* strongly condemned what had been done in the name of eugenics, and Premier Ralph Klein (1942–2013) delivered an apology to Leilani Muir in person.[1] The Muir trial explored the illegality of many things done by the Alberta Eugenics Board (AEB), but it did not delve into the scientific basis for eugenics itself. No experts in population genetics testified at the trial.[2] This chapter examines the science available to the AEB in the 1950s and 1960s, when hundreds of Alberta children, among others, were sterilized, and estimates the likely effects of all those sterilizations.[3] This estimate was not made at that time, so let us do it now. For historical and contemporary reasons, it is also informative to compare the likely genetic consequences to enhancements in children's intelligence that could have been achieved by improving their environments, according to knowledge available at that time.[4]

The author specializes in the study of genetic influences on behaviour and has published several scientific articles on heredity and human intelligence.[5] He attended much of the trial, became familiar with the Muir case in detail, and later served as an editor of her book, *A Whisper Past*.[6] After her stunning victory in court, many others who had been sterilized by order of the AEB initiated their own lawsuits. The author was then asked to serve as an expert witness in the resulting trials, in the capacity of which he reviewed many complete case files and prepared a scientific assessment of the actions of the AEB.[7] These cases were later settled out of court, and the identities of most of the plaintiffs are now protected.

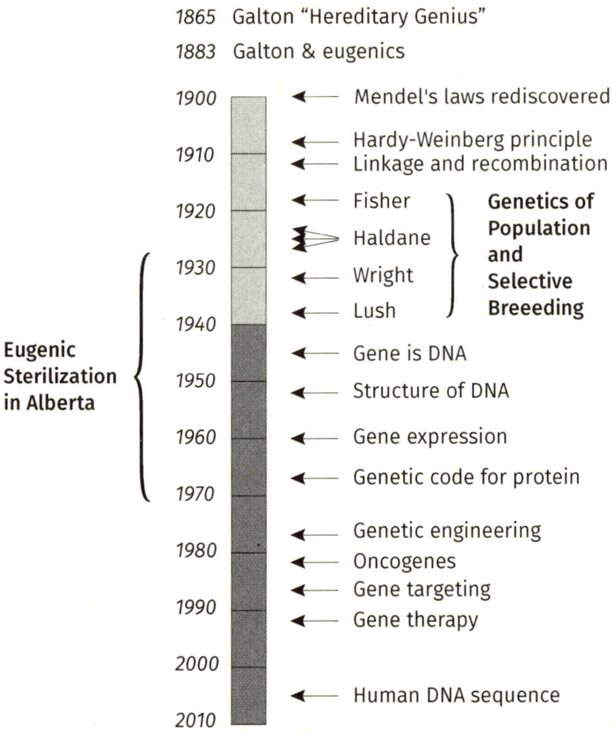

Figure 2.1 Timeline of genetic advances. The Sexual Sterilization Act of Alberta was passed in 1928 and repealed in 1972. The scientific principles of genetic inheritance were understood before the act was passed but were not taken into account. Figure compiled and designed by Douglas Wahlsten, 2013.

EUGENICS PREDATED GENETICS

History reveals that the practice of eugenic sterilization, before Alberta's Sexual Sterilization Act was passed in 1928, was conceived before the scientific principles of genetics and heredity were understood. It is quite a telling fact to see that the Mendelian laws of genetics and early scientific insights from the field of synthetic evolution had not been integrated with eugenics legislation until the act was repealed in 1972 (see Figure 2.1).[8] By the 1920s, when eugenic policies were adopted in Alberta and several US states, scientific knowledge of heredity had advanced greatly,[9] but there are serious doubts as to whether those responsible for implementing eugenic policies in Alberta had even a basic understanding of the scientific basis for what they wanted to accomplish.

British psychologist Francis Galton (1822–1911),[10] cousin of evolutionary biologist Charles Darwin (1809–82), published *Heredity Genius* in 1869 on the basis of his observations of the achievements of eminent British men and their male offspring.[11] High achievement tended to follow the male line in those days, and Galton interpreted his observations as support for a "like begets like" view of heredity. He concluded, "I find that talent is transmitted by inheritance in a very remarkable degree."[12] In 1883 he fathered the doctrine of eugenics, which he defined as "the study of the agencies under social control, that improve or impair the racial qualities of future generations either physically or mentally."[13] Galton advocated that government policies should be applied to foster breeding by the best specimens and restrain the breeding of supposedly inferior individuals. Although the Bohemian Augustinian monk and naturalist Gregor Mendel (1822–84) presented his brilliant experiments with the garden pea to the Bruenn Natural History Society in 1865, and the work was published in 1866, Galton took no account of Mendel's work at all—nor did biological science appreciate its significance until 1900, when it was rediscovered and Mendel's results were confirmed in a wide variety of species.[14] From that time, the science of genetics developed rapidly.[15] The mathematical aspects of genetics and risks of genetic disease in different kinds of relatives were well understood in the period when eugenic policies were active in Alberta, and mathematical methods for applying them to animal breeding in farming had become widely accepted.

LEVEL OF KNOWLEDGE

The AEB's decisions involved primarily the disciplines of genetics, the psychology of child development, and intelligence testing. The board included people with higher education but not specific expertise in those fields. It would be reasonable to expect the AEB to have had at least a level of knowledge that students in undergraduate (bachelor's degree) and graduate (master's degree) programs in those fields at the University of Alberta would have acquired during that period. The University of Alberta calendar as well as the syllabi or course outlines deposited in the university archives for many pertinent courses were therefore consulted.[16] The principles of genetics were well understood in the 1920s,[17] and undergraduate courses at the university presented Mendelian genetics to students *before* the Sexual Sterilization Act was passed in 1928. In 1917, the course Animal Husbandry 52(a): Animal Breeding taught "the principles of animal breeding, variation, selection, heredity and modern methods of practice." A new course, Biology 51: Comparative Anatomy and Genetics, was offered in 1918, and, in 1920, Biology 1: General Elementary Biology included "Mendelism, Genetics." In 1922, Animal Husbandry 53: Animal Breeding was described as an "application of the principles of genetics to the improvement of domesticated livestock" and its text was *Genetics in Relation to Agriculture*.[18] The first University of Alberta course devoted entirely to genetics was Field Husbandry 61: Genetics in 1923.

Selective breeding to improve the genetic quality of Alberta's population was the principal rationale for eugenic sterilization at this time.[19] The University of Alberta calendar for 1950–51 lists the course Animal Husbandry 65: Animal Breeding, which applied the principles of genetics to the improvement of farm animals, and the more general course Genetics 51, which introduced the basic principles of heredity. The texts for those courses, as listed in the calendar, were *Animal Breeding Plans* by the pioneering Kansas animal geneticist Jay Lawrence Lush (1896–1982) and *Genetics* (1945) by Texas-based *Drosophila* geneticist Edgar Altenburg (1888–1976), respectively.[20] These books indicate what ought to have been known by anyone using a scientific approach to selective breeding. After all, if contemporary genetic science was used to choose parents for propagating farm animals, surely the level of knowledge applied to the selective breeding of humans should have been at least as high as for work with domestic fowl and cattle.

The AEB relied heavily on data from intelligence testing.[21] During the academic year of 1950–51, and for many years thereafter, the undergraduate course Psychology 63: Elementary Psychometrics taught students about "the nature of psychological tests, with practical work in administration, scoring and interpretation of tests," and the graduate course Psychology 107: Clinical Psychometrics taught of "diagnostic clinical tests: Wechsler-Bellevue, Binet ... with practical work in administration, scoring and interpretation." Education 172–176 was a course to be taken by all students in education and included instruction about "the intelligence testing program, and the wise employment of test results." The text for the course was *Educational Psychology* by the Washington-based child psychologists Lester D. Crow (1897–1983) and Alice Crow (life dates unknown), and supplementary references used as required reading included *Differential Psychology* by New York-based test psychologist Anne Anastasi (1908–2001) and *Educational Psychology* by the Columbia psychologist Arthur I. Gates (1898–1989) et al.[22] The 1950–51 reading list for Education 476: Educational Psychology included *The Meaning of Intelligence* by University of Illinois education professor George D. Stoddard (1897–1981), *Measuring Intelligence* by the American psychologists Lewis M. Terman (1878–1956) and Maud A. Merrill (1888–1978), and *Measurement of Adult Intelligence* by the Romanian American psychologist David Wechsler (1896–1981).[23] Students in the course Education 476 were later assigned *Intelligence and Experience* by educational psychologist Joseph McVicker-Hunt (1906–91) as a reading, as indicated by annotations in copies of the book in the University of Alberta Library.[24] The library also held multiple copies of Anastasi's *Psychological Testing*, for use as a required reading in the Edmonton university's psychology courses.[25]

ALBERTA LAW

Admission of a mentally deficient person to a provincial mental institution was governed by the Mental Defectives Act, whereas operations of the AEB and requirements for sterilization were governed by the Sexual Sterilization Act.[26] The Mental Defectives Act defined a "mentally defective person" as a "person in whom there is a condition of arrested or incomplete development of mind existing before the age of eighteen years, whether arising from inherent causes or induced by disease or injury."[27]

Section 14(4) of the Mental Defectives Act anticipated eugenic sterilization where it stated, in part, "The Superintendent (a) may discharge a mentally defective person from an institution in any case in which the Superintendent considers . . . that the power of procreation of such person no longer exists."

The Sexual Sterilization Act used the same definition of a "mentally defective person" and stipulated,

> The medical superintendent or other person in charge of a mental hospital may cause a patient of a mental hospital whom it is proposed to discharge therefrom, to be examined by or in the presence of the [Alberta Eugenics] Board.[28]

Section 6(1) further stated, with respect to the examination process of so-called mentally defective persons,

> If . . . the Board is unanimously of the opinion that the exercise of the power of procreation by that person (a) would result in the transmission of any mental disability or deficiency to his progeny, or (b) involves the risk of mental injury either to such person or his progeny, the Board may in writing direct such surgical operation for the sexual sterilization of that person as may be specified in the written direction.[29]

Thus, the law clearly required that a person be judged mentally defective both at admission to an institution and when considered by the AEB. Surgical sterilization could be directed if the board believed the person's mental disability or deficiency would otherwise be transmitted to progeny.

INTELLIGENCE

There have long been two general approaches to establishing mental deficiency: the *psychometric* and the *social*.[30] The psychometric method assesses mental ability using a standardized psychological test, generally known as an intelligence quotient (IQ) test; the resulting IQ score does not indicate why a child may score exceptionally low. The social method assesses the child's progress in school and whether he or she is able to carry out the basic requirements of daily living, but it also explores the possible environmental sources of mental deficiency. The AEB considered only the psychometric evidence, primarily the IQ score.[31]

There was no general agreement among psychologists in the 1950s on the precise nature of intelligence, and much the same situation prevails today.[32] The French psychologist Alfred Binet (1857–1911) and physician Théodore Simon (1873–1961) devised the first formal tests of intelligence, in 1908.[33] Binet's original objective was to detect children doing poorly in school, who he believed would be aided by a program of special education.[34] Having explained how to measure intelligence, he stated, "After the evil comes the remedy. After identifying all types of intellectual defects, let us pass on to their treatment." He presented a new course of "mental orthopaedics exercises" that "make the child an active individual instead of reducing his role to that of a listener."[35]

When Binet's test was imported to the United States, however, it was initially adapted and applied by psychologists who placed a much greater emphasis on biological determinants.[36] The test was translated and adapted by Lewis M. Terman at Stanford University.[37] The Stanford-Binet test was intended by Terman and Merrill to provide an "all-round clinical appraisal of a subject's intellectual ability" using a "method of standardized interview which is highly interesting to the subject."[38] The test obtained a general estimate of intelligence by tapping a wide range of capacities and then using the total score on all items. According to the author of a competing intelligence test, the Wechsler Intelligence Scale for Children (WISC), "*Intelligence is the aggregate or global capacity of the individual to act purposively, to think rationally and to deal effectively with his environment* [emphasis in the original]."[39] Wechsler's conceptualization went beyond intellectual or reasoning ability *per se*. He argued that non-intellective and personality factors were essential parts of intelligence. For him, intelligence depended strongly on the individual's drive or incentive to perform well on several tasks, the "persistence in attacking them" and "zest and desire to succeed."[40]

While differing to some extent on what intelligence is, leading experts from the mid- to the late twentieth century generally agreed on what it is *not*. Specifically, an intelligence test is not a measure of some innate or biologically fixed entity. According to George D. Stoddard, "A definition of intelligence may be expressed independently of the way in which abilities are developed in the organism. . . . But to *define* intelligence as a composite of inherited factors, or as a derivative of environmental pressures, would beg the question." He criticized earlier theorists such as Cyril Burt who said intelligence is "inborn." Stoddard reviewed numerous authorities on intelligence and discerned a change since the 1920s and 1930s: "a noticeable departure from flat statements about the constancy of the IQ and the inheritance of intelligence."[41] Similarly, McVicker-Hunt observed that "most of the general textbooks written before World War II tended to present the view that the IQ is essentially constant because intelligence is fixed." He also noted that "a transformation has been taking place.... Evidence from various sources has been forcing a recognition of central processes in intelligence and of the crucial role of life experience in the development of those central processes."[42] According to David Gibson, all of the texts on mental testing used in the 1950s taught that cultural impoverishment could reduce scores on IQ tests.[43] Writers who asserted that intelligence is a hereditary trait were considered to be out of the mainstream of contemporary expertise. Altenburg criticized "extremists" on the political right who said heredity was everything as well as those on the political left who said heredity was irrelevant to intelligence.[44] Gates and colleagues also abjured "dogmatic statements of extremist viewpoints."[45] It is evident that, according to the opinions of leading experts in intelligence testing in the 1950s, the AEB would unquestionably have qualified as a group of extremists on the political right.

Psychometric IQ

In the psychometric approach to measuring intelligence, a series of test items is first devised that is appropriate for children across a certain range of ages. Some items are quite easy for all but the youngest children, whereas others are beyond the capabilities of all but the brightest among the oldest children. The number of items a child can answer correctly is the *raw score*. On a well-designed test, the average raw score increases rapidly with age as mental growth occurs. Next, the test is administered to a large standardization sample of children that is supposed to be representative of the population to which the test will be applied in the future. This sample is used to establish age-specific norms for average, high, and low scores.

The WISC used a *scaled deviation score* to obtain the IQ. At each age, the average or mean score and the variability of scores among the different children in the standardization sample are computed. The statistical measure of variability is the standard deviation, which on the Wechsler tests is set at 15 IQ points. For any one child, the IQ score is based on the number of standard deviations by which the child exceeds or falls short of the mean. The Wechsler tests are scaled so that the formula for IQ is IQ = 100 + 15 (scaled deviation score). Tables in the test manual convert raw test scores to scaled scores at each age. For a child who remains consistently at the average score for her age over several years, the deviation score will be 0 and the IQ score will remain near 100. For one who scores two standard deviations above the mean, the deviation score is 2.0 and the IQ = 130, whereas a child scoring two standard deviations below the mean has IQ = 70. The theoretical distribution of IQ scores in a large population generally resembles a normal bell-shaped curve (see Figure 2.2a), with most people scoring near 100 and relatively few scoring very high or low. Because of the way the IQ score is scaled, it is possible to know how a child did on the test relative to his or her peers simply by knowing the IQ, even if the child's age is not known. When another intelligence test, the California Test of Mental Maturity, was given to all Edmonton schoolchildren in 1956, the actual distribution of scores on an IQ test was very similar to the theoretical bell-shaped curve (see Figure 2.2b).[46]

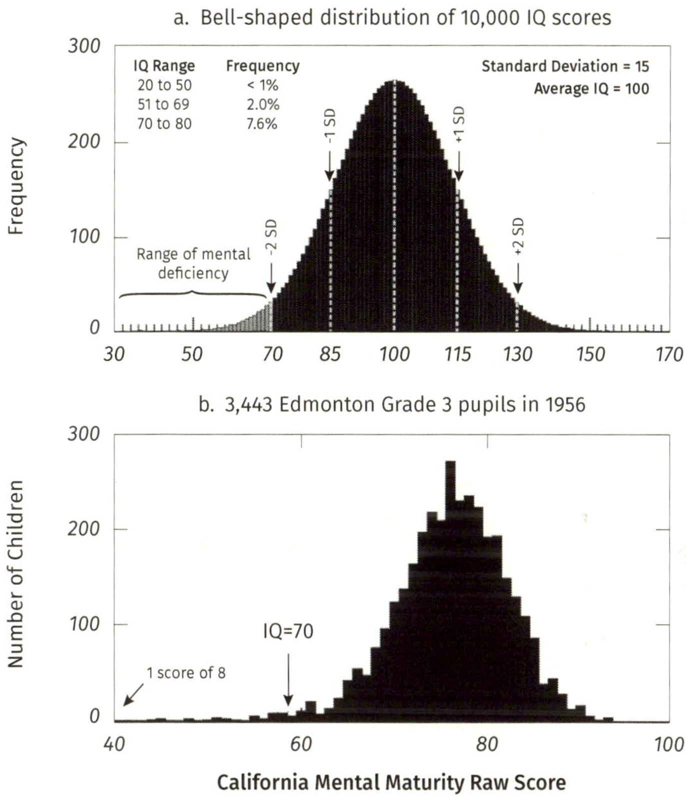

Figure 2.2 (a). Theoretical distribution of IQ scores when they occur as a normal bell-shaped curve. (b). Actual distribution of scores on an IQ test given in 1956 is close to a bell shaped curve (Clarke, et al., 1978).

Psychometric Criterion for Mental Deficiency

The psychometric definition of mental deficiency is generally based on the IQ score. Several leading authorities classified *mental deficiency as an IQ less than* 70, and this criterion was widely adopted by professional organizations, including the World Health Organization in 1954.[47] The terms used to describe different levels of mental deficiency differed between countries and underwent revision to reflect social attitudes toward the mentally deficient in degrees of "mental deficiency" and "subnormality" (see table 2.1). In practice, Alberta also adhered to this criterion for clinically diagnosed mental deficiency; it was applied by the AEB. Dr. R. Kenneth Thomson (d. 1999), an internist, psychiatrist, and board member for more than twenty years and board chair from 1965 to 1972, stated explicitly that the cut-off score for mental deficiency was an IQ of 70.[48]

Table 2.1 Categories of mental deficiency in relation to IQ score range

Degree of mental deficiency	British (Penrose, 1949)	American (Terman and Merrill, 1960)	World Health Organization (Anastasi, 1958)	IQ range
Mild	Feeble-minded	Moron	Mild subnormality	50–69
Severe (mid-grade)	Imbecile	Imbecile	Moderate subnormality	20–49
Severe (low-grade)	Idiot	Idiot	Severe subnormality	0–19

Source: Table adapted from Penrose (1949), p. 9, and updated as indicated.

Terman and others also recognized the range from IQ 70 to 80 as "borderline," but it is clear that authorities on intelligence testing generally did not consider this range to constitute psychometric grounds for diagnosing mental deficiency. In 1955, the total patient population in each of the three diagnostic categories plus "borderline" mental deficiency in Alberta mental institutions (shown in table 2.2) revealed a scarcity of "borderline" cases.

Table 2.2 Diagnoses of 1,042 patients in Alberta mental institutions on December 31, 1955

Category	Idiot	Imbecile	Moron	Borderline	"Mongolism"	Epilepsy	Other
ICD class	325.0	325.1	325.2	325.3	325.4	325.5	325.6
Number	223	495	242	10	6	15	51

Source: Annual Report of the Department of Public Health (1955), Province of Alberta, p. 87, p. 95, and p. 113. ICD is the International Classification of Diseases established by the World Health Organization in 1948 under auspices of the United Nations.

After several years of experience with IQ testing and school performance measures, psychologists began to define mentally deficiency using a statistical criterion: the lower 2 percent or 2.5 percent of the population.[49] To some extent the figure of 2.5 percent was based on social rather than strictly psychological criteria. As Wechsler pointed out, "Arbitrary and callous as it may seem, the definition of mental deficiency in terms of social criteria is a function of the number of individuals which a given community can afford to call so, that is, is able to institutionalize, or believes ought to be institutionalized if it had the resources to do so."[50] In Alberta in 1955, a rather small proportion of the school-age population of children was institutionalized for diagnosed mental deficiency. The Department of Public Health's annual report for that year reported that 193 patients in the Provincial Training School for Mental Defectives (PTS) at Red Deer were in the age range of ten to fourteen years.[51] The Provincial Mental Hospital in Ponoka housed 80 patients with a primary diagnosis of mental deficiency in 1955, but only 2 of 482 admissions that year involved persons less than fifteen years of age. The Oliver Mental Hospital housed 191 patients with a primary diagnosis of mental deficiency, and comments in the annual report made it clear that some of these were "in the school age group."[52] If the age distribution was approximately the same as in the PTS (27.6 percent in the age range of ten to fourteen years), then there might have been another 53 mentally deficient children housed in Edmonton. Thus, about 246 Alberta children between the ages of ten and fourteen were institutionalized for mental deficiency in 1955. The annual report of the Department of Education reveals that 90,393 children in this same age range were enrolled in school at the time.[53]

Undoubtedly there were other children in this age range who were neither in school nor in a mental institution. Thus, if roughly 246 out of more than 91,000 children aged ten to fourteen years were institutionalized for mental deficiency in 1955, this amounts to about 0.3 percent or 1 per 300 Alberta children, a figure somewhat higher than in most industrialized countries in the 1930s.[54] Nonetheless, the patient population in that age range was *much* smaller than the expected 1,800 mentally deficient children in Alberta at the time 2 percent of 91,000 children.

That is, no more than 14 percent of the children expected to have an IQ score of less than 70 were actually institutionalized for mental deficiency. It was also expected that far more Alberta children would be in the IQ range of 50 to 69 than in the range of 20 to 49 (see Figure 2.2), yet the latter category was much more common in Alberta mental institutions (see table 2.2). Hence, most children in the 50 to 69 IQ range were *not* in a mental institution at the time. Some of them were attending special schools but children in these schools were never presented to the AEB for sterilization.[55] Many others were simply kept at home and did menial chores.

All leading authorities at the time stressed that mental deficiency in the clinical or legal sense should *never* be diagnosed solely on the basis of an intelligence test.[56] Wechsler remarked, "Intelligence, like personality, is too complicated an entity to be defined by a single number. . . . [I]ndividuals having the same IQ's may differ considerably in either their actual or potential capacity for intelligent behaviour."[57] American psychologist Florence L. Goodenough (1886–1959) referred to one of the "unfortunate errors in thinking . . . [of] those who, on the basis of a single test, even when given at a tender age, are ready to 'diagnose' the child's present mental level, make predictions as to his future, perhaps even take action with respect to matters of vital importance for his future."[58] The problem of test interpretation was especially apparent for children living in rural areas, who tended to score lower than urban children because of their poorer schooling. The average IQ score in an Alberta survey was fully ten points lower for children from ungraded (one-room) rural schools than those from large urban centres, and it was also ten points lower for children living in homes where a language other than English (mostly French or Ukrainian) was spoken.[59] Goodenough observed that IQ tests "deal with the results of learning, from which capacity to learn is inferred. When opportunity and incentives have been reasonably similar, the inference is sound, but its validity may be questioned when a comparison is to be made between two or more groups for whom these factors have been markedly different."[60]

CONSEQUENCES OF STERILIZATION FOR THE GENETIC QUALITY OF THE POPULATION

The original purpose of the 1928 Sexual Sterilization Act was to reduce the frequency of social failure and misconduct in Alberta by preventing the reproduction of individuals who were believed to possess defective genes.[61] The crusaders for passage of the act in the 1920s included women's rights activist Emily Murphy (1868–1933), a police magistrate, and the United Farm Women of Alberta (UFWA). The minister responsible for the act in 1928 was George Hoadley (1867–1955), a farmer. There was no indication that any of these people understood genetic principles. Later, in 1950, a government committee said the object of the AEB was "to reduce the level of hereditary mental defects,"[62] yet no person competent in genetics was appointed to the AEB or advised the board on technical matters until May 27, 1960, when Margaret Thompson (1920–2014), assistant professor of human genetics at the University of Alberta, was appointed.[63]

Heredity

When considering mental deficiency, two basic kinds of hereditary defect may be involved: *discrete* or *multi-factor.* These kinds of defects are diagnosed in fundamentally different ways, and they differ in the likelihood of transmission to progeny. The consequences of sterilization can be computed for both kinds of defects using appropriate methods readily available in the 1950s and 1960s. Discrete defects of heredity are changes (mutations) in a single gene (DNA) and are inherited according to distinctive patterns known as the Mendelian laws.[64] The DNA contains a code for the structure of a protein molecule, and a mutation can lead to an altered protein that does not function correctly. This in turn can lead to mental deficiency. Mental deficiency itself is not transmitted from parent to offspring. Clearly, those who decided on the wording of Alberta's Sexual Sterilization Act did not possess an adequate understanding of heredity. Multi-factor defects involve the combined effects of several defective genes as well as adverse environmental factors. More elaborate statistical methods are used to study and predict them.[65] Discrete defects were discussed at length by Canadian biology professor Roy Fraser (d. 1956), British psychiatrist Lionel S. Penrose (1898–1972), American geneticist and eugenicist Shelden C. Reed (1910–2003), and others, and those works on human genetics were widely available at the time.[66] Table 2.3 lists disorders that in the mid-1950s were believed to be caused by a genetic defect and were also known to cause mental deficiency in most cases. Most involved relatively severe abnormalities and were therefore relatively rare in the population. These disorders were also accompanied by characteristic physical or physiological symptoms and were not purely mental. A genetic disorder would ideally have been diagnosed by someone with expertise in both human genetics and pediatric medicine, although in the 1950s the profession of medical genetics and genetic counselling was in its infancy in Canada.[67] In that decade, three kinds of specific genetic transmission were recognized: recessive, dominant, and sex-linked inheritance. The sex-linked form was not encountered by the AEB and is therefore not discussed here.

Table 2.3 Genetic defects known in the 1950s to cause mental deficiency

Name of disorder	Frequency	Physical signs
	Dominant transmission	
Achondroplasia	1/10,000	Gross shortening of limbs
Aniridia	1/100,000	Absence of iris in eyes; often blind
Epiloia	1/50,000	Sebaceous adenoma or "butterfly" rash
Huntington disease		Adult onset muscle spasticity
Neurofibromatosis		*Café-au-lait* spots, small tumours in skin
	Recessive transmission	
Juvenile amaurotic idiocy	1/40,000	Loss of muscle power; progressive blindness
Phenylketonuria	1/25,000	Phenylacetic acid in urine; musty odour
Retinitis pigmentosa	1/10,000	Progressive degeneration of retina
Tay-Sachs disease	1/250,000	Degenerative; death within 2 years

Source: Fraser (1949), Penrose (1949), Reed (1955). Population frequencies from Fraser (1949) and Reed (1955) may be higher for some ethnic groups and even zero for others.

Recessive disorders

The effects of sterilization depend strongly on the mode of inheritance, whether recessive or dominant. In the 1950s several recessive genetic disorders, such as phenylketonuria, were well documented (see table 2.3) and must have appeared in Alberta institutions for the mentally deficient, although several recessive genetic disorders may not have been diagnosed as mental deficiencies. Most of them were relatively rare in the population because afflicted individuals were usually unable to reproduce because of infertility or simply lack of viability. That is, natural selection had over the centuries reduced the defective form of the gene to a rather low frequency in the population. The idea behind eugenic sterilization was that deliberate prevention of reproduction would reduce the frequency of the defective gene even further and thereby prevent many future cases of the disorder. Yet how great would that reduction actually be? This can be calculated with the aid of principles well established in the 1950s.

A recessive disorder is one in which the child must inherit *two* defective copies of the gene, one from each parent, in order to have the disorder. A child who inherits one defective and one normal form of the gene will be normal, although he or she will be a carrier of the defect. Cystic fibrosis is a well-known example of such a disorder.[68] The typical pattern for a rare recessive disorder is that neither parent has the disorder (although both are carriers of one defective gene) and only 25 percent of their children have it. This kind of disorder often occurs in an otherwise normal, healthy family. Thus, *recessive genetic disorders do not appear to run in families*. The afflicted child does *not* resemble the parents' mental abilities. The defective gene is hereditary, but the disorder itself is not.

Let us consider a numerical example. Suppose a recessive genetic disorder afflicts one child in 2,500 in the population. This would be more common than any serious genetic disorder known to cause mental deficiency in the 1950s (see table 2.3) and overstates the likely effects of sterilization. Knowing the frequency of the disorder, the gene frequency can be calculated. Suppose there are only two forms of the gene present in the population, one being quite normal (+) and the other being a harmful recessive mutation (*k*). Genes occur in pairs in each person—one inherited from the father and one from the mother—and the specific pair constitutes the person's genotype. If there are only two kinds of genes (+, *k*), there can be only three possible genotypes (+/+, +/*k*, *k*/*k*); only genotype *k*/*k* will have the disorder, whereas persons +/*k* will be carriers of the mutant gene but not manifest the condition.[69] Table 2.4 presents the most likely frequency of each kind of individual in a hypothetical population of 100,000 people, each with two genes for a total gene "pool" of 200,000 genes. The table reveals a well-established fact about rare recessive disorders: the vast majority of abnormal genes are carried by individuals who show no clinical signs of the condition itself. In this example, 98 percent of the *k* genes are possessed by carriers. In the 1950s there was absolutely no way to determine who was a carrier except by observing their offspring. If a person had an afflicted child, that person must have been a carrier.[70]

Table 2.4 Population frequency of a rare recessive disorder

Type of person	Genotype	Number of people	"+" genes	"*k*" genes
Non-carrier	+/+	96,040	192,080	0
Carrier	+/*k*	3,920	3,920	3,920
Afflicted	*k*/*k*	40	0	80
Totals		**100,000**	**196,000**	**4,000**

The second step in this exercise is to consider reproduction. For purposes of explanation, let us presume that each person, even one afflicted with the disorder, is fully fertile and that couples have an average of four children, a reasonable number for the 1950s. Because there is no way to detect a carrier prior to mating, we may fairly expect that mating relationships are random pairings with respect to the three genotypes, although mating relationships will of course not be random with regard to other valued and visible qualities. In the population of 100,000 people, half males and half females, there will be 50,000 pairings that yield a total of 200,000 children.[71] Table 2.5 depicts the expected frequency of each kind of pairing and the composition of the offspring generation. Two salient points are evident from the table. First, almost all of the afflicted children are produced by couples where neither father nor mother showed any indication of the specific mental disability, because they were carriers, not genotype *k*/*k*. Second, the vast majority of mutant *k* genes are contributed to the gene pool of the next generation by couples who appear normal and have no afflicted children.

Table 2.5 Numbers of matings and children from a population of 100,000 parents

Mating type	Relative frequency	Number of matings	Number of children	Afflicted children	Number of "*k*" genes
Non-carrier x non-carrier	.9224	46,118	184,472	0	0
Carrier x non-carrier	.0753	3,765	15,060	0	7,530
Carrier x carrier	.0015	77	308	77	308
Afflicted x non-carrier	.0008	38	**152**	0	**152**
Afflicted x carrier	.00003	2	**8**	**4**	**12**
Afflicted x afflicted	.0000002	<1	0	0	0
Totals	1.0000	50,000	200,00	81	8,002

Note: Numbers in bold are those who might be eliminated by eugenic sterilization.

Knowing these figures, we can take the crucial third step to see what difference eugenic sterilization would make. The Sexual Sterilization Act of Alberta was supposedly intended to curtail reproduction of those actually afflicted with mental deficiency and would have had no impact whatsoever on the breeding of carriers, who would have been mentally normal.[72] The process would be highly inefficient because only 164 of the 8,002 abnormal *k* genes would be possessed by people showing the disorder. Suppose that all afflicted children with genotype *k/k* were institutionalized and then sterilized. This would result in no reproduction by two categories in table 2.5: afflicted x normal and afflicted x carrier. Of course, the afflicted by non-carrier mating would never yield any afflicted offspring, even with no sterilization, but there would be about 152 carriers among their offspring. The consequence for the next generation is that there would be 160 fewer children, 4 fewer afflicted children, and 164 fewer mutant genes in the gene pool. Thus, the frequency of the disorder in the population would decline from 1 per 2,500 to 1 per 2,595, and the frequency of the mutant gene would decline from 2.0 percent to 1.96 percent. In order to prevent the birth of 4 afflicted children, the birth of 156 children not afflicted with the disorder would also be prevented by eugenic sterilization of afflicted persons. From a purely genetic standpoint, then, sterilization of those afflicted with a rare recessive genetic disorder would have a trivially small impact on the future generation of children in that population. As British geneticist Lancelot Hogben (1895–1975) pointed out, to have a major impact on the frequency of mentally defective children in a future generation, it would be necessary to sterilize the prospective parents who were definitely carriers, plus the siblings, most of whom were carriers, not just individuals with the disorder.[73] In practice, the process would be even less efficient because (a) it is unlikely that every child with the disorder would be institutionalized unless it was a severely disabling defect, and (b) if it did cause severe disability, reproduction would most likely be curtailed without any order by a eugenics board. Furthermore, there would be diminishing returns: the change in gene frequency would become even smaller each generation as the defective gene becomes rarer. Indeed, as shown by Lush, to reduce the frequency of a harmful recessive gene from 2 percent to 1 percent in a population by sterilizing all afflicted children would require *fifty-one generations* of selective breeding, or more than one thousand years.[74]

Dominant disorders

A dominant disorder occurs when every person carrying just one copy of the mutant gene shows signs of the defect. A classic example is the genetic neurodegenerative disease identified by the American physician George Huntington (1850–1916), a neurological syndrome of mental and motor deterioration beginning in middle age. In such a case, there is almost always one parent who died from the same disease, and about half of the children are afflicted if they live long enough. This defect does indeed occur in families and the risk of it occurring in the offspring of a carrier is quite high, 50 percent.[75] If all children harbouring a defective dominant gene were institutionalized because of the disorder and later sterilized, the scourge could be purged from the population in one generation and never reappear, except in the extremely rare eventuality of a new mutation caused by radiation or a dangerous chemical. State-mandated eugenic sterilization could have a major impact on a dominant genetic disorder if the symptoms are typically obvious and manifest in childhood.[76] It would have virtually no impact on a neurological disorder such as Huntington's disease, where symptoms typically appear after the age of reproduction and carriers cannot be detected until symptoms appear.[77]

Non-specific, multifactorial disorders

For characteristics such as IQ, instances where a single genetic mutation has major effects are very rare; instead, development is influenced substantially by both heredity and environment. The hereditary factor likely involves defective variants of several genes.[78] The only recourse here is statistical. The method involves the coefficient of "heritability" (h^2), which estimates the percentage of variation in IQ in the population that is attributable to genetic variation. If the value of heritability of a characteristic is known, the response to selective breeding can be estimated from the formula $R = h^2S$.[79] The selection differential S is the difference between the average score of the original population and the average score of those individuals chosen to be parents of the next generation. In agricultural or laboraory applications with animals, usually a small fraction of the population is chosen for breeding, perhaps the top-scoring 5 or 10 percent, and the selection differential is quite large.[80] The response to selective breeding (R) is the difference between the average of the original population and the mean score of the offspring of the selected parents. The h^2 coefficient is very difficult to estimate accurately with humans and its interpretation is controversial.[81] Nevertheless, a numerical exercise can be done to get a very rough idea of the prospects for eugenic improvement of human intelligence. Let us assume $h^2 = .5$, being neither particularly high nor low. When the American psychologists John L. Fuller (1910–92) and W. Robert Thompson (d. 1960?) first reviewed the literature on heritability of intelligence in 1960, they made an educated guess that the weighting for heredity should be a little heavier than for environment.[82] More recently, Devlin et al. arrived at a smaller value of about $h^2 = .4$.[83]

In order to calculate the expected response to selective breeding, we first need to know the mean score and variation about the mean for the original population before selection begins. The precise distribution of IQ scores of all Alberta children in the 1950s was probably was not too far away from a bell-shaped curve with a mean IQ of 100 for Alberta school children (see also Figure 2.2).[84] Thus, for the purpose of this exercise, the number of children in each IQ score range in the population is computed from a bell-shaped curve. The most challenging task is to find the average

IQ of those allowed to breed. This is done for two situations: the first uses data on Alberta children actually sterilized to make an educated guess; the second presumes that every child in Alberta with an IQ score less than 70 was sterilized, regardless of whether he or she was in an institution. This involves far more children than were actually sterilized, and consequently it yields an estimate of what the AEB might have achieved with a maximally efficient program based on IQ alone.

Table 2.6 Sterilization of 14-year old children in a population of 18,000 children

IQ range	Expected # of Alberta children in IQ range	# sterilized, estimated from actual data	Hypothetical # if all with IQ < 70 were sterilized
50 to 54	15	10	15
55 to 59	41	10	41
60 to 64	99	10	99
65 to 69	217	5	217
70 to 74	424	1	0
75 to 79	743	1	0
Totals	**1539**	**37**	**372**

For the first calculation, the numbers of Alberta children of a particular age and IQ range who were sterilized in 1955 are estimated. In 1955, in Alberta, there were about 18,000 fourteen-year-old children.[85] The AEB knew exactly how many of which age and diagnosis were considered for sterilization, but we must assemble the picture from shards of evidence. Seven of the cases I reviewed were seen by the board at the age of fourteen, and this is also an age when most normal children were still enrolled in school, so let us use the numbers for fourteen-year-old children. Available evidence indicates about 37 such children in the IQ range from 50 to 79 would eventually be sterilized and then discharged, as shown in table 2.6, amounting to about half of the 75 institutionalized children at that age. Because those in the IQ range below 50 would likely not have been considered for discharge in any event, or would almost certainly have been infertile,[86] with or without the Sexual Sterilization Act, the infertility of only the 37 individuals in the IQ range 50 to 79 should be ascribed to the eugenic sterilization policy. Removing those 37 from the population of 18,000 children born in 1941 would yield a mean IQ of the remaining 17,963 children equal to 100.086. Thus, the selection differential would be $S = 100.086 - 100.0 = 0.086$, the selection response would be $R = 0.5(.086) = 0.043$, and the expected mean IQ of the next generation would be 100.043. An increase in average IQ score in the population of 0.043 points is trivially small.

Next, suppose the act required the AEB to seek out and sterilize *every* child in Alberta with an IQ score of less than 70 while not tampering with the reproductive organs of those with an IQ of 70 or more. There would have been about 49 of those children with an IQ of less than 70 but more than 372 among a total of 18,000 children at that age. The mean IQ of those allowed to breed under this scenario would have been 100.758. The selection differential would have been $S = 100.758 - 100.0 = 0.758$. Thus, the improvement in average IQ of the Alberta population would have been about $R = 0.5(0.758) = 0.379$ or about one-third of an IQ point. This would have been difficult to support politically, because it would have included *every* child below IQ 70, including those dearly loved, nurtured, and sheltered by their parents. The point of this second calculation is to show that even a tenfold increase in the number of children sterilized would have had very little impact because it would still entail a small minority of all children.

To have an appreciable impact on the next generation of Alberta children, unrealistically large numbers would need to be subjected to the eugenic surgeon's knife.[87] For example, if only children in the top 10 percent of the IQ distribution were approved for parenthood, the average IQ of this elite group would be 126.3 and the selection differential would be 26.3 IQ points. The response to selective breeding in the first generation would then be about 10.5 IQ points and the new population average score might rise to 110 points. The parents would need to contribute at least twenty children per couple to the next generation to compensate for all the forced infertility.

The conclusion from this exercise is that, according to well-known genetic principles that were well understood in the 1950s and taught at the University of Alberta at that time, the likely effect on the average IQ of Albertans from a program of eugenic sterilization similar to what was implemented under the Sexual Sterilization Act would have been trivially small. This is one of the major reasons why many reputable geneticists deserted the eugenics movement in the 1920s and 1930s after the genetics of human populations became better understood. Stoddard, in 1945, observed wryly that "there has grown up a certain disjunction between the sober writing of geneticists and the expectation of eugenicists."[88]

SOCIAL AND EDUCATIONAL ENVIRONMENT

Having found that the genetic consequences of eugenic sterilization in Alberta in the 1950s would have been small indeed, it is informative to consider what degree of change in IQ was to be expected from improved environments. Thorough discussions of social and educational factors related to childhood intelligence were provided by Stoddard, Harold E. Jones, Anastasi, and McVicker-Hunt.[89] There was considerable dispute in the 1950s and 1960s about the potency of the psychological environment in shaping intelligence. Authors such as Jones tended to minimize environmental effects while others, including McVicker-Hunt, believed intelligence to be quite malleable, especially in early childhood. However, there was little dispute as to whether environment had *any* effect. Virtually all authorities acknowledged the importance of upbringing, especially extreme departures from the normal mode of life. The big unknown was the precise strength of the influence of specific kinds of experience in terms of points on the IQ scale.[90] In many examples, the change in IQ amounted to five to fifteen points. Table 2.7 summarizes results of several studies of environmental effects that were well known in the 1950s. The difference in IQ score attributed to each effect represents the difference between two groups of people: one with and the other without the environmental treatment in question. The IQ point differences provide an approximation of the kinds of effects that were to be expected in the 1950s.

The *cohort effect* was a direct test of the predictions of many leading voices in the early eugenics movement who claimed that people of lower intelligence usually had larger families and, therefore, intelligence would decline over the years. Birth cohorts are entire populations of children born in different years. If national intelligence is changing, those born many years apart should differ substantially on an IQ test. Of course, improved medical care and education over a period of several decades could increase intelligence if environment plays a major role. There was clear evidence of a general *increase* in the intelligence test performance of

Americans. For instance, soldiers taking an IQ test during World War II scored almost twenty points higher on average than those in World War I.[91] A portion of this improvement was evidently related to education; the average years of schooling of American men in World War I was eight and in World War II was ten. When the Stanford-Binet test was re-standardized in 1960, children scored about five IQ points higher on the older 1937 version of the test that had become culturally out of date than did the 1937 standardization sample.[92] In 1936 and 1937, Raymond Bernard Cattell (1905–98), personality psychologist and eugenicist from the University of Illinois, compared IQ scores of parents and their children and reported data showing the children scored ten to fifteen IQ points higher than their parents.[93] Cattell predicted a subsequent decline in national intelligence but thirteen years later was surprised to find evidence of an increase in IQ.[94]

Table 2.7 Environmental effects on children's IQ scores

Kind of environmental difference	IQ difference	Sources of information
Cohort effect of birth year	Up 5–15 pts / generation	Tuddenham (1948); Cattell (1936/7, 1950); Terman and Merrill (1960)
Rural home and schooling	Down 10 pts	Stoddard (1945); Reid (1954)
Institutional rearing	Down 10–30 pts	Stoddard (1945); Hunt (1961)
Foster and adoptive home	Up 15–30 pts	Stoddard (1945); Skodak & Skeels (1949)
Early language stimulation	Up 10–15 pts	Stoddard (1945)
Day care and nursery school	Up 5–11 pts	Stoddard (1945)

Rearing in a rural environment was associated with lower IQ scores, and the longer a child remained in a rural setting, the greater was the disadvantage.[95] Medical care and education were generally inferior in rural settings from the 1930s to the 1950s, and much of the IQ difference from urban children might have been caused by the environmental difference. Some academics speculated that the pattern might have resulted from selective migration, whereby the genetically brightest people moved to the cities, leaving the biological dolts and laggards behind on the farm. Evidence in support of this view was generally lacking. In more recent times in Alberta, the government has done much to improve rural health and education, and the urban-rural difference has now largely disappeared.[96]

Institutional rearing, especially in orphanages where staff were overworked and had little time to give their wards individual attention, was widely known to impair intellectual growth.[97] The longer the residence in the institution, the lower the IQ score compared with the cohort of the same age living at home and attending regular schools. This finding was based on IQ testing from the Iowa Adoption Study of 1949; these biases from the poor staffing conditions and low adherence to observational and testing standards of course influenced the numerical distributions of IQ scores when they occur as a normal and the actual distribution of scores on an IQ test given in 1956 being close to a bell-shaped curve (see Figure 2.3). Poor development was not an inevitable consequence of being in an institution, however. An enriched training program could avoid most of the retardation usually occasioned by neglect.

Foster home rearing and adoption were known to facilitate mental growth when an infant from an impoverished background was placed into a prosperous home with well-educated parents. One of the most widely cited studies involved adopted children in the state of Iowa.[98] Each child chosen for study had been adopted prior to the age of six months and IQ test scores were available for both the birth mother and, later, her biological child during school years. One hundred children were given three IQ tests over a period of several years. As shown in Figure 2.3, the average IQ score of the sixty-three birth mothers was 85.7, whereas the average score for their one hundred children was 114.8, a difference of about 30 IQ points. Fourteen of the mothers had IQ scores in the range of mental deficiency, but none of their children was below an IQ of 80. A major portion of the improvement must have been environmental.

A variety of enriched early education programs, especially those involving special language training for normal children, were known to enhance IQ test results by a few points.[99] Since the studies cited above were done, many further research projects have been conducted with better controls and better methods of testing. As summarized by Douglas Wahlsten, major improvements in environment are now well established as causing an upward change of as much as fifteen points on IQ tests.[100] The cohort effect has become very widely known.[101] The early eugenics movement raised an alarm about a pending decline in national intelligence if people with low IQ scores were allowed to reproduce. Now we are witness to perhaps the ultimate refutation of this *raison d'être* for the eugenics movement. Since

World War II, intelligence, as measured by IQ tests, has in fact increased very substantially in every industrialized country where large-scale IQ testing has been done.[102] The precise magnitudes of environmental effects were not known in the 1950s and 1960s, but there was sufficient evidence at the time to show that the effects were at the very least increases of several IQ points, far larger than any paltry boost from eugenic sterilization on the scale that was actually practised in Alberta.

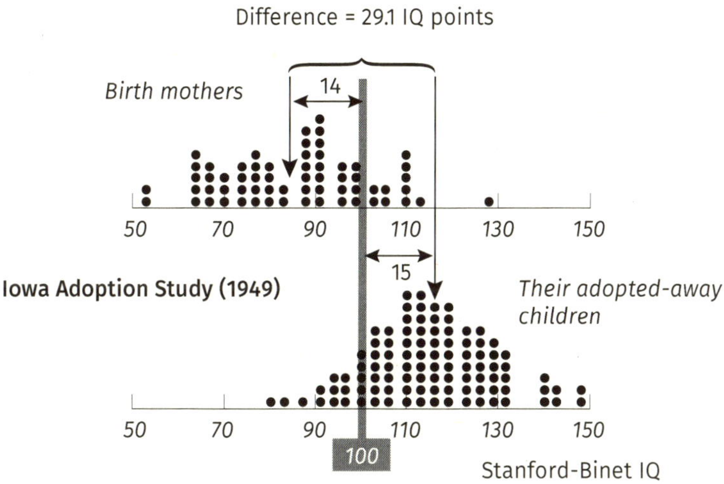

Figure 2.3 Illustration of the IQ testing from the Iowa Adoption Study, 1949. Top: IQ scores of birth mothers having little formal education who gave up at least one child for adoption. Bottom: IQ scores of 100 adopted-away children of those mothers who were reared in good homes. Based on data provided by Skodak and Skeels, 1949, compiled and designed by Douglas Wahlsten, 2013.

BLINDED BY THE EUGENICS CREED

It is a chilling and distressing experience to read patient files from the PTS and realize the utterly horrid conditions in which many had been living prior to admission to the institution. The AEB ignored this information completely. For those devoted adherents of the eugenics creed, intelligence was fixed by heredity. Consequently, no additional influences needed to be considered, and they were not. The board simply accepted the recommendations of the superintendent of the PTS, presented in a brief case summary, which affirms the contention of Hansen and King that the superintendents of mental institutions played crucial roles in decisions for sterilization.[103] Cases were heard by the AEB at a rate of about one case every five minutes.[104] For many of the children confined in the PTS, life there was actually better than at home. Leilani Muir (b. 1944), for example, had been starved and beaten at home, but in the PTS she began to gain weight and made some lifelong friends. Her IQ score in 1957, shortly before she was sterilized, was 71, which is in the normal range, but she was sterilized anyway as the result of an error in totalling her scores that placed her at an IQ of 63.[105] Several years after leaving the PTS, as an adult, she scored in the range of 85 to 90, which was a clearly normal performance. In another example, a boy in the PTS was tested four times from 1957 to 1961 and showed a clear improved pattern of IQ each time he was tested; his score increased from 42 to 76—until he was above the cut-off for mental deficiency—yet he too was sterilized (see Figure 2.4).

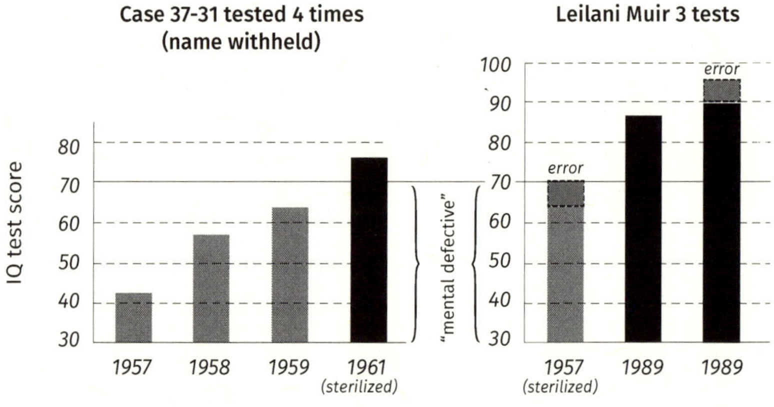

Figure 2.4 IQ test comparisons from the Leilani Muir Case, 1957 to 1989. Left: A boy in the Provincial Training School in Red Deer was given an IQ test four times and improved each time until he was above the cut-off for mental deficiency, but the Alberta Eugenics Board ordered him sterilized. Right: Leilani Muir also scored above 70, but an error in totalling her scores placed her at an IQ of 63. As an adult, she scored higher than 85, a clearly normal performance. Reproduced by permission from Douglas Wahlsten.

In one case reviewed by the author, police and social worker reports of the home situation provided vivid testimony about the circumstances of Ilsa Anderchuk (a pseudonym):

> [Report of July 8, 1949:] There are about 5 or 6 small children . . . and the parents living in a small one room shack. The shack is filthy and is practically without furniture. The mother and children are filthy and are practically without clothing. . . . The mother is a mental defective who cannot speak English. The father can talk English but does not appear to be overly bright. . . . I have seen plenty of pretty poor homes in this and other districts but this is one of the very worst and conditions can only be described as deplorable. . . .
>
> August 24, 1949 (W. Filewych, Welfare Inspector): I don't believe I have ever seen anything like it before. The mother is a mental case. She has been in the Ponoka Mental Institution for quite a while. The husband took her out in 1944 knowing that her condition was not in any way bettered. I spoke to her for a few minutes and she is definitely not in her right mind. . . . She was only scantily dressed. . . . She sometimes wanders away from home. . . . She does not wash or feed the children. . . . There have been four children since the mental condition set in. . . . These children should either be placed in a children's home or perhaps be looked after by relatives. It is hard to believe that in the twentieth century conditions such as these exist. There is evidence of severe neglect on part of both parents. . . .
>
> [Nov. 10, 1949 (RCMP): The home] was found to be in the filthiest condition imaginable. The children were only partially clothed. . . . Two basins of slops sat on the stove which had been there for seven days at least. . . . Mrs. ANDERCHUK's major problem has undoubtedly been the raising of her children, and their ages will give an indication of the strain the woman has undergone, and which no one can gainsay is the reason for her present mental condition.[106]

This report then identifies the children, aged one, two, four, five, eight, and nine years. It is apparent that young Ilsa, the nine-year-old, was the eldest sister, who must have actually borne the principal responsibility for raising her younger siblings under extremely difficult circumstances. There would have been no time to devote to schoolwork. Ilsa was later interviewed briefly by the AEB, at the age of thirteen, one month after scoring 63 on an IQ test. The report of the 1954 Stanford-Binet IQ test described the girl as a "mid-grade moron" and included comments—"Rather tense—short of breath. 'sob breathing.' Poor in attention and memory"—indicating she was very anxious during testing. Ilsa was ordered to be sterilized, for the following reason: "Danger of the transmission to the progeny of mental disability or deficiency, also incapable of intelligent parenthood."[107] Evidently the eugenics creed blinded both the superintendent of the PTS and the eugenics board to what was happening right before their eyes. They held fast to their belief in hereditary intelligence despite abundant evidence to the contrary. They boldly asserted genetic explanations without having an adequate understanding of the genetic or psychological science existing at the time.

CONCLUSION

Many important human traits such as intelligence, personality, and emotions are very complex, cannot be traced to simple genetic origins, and are influenced in a substantial way by experience. There are only a few well-defined disorders of the nervous system that are caused by a defect in a specific gene (as Mendelian inheritance) that is inherited from the parents. The more severe defects are generally very rare. A eugenics program to reduce the frequency of these defects in the population can be founded on good scientific principles that were fully elucidated by the 1930s. Whether such a program should be voluntary and implemented through education and counselling or forcible by edict of the government is a question of ethics and politics, not biological science.[108] A eugenics program to alter these traits in the population was proposed in Alberta based on principles used to selectively breed improved strains of farm animals. Those principles were well understood by about 1940 and were widely taught in schools of agriculture during the 1950s. There is, however, no evidence—as this chapter has argued—that the AEB (since its functional existence from 1929 onward) was well aware of or cared about those scientific principles. The practices of the board were apparently based on social prejudice, not genetic knowledge, and membership on the board evidently was determined by allegiance to a pseudo-scientific creed. That creed allowed the government of the time and the AEB to deny the fundamental humanity of their victims and authorize actions against them that were without a doubt crimes under Canadian law.

3

The Involvement of Nurses in the Eugenics Program in Alberta, 1920–1940

Diana Mansell

The opening decades of the twentieth century were years in which the Canadian government actively recruited immigrants from the United Kingdom, Europe, and the United States to assist in the settlement of western Canada. The immigration waves that followed contained large numbers of non-English-speaking people of eastern European heritage.[1] As these numbers increased, the white Anglo-Saxon Protestant minority feared a "multiplication of the inferior."[2] Indeed, during the first half of the twentieth century, Canadians felt threatened by the rising numbers of what were considered "unfit" and "inferior" citizens, on whom they blamed a wide variety of social problems such as divorce, alcoholism, and economic instability.[3] To that end, according to public health researchers Kowalewski and Mayne, "the mentally ill, new immigrants, and social deviants were very often considered unfit."[4] Alberta's solution was the passage of the Sexual Sterilization Act in 1928 and the creation of the Alberta Eugenics Board (regarding the more detailed social and political context, see also chapters 1 and 4). The act remained law until 1972 and its repercussions continued into the 1990s, when the Progressive Conservative government of Ralph Klein (1942–2013) was taken to court by many victims of sterilization.[5] The act was supported by many prominent first-wave feminists, including Nellie McClung (1873–1951) and Emily Murphy (1868–1933). Nurses too supported the act and the philosophical ideology on which the need for sterilization was based: "on available means for racial improvement," as was prominently pointed out by the Toronto-based psychiatrist Clarence B. Farrar (1874–1970) in his 1931 editorial in the *Canadian Journal of Public Health*.[6]

The historical argument made in this chapter is that nurses, with their concerns for the overcrowding and overburdening situation and working context in hospitals and mental institutions of the time, were especially drawn to contemporary eugenic ideals that seemed to offer an easy way out of the often-unbearable care and administrative situations in those hospitals and asylums. The chapter will explore the role nurses played in promoting eugenics in Alberta through referrals to the AEB and the promotion of birth control material in public and institutional advertisement and prevention campaigns. It includes contributions made by public health nurses since much of their work was devoted to the socialization of new immigrants to Canada. Class, gender, and ethnicity are central themes to this discussion because the majority of individuals who were sterilized were unemployed female immigrants from eastern Europe.[7] The 1920s to the 1940s represent a time in nursing history when a nurse's duty to care was complicated by the attitudes and values of the society in which she existed. Patricia Dantonio highlights the importance of revisiting nursing history:

> History matters to nursing . . . more today now that issues of health care policy and practice, so central to the mission of the profession, have re-engaged the public agenda. . . . [However,] there seems to be only one familiar history to which nurses turn as they consider their place in this process. This history has often been written from the stance of educators deeply concerned about the inability of the profession to control the many different educational routes to nursing practice. Its sources have been a long list of twentieth century reports on the status and future of nursing education.[8]

THE LEILANI MUIR LAW CASE

In the 1990s, a high-profile court case in Alberta drew attention to the topic of eugenics and the controversial issues that surrounded it. In the case of *Muir v. Alberta*, a fifty-one-year-old woman was awarded $740,000, to be paid by the Alberta government, for having been sexually sterilized while wrongfully confined to a provincially run mental institution.[9] In her ruling on January 26, 1996, Madam Justice Joanne Veit stated, "The circumstances of Ms. Muir's sterilization were so high-handed and so contemptuous and so little respected Ms. Muir's human dignity that the community's and the court's sense of decency is offended."[10] At fourteen years of age, Leilani Muir (1944–2016) had been classified as a "mental defective" following an IQ test that rated her as subnormal. On January 19, 1959, she was sterilized without her knowledge.[11] This procedure was done in accordance with the Sexual Sterilization Act. The provincial act, which became law on March 21, 1928, and was finally repealed in 1972, directed the Lieutenant Governor in Council to appoint a board that would include two medical practitioners. This board became known as the Alberta Eugenics Board (AEB). It was established to examine all patients residing in Alberta mental hospitals for the purposes of sterilization prior to their discharge. In this way, according to the AEB, "the danger of procreation with its attendant risk of multiplication of the evil by transmission of the disability to progeny" would be eliminated.[12]

The Muir case raised a number of socio-legal and health-care-related questions. To what extent is a current government accountable for consequences of previous social policy going back as far as 1928? Furthermore, as one newspaper editor noted, "It is worth considering the parallels between eugenics, a faith in human engineering that at one time was embraced by reputedly progressive thinkers of the right and left and the new science of genetic engineering."[13] For nursing, however, a group that is always associated with health and health-care issues, the questions are different. Past nursing activities are often viewed through the lens of "caring."[14] In what way was caring manifested as nurses assessed and referred individuals for sterilization and assisted in the actual operative procedure? In the Muir case, for example, the nurse was not entirely honest when she told Leilani that she was only going to have her appendix removed.[15] On the surface, this might appear to contradict her duty of care, but "caring" was perceived quite differently during past decades than it is understood today.[16] The point is that nursing did not develop in isolation but participated in, and became very involved with, the lives of all Canadians. As a result, much of the profession's development was in response to the needs of Canadian society often identified by individuals and groups external to nursing. This chapter, therefore, examines the role of women in the eugenics movement and raises questions regarding the role of nurses in that movement.[17]

Eugenicist ideas emerged out of nineteenth-century notions developed by British polymath Charles Darwin (1809–82) and became very popular in the United States through Herbert Spencer (1820–1903), a Social Darwinist.[18] Sir Francis Galton (1822–1911), a cousin of Charles Darwin, took these theories further, becoming known as the founder of eugenics. According to Galton,

> Eugenics is the science which deals with all influences that improve the inborn qualities of a race; also with those that develop them to the utmost advantage. The improvement of the inborn qualities, or stock, of some one human population.... All creatures would agree that it was better to be healthy than sick, vigorous than weak, well-fitted than ill-fitted for their part in life.[19]

NURSING BETWEEN CARE AND COMPASSION

The international climate into which these ideas parachuted was receptive because evolution suggested that the race was moving forward and there existed a possibility of improving the race through selective breeding.[20] The Canadian milieu for the reception of these ideas was fertile. This was due in part to the large influx of eastern and southern European immigrants between 1896 and World War I. Their numbers added to the anxiety of Canada's middle-class reformers, who considered themselves to be from sound Anglo-Saxon stock and were highly conscious of the warnings about the degeneration of the race.[21] The emerging view of the new immigrants was linked to notions of social purity by those moral reformers who favoured a "whiter" skin colour. It was thought that the darker the skin, the lower the race and, as a result, the lesser the ability to control sexual desires.[22] According to Kowalewski and Mayne, for example, physicians were among the main proponents of eugenics and their increasing authority in society led to a widespread belief in the power of science to solve social problems.[23] Additionally, the social problems and public discourses in Alberta and its neighbouring province Saskatchewan were similar, while nurses and nursing teachers frequently moved from Alberta to Saskatchewan and vice versa. This was particularly the case in the 1930s, when their similar challenging experiences of the Great Depression and the Western Dust Bowl necessitated personal exchanges and interprovincial mobility of nursing and warden staff. Indeed, the argument was made "that only professionals educated in scientific biological thought could possibly cope with the complex problems facing a society on the brink of degeneration."[24] Physicians then convinced the Canadian public that social problems were medical issues, thus reflecting the beginning of a trend toward medicalization and an easy opportunity to increase the power of the medical profession.[25]

At the same time, psychiatrists Charles Kirk Clarke (1857–1924) and Clarence Hincks (1889–1964) founded the Canadian National Committee for Mental Hygiene (CNCMH) in 1918.[26] The committee encouraged a public health movement predicated on assessing the severity of mental health problems across Canada.[27] As historian Erika Dyck notes, these Canadian reformers "believed that there was a strong correlation between mental abnormalities, or levels of intelligence, and criminal or, immoral behaviour, and likened these categories to a social disease or epidemic that threatened to infect mainstream society."[28] In Alberta, psychiatrists, superintendents, and mental hygiene practitioners conducted a survey and concluded that it would be ideal to reject the insane and mentally deficient because they were more threatening than any other group. And further, "immigrants have contributed more than their fair share to the insane and feeble-minded population, and to other undesirable groups."[29]

Another factor that contributed to Canadian receptivity of eugenic ideas was that the control of reproduction in segregated asylums for those classified as "feeble-minded" was being criticized as expensive and inefficient.[30] Although these ideas received much attention in eastern Canada, the western provinces provided a more hospitable climate for the growth of hereditarian doctrines.[31] In western Canada the language of eugenics focused on foreign weeds in the gardens of Alberta, a reflection of an economy based on agrarian activities. The topic of immigration posed questions that fused the "elements of class, race, and intelligence, using 'foreigner' as convenient shorthand for undesirable." According to Dyck, "at the heart of eugenics programs ... lay a desire to exert power and surveillance over families that did not suit the national regional plan."[32] The plan would have been to focus on the growth of the white Anglo-Saxon Protestant population, and this was further endorsed by that demographic, which was strongly represented in the farming community. The United Farmers of Alberta (UFA) was formed as a political entity and entered the political arena in 1917. Its main areas of concern were public health and social ethics. At the UFA's annual convention in 1918, its members asserted that "the insane and feeble-minded constitute a source for a large proportion of the paupers, criminals and prostitutes in Alberta."[33] Given the timing, the UFA decided to take this opportunity "to build a new, healthier post-war society ... through prohibition, health care, eugenics, social welfare, and progressive taxation."[34] Along with the United Farm Women of Alberta (UFWA) the UFA endorsed "eugenic solutions to keep Canada racially virile," thus providing fertile ground in this western province.[35]

In 1921, the UFA formed the provincial government in Alberta. The UFWA carried a significant amount of influence with the UFA, as had been reflected in the fact that both organizations supported suffrage for women, which resulted in women obtaining the provincial franchise in 1916.[36] The suffragists were Anglo-Saxon, Protestant, and middle-class and shared the anxieties and expectations of this group; they also viewed social problems through glasses tinted with values shaped by this allegiance.[37] According to Dyck, these early feminist reformers in the UFWA "linked poverty and reproduction even more explicitly with feeble-mindedness, and eugenics became a significant part of their campaign in Alberta, embracing the ethos of eugenics as a progressive approach to improving the province's families."[38] In 1924, Irene Parlby (1868–1965), as the acting UFWA president, noted in a speech the grave concerns surrounding mental deficiency and prostitution "and the urgent need for the public to consider its role in assuaging the calamitous effects of prostitution, illegitimacy, drunkenness, and criminality in society."[39] According to Parlby, "the main problem ... remained the high birth rate among people in the defective category, for which she recommended regulation of marriage, segregation of all defectives, and sterilization."[40] Further defence of their domestic turf involved the prevention of entry by immigrants. The UFWA asserted that immigrants "were over-represented by the feeble-minded, the epileptic, the idiotic, the tubercular, the dumb, the blind, the illiterate, the criminal, and the anarchistic."[41] Eugenic principles would bring about the betterment of the state through scientific breeding—a notion not unfamiliar to the farming community.[42] Their ideology has been labelled "maternal feminism" in that they demanded the vote so that they could more adequately defend their homes and children.

During the 1920s, "disease prevention and health promotion took on a major role in the health care services provided by the federal and Alberta provincial governments." Included in this was the importance of early detection of disability and disease, thus resulting in the need for "periodic health examinations, medical inspection of schools, and the promotion of prenatal care."[43] Furthermore, at that time, only 50 percent of women calling themselves nurses were registered with the professional association, the Alberta Association of Registered Nurses (AARN). Indeed, these women were operating quite autonomously in their nursing practice.[44] In 1923, the Calgary Graduate Nurses Association influenced a change in policy by recommending that "patients in the country needed the services of the most highly skilled nurses as well as those living in the city."[45] This notion would lead to the creation of the District Nursing Services.[46] At this time, the nursing service ideal was based on Christian values rooted in church attendance.[47] Yet, the District Nursing Services happened as a direct result of political activism by organized women's groups, especially the UFWA, not the Alberta Association of Registered Nurses.

It should also be noted that during the 1920s, licensure with the professional association was not pursued by graduate nurses in Alberta. Furthermore, the AARN was not involved in any "political activism relating to health care issues" and although the association "did little overtly to impede creation of the District Nursing Service, it similarly offered no concrete support."[48] Indeed, the AARN did not see any value in "allying themselves with other organized women's groups," because their goals were different.[49] This view was accepted among nursing associations on both provincial and national levels. As the University of Alberta's nurse historian Sharon Richardson has pointed out, the "creation of the Alberta District Nursing Service became the exclusive result of extensive and persistent political activism by organized women's groups, especially the UFWA," and not of influence by organized nursing or graduate nurses.[50] Indeed, early Alberta nurse leaders divorced themselves and members of their nursing organizations from health-care issues such as rural and homesteading women's need for reproductive health care.[51]

PUBLIC HEALTH PERSPECTIVES

The Canadian government built a railway across Canada to link the East and the West and, in 1872, passed the Dominion Land Act, which provided "free homesteads to settlers locating in the west." The first homesteaders were primarily "English-speaking and [of] Anglo-Saxon origin."[52] Once this influx of settlers tapered off, large campaigns were launched to entice eastern Europeans—targeted because the government believed the land in the Canadian West was similar to that of eastern Europe and thus these peasants would be suited to Prairie farms. As a result, between 1901 and 1931 the population of Alberta increased from 73,033 to 732,605, resulting in a dramatic change in the ethnic composition of the province; the Prairies had become a "mosaic of distinct ethnic and linguistic communities."[53] This immigration impacted nursing and the provision of health care. Alberta developed public health-care services in 1918 through its new Department of Public Health, because—as a Public Health report noted—"at this period in our history, a great many deaths among the infant population, especially among our immigrants, were never reported; burials being made in the back yard."[54] This was probably the underlying reason for the employment of nurses: to investigate these deaths and to educate people as to what might be done to prevent them.[55] In Manitoba, public health nurses were meant to detect "symptoms of disease and physical defects, unreported communicable diseases, unreported births, malpractice in midwifery, and unsanitary conditions, especially detrimental to the welfare of mothers and children."[56] These tasks would have been the same for public health nurses across the Prairies, in Saskatchewan and Alberta, as well.

The Department of Public Health's report of 1921 was particularly concerned with the living habits of eastern Europeans that were viewed as "disgusting" and a threat to the health of the "whole province." It was suggested that inspectors along with public health nurses investigate these immigrants' homes and "force sanitary conditions upon these people."[57] The problem of mentally defective immigrants raised alarms for the Department of Public Health as well. In 1924, the minister, George

Hoadley (1867–1955), brought his concerns to Premier Herbert Greenfield (1869–1949), noting that medical examinations at point of entry were at that time only cursory.[58] Hoadley argued that "this practice had resulted in a large number of foreign-born individuals residing in the Provincial Hospital for the Insane. Canadians, for example, represented 49 percent of the provincial population and 27 percent of patients in the asylum, while immigrants from the British Isles, Europe, and the United States, although they represented 17, 14, and 18 percent of Alberta's population, respectively, were a disproportionately higher 25, 24, and 22 percent of asylum patients."[59]

The UFWA moved in concert with the UFA.[60] Parlby was the first president of the UFWA and the first female cabinet minister in Alberta in the newly elected UFA government. In 1921, however, she was succeeded by Marian Sears (b. 1862?), who was particularly interested in hygiene, birth control, sterilization of the mentally unfit, and sterilization legislation.[61] In 1928, UFWA members fully supported the Sexual Sterilization Act.[62] Their goal was the protection of their community or, as Emily Murphy (who was then the first female magistrate in the British Empire) said, "to prevent these deviants from plucking the plum and the cream from the upper crust."[63] In 1929, the UFWA immigration convener made a plea for the maintenance of "superior British stock" in Canada, a country for "virile races."[64] She then moved that "we urge our Canadian government to regulate the flow of migrants to Canada so that in no year would the number from other countries exceed [those] of British birth."[65] Society in general feared that alcoholism, epilepsy, social dependency, delinquency, borderline intelligence, congenital syphilis, physical weakness, and criminal behaviour might be transmitted from parent to child.[66] As noted by sociologist Jana Grekul, the provincial director of mental health and the superintendents of the province's mental institutions concluded that "sterilization is the only rational procedure for dealing with mental defectives who were unduly prolific both within and without marriage and bring into the world children double handicapped by both heritage and early environment."[67]

As the influence of psychiatry and medicine grew, it was believed that their "scientific" proof allowed for the promotion of the link between feeble-mindedness and social problems, the solution to which was to be found in "involuntary sterilization" and "racial betterment through the weeding out of undesirable strains."[68] The AEB first appeared in the Department of Public Health's annual reports in 1932. A profile emerged of those individuals who were referred to the board. As legal scholar Timothy Christian concluded from his research,

> They tended to be female rather than male, young and inexperienced rather than mature, not employed and dependent rather than self-supporting, employed in low status rather than prestigious jobs, residents of small towns rather than cities, members of ethnic minorities rather than the dominant ethnic group, single rather than married, and had been defined as sexual deviants. In addition, those persons dealt with by the Eugenics Board had been branded with the most socially debilitating label of all—a psychiatric diagnosis.[69]

Most cases approved for sterilization were those in which a patient was diagnosed as mentally defective. However, psychotic, "manic-depressive" (today's notion would be bipolar disorder), and schizophrenic patients represented 42.7 percent of cases and the bulk of the remaining individuals approved for sterilization. Further, by 1929, the UFA was looking to enlarge the community of health-care professionals to include physicians and public health nurses in order to identify potential candidates for sterilization who had not been admitted to an institution.[70]

Since women were viewed as more promiscuous than men and as having a greater potential for evil than men, cumulative totals for female sterilization were much higher than those for men. This was in spite of the fact that from 1934 until 1943, the number of men recommended for sterilization annually outnumbered women. In 1934, 132 men were recommended for sterilization and 46 operations were performed: in the same year, 82 women were recommended and 59 were sterilized.[71] Given the fact that a vasectomy is much simpler to perform than a salpingectomy (removal of a Fallopian tube), this situation can also be seen to reflect both the domination of men within the AEB and the low social status held by women.[72] Nurses joined virtually all Canadians in working toward the maintenance and preservation of a white Anglo-Saxon Canada. Since all aspects of nursing are closely connected to hygiene, it is not surprising to learn that nurses were also concerned with "mental hygiene," "social hygiene," and mental illness. To this end, articles published in the *Canadian Nurse* addressed the sexual attitudes of nurses.[73] It was generally agreed that sex was at the root of a great number of the ills from which the world was suffering—ills that nurses also combated. One such "ill" was masturbation, which was closely linked to insanity and criminal or anti-social behaviour.[74] The language of eugenics also appeared in articles in the *Canadian Nurse* that discussed the type of young woman that should be accepted into training schools. The ease with which nurses made use of the vocabulary of eugenics reflects the interactivity of nursing with society at the time.[75] Similar rhetoric appeared in the pages of the *Canadian Public Health Journal*, a journal in which both nurses and physicians expressed their views.[76] Health-care workers seemed to agree that sterilization provided a path to racial improvement.[77]

Support for this idea is particularly exemplified in the role played by the public health nurse, who was very much involved with "public hygiene" in that she often worked with children and thus had the opportunity to identify those commonly referred to as "idiot" or "feeble-minded." The appearance of these children in a family was usually attributed to a history of insanity, poor environment, or poor hygiene on the part of the mother.[78] The services of a public health nurse might also be viewed as a "Canadianizing" influence on the eastern Europeans. Health education and prevention of disease in this population contributed to the perceptions that the nurse acted as an agent of socialization and surveillance, owing to the frequency of the visits. As one public health nurse wrote, "I have tried everything as perfectly as possible under the circumstances, and also to explain to them just why we think our way better than theirs."[79] The preferred way for a new Canadian to arrive in Canada was "in a cradle in a Canadian home."[80] These views were in keeping with mainstream Canadian society. The support that nurses gave eugenics mirrors the assent of Canadian society in general and demonstrates the integral role of nursing in these social developments. It also reveals their prejudices and the kind of attitudes they would have had toward the people they were trying to help.

In Alberta, public health nurses and the UFWA were closely connected. As early as 1916, the UFWA initiated investigations into the need for public health nurses, rural hospitals, and health units. The organization's efforts were rewarded when the Department of Public Health was established in 1919. This, in turn, led to the creation of a system of public health nurses, municipal hospitals, and travelling clinics throughout Alberta. Nurses collaborated with the Women's Institute, the Red Cross Society, and the UFWA to ensure that hospital care and nursing care were available to all Albertans.[81] By 1935, nurses staffed the twenty-two hospitals operating under the Municipal Hospitals Act. In addition to offering their services within these institutions, nurses provided professional help when called upon by the communities in which they lived. Throughout Alberta, nurses who were married were on call and often performed public health nursing functions in their homes. Nursing had become an essential service and the status of those women involved in delivering the service had been further enhanced by the approval in 1923 of a degree program that would lead to a bachelor of science in nursing at the University of Alberta.[82]

PUBLIC HEALTH NURSES AND THE ALBERTA EUGENICS PROGRAM

Public health nurses worked diligently to maintain the standards of public health set by the dominant group.[83] These standards were fuelled in part by eugenic ideology as well as by fiscal restraint. As Jean Field of Kinuso, Alberta, member of the AEB, noted in her address to the eighteenth annual convention of the UFWA in 1932,

> I am convinced that the Eugenic Sterilization Act brought into being a new phase of health work, which will be of great benefit to the future of our citizenship in Alberta.... It is not a cure all. ... But it is one of many sane and practical and humane methods which must be adopted in all effort to relieve in a slight degree, the appalling problem of the mentally incompetent, and the result to our future citizenry of the unimpeded transmission of mental defects to progeny. Also, when we consider that, out of every hundred dollars spent in this Province in public health, eighty dollars is spent in mental health, one must consider this question in its economic aspects as well.[84]

Farm women and public health nurses were not alone in their support of these views. The citizens of Alberta strongly supported the sexual sterilization activities approved by the AEB.[85] One fascinating example of this closer interaction between groups of farm women and public health nurses occurred in 1937, when the Wesley United Church in Calgary established the Family Planning Association, to educate women to have "children by choice—not by chance." To this end, the Family Planning Association hired a Kaufman nurse.[86] Alvin Ratz Kaufman (1885–1979) already had one nurse in Alberta when Ann Hammill (d. 2007?) accepted the position to assist in the promotion of birth control material for the Family Planning Association.[87] Hammill was paid $19.95 per month plus an additional $1.00 for every application for birth control that she sent to the Parents' Information Bureau at 410 King Street West in Kitchener, Ontario. The application incorporated a brief medical history of the client, a description of the client's home conditions, and information relevant to birth control devices. Information was available in English, Polish, Ukrainian, or French and all supplies were free of charge. Hammill cooperated with the AEB and described the board as "very helpful."[88] All of the "abnormal" cases were referred to the board; for Hammill, "abnormal" meant families in which one or two children out of five or six had a physical deformity.[89]

This nurse was committed to her work. Indeed, in her opinion, given the economic climate of the 1930s, the government could not bear the cost of the many children who eventually became wards of the state. Hammill herself recounted one case in which she felt she had "picked the wrong one to sterilize":

> We had one or two women here in town whom I am sure were responsible for turning over 15 to 20 babies to the Relief Department here. Every year they would present another one. . . . After having about 12 children, we finally caught up with the family and suggested possible sterilization and we picked the wrong one to be sterilized—we sterilized the husband. So, she turned up again a few years following this and when Mrs. W came into the clinic at City Hall, she called me and she said: "I have a baby in east Calgary left with a babysitter and the mother has not come back for the baby and I recognize the features and I know where [it] belongs." Do you suppose you could possibly get a hold of this patient and maybe it's not too late to have her done. So we finally did have her sterilized. But this was over a period of years. These babies were taken over and became government wards. . . . This is why Commissioner X said that we had saved them so much money.[90]

Those individuals referred to the AEB by nurses such as Hammill were seldom from the dominant class, with whom nurses shared concerns regarding the burden that unwanted children placed upon both the poor and the state. The goal of these socially conservative women was to control the health and well-being of women, children, and the families in the community where the poor, as a group, constituted a socially disruptive force.[91]

The direct role that nurses in Alberta played in the eugenics movement with its focus on questions concerning procreation by individuals with mental disorders involved the assessment, referral, operating room assistance, and post-operative care. Anecdotal evidence suggests that on an individual basis, some nurses refused to participate, but this was usually rooted in a deep religious conviction. In particular, at the Alberta Hospital, Edmonton, student nurses in their psychiatric nursing training refused to assist in the operating room during a sterilization procedure. Most nurses, however, recognized it as law.[92] In 1937, the Social Credit government wanted to reassure voters about their fiscal credibility, and to demonstrate this, they "removed the Board's need to obtain consent in cases where the client was deemed mentally defective."[93] The revised act included the following:

> If, upon examination of any mentally defective person, the Board is unanimously of the opinion that the exercise of the power of procreation would result in the transmission to such person's progeny of any mental disability or deficiency, or that the exercise of the power of procreation by any such mentally defective person involves the risk of mental injury either to such person or to his progeny, the Board may direct, in writing, such surgical operation for the sex sterilization of such mentally defective person as may be specified in the written direction.[94]

This shift in the consent process coincided with a growing silence around the subject of eugenics in medical journals and the press, so that by the end of World War II, the surgeries had increased but reporting on them had disappeared completely (compare with tables A1 to A4 in the appendix).[95] This would suggest that other problems were taking up the attention of society, with the returning soldiers and the postwar relief to which people turned following the trauma of war. In December 1940, psychologist John M. MacEachran (1872–1947), then chair of the AEB, reported that a total of 801 males and 774 females had been presented and passed for sterilization but "only" 277 males and 450 females had actually been sterilized during the first twelve years of the existence of the eugenics program in the province (see also chapter 1).[96] Given the aims of the Sexual Sterilization Act, these numbers suggest that some success was obtained. In fact, by the time the act was repealed, 2,835 women and men had been sterilized.[97] What does this tell us about nurses and their participation in these sterilizations? Nursing historian Hilde Steppe viewed the support that nurses in Germany gave to the National Socialist Party during the 1930s and 1940s as the darkest chapter in the history of her profession.[98] She attributed the willingness of those nurses to participate in National Socialist policy to what she describes as the four pillars on which secular nursing in Germany was based: humility, sacrifice, selflessness, and obedience.[99] National Socialist nurses followed orders and experienced an internalized sense of obligation that moved one nurse to state, "I was personally of the opinion that if the doctor prescribed it and the law prescribed it, then it must be right."[100] A similar explanation can be applied to nurses in Alberta between 1920 and 1940. Tradition dictated that a "good" nurse was an "obedient" nurse. Indeed, one school of nursing in Alberta made the following demands:

> All pupils are required to be honest, truthful, trustworthy, punctual, orderly, neat and obedient. In a word, they are expected to keep in mind the importance of their position and to evince at all times the self-denial, good temper and gentleness so essential to successful service.[101]

Not surprisingly, this school is credited with making a significant contribution to nursing in Alberta, particularly through the provision of matrons in hospitals throughout the province.[102] Ultimately, sterilization decisions were medically driven and the rationale was understood to be for the protection of, and in the best interests of, the patients.

DISCUSSION

As this chapter has sought to demonstrate, predominantly those nurses in Alberta—who were organized in the Provincial Nursing Association of Alberta—supported the notion that society was protecting these patients, especially female patients, from exploitation, unwanted pregnancies, and the burden of childrearing by applying both positive and negative forms of eugenics measures.[103] As I have argued here, nurses were working obediently in a medical culture—at the time led largely by white, male, Anglo-Saxon Protestant physicians, scientists, and administrators—that was pro-eugenics, despite likely personal reservations about the program. In particular, the nurses were, by job description and function, peripheral to the matter of eugenics as a medico-legal matter. In this way, the caring demonstrated by these nurses is similar to that discussed by Thomas Olson in that the nurses handled, managed, and controlled individuals in order to maintain a society that adhered to the wishes of the dominant group, of which they were a part.[104] As Dyck has previously determined,

> The history of reproductive politics is complicated through the swirl of debates surrounding sterilization, contraception, and abortion, loud voices have often been raised to condemn seekers of such choices for their carelessness and irresponsibility. Carelessness has been framed in terms of personal hygiene, proximity to mainstream values . . . and intelligence or ability. Irresponsibility has been used to justify intervening in people's lives, sometimes coercion, and in the case of eugenics, to curb their fertility.[105]

These conclusions also hold for my own argument here regarding the involvement of nurses in the centralized eugenics program in Alberta between 1920 and 1940.

Finally, however, there is no evidence to suggest that the Provincial Nursing Association attempted to influence social policy on any level, one way or the other.[106] This was not a time when the topic of human rights was on the social agenda of provincial or national politics; therefore, there is little reason to suspect that the attitudes of nurses differed from those held by the society within which they functioned. In terms of eugenics in Alberta, this chapter has stressed that nurses clearly represented the thinking of Canadian society at large. If opposition to the eugenics movement existed among nurses, failure to articulate it or act upon it might he attributed to "I see and I am silent," the motto chosen for the first school of nursing in Canada.[107]

4

The Alberta Eugenics Movement and the 1937 Amendment to the Sexual Sterilization Act

Mikkel Dack

The scholarly study of eugenics in Alberta has been seriously limited, as concentration has been restricted to the province's original Sexual Sterilization Act, passed in March 1928, and to the political, social, and economic conditions of the 1920s. Although the 1928 act was of great significance, being the first sterilization law passed in Canada, it was its 1937 amendment and the permitting of involuntary sterilizations that made the Alberta eugenics movement truly distinct. During the mid- to late 1930s—a time when the majority of regional governments in the United States and Canada were either decommissioning or disregarding their sterilization laws due to a lack of funding, the discrediting of hereditary science, and an increase in public protest—Alberta expanded its own legislation. Although similar laws were met with fierce opposition in other jurisdictions, the 1937 amendment remained largely unopposed in Alberta. As such, while this chapter explores the legislative and cultural history of one Canadian province, it also considers how eugenics laws in Alberta compared to similar legislation in other provinces and in the United States and Europe.

Explanations of why the act was amended and why resistance to non-consensual sterilization remained minimal during the 1930s and 1940s have been based almost entirely on political and social assumptions and not on sound evidence. In the existing scholarship, the 1937 amendment is either characterized as legislation that accurately reflected the political and social climate of the 1920s or included in the narrative of the "quiet longevity" of sterilization practices after the Second World War. By elevating the 1937 amendment into an arena of scholarly discussion and dismissing the preconceived notions and arguments of the past we are left with a new grounding from which to build future propositions and with a new set of sharpened questions to help determine why the Alberta government, and presumably its citizens, were willing to condone such regressive legislation when it was being ignored and rejected elsewhere on the continent. By doing so, new theories arise, such as the influential role of individual personalities within the provincial government and medical community, the definition and diagnosis of "mental deficiency" in Canada, and the means by which political opposition and public protest could be expressed in the 1930s.

THE INTERNATIONAL EUGENICS MOVEMENT

The modern eugenics movement, which developed at the turn of the nineteenth century under the English anthropologist and natural philosopher Sir Francis Galton (1822–1911), promoted "healthy living" and "social purity" and focused on both positive and negative eugenics practices as a means to eliminate hereditary disease and "feeble-mindedness."[1] The British upper and middle classes of the late nineteenth century feared social degeneration and a "racial suicide." However, it was not in Britain where such socio-scientific concepts were first introduced into the political sphere, or even in Europe; instead, it was the United States that pioneered eugenics legislation. By 1917, sterilization laws had been enacted in fifteen states and by 1937, in thirty-one.[2] These acts were often accompanied by newly revised marriage and immigration laws, many of which possessed strong undertones of racial prejudice.[3] In 1910, the Eugenics Record Office (ERO), headed by Dr. Charles B. Davenport (1866–1944), was established in Cold Spring Harbor, Long Island, and it soon became the institutional nerve centre for human hereditary research in North America.[4] Backed by a belief in the legitimacy of hereditary science, inspired by an age of modernization and progressivism and accompanied by a fear of unregulated immigration and "race defilement," the United States became the international leader of eugenics in the 1920s, and by 1935 over twenty-one thousand sterilizations had been performed.[5]

Although eugenics as a social and scientific movement had officially existed in Germany since 1905, and the liberal-democratic government of the Weimar Republic often applied eugenics-based theory to various health and social programs, it was during the National Socialist period that Germany would surpass the United States in its total number of eugenic laws.[6] On July 14, 1933, the Law for the Prevention of Offspring with Hereditary Diseases was passed, permitting the sterilization of German citizens affiliated with "feeblemindedness," schizophrenia, epilepsy, and other "incurable diseases."[7] In November 1935, the so-called Nuremberg (Race) Laws were enacted, detailing strict racial classifications and forbidding sexual and marital relations between Jews and "citizens of German or kindred blood."[8] Although the German eugenics programs during the 1930s were far more radical than those in any other country, sterilizing nearly 375,000 people between 1933 and 1945, its collaboration with eugenicists in the United States cannot be overlooked.[9] Not only did Germany attempt to emulate the United States in its sterilization practices; the ERO and the American Eugenics Society (AES) eventually became the strongest foreign supporters of Nazi eugenics, regardless of its extreme nature and racial tone.[10] After a visit to Germany in 1934, the head of the AES, Leon Fradley Whitney (1894–1973), remarked that he was determined to work toward "something very like what [Adolf] Hitler has now made compulsory" and that Nazi eugenics measures corresponded with the "goals of eugenicists all over the world."[11]

THE EUGENICS MOVEMENT IN ALBERTA AND THE 1928 SEXUAL STERILIZATION ACT

The Canadian eugenics movement was informed by both the American pioneers of the 1920s and the German radicals of the 1930s.[12] The mass influx of immigrants into the young country, beginning in the 1890s, and concern about the mentally ill and "feeblemindedness" in Canadian society had dominated debates on eugenics well into the 1920s. The

Canadian National Committee on Mental Hygiene (CNCMH), which was established in 1918 with the goal to "fight crime, prostitution and unemployment," conducted province-wide surveys on the health and wellness of the nation's residents, all of which reported "negative results."[13] Although eugenics organizations were formed in all Canadian provinces during the 1920s, the warnings of the CNCMH found their greatest resonance in Alberta. Western Canada in the 1920s provided an ideal climate for the acceptance of eugenics science, not only because of the fear produced by a large and ever-growing immigrant population (see also chapter 3), but also because it was a reforming society rife with social gospellers, radical politicians, and women's suffragists, many of whom advocated a philosophy of progress based upon the application of science. In 1921 the United Farmers of Alberta (UFA) formed a majority in the provincial legislature, immediately advocating for the establishment of sterilization laws.

The United Farm Women of Alberta (UFWA), an auxiliary of the UFA, spearheaded efforts to enact compulsory sterilization, seeking "racial betterment through the weeding out of undesirable strains."[14] In 1922, the province's minister of health, Richard G. Reid (1879–1980), announced that the government was in favour of sterilization. However, it would be six years before his position would materialize into provincial legislation.[15] On March 21, 1928, the UFA government enacted Canada's first legislation concerning the sterilization of mentally disabled persons.[16] Passed by the legislative assembly after three separate readings, the Sexual Sterilization Act established a four-person eugenics board, composed mostly of senior physicians, who could authorize the sterilization of individuals discharged from mental institutions. During its forty-four years of existence, the Alberta Eugenics Board (AEB) reviewed 4,785 cases for potential sterilization, of which 2,835 were performed.[17] Candidates were selected from four "feeder-hospitals" throughout the province, which included Alberta Hospital (Ponoka), Provincial Training School for Mental Defectives (Red Deer), Alberta Hospital (Oliver), and Deer Home (Red Deer).[18] Physicians or psychiatrists at these institutions would recommend patients for sterilization and present their cases to the AEB, along with information on the patient's family and a detailed history of their sexual activities, education, criminal behaviour, and finances. The board would then interview the patient and ask for personal consent from them or their legal guardian. On average, the AEB reviewed thirteen cases during each of its hour-long sessions, with sometimes not even five minutes of discussion for each recommendation (see also chapter 1).[19]

Although legal equivalents to the Alberta sterilization law could be found throughout the United States, by the mid-1930s important scientific and political groups in both countries had grown more skeptical about the practice of eugenic science. The rising status of Nazi Germany in world affairs had led to a closer examination of the Reich's health programs and racial laws, resulting in a decline in negative eugenic practices in North America.[20] The Nazi regime's tendency to use racial hygiene to justify sterilization and euthanasia began to severely discredit the eugenics movement.[21] In the United States politicians debated over the "absurd premises of Nordicism" claimed by the National Socialist government and the scientific basis of discrimination against Jews.[22] One anti-sterilization pamphlet, published in Canada in 1936, announced that "eugenics rests entirely on a few unproved and even dubious theories. Consider for example the myth of 'racial superiority.'"[23] This decline was perpetuated by a loss of financial support from wealthy sponsors, a general questioning of simplistic genetic claims by the scientific community, and the retirement or death of many prominent figures who had supported programs of racial eugenics.[24] Furthermore, in the late 1930s a new generation of progressive social eugenicists began to promote positive eugenics. By the late 1930s sterilization operations in the United States had dropped to 1.68 per 100,000 population, while Alberta's sterilization rate had reached 6.21 per 100,000, or nearly four times the American average.[25]

During this period of international decline in the practice of negative eugenics, the majority of sterilization laws in the United States were simply ignored, though they remained in the statute books; however, Alberta continued to apply its legislation fairly widely.[26] In fact, in 1937 the Social Credit minister of health, Dr. Wallace Cross (1887–1973), complained to the legislature that in the nine years since the passing of the province's sterilization law *only* four hundred "abnormal persons" had been sterilized and *not* the two thousand that he believed were qualified.[27] His government considered the Sexual Sterilization Act too restrictive and therefore proposed an amendment to the law that would grant the AEB authority to compel the sterilization of patients without consent. The director of the mental health services for the province, Dr. Charles Baragar (1885–1936), also advocated for the removal of the consent requirement for "mental defectives," writing that "the Sexual Sterilization Act is a very mild one. On account of the necessity for securing consent in all cases there are a number of cases in which sexual sterilization would be strongly advisable ... to whom consent cannot be obtained."[28] An editorial in the *Edmonton Bulletin* voiced similar concerns, explaining that "only ten years ago there were three hundred hopeless mental defectives in Alberta and now there are three thousand."[29] Amid such popular sentiments, the sterilization act was amended in March 1937 and the AEB given consensual rights to perform sterilization on those patients whom they believed posed a "risk of mental injury, either to the individual or to his or her progeny."[30]

A second amendment of similar features was passed in 1942, before the law was abolished by the government of Peter Lougheed (1928–2012) in 1972.[31] While most provincial and state governments were either decommissioning or disregarding their sterilization laws due to a lack of funding, an increase in public scrutiny, and the discrediting of hereditary science, Alberta's expanding legislation appeared to remain virtually unopposed by government officials, health administrators, and the general public. The 1928 Sexual Sterilization Act and its public discourse have since been thoroughly investigated by scholars searching for a rationale as to why no significant form of protest accompanied the law's enactment.[32] However, the study of eugenics in Alberta has been importantly restrained, as scholars have concentrated largely on the original sterilization act and on the political, social, and economic conditions that existed in Alberta during the 1920s. More recent studies have looked to the longevity of sterilization legislation in Alberta to account for the passing of the amendment of 1937, arguing that by the time negative eugenics science had been discredited internationally, the sterilization legislation in Alberta had moved beyond the purview of the general public, allowing for the quiet continuation of such practices.[33] Although the 1928 act was of great significance, as it was the first sterilization law passed in Canada, within a larger context of North America, its enactment was quite ordinary.[34] The 1937 amendment and the relatively late onset of legislation that permitted involuntary sterilizations, on the other hand, was not; this is where the Alberta eugenics movement was truly distinct and where further study must be conducted.

Due to a heavy concentration on the original sterilization law and to the overall longevity of involuntary sterilizations in Alberta, scholarly explanations for why the act was amended in 1937 and why resistance to sexual sterilization remained minimal during the 1930s and 1940s have been unsatisfactory. The four most common explanations given by historians and scholars for why resistance did not emerge in Alberta during the 1920s and 1930s are (1) that the province experienced a mass influx of immigrants, resulting in fears that an "inferior stock" was polluting the local community, (2) that the general public was unaware of the sterilization laws themselves, as such legislation was confined to the conversations and debates of politicians and health administrators, (3) that the public was unaware of the racial eugenic programs in Nazi Germany, the discrediting of hereditary science, and the decline of eugenics movements throughout North America, and (4) that there was a popular belief that eugenics legislation would improve the economic conditions of the province and that sexual sterilization would help reduce frivolous government spending. Although all these explanations for the public acceptance of government-sanctioned sterilization are plausible within the political, social, and cultural context of the 1920s, they quickly lose their relevance when applied to the 1930s. To obtain a greater understanding as to why Alberta seemingly embraced eugenics legislation with such enthusiasm and why involuntary sterilization appeared to be socially uncontested, the 1930s must be studied in isolation and not merely as an extension of the 1920s eugenics movement or the thirty years of unpublicized and discreet sterilization practices that followed the Second World War. Only then can a new scholarly investigation be conducted and the question of why Alberta remained one of the strongest advocates for sexual sterilization in North America during the twentieth century answered.

IMMIGRATION

In his doctoral dissertation, Terrence Chapman argues that mass immigration to Alberta during the 1920s was the single largest motivator for the passing of the Sexual Sterilization Act in 1928.[35] At the turn of the century, Canadian immigration was still governed by the terms of the 1869 Immigration Act, a more or less open-door policy for European immigrants that required no medical inspection upon disembarking at Canadian ports.[36] From 1901 to 1911, the population of Canada increased by 43 percent, and in 1913 alone more than four hundred thousand immigrants were permitted residency in the country, a large proportion of whom migrated west to the Prairie provinces.[37] In combination with the effects of the First World War and Great Depression, the increasing immigrant population caused many middle-class Canadians to fear national degeneration. Historian Timothy Christian supports such claims, drawing considerable attention to the Mental Hygiene Survey published in 1921 that reported that only 49 percent of people living in Alberta were born in Canada and that the high level of "unfit elements" was largely due to immigration, specifically from eastern Europe.[38] In 1922, the former minister of the interior, Clifford Sifton (1861–1929), renounced Canada's immigration policy, arguing that Alberta had been overrun by undesirable immigrants and that the Canadian federal government had "not been admitting those individuals of the most rugged fibre."[39] The *Farm and Ranch Review* expressed similar grievances, explaining to its readers that "the immigrants [in Alberta] are beaten men from beaten races."[40] As early as 1924 the UFWA began to organize a campaign against the immigration of the "insane and feeble-minded" into the province, calling for either physical segregation or social assimilation; they chose assimilation and sexual sterilization as means to achieve eugenics results.[41]

However, a review of government statistics and of popular media of the time suggests that such trends in western immigration, and the fears that accompanied them, changed substantially in 1930s. When Richard Bedford Bennett (1870–1947), the first leader of the Alberta Conservative Party, won the federal election in 1930, he promised not only an end to unemployment, but also a drastic reduction in immigration.[42] Within three months of taking office, Bennett's Conservative government imposed a series of legal restrictions resulting in the most rigid immigration admissions policy in Canadian history.[43] While as many as 165,000 immigrants had entered Canada in 1929, in 1936 that number was only 12,000—more than a 90 percent drop in only seven years.[44] The early 1930s also saw the deportation of more than 25,000 immigrants who had been recipients of public assistance and considered to be a "drain on Canadian society."[45] In the 1920s Alberta itself had admitted upwards of 20,000 immigrants per year; by the mid-1930s, however, due to government's response to a popular fear of rising unemployment, that number had fallen to under a thousand.[46] In 1935 only 735 immigrants arrived in Alberta.[47] Furthermore, of the small number of immigrants received by the province during these years, few were from eastern Europe and other regions that the CNCMH and the UFWA had targeted during their original sterilization campaign in the 1920s.[48]

Christian has argued that despite any decrease in Alberta's immigration rates in the 1930s, the fear of immigration among the resident population had remained unchanged, owing to such a large influx of foreigners during the four previous decades.[49] However, a close examination of popular newspapers of the time challenges this argument. News of Bennett's restrictive admission policy and Alberta's dramatic drop in immigration was widely published in local newspapers; in fact, from 1930 to 1935 such stories were often found on the front pages. On March 7, 1929, the *Edmonton Journal* reassured its readers with the headline "Immigration Activities Will Be Curbed" and noted that, in the future, "the proper restrictions shall be exercised over the character of immigration in the country's interests."[50] The *Calgary Daily Herald* ran similar headlines, informing the public that an immigration advisory body had been formed and that "immigration ... to Canada has fallen off greatly."[51] Not only had immigration to Alberta been nearly eliminated by the mid-1930s, but the population knew that it had been. The fear of mentally deficient immigrants who were already living in the province may have lingered, but it can be assumed that during the 1930s Albertans saw the problem of immigration in a much different light; it was no longer seen as a growing threat, one that required extreme and immediate action to prevent its expansion.

LACK OF PUBLIC KNOWLEDGE OF THE STERILIZATION LAWS

A common explanation given by scholars for why Albertans did not oppose the sexual sterilization program is that there was a general lack of public knowledge of the laws themselves and that such information was confined to conversations and debates among politicians and health administrators. This argument at first glance is believable, as all AEB sessions were closed to the public and the majority of debates surrounding eugenics legislation were carried out either in the provincial legislature and the office of the minister of health or within medical journals that few Albertans read. However, the examination of newspapers and other publications of the time casts doubts on the applicability of this argument to the 1930s. The original Sexual Sterilization Act of 1928 was loudly announced in the media the very day of its enactment. On March 7, 1928, the front page of the *Edmonton Bulletin* declared, "Sterilization Bill Passes Third Reading."[52] During the period of political debate that preceded the act, newspapers spoke of the "sterilization of defectives," arguing that such proposed legislation was necessary due to the "appalling growth of the mental defectives in the various provincial institutions."[53]

On December 9, 1935, the *Edmonton Bulletin* published a special report on the eugenics debate in Canada, highlighting the various sterilization laws that had been passed in the United States and Europe and their influence on provincial legislation.[54] The *Calgary Daily Herald*, in its coverage of the 1937 amendment, questioned the authority of the AEB, explaining to its readers how "this medical body is able to order operations on under age mental cases."[55] Furthermore, a number of pamphlets and books were published in Canada in the mid-1930s, mostly by religious organizations, which were widely distributed across the country and spoke out specifically against Alberta's sterilization law. In 1934, Canadian lawyer Lettilia Fairfield's (1885–1978) *The Case against Sterilization* was published, as was Canadian physician Helen MacMurchy's (1862–1953) *Sterilization? Birth Control? A Book for Family Welfare and Safety*; two years later, Québec-based theologian Antoine d'Eschambault (1896–1960), wrote *Eugenical Sterilization*.[56] All of these works condemned Alberta's sterilization practices on moral, scientific, and economic grounds.

Due to the wide exposure of Alberta's sterilization laws in the popular press, and the availability of anti-eugenic literature, it is difficult to believe that the province's population, or at least the proportion that actively read, remained ignorant of sterilization activities during the 1930s. Media sources not only printed the details of the 1937 amendment but also reiterated the discussions and debate that surrounded the new and existing sterilization legislation (on the comparative role of the media in the US see chapter 6). Albertans may not have been informed of the day-to-day administration and operation of sterilization activities, as such information was reserved for politicians and the medical community, but they *were* well informed of eugenics legislation that had been passed in the Legislature, the political and social ramifications that it entailed, and the amendment to the law in 1937.

NAZI RACIALISM AND THE DECLINE OF NEGATIVE EUGENICS PROGRAMS

Another common explanation for the lack of opposition to Alberta's sexual sterilization program, including the 1937 amendment, is twofold: that the province's media did not provide sufficient coverage of racial eugenic practices in Nazi Germany, and that, as historian Angus McLaren has argued, "the general public was not made aware of the declining scientific respectability of eugenics."[57] This argument is of relevance because many other jurisdictions in North America witnessed a loss of popular support for eugenics reputedly due to Nazi activities in the same field. In examining the available evidence, it becomes clear that the general public in Alberta *was* exposed to a considerable amount of information regarding Nazi racial ideology and eugenics legislation, as well as to the international decline of negative eugenics, mainly through the popular press. On July 16, 1933, the *Edmonton Journal* published a full-page editorial entitled "Whither Germany?" in which a review of the current conditions of the new regime was conducted. What inspired this special inquiry was the passing two days prior of a new eugenics law in Germany, the Law for the Prevention of Hereditarily Diseased Offspring. In this editorial, the paper not only detailed the specific terms of the new law, but also reviewed other controversial legislation and government programs that had been implemented in Nazi Germany. It criticized Germany's racial health programs, its determination to "decry everything foreign," and its attempts to "reintegrate the whole of the German race."[58] Close coverage of Nazi health legislation again appeared with the passing of the first two measures of the Nuremburg Laws in September 1935. The *Calgary Daily Herald* ran front-page headlines announcing "Nazis Bar Jews from Citizenship" and "New Laws Persecute German Jews."[59] These articles recounted the details of the new racial laws, explaining to their readers how "race now determines German status" and how "marriage laws are governed by race."[60]

Newspapers were not the only sources that delivered news to Albertans about German anti-Semitic legislation and racial health practices. The international boycott movement that had preceded the 1936 Summer Olympics in Berlin had found strong support among sporting organizations in Alberta and had sparked a considerable amount of protest against German acts of racial persecution and violence.[61] Furthermore, during a trip to Germany in 1936, future premier of Saskatchewan Tommy Douglas (1904–86) admitted to the press that he had been "turned away from eugenics" after learning more of the Nazis' sterilization laws, calling them "frightening."[62] Whether informed by the local press, by sports organizations and returning athletes, or by politicians, Albertans had knowledge of Nazi social and health programs—all of which were grounded in racial ideology and enforced through oppression and violence.

There is substantial evidence to suggest that Albertans were also aware of the general decline of the eugenics movements throughout North America beginning in the mid-1930s. The *Edmonton Journal*, the *Edmonton Bulletin*, and the *Calgary Daily Herald* all printed articles on the debates and discussions that were occurring in various state legislatures in the United States regarding existing sterilization laws. On January 16, 1936, the *Edmonton Bulletin* reprinted a *New York Times* editorial entitled "Against Sterilization," in which the scientific qualifications of eugenics was challenged.[63] Similar articles from the Associated Press and the *Washington Post* also appeared in Alberta newspapers, with headlines reading "Sterilization Forced upon Her by Mother, Heiress Charged" and "Woman Is Saved from Sterilization."[64] This popular questioning of sterilization as a means to solve social, economic, and health problems renders it unlikely that Albertans were unaware of the decline of eugenics movements and the discrediting of heredity science.

ECONOMIC CONSIDERATIONS

The final, and possibly strongest, argument made by scholars to account for the lack of opposition to the province's sexual sterilization program proposes that there was a popular belief among Albertans during the 1930s that sexual sterilization would improve the province's economic situation. McLaren argues that mentally deficient patients who were institutionalized in hospitals and psychiatric wards were often seen as an economic burden to the province and its taxpayers.[65] It can be assumed that such sentiments would only have been amplified during the 1930s as the nation sunk deep into economic depression. Sociologist Jana Grekul explains how the CNCMH announced in 1932 that its long-term goal was to fight "crime, prostitution, and unemployment," all of which it claimed were related to the economic burden of "feeble-minded" individuals.[66] A contributor to *The Canadian Doctor* expressed a similar opinion in the journal's January 1936 issue, arguing that Alberta's Sterilization Act should be expanded due to the fact that it would save "immense amounts of money."[67] However, newspaper articles, popular literature, political interviews, and debates in the legislature from this period challenge this argument as well.

Dr. Clarence M. Hincks (1889–1964), University of Toronto professor and co-founder of the Canadian Mental Health Association, in his federally commissioned survey of Alberta's "mental hygiene" argued that sexual sterilization operations should be expanded within the province in order to eliminate the "unfit."[68] In his assessment he warned that if the province did not amend its Sexual Sterilization Act then the "moral sense of Alberta" would be jeopardized. Nowhere in his comprehensive report did Hincks mention the economic considerations of sterilization.[69] Dr. Charles Baragar (1885–1936) presented a similar case to the minister of health in June 1936, arguing that "on account of the necessity for securing consent in all cases . . . the quality of citizens of this province has been lessened."[70] During the second reading of the proposed bill, George Hoadley (1867–1955), Alberta's minister of agriculture and health, referred to the need for the province to be "protected from the menace which the propagation by the mentally diseased brings about" and that the "mentally unfit" were a "menace to the community."[71] Hoadley was referring to not an economic menace, but instead a menace to the "civilized world," closely resembling the Nazi racial interpretation of *Volk* and the burden of the *Untermensch* (subhuman). Hoadley concluded his speech by stating that "if it is quantity of production of the human race that is required, then we don't need this Bill, but if we want quality then it is a different matter."[72] It becomes abundantly clear through these recorded statements that the most important figures in the sterilization movement in Alberta during the 1930s viewed the amendment as, above all things, a remedy for social and cultural ailments, and not as an answer to economic depression and frivolous government spending.

This tendency to concentrate on the quality of the human race rather than on economic factors was not confined to the opinions of politicians. Newspapers and popular literature of the 1930s produced a similar message. In an editorial discussing the possibility of amending the sterilization act, the *Medicine Hat News* stated that it is the "quality of humanity that is in question."[73] An article published in the medical journal *Mental Health* spoke similar rhetoric, with one member of the medical community suggesting that Albertans should "get away from the concerns of sterilization as a cost form of sentiment and give more attention to raising and safeguarding the purity of the race."[74] An editorial in the *Lethbridge Herald* continued this line of reasoning, arguing that "the remedy is obvious. It is a question of humanity. Insane people are not entitled to progeny."[75] The words of UFWA president Margaret Gunn were also published; she stated that "the government should pursue a policy of racial betterment" so that the "vitality of our civilization" would not be lowered.[76] The economic argument for the amendment of the Sexual Sterilization Act was seen by most politicians and eugenicists as second to the primary concern of preventing social negligence and crime. Economic factors were surely considered, both in private circles and within the public arena; however, they were not the strongest motivator for the expansion of eugenics legislation in the 1930s. If they were, they were not publicly promoted as much as other factors were, whether by those who wrote the amendment, by those who passed it in the Legislature, or by those who conveyed its details to the public. The politicians, medical administrators, and media sources were concerned with the intellectual and racial quality of Alberta's citizens rather than the economic burdens that might be placed upon them.

CONCLUSION

After reviewing and re-evaluating the various arguments employed by scholars to account for Alberta's support for or indifference to sterilization legislation in the 1930s, it becomes clear that such claims may be exaggerated, or their relevance misinterpreted. Immigration to Alberta was drastically reduced in the 1930s and the public was aware of this; the province's sterilization law and the moral debate that surrounded it were widely published in the media, as were the details of eugenic practices in Nazi Germany. Furthermore, the economic motivations for sterilization were constantly superseded by racial and cultural motivations. These realizations are not sufficient in answering the question of why Alberta politicians and members of the medical community—and presumably the greater public—continued to embrace negative eugenics during its international decline. However, they do bring us closer to an answer to these challenging historical questions.

This explorative chapter has made two arguments, or perhaps suggestions, regarding the future study of the history of negative eugenics in Alberta. First, scholarly attention on the subject should shift from the 1928 Sexual Sterilization Act to its 1937 amendment and, more generally, to the eugenics movement and eugenic practices in Alberta during the 1930s. The much studied 1928 act, while significant, was not unique in its content, scope, or popularity; many state governments in the United States, as well as other countries, passed similar legislation around the same time. The 1937 amendment and the legalization of non-consensual sterilization, however, was a dramatic and unusual deviation from the national and international eugenics movement. The Alberta doctors, social reformers, and legislators who endorsed this amendment were going against the grain. The second suggestion is that when examining the unorthodox decision to expand sterilization in Alberta, researchers should discard familiar lenses of interpretation. Much had changed in Alberta, and in Canada, between the passing of the original sterilization act in 1928 and its amendment in 1937: politics, the economy, immigration, the media, even cultural norms had shifted. To understand the uniqueness of the 1937 amendment, an original scope of analysis should be applied and new variables considered.

This author suggests that future inquiries into the radicalization of eugenics legislation in Alberta should begin with the study of individual personalities: the eugenicists, politicians, and social advocates who played an instrumental role in the implementation of sterilization laws and practices. Figures such as Hoadley, the minister of health; Gunn, the UFWA president; and Dr. John MacEachran (1877–1971), long-time chair of the AEB, should be examined, their personal opinions further investigated, and the extent of their political influence considered.[77] This avenue of research is already being pursued, with studies being conducted on Hincks and Hoadley (and in chapter 1, Henderikus J. Stam and Ashley Barlow scrutinize MacEachran's contribution to eugenics in Alberta). Still, other individuals should be researched, such as University of Alberta president and outspoken advocate of eugenic sterilization Robert Charles Wallace (1881–1955); Alberta's minister of health, Richard G. Reid (1879–1980); and geneticist and former AEB member Dr. Margaret Thompson (1920–2014).[78] Furthermore, a clear distinction needs to be made between the opinions of such influential figures and the popular public opinion in the 1930s, as it is often assumed that one simply mirrored the other.[79]

Next, a closer study of the immigrant population of Alberta should be conducted, with regard not only to their "mental state" but also to their social and economic origins.[80] Were immigrants who entered Alberta more prone to mental deficiencies, resulting from either the emotional endeavour of their displacement or their economic background? Also, is it possible that the diagnosis of "mental deficiency" in immigrants did not account for certain emotional factors and cultural differences? A close study should also be made of the various means by which political resistance could be expressed in Alberta during the 1930s. What organizations and means of correspondence were available through which to voice protest? Perhaps opposition to sterilization laws was present but unable to be heard outside of the political and medical realms. Particular attention should be given to the influence (or lack thereof) of the Roman Catholic Church in Alberta, the liberal politicians of the provincial opposition, and the nature of editorial columns in major newspapers.[81] In chapter 5, Erna Kurbegović shows that the Catholic Church voiced significant opposition to sterilization legislation in Manitoba; was similar protest expressed by the church in Alberta?

Finally, the international exchanges of the Canadian eugenics landscape should be explored in detail. Alberta eugenicists not only worked to emulate their American and European forebears, they corresponded directly with them, including physicians working under the Nazi regime (see, for example, Frank W. Stahnisch's chapter 7 on holist neurologist Kurt Goldstein). This international collaboration has only begun to emerge in the scholarship and is the reason why this current edited volume is so valuable. These questions and others can and should be asked with much more precision and confidence now that the arguments and explanations of the past, having long misled and hindered the study of this important historical topic, have been dismissed.[82]

5

Eugenics in Manitoba and the Sterilization Controversy of 1933

Erna Kurbegović

In February of 1933, Robert A. Hoey (Progressive, St. Clements, 1883–1965), Manitoba's minister of education, introduced the Mental Deficiency Act with a section on the sterilization of "mental defectives."[1] The act was introduced following pressure from the medical community in the province. The proposed bill led to debates not only in the provincial legislature but also in communities across Manitoba. From February to May of 1933, the bill travelled back and forth between the House, the Law Amendments Committee, and the Committee of the Whole in an attempt to reach a decision regarding the clause. In May of 1933, the Mental Deficiency Act eventually passed, but without the sterilization section, which was defeated by just one vote.[2] This suggests that Manitoba was very close to adopting a eugenics program, though in the end it did not. Yet this does not mean the province lacked enthusiasm for eugenic measures.

The nearly myopic focus on provinces that passed eugenics legislation, namely Alberta and British Columbia, belies the popularity of the movement elsewhere in Canada. Eugenics was a powerful movement in the early twentieth century that captivated many medical professionals, social reformers, and interest groups. In particular, despite coming within only one legislative vote of adopting eugenic measures in 1933, Manitoba's dynamic and vigorous eugenics debate has been understudied. Looking at provinces that had an active eugenics movement irrespective of the legislative outcomes allows us to better see the presence and place of eugenic ideology within early twentieth-century Canadian society. Manitoba presents us with a particularly good case study because in contrast to provinces that have received much scholarly scrutiny, such as Alberta, the process was not controlled by a small number of individuals.[3] Rather, as this chapter demonstrates, the debate in Manitoba was open and allowed for the engagement of broad swathes of society, including medical professionals and religious groups. Within the political realm, the legislative vote in Manitoba was not whipped, as it was in Alberta, and individual members of the legislative assembly were able to split with their party and vote according to their own beliefs. Thus, in Manitoba it is possible to more accurately see the specific beliefs of individuals and groups and analyze the arguments they mustered for and against eugenics legislation. By doing so, we can better understand how eugenics and sterilization were viewed by different strata of society in the interwar Canadian West.

The study of the eugenics movement in Canada has unfortunately not received as much attention from historians as would be appropriate given the long-term social, legal, and medical reverberations to which it has led, but this is changing. Historians have focused primarily on Alberta's eugenics program prior to 1945, discussing the implementation of the Sexual Sterilization Act (1928) and placing the eugenics movement in the province within the larger context of social reform movements.[4] Historians have also shed light on eugenics in the second half of the twentieth century, focusing on Alberta's long eugenic history, as well as connecting the "old eugenics movement" in Canada with current discussions about reproductive rights and with new reproductive technologies in medicine.[5] While these scholars have offered important insights into the history of eugenics in Canada, there still remains a strong historiographical need to further address eugenics in other Canadian provinces. As this chapter proposes, adding Manitoba into the history of eugenics in western Canada demonstrates that significant enthusiasm for eugenics existed even in provinces without sexual sterilization legislation. Further, the Manitoba case allows for a better understanding of eugenics and its place in western Canadian society in the early twentieth century.

Many historians trace the origin of eugenic thought to the ideas of British naturalist Charles Darwin (1809–82) and his major work *The Origin of Species by Means of Natural Selection, Or the Preservation of Favoured Races in the Struggle for Life*.[6] Although scientists discussed heredity and evolutionary thought before 1859, Darwin's theory of evolution by natural selection set the foundation for eugenic ideas to emerge later in the nineteenth century.[7] Any study on eugenics must also begin with a discussion of Francis Galton (1822–1911), Darwin's cousin and the acclaimed "father of eugenics." Darwin's ideas influenced Galton, who was interested in heredity and the "betterment of the human race."[8] In 1883, Galton coined the term "eugenics" and described it as "the science of improving stock, which is by no means confined to questions of judicious mating, but which, especially in the case of man, takes cognizance of all influences that tend in however remote a degree to give to the more suitable races or strains of blood a better chance of prevailing speedily over the less suitable than they otherwise would have had."[9] It is important to note that the idea of improving a society's strength through the selective breeding of its population ("improving stock") was not a new one, and it can be traced to a period before Galton's work on eugenics became widespread.[10] Nevertheless, Galton's ideas gained popularity in many Anglo-Saxon countries, including the United States and Canada, and contributed to the development of eugenics movements there.

The economic, social, and technological developments that occurred at the turn of the twentieth century in Canada led to deep anxieties about the decline in the health and well-being of the nation and the fear of biological degeneration. Concerns over degeneration were linked to the larger international eugenics discourse that sought a biological explanation to problems of modernity.[11] Moreover, during the late nineteenth and early twentieth century, a significant number of new non-British immigrants settled in Canada, and many Canadians believed that this influx threatened the social and cultural character of the country. As a result of increased immigration, World War I, and the Great Depression, Canadian politicians, social reformers, and medical professionals became concerned about "mental deficiency" and "feeblemindedness" in their society.[12] In order to assess the mental health status of the country,

Canadian psychiatrists Clarence Hincks (1889–1964) and Charles Kirke Clarke (1857–1924) founded the Canadian National Committee for Mental Hygiene (CNCMH) in 1918.[13] The committee had an extensive mandate, including providing care to soldiers suffering from mental disabilities, but it was also interested in the prevention of mental diseases and "deficiency."[14] Hincks and Clarke conducted their first mental hygiene survey in Manitoba in 1918, in response to an invitation from the provincial government, and concluded that the province's institutions were inadequate for the care of the mentally ill.[15] The survey also revealed that the rate of "mental deficiency" in the province was high and recommended segregation in separate institutions or farms as well as eugenic measures.[16] Shortly after, similar surveys were conducted in several other Canadian provinces, and all suggested that the high rates of poverty, crime, and prostitution were linked to "mental deficiency."[17] The commissions' findings regarding "mental deficiency" were taken up by social and medical eugenicists in western Canadian provinces, particularly Alberta, and transformed into eugenics legislation.[18] These reformers embraced eugenics because they believed it was scientific and progressive and, more importantly, that it provided a new approach to explaining many of Canada's social problems, including poverty, alcoholism, and crime.

MANITOBA'S STERILIZATION DEBATE: THE SUPPORTERS OF EUGENICS LEGISLATION

The provincial government in Manitoba had been concerned about "feeblemindedness" and "mental deficiency" in the province since its request for the mental hygiene survey, yet it was not until 1933 that it seriously considered sterilization as a solution to "mental deficiency."[19] Hoey introduced the sterilization bill following pressure from the medical community, particularly psychiatrists, who believed that Manitoba needed to improve the care of those suffering with mental conditions. At the same time, medical professionals viewed "mental defectives" as a serious threat to the future of society because of the supposed heritability of their condition.[20] Psychiatrists called for sterilization measures in order to reduce the numbers of "mental defectives" in institutions.[21] The activities and arguments of psychiatrists were connected to the problem of professionalization of psychiatry during the interwar period. As sociologist David MacLennan points out, psychiatrists "urged the state to assume a greater role in the treatment of social problems and, by making a case for the value of their specialized knowledge, they were able to position themselves squarely between the state and the social problems."[22] Eugenics proved to be one of the ways in which their expertise could be utilized, and it provided them with the opportunity to assert, maintain, and extend their authority and advance their professional interests.[23]

The fear of the "mentally defective" in Manitoba was exacerbated by the findings of the 1918 mental hygiene survey conducted by the CNCMH. The Manitoba survey found that the provincial institutions were not only overcrowded, underfunded, and understaffed but also lacked qualified personnel and adequate treatments.[24] What is more, the institutions were allegedly overrun with "defective classes."[25] These concerns were taken up by psychiatrists in Manitoba, particularly Alvin Trotter Mathers (1888–1960), who argued that "mental deficiency" and "feeblemindedness" were significant issues that required prompt response from the province. For example, Mathers recommended that the government implement legislation "establishing registration, care, training commitment, parole and discharge and community supervision of the feeble minded."[26]

The Mental Deficiency Act of 1933 was a direct response to Mathers's recommendations. With their concerns over "mental deficiency," psychiatrists in Manitoba placed pressure on the provincial government to deal with this supposed issue. While those deemed to be "mentally defective" were segregated in institutions such as the Portage la Prairie School for Mental Defectives, the overcrowding in these institutions, together with the economic downturn in the late 1920s and early 1930s, led medical professionals to lobby the Manitoba government for radical eugenic measures such as sterilization.

In their lobbying efforts, medical professionals framed their concerns within an economic context in order to enlist support of politicians, arguing that eugenic measures would save the province a significant amount of money.[27] For instance, psychiatrist Thomas G. B. Caunt argued that if the number of "mental defectives" continued to increase across the country, more resources would need to be spent on mental institutions, stating requirements of "$3,500,000 for buildings and equipment, and an annual maintenance charge of $650,000. This meant an additional expense of over $4,000,000 in 1931."[28] Similarly, Byron M. Unkauf

(1905–83) focused on the issue of cost. He argued that measures needed to be taken in order to deal with the extreme overcrowding of the mental hospitals and that Manitoba taxpayers should not have to spend money to support these institutions. He claimed that "taxpayers spend annually, twice the amount of money, approximately to care for these people, as for the provincial university for higher education."[29] Unkauf clearly believed that public funds should be spent elsewhere, particularly in areas that would benefit the middle class. Focusing on the economy was an effective strategy especially during the years of the Great Depression, when the provincial government needed to cut spending. Similar to other Prairie provinces, Manitoba was hit hard by the Depression as grain prices collapsed, but its diverse economy and fiscally conservative government enabled the province to remain solvent during the economic recession. Nevertheless, the government's strategy led to significant cuts to various services, including public works programs.[30]

Aside from making an economic argument, medical professionals also used the open debate setting to their advantage to "inform" the public of the necessity of the sterilization procedure on humanitarian grounds. For example, Unkauf was an active member of the community and, according to the *Winnipeg Tribune*, during 1933 organized several meetings in Winnipeg at which to speak about sterilization. Unkauf believed that the public's opinion was important and that they needed to hear the arguments for and against sterilization. According to the *Winnipeg Tribune*, the presentations would be unbiased and Unkauf was interested only in "imparting information."[31] Unfortunately, the newspaper did not report on the full content of these meetings; therefore, it is difficult to determine what information was made public. Yet if Unkauf's meetings were anything like his published articles, then he clearly had an agenda to sway public opinion in favour of involuntary sterilization. In the article "The Sterilization of the Mental Defective," Unkauf argued that provincial governments needed to speed up the process of sterilization because "intelligent, healthy and useful families are becoming smaller, while irresponsible, diseased and mentally defective families are becoming larger and larger."[32] This was a common argument made by eugenicists who claimed that "defective" genes were the main result of "mental deficiency" and that even if these individuals had "normal" children, those children would still suffer due to lack of care from the "defective" parents.[33]

During the Law Amendments Committee hearings, physician Frederick Wilbur Jackson (1888–1958) and psychiatrist Henry Sheridan Atkinson (1901–65) informed the committee about the sterilization procedure. The *Northwest Review* and the *Winnipeg Free Press* summarized the arguments made by Jackson and Atkinson. Both doctors pointed out that sterilization was necessary because it would decrease the number of "feebleminded" individuals in the province. While Atkinson admitted that the procedure was not a "cure-all," it would nevertheless "go a long way in reducing the number of hereditary cases."[34] Additionally, Atkinson and Jackson made arguments on humanitarian grounds, suggesting that sterilization would be beneficial to the "feebleminded" individual. For example, they claimed that the procedure would reduce the number of "feebleminded" persons in institutions and would allow them to freely participate in society.[35] Historian Angus McLaren has pointed out that many sterilization proponents across Canada believed that the procedure would benefit the "abnormal individual" in that it would allow them to leave mental institutions and have more freedom instead of being segregated from the rest of the society.[36] The opinion of psychiatric and medical experts was important in the debates and discussions over Manitoba's sterilization clause. Not only did medical professionals inform the committee and the public of their position regarding sterilization, but they were also instrumental in framing the Mental Deficiency Act.

Hoey's introduction of the sterilization bill must be understood within the context of the economic downturn during the 1930s and the pressure exerted by medical professionals on the provincial government. Hoey cited two main reasons for the introduction of the sterilization clause, according to the *Winnipeg Free Press*, which echoed the arguments of the province's physicians: "that the cost to the province incurred by families of hereditary mental deficiency was tremendous" and that the procedure was necessary for humanitarian reasons as "nothing was more tragic and pitiful than the spectacle of an imbecile mother with her offspring."[37] In her study on eugenics in California, historian Alexandra Minna Stern connects sterilization to the wider history of public health, suggesting that eugenicists often presented sterilization as "protection" of both state resources and society. In other words, sterilization would save the state money by ensuring that fewer "mentally defective" individuals were born, and it would also allow patients to be discharged from mental institutions since their ability to reproduce would been removed.[38]

Sterilization as "protection" could also be extended to the second part of Hoey's argument, dealing with the humanitarian aspect of the procedure. Sterilization would allegedly "protect" "imbecile" women from pregnancy and from the burden of parenthood.[39] As historian Wendy Klein has demonstrated, from the 1910s onward, eugenicists became increasingly interested in female sexuality and behaviour, especially because women were seen as the reproducers of the future. As a result, eugenicists differentiated between women who would preserve the "race"—primarily those who were white and middle class—and those deemed "unfit" who would destroy it.[40] It is evident from Hoey's humanitarian argument that he believed some women should be prevented from having children.

The fact that the education minister employed arguments similar to those of the province's psychiatrists demonstrates the effectiveness of the latter's claims in support of eugenics legislation. Seeking eugenics legislation for humanitarian reasons was a common approach among eugenicists and bringing an economic perspective into discussions of the benefits of sterilization was particularly effective. During the economic depressions of the late 1920s and early 1930s, the Manitoba government welcomed any measures that would allow it to reduce spending, particularly in provincial mental hospitals. However, despite significant enthusiasm for eugenics, the proposed sterilization bill faced much opposition.

MANITOBA'S STERILIZATION DEBATE: OPPOSITION TO EUGENICS LEGISLATION

Hoey's bill sparked serious discussions about the morality of sterilization, the necessity of the procedure, and the credibility of the science behind eugenics. While significant support for eugenics existed among medical professionals in Manitoba, the most vocal group opposing sexual sterilization was the Roman Catholics. A number of church leaders in the province presented the views of their communities to the lawmakers during the 1933 sterilization debates. In doing so, they played an important role in the public discussions and debates over the sterilization bill. Primarily, Catholics argued that sterilization was immoral because it took away an individual's dignity and bodily integrity, and secondly, they attacked eugenics on scientific grounds, arguing that sterilization policies were based on flawed science.

The Catholic opposition to eugenics has been discussed by a number of historians, including McLaren, Erika Dyck, Sebastien Normandin, and, more recently, Alex Deighton, yet it is an area in Canadian historiography that still requires further study. We know from these scholars that Roman Catholics were the most active in opposing eugenics legislation; however, little has been written about their activism in this respect. McLaren credits the Catholic opposition, among other factors, for averting the passage of sterilization bills in provinces east of Alberta. He suggests that in areas where Catholics composed a significant portion of the population such negative eugenics measures could not flourish, and even in provinces with a strong Catholic minority, such as Manitoba and Ontario, sterilization bills were defeated.[41] While it is true that Catholics tended to be the most ardent opponents of sexual sterilization policies—and certainly played an important part in eugenics debates—a closer examination of local political and social contexts is necessary to gain better insight into why sterilization bills passed in some provinces but not others.[42] In his work on Québec, Normandin paints a more complex picture of Catholic resistance in that province by suggesting that while the church doctrine opposed any measure that limited reproduction, it had little to say about positive eugenics. In addition, he shows that the resistance to eugenics came primarily from French-speaking Catholics who objected on cultural and religious grounds.[43] Dyck provides a sample of the Roman Catholic opinion on eugenics in the province of Saskatchewan through an analysis of a Catholic newspaper, the *Prairie Messenger*. She shows that the newspaper's approach to eugenics was sometimes softened, particularly in its response to marriage of those deemed to be "mentally defective." At other times, it stuck strictly to the Catholic doctrine.[44]

Historians studying Catholicism and eugenics in the United States have shown that opinions varied, even among Catholic clergy, regarding eugenics particularly before 1930. Some voiced strong opposition, while some accepted positive eugenics, and others joined eugenics organizations such as the American Eugenics Society.[45] Prior to 1930, there was no official Catholic position on eugenics; that is, the Vatican did not officially comment on the issues until Pope Pius XI's (1857–1939) encyclical letter, *Casti connubii*, of December 1930. As historian Christine Rosen points out, the lack of an official Catholic position allowed Catholic leaders to form their own arguments about eugenics, but these were often carved out with church doctrine in mind: specifically, race improvement was a good thing but the means to achieve it must be legitimate.[46] What all of this suggests is that Catholicism was not monolithic. Catholics had varied views on a number of social issues, including eugenics, that were often shaped by particular local circumstances.

Roman Catholics had been engaged in debates about eugenics since the late nineteenth century but it was not until the 1920s and 1930s, at the peak of the eugenics movement, that they became vocal in resisting it.[47] Eugenics challenged the Catholic doctrine because, as historian Nancy Stepan explains, eugenics "attacked the rights of individuals within marriage, deformed what the church believed was the proper function of sexuality, and perverted the moral sense of the human species."[48] In other words, the goal of eugenicists to limit reproduction through sterilization ran counter to the Catholic doctrine, plus Catholics opposed the practice because it violated an individual's bodily integrity. Further, it led to "mutilation" of the body and interfered with procreation. Catholics only permitted such intervention for therapeutic reasons.[49] Some Catholics were also concerned about the scientific credibility of eugenics. In the 1920s, geneticists were already questioning the credibility of eugenics as a science, acknowledging that heredity is complex and is not as simple as the eugenicists claimed (see also chapter 2 by Douglas Wahlsten). The geneticists' conclusions about heredity were also based on rigorous research and not on broad conclusions influenced by racial, ethnic, and class prejudices. With the growing critique of eugenics, many Catholics felt confident that they could successfully challenge the arguments in favour of eugenic measures.[50]

While Catholics engaged in multiple discussions about eugenics, a single issue created the largest division between them and the movement: sterilization. The Catholic disapproval of sterilization, or any other contraceptives, was not new; for instance, Pope Leo XIII (1810–1903) condemned sterilization in 1895, calling it immoral.[51] The church then remained silent on the issue of sterilization and eugenics until 1930, when Pope Pius XI issued a papal encyclical on Christian marriage, *Casti connubii*. The decree was issued in response to social, cultural, and economic changes in the early 1900s. The Catholic Church regarded traditional gender roles and the sanctity of marriage as being under threat from these changes. While the encyclical covered a number of subjects, the sections that stood out for most Catholics dealt with eugenics:

> For there are some who, over solicitous of the cause of eugenics, not only give salutary counsel for more certainly procuring the strength and health of the future child—which, indeed, is not contrary to right reason—but put eugenics before the aim of a higher order, and by public authority wish to prevent from marrying all those who, even though naturally fit for marriage, they consider, according to the norms and conjectures of their investigations, would, through hereditary transmission, bring forth defective offspring. And more, they wish to legislate to deprive these of that natural faculty by medical action despite their unwillingness. . . . Public magistrates have no direct power over the bodies of their subjects; therefore, where no crime has taken place and there is no cause present for grave punishment, they can never directly harm, or tamper with the integrity of the body, either for the reason of eugenics or for any other reason.[52]

The encyclical essentially affirmed the Catholic position on sterilization: namely, that the procedure conflicted with Catholic doctrine because it interfered with reproduction and that it unnecessarily encroached upon an individual's God-given rights. The above passage suggests that while the Catholic Church still believed in human betterment and in having healthy children, it rejected the methods eugenicists employed, especially sterilization and, later, birth control. The papal statement provided Catholics a clear position on a number of issues including marriage, divorce, birth control, and eugenics; second, it questioned the role of the state in the eugenics movement and its power over the bodies of its citizens; third, as historian Sharon Leon notes, "the far-reaching teaching raised questions of the proper relationship between the church and state with respect to marriage and reproduction."[53] Having the support of the church authority behind them, many Catholics were motivated to continue their fight against eugenics and particularly against involuntary sexual sterilization.

Roman Catholics in Manitoba were particularly active in their opposition to the sterilization bill. During the early months of 1933, members of the legislative assembly and Premier John Bracken (Progressive, The Pas, 1883–1969) received letters and petitions from constituents protesting the proposed legislation and urging their political representatives to vote against the bill. Catholics in the province presented their perspectives on eugenics theory and sterilization through letters, petitions, publications, letters to the editor in local newspapers, and Law Amendments Committee hearings, as well as within their communities. The majority of the documents sent to the provincial government were written by Catholic officials on behalf of their parishioners, and these arrived primarily from French-speaking communities. Some of the letters were written as basic protests to the introduction of the sterilization clause while others were much more detailed. For example, a number of the writers opposed eugenics legislation because they believed it to be immoral, as it violated an individual's integrity; others challenged the science behind the eugenics theory, pointing to studies that disproved eugenicists' claims.

In a letter to the editor of the *Winnipeg Tribune*, F. W. Russell, chair of the Council of Catholic Action, objected to sterilization on scientific grounds: "I see you declare that Mr. Hoey's sterilization bill 'embodies results of extensive study and observation.' I wonder!" He pointed out that "the British Medical Association . . . declared that incidence of mental deficiency would not be decreased to any degree worth considering by sterilization."[54] In other words, Russell accused the provincial government of being ill informed on the issue of sterilization, and by citing the British Medical Association, he brought in "expert knowledge" to refute the eugenicists' claims.[55] Similarly, Reverend Wilfrid L. Jubinville (1872–1946) from Saint Boniface wrote to Premier Bracken in protest to the sterilization bill: "It is an acknowledged fact that mental deficiency proceeds . . . from social plagues such as alcoholism, tuberculosis, syphilis. . . . That such vices do affect normal parents as well as abnormal ones, is obvious. . . . This being the case sterilization would be no cure."[56] Jubinville also relied on the arguments made by the British Medical Association that focused on environmental causes of "mental deficiency" and suggested that the majority of those diagnosed as "mentally defective" had "normal" parents. Therefore, sterilization would not lead to human betterment. As historian Garland Allen demonstrates, in their critique of eugenics, some contemporary scientists suggested that "even if genetic factors might be involved in leading to certain social or mental conditions, it would make far more sense to search out the social components involved, since those could be changed more readily." In other words, rather than arguing that poverty, alcoholism, criminality, and "mental deficiency" were the results of "defective" genes, it would be easier to solve those problems through social reform.[57] Leon has pointed out that scientific objections presented by the Catholic clergy to a lay audience were much more successful in casting doubt on eugenicists' claims than those made by scientists and medical professionals. By making secular arguments against eugenics, Catholic officials could mobilize a large group of people, sometimes even non-Catholics, and speak on their behalf.[58]

A number of Catholic representatives wrote letters to Premier Bracken objecting to sterilization on moral grounds. For example, the rector of St. Boniface College, Reverend F. Faure, objected on the following grounds: first, "the Government has no authority to impose mutilation against innocent persons nor have individuals any right to accept it"; and second, "that part of the Bill will be the cause of many moral evils much more serious than those it is called to cure, not to speak of the social evils."[59] Essentially, Faure argued that no law should give the government the power to violate the body of an individual, and that no individual should be forced to accept such an intrusion. Moreover, he argued that the sterilization clause would not solve the social problems that eugenicists connected with "deficiency," namely, prostitution, criminality, and poverty. The *Winnipeg Tribune* published an anonymous letter to the editor—signed by "A Seeker of Truth"—that argued that the right to one's integrity is at stake when a state introduces policies such as sterilization and that an individual's "rights and privileges are to be protected by the state instead of being sacrificed at random," or for the public good.[60] Likewise, J. H. Daignault, secretary of the Association d'education des Canadiens-français du Manitoba, wrote on behalf of the association that "in view of the important moral principles involved in this rather hurried move, we as a body, beg to protest very emphatically against it and we earnestly hope that the bill may not be urged further."[61] Daignault implied that the government's introduction of the sterilization bill was rushed and that perhaps they had not considered the moral side of the issue. Similar views were expressed by Reverend Antoine d'Éschambault (1896–1960), who accused the provincial government of not consulting Catholics on this issue even though they were aware that Catholics would object on moral grounds. What is more, d'Éschambault believed that the representatives in the legislature had misled their Catholic voters by suggesting that they had no intention of introducing a sterilization clause; this he called a "true calumny."[62]

In Manitoba, sterilization was clearly a significant issue for Catholics, who put forward important arguments in the debate over the proposed sterilization clause. Catholics were effective in framing their arguments against sterilization. They did not only oppose the procedure because it ran counter to Christian principles; they also questioned the science behind eugenic theory. The approach of the province's Catholic clergy was much broader because they realized that Catholics would not likely be the only group to oppose the sterilization clause.[63]

MANITOBA'S STERILIZATION DEBATE: THE VIEWS OF THE POLITICIANS

The political climate in Manitoba during the 1920s and 1930s allowed for an open debate on the eugenics issue. By 1933, the province was led by a Liberal-Progressive coalition government under Premier Bracken (1883–1969). Bracken believed in non-partisanship, businesslike administration, and coalition governments. This governing philosophy, which became known as Brackenism, informed Bracken's approach in all areas of politics.[64] Controversial legislation was particularly problematic for the Bracken administration, which consistently sought unity and was sensitive to policies that could generate intense minority opposition. While eugenics policy was in line with the progressive mindset of the administration, it was at odds with its consensus-driven approach to governing. Therefore, when the government put section 30 of the Mental Deficiency Act to a vote in the legislature, the MLAs were given a free vote.

Once Hoey had introduced the Mental Deficiency Act in the legislature, it was subjected to immediate opposition from several members of the legislative assembly, including Albert Préfontaine (Liberal-Progressive, Carillion, 1861–1935), who called for the sterilization section to be removed. In response, Hoey argued that the province needed such a measure because of the rising costs of running the mental institutions and for humanitarian reasons. More importantly, Hoey believed that such a measure would benefit the individual affected.[65] Other members of the House did not necessarily support or oppose the clause; instead, many were unsure whether the province needed such a measure and wanted Hoey to provide additional information about the bill before they were required to vote on it.[66] It is unclear what other information the MLAs were asking from Hoey or whether he provided them with it.

The MLAs who opposed the legislation did so due to religion, pressure from constituents, or uncertainty over the bill. Those who supported it did so for economic and humanitarian reasons. Once the MLAs started their debate, John A. Munn (Liberal-Progressive, Dufferin, 1882–1941) stated that if the sterilization section was not removed, he would "move an amendment that it will not apply to Roman Catholics."[67] Similarly, Nicholas V. Bachynsky (Liberal-Progressive, Fischer, 1887–1969) stated that he not only objected on religious grounds, but also questioned the proponents' claims that linked heredity and "mental deficiency."[68] Harold F. Lawrence (Labour, Saint Boniface, b. 1887) also opposed the bill on religious grounds. He pointed out that while he was not a Roman Catholic, the majority of his constituents were of Roman Catholic faith. They had presented him with many letters urging him to vote against the clause, which he said he would. Lawrence also stated that the House must remember that Manitoba was home to two hundred thousand Roman Catholics and that their opinions needed to be considered.[69] As noted above, Catholic clergy and lay Catholics were active members of the campaign against sterilization and presented both theological and secular arguments in challenging the proposed bill.

Other members of the legislative assembly stated that they were divided between two opposing viewpoints. For example, Seymour James Farmer (Labour, Winnipeg, 1878–1951) told the House that while some arguments for sterilization had strength, he was "suspicious" of others. He believed that the sterilization measure was being used as a "short cut" to solve a "mental deficiency" rather than focusing on what caused the "problem" in the first place. Moreover, Farmer stated that he was "becoming more and more convinced that a great deal of mental deficiency was due to conditions of environment."[70] In other words, in order to understand the causes of "mental deficiency" it was necessary to focus on factors beyond heredity. As Allen has noted, eugenicists faced criticism from the scientific community, including scientists Leonard Darwin (1850–1943) and Alexander Carr-Saunders (1886–1966), who argued that too much emphasis was placed on the heritability of "mental deficiency" without significant evidence.[71] Much like Farmer, Conservative MLA Ralph Humphreys Webb (Assiniboia, 1886–1945) told the House that he knew little about sterilization but that after consulting with experts he did not think it would "provide the remedy its sponsors hoped for." Additionally, he argued that "scientific information was not complete.... There was not enough authoritative information available ... to give intelligent consideration to the matter."[72] What this suggests is that the arguments presented by eugenicists were not convincing enough to sway Farmer and Webb to support the sterilization bill. Too many unanswered questions remained about the supposed benefits of sterilization, and for Webb and Farmer this was enough reason to object to the clause.

The legislative representatives who were convinced by the medical opinion that "mental deficiency" was a significant problem in the province voiced their views in favour of the sterilization clause. For example, Douglas Lloyd Campbell (Liberal-Progressive, Lakeside, 1895–1995) cited economic and humanitarian reasons for his support of the bill. He argued that the sterilization procedure would ensure that the province did not have to build any more mental institutions and therefore would save resources. More important for Campbell was the humanitarian reason. He had allegedly visited the provincial institutions and "had seen mentally defective children condemned to a life of misery, which this bill could eliminate."[73] Specifically, sterilization would allow those deemed "mentally defective" to be discharged from institutions, but more importantly, it was believed that it would prevent them from passing their "defect" to the next generation. Similarly, Marcus Hyman (Labour, Winnipeg, 1883–1938) argued that while the religious opinion must be respected, he favoured sterilization. He suggested that the opposition had nothing to fear, especially because the procedure required the consent of the patient or their guardian. Instead, he suggested, the opposition needed to consider the benefits of the legislation.[74] Lastly, Premier Bracken voiced his view on this issue, stating that while he supported the clause, he was aware that many objected to it on religious grounds. Further, he would not force members to vote for it or to force the bill through with so much opposition.[75] The fact that the vote on the sterilization bill was not whipped is significant. This meant that MLAs did not have to follow the voting intentions of their party but were free to vote based on their own beliefs.

After serious debate in the legislature, the bill was defeated in a very close vote of 20 to 21.[76] This outcome illustrated five points. First, since Bracken was leading a coalition government, he was clearly aware that there were various perspectives on the topic of eugenics within the party and therefore could not risk pushing through controversial legislation. Instead, the subject of sterilization of "mental defectives" was debated in public and MLAs were given a free vote on the bill. Second, the legislative result also points to the importance of medical professionals and Roman Catholics in the debate over sexual sterilization. Their arguments likely swayed those legislative representatives who were "on the fence" about the issue, such as Farmer and Webb. While some of the MLAs, such as Campbell and Hyman, supported the proposed sterilization legislation, citing societal and economic benefits, others objected primarily on religious grounds, whether for their own religious reasons or on behalf of their constituents. Third, not all of the MLAs voted against eugenics legislation because they were pressured by their constituents to do so. Others would not vote for it because of their own conscience. Fourth, for members such as Farmer, the claims regarding the benefits of sterilization were unconvincing; he did not think that sterilization would solve the supposed problem of "mental deficiency." He was likely not the only one to vote against the clause for this reason. Lastly, the result suggested that there was significant support for eugenic measures in Manitoba and that the province was very close to following the footsteps of Alberta and British Columbia in implementing a eugenics program.

CONCLUSION

The controversial sterilization section of Manitoba's Mental Deficiency Act produced many debates within the legislature and in communities across the province. The claims of medical professionals that the legislation was needed for economic and humanitarian reasons were effective in influencing the provincial government to introduce the clause in the first place. The politicians who supported the bill did so for similar reasons. On the other side, Roman Catholics objected to the sterilization section on theological and scientific grounds, arguing not only that was sterilization immoral but that eugenics was based on a simple understanding of heredity. The fact that both pro- and anti-sterilization groups were encouraged to voice their views in a public debate is important because it shows that the provincial government recognized the controversial nature of the proposed bill. This is further evident by the fact of the non-whip political process on this issue, which allowed MLAs to freely vote based on their own views. This overview of the sterilization debate in Manitoba demonstrates that the lack of legislation did not necessarily mean that there was a lack of enthusiasm for eugenic measures. Furthermore, the fact that Manitoba never implemented a formal eugenics program has meant that historians have overlooked its eugenics history. The sterilization debate of 1933 illustrates that Manitobans did in fact engage with eugenic discourse. By understanding the various perspectives on sexual sterilization held by individuals and groups in the province, we gain a better insight into the history of eugenics in the Canadian West.

6

"New Fashioned with Respect to the Human Race"

American Eugenics in the Media at the Turn of the Twentieth Century

Celeste Tường Vy Sharpe

> *Tendencies fostered by the modern social organism are injuring the race. . . . War itself, once a valuable selective agency, exposes the strongest and the fleetest to the bomb and the bullet, to the diseases and temptations of military service, to irregular habits, delayed marriage, and diminished families. The confinements of the industrial organization kill off the biologically fitter. The institution of property replaces "natural mating" with mating of the less fit to perpetuate the race. Celibacy, the custom of later marriage, and the restriction of families cut down the ranks of the fittest. Even the development of medicine, hygiene, and dietetics rears to maturity fathers of weakly families who might have fallen early beneath the scythe of natural selection. Excessive humanitarianism fosters parasitic and pauper growths, propping ill-favored individuals at the expense of the social group.*
>
> —Albert Galloway Keller, *New York Times*, 1908

During the second half of the nineteenth century and early decades of the twentieth century, rapid industrialization and the related large-scale transatlantic patterns of migration to urban centres lay at the centre of Progressive Era concerns, which echoed earlier and parallel European developments (as chapters 7 and 8 also argue with respect to coerced experimentation and sterilization, or the application of eugenics ideology in the psychiatric and mental health field). In the United States, the period from the 1890s to the 1920s was characterized by profound social discourses and medical reform movements, which were likewise motivated by political attempts to eliminate the ills caused by urbanization, industrial labour conditions, immigration challenges, and corruption in the federal government. The "modern social organism," as Yale sociologist Albert Galloway Keller (1874–1956) described so vividly,[1] caused grave concern in that it seemingly altered the existing mechanisms for ensuring that the physically strongest and mentally fittest people continued "the race." Fear of the fertility of newly arrived immigrants to American cities almost sparked a panic about "race suicide," the belief that the reckless breeding of the lower classes and "unfit" would eventually overwhelm the approved reproduction of the white middle and upper classes and also hurt the level of culture and social behaviour of the nation as a whole.[2] These changing times, according to eugenicists, needed dedicated, thoughtful, and far-reaching responses and solutions to preserve the "best stock" and eventually produce "a race of superior beings," including their mental functions and social capabilities.[3]

Eugenics gained traction in the United States around the turn of the twentieth century as a response to the perceived imminent degeneration of society, with psychiatrists and physicians often at the forefront of this new scientific and social movement. Eugenics—defined by Francis Galton (1822–1911) in 1882 as "the science which deals with all influences that improve the inborn qualities of a race; also with those that develop them to the utmost advantage"—appealed to many in the Progressive Era as a new science-based approach to the pressures of modernization on human development.[4] Varying incarnations of this popular and medico-scientific ideology permeated North American and European policy and society during the early twentieth century, resulting in the establishment of numerous laws and organizations advocating for and designed around eugenic principles (see, for example, Mikkel Dack's chapter on the social and legal context of the 1937 Amendment to the Sexual Sterilization Act in the province of Alberta).

This chapter primarily examines the discourse in American print media on eugenics and its relation to mental and public health from 1900 to 1915, with attention to how this rhetoric introduced eugenics to the public and laid a foundation for its later popularity during the interwar period. While historical studies using media as their main content source face frequent methodological difficulties in measuring the effects of media content, messages, and formats, this approach is here triangulated between the strengths and weaknesses of newspapers as historical sources, scientific and political publications from the time period, and secondary literature accounts. The emergent media discourse on eugenics and public mental health successfully blended established nineteenth-century preoccupations with racial taxonomies and reproductive control with Progressive Era ideas of behavioural control and social collectivism, thus situating eugenics as a response to old and new problems alike. The American eugenics community's self-perceived status from 1900 to 1915 as a latecomer to eugenic policy and study provides deeper context for the sharp rise in support by scientists, administrators, and public health workers for eugenic organizations, forced sterilization laws (for a comparison, see chapter 8 and 9), and the eugenic movement as a whole between World War I and World War II. Eugenic policies and regulations thereby emerged in many North American jurisdictions, including in more than thirty American states and Canadian provinces; Canada saw the introduction of Alberta's Sexual Sterilization Act in 1928 and a derivative act in British Columbia in 1933. In recent years, historians and other researchers and community activists have drawn attention to the broader reach of the eugenics movement across the globe.

While eugenics infused a range of topics in public conversation, in this chapter I will focus on two of the most prevalent themes: the science of heredity and eugenicists as vehicles for progress; and the ramifications of eugenics for the social institution of marriage, childbirth, and family health. These two thematic areas are significant in that they suffused conversations on eugenics in the early years of the movement. While I am analyzing them separately, it is important to acknowledge that newspaper articles on eugenics often employed combinations of the themes to better support the eugenicists' particular positions. Another significant feature of the discourse is that beyond frequent references to Galton and Charles Darwin (1809–82), the newspaper articles indicated that American eugenicists, psychiatrists, and neurologists were attuned to the conversations and scientific studies being conducted in Europe, particularly in England, during the period of analysis. Taken together, the two thematic areas laid a foundation that the eugenics movement would build on and adapt in the years to come.

HISTORIOGRAPHY

The scholarship on eugenics and psychiatry in the United States[5] has typically focused on the most renowned figures and institutions of the movement, such as Charles Davenport (1866–1944) and the Eugenics Record Office (ERO)—located in Cold Spring Harbor, New York—although the scholarly research has diversified considerably in the last two decades.[6] Key points in the more traditional narratives include the establishment of a few East Coast–based eugenics and mental institutions, the support of various eugenic policies and programs by wealthy corporations, and the charisma of the movement's male leaders in advocating for eugenic-based legislation at the state and national level. A common periodization of eugenics history on the international level, one that is still often used, begins with World War I and ends with the eugenics community's retreat in light of the horror of, and public revulsion to, German eugenic and euthanasia programs during World War II. Studies of this kind include, for example, historian of biology Garland E. Allen's *The Ideology of Elimination: American and German Eugenics, 1900–1945* and Edwin Black's *War against the Weak: Eugenics and America's Campaign to Create a Master Race.*[7] While Allen and Black acknowledge the diffuse nature of eugenics organizations and figures in the United States, their studies still focus largely on the most prominent—typically East Coast—psychiatric and research institutions, along with male eugenicists who were also scientists. This focus, while vital to understanding the larger narrative of the eugenics movement, overemphasizes the efforts of these few institutions and individuals and obscures the diversity of perspectives and approaches of eugenics advocates across time and space.

More recent scholarship has shifted the study of eugenics away from the stricter chronological and limited geographic focus to deepen and enrich understanding of eugenics in American history by demonstrating how eugenics policy and rhetoric developed at different rates and in different ways across the country. Historian Alexandra Minna Stern, for instance, emphasizes the importance of place to the development of eugenics in the United States and, in relation to the movement in the western states, argues that "by turning our gaze thousands of miles west, away from the headquarters of the ERO, we encounter a history that was both paradigmatic of large-scale national trends and particular to the region."[8] Historian Nathaniel Deutsch discusses the development of eugenics programs and attitudes in Indiana, the first state to successfully pass sterilization legislation, in 1907, informed by specific neurological and psychiatric medical concerns. His work on the "Tribe of Ishmael," a pejorative phrase for the poorest white class, examines eugenics from the perspective of a group targeted by the eugenics proponents and the government for sterilization.[9] Eugenics legal scholar Edward J. Larson's study of the shape of eugenics in the Deep South highlights the different mechanisms and ways in which eugenics was used by (predominantly) white southerners to maintain economic, political, and social control.[10] Taken together, these scholars largely argue that the form taken by eugenics policies and rhetoric was often shaped more by the particular views of individual local and state societies than by the agendas put forward by the big northeastern institutions. Following the work of these researchers, this study likewise seeks to shift attention away from the northeast part of the United States to the articles and conversations that took place in newspapers across the country.

Scholarly interest in eugenics rhetoric is perhaps best exemplified by Marouf Arif Hasian's monograph *The Rhetoric of Eugenics in Anglo-American Thought*. He applies an ideographic approach to show how the "rise and (temporary fall) in the popularity of eugenic explanations of individual and social behaviour reflects the changes that were taking place in the public vocabulary." His analysis of eugenics rhetoric seeks to get at the "instantiated particular views of the relationship between citizens and the government."[11] Hasian's arguments are framed largely in response to a concern that public and health discourses around genetics in the 1980s and 1990s misrepresented eugenics as a temporary aberration in history before World War II driven by mistaken, unscientific individuals. He also places considerable weight on the frequency of keywords he identified, such as "necessity," in tracing the warp and weft of eugenics rhetoric. My own study diverges from Hasian's in that I am placing more emphasis on the historical context of the Progressive Era, and specifically on how newspaper articles on eugenics and the emerging movement functioned as a space for various individuals and expert groups across the country to express their visions of the future. By focusing on the earlier years of the movement, this chapter also argues for more scholarly attention to the overlap between the eugenics movement and transatlantic progressivism.

The scholarship on Progressive Era reform provides the backdrop for this study. Daniel Rodgers's monograph *Atlantic Crossings: Social Politics in a Progressive Age* in particular provides several starting points for this project. Although Rodgers does not delve into the growing discourse around eugenics specifically in his book, his work on city planning, social insurance, wartime collectivism, and cooperative farming resonates in that it shows an America that sought and contributed to these transatlantic discussions, although often with different results than European states. He argues that America's laggard position on these issues actually had some advantage by opening opportunities to "leapfrog over their competitors," namely, to see how experimental work had played out and avoid costly mistakes.[12] This view can also be applied to the arc of the American eugenics movement, which is commonly considered to have started slowly in Britain, where the movement was founded but did not develop as much as in America and Germany (in terms of laws, social programs, mental institutions, and forms of psychiatric diagnostics and control). This was truly an international movement that reached well beyond the "big three" eugenics countries and had its peak in the interwar period with an emphasis on so-called negative eugenics, in line with its implementation and practice in Germany. Timing and precedent, then, as Rodgers demonstrates, are as significant as ideology in shaping public sentiment and policy decisions.[13] The sentiments expressed in the earlier years of the eugenics movement provided precedents upon which later eugenicists could build.

Critical scholarly interest in eugenics has provided a rich body of work. In examining newspaper items on eugenics published across the country, this study seeks to highlight how the eugenicists working in the early years of the movement carved out a vital space in the public conversation for their particular plans for society. Early eugenicists—mindful that the United States was slightly behind its European peers on eugenics policies and studies—built a discursive foundation for the movement that drew expressly on interest in breeding science, racial taxonomies, psychiatric nosologies, and systematic responses to mass industrialization, urbanization, and immigration.

The language of breeding—namely, discussions on animal- and plant-breeding principles as a springboard for human eugenics—was strongest during the first decades of the twentieth century. Connections with agricultural breeding provided common references and explanations with which to educate a broader public on the expertise of the eugenicists and the rationale of applying eugenic principles to questions of human reproduction. Such advocates argued that while America had long struggled with demographic pressures, developments in science and breeding meant a conceivable end to mental health concerns about drunkenness, epilepsy, social deviance, race, and other undesirable aspects of human difference plaguing the nation. The process of identifying problem groups, adapting animal- and plant-breeding techniques for humans, and outlining legal and social mechanisms to enact eugenic programs would, according to the early eugenics discourse, propel the chosen American and European races to greatness.[14]

Yet what identified an ideal eugenic person? Typically, people from the middle class were identified as the best breeding stock, with special emphasis on intellectuals, artists, and scientists—reflecting the kinds of people who were the strongest advocates in the movement. A combination of German, Nordic, and white Anglo-Saxon Protestant characteristics was thought to be the best.[15] Amory C. Stevens of New York described the ideal type of man as one "who will combine the large frame and strength of the ideal Anglo-Saxon or Scandinavian, the practical intelligence of the American, the intellect of the high German, the art-loving qualities and sunny temperament of the Latin, and so forth."[16] In predominantly white areas of the country, the definition of "race" shifted to include more attention to class and social factors in addition to ethnic differences. Eugenicists created all sorts of social boundaries and categories among whites, as Stern points out, by "dividing northerner from southerner, employed from unemployed, . . . schooled from unschooled, sound from unsound and ordered from disordered."[17] The complex characterizations and distinctions created to delineate the ideal from the degenerate highlighted the white middle- to upper-class core of the movement and further demonstrated the ways that eugenicists wove together their own notions of race, class, and ability in categorizing people as eugenically healthy or not. These notions visibly informed the early eugenics discourse, particularly the conversations on how to extrapolate from agricultural breeding to human breeding and on how to overcome existing social norms that might impede the progressive eugenics programs.

Printed in newspapers across the United States, triumphant reports from prominent scientists on the formation of new scholarly societies and on their latest findings sought to impress upon the public the cutting-edge relevance of eugenics. Turn-of-the-century articles and some editorials reinforced this view by describing eugenics as the natural extension of breeding programs for animals and plants that yielded stronger, faster-growing specimens. Eugenics advocates claimed that American horticulturalist Luther Burbank's (1849–1926) well-documented successes in creating new varieties of plants, for example, paved the way for applications of breeding science to human beings. A 1906 *Blue Grass Blade* article on Burbank cheerfully declared that his "achievements with the fruits, the flora and the trees coupled with his own practical human and aspiring intelligence have come opportunely to help our species further onward and upward."[18] The discoveries he made with plants were portrayed largely as a model of the possibilities of heredity and breeding science, and eugenics advocates depicted Burbank himself as an exemplar of human achievement, ingenious intellect, and progressive scientific thought.

Early attempts to educate the public on the potential of eugenics widely acknowledged that human nature and individuality will presented significant obstacles to any direct translation of agricultural breeding to humans. Belief in the goals of eugenic science, however, provided hope that eugenicists would create new knowledge about human heredity. As German historian Peter Weingart argues, "Given the concern about degenerative development, traditional demography seemed inferior because it focused only on the quantitative aspects of the population, whereas eugenics could deal with the quality."[19] Assistant secretary of agriculture Willet M. Hays (1879–1954) released a cautiously optimistic statement highlighting the potential of eugenics: "The subject of investigating the heredity of man is comparatively much more difficult than in the case of plants and animals. It is so important that science and religion should join in an investigation at once conservative, careful, and possibly constructive."[20] Eugenicists educated in a range of fields, but primarily from the sciences, medicine, and psychiatry, promoted a belief that their work was a natural extension of agricultural breeding, "improving the human species in much the same ways as a breeder improves a flock or herd," albeit with greater consequences for the future.[21] Eugenic science, then, held the key to eliminating degenerate groups identified as "injuring the race."[22]

In 1906, the Department of Agriculture held a series of high-profile meetings of eugenicists in the United States. Statements and reports from the meetings, published in newspapers across the country, outlined the objectives of eugenics and how these principles should be applied in practice for the good of society, especially in America. The meeting delegation was made up of prominent eugenicists chosen by Assistant Secretary Hays: Alexander Graham Bell (1844–1929) as chair, Stanford University president David Starr Jordan (1851–1931), University of Chicago professor Charles R. Henderson (1848-1915), Dr. Charles Woodruff (1846–1927), C. W. Ward (1867–1931?), and Reverend J. E. Gilbert (1886–1963?). Hays described the committee's four areas of activity: "to investigate and report on heredity in the human race; to devise methods of recording the values of the blood of individuals, families, peoples, and races; to emphasize the value of superior blood and the menace to society of inferior blood, and to suggest methods of improving the heredity of the family, the people, or the race."[23] Hays's own background as a founder of the American Breeder's Association, and an avid animal and plant breeder, is apparent in the men he selected for the committee and its initial stated goals.

As framed by eugenics articles, social progress and selective breeding measures went hand in hand—though the language allowed considerable room for various interpretations of what improvement to the human race might look like. As a tangible first step, while those investigations into translating principles of animal and plant breeding were conducted, the committee agreed that the "immediate object of the committee . . . is to spread information in regard to the ill effects of the marriage of defective persons, including imbeciles, idiots and feeble-minded." Insane persons, confirmed drunkards and moral degenerates were to be "restrained in colonies and kept from marrying."[24] Starting with those groups, the Department of Agriculture's committee could use public education in eugenic rhetoric to lay the foundation for broader legislative, mental health, and social actions. As these ill-defined groups had long been blamed as morally and genetically bereft and targeted by nineteenth-century reformers of all stripes, eugenicists needed only to put a bit of their own gloss on how best to "solve" the contemporary societal problems of poverty, addiction, decreasing social coherence, and immigration rather than devise an entirely new position. The vagueness of eugenics generally, and the 1906 committee's reports specifically, opened a discursive space for differing groups to describe and promote a wide range of actions and policies to further eugenic aims.

The shift from Galton's more benign definition of eugenics to the more active selection process and set of tactics outlined in the 1906 reports and articles established eugenics as a science and a social program. Early eugenic discourse aimed high: to produce scientific knowledge about optimal partnering and reproduction, to prove its utility in American society through demonstrated results, and to align with American notions of progress. Sweeping statements became increasingly common, such as Garrett P. Serviss's (1851–1929) bold declaration on page 1 of the *Blue Grass Blade* that "the new men and women raised up by the new science of 'eugenics' will have, by the mere effect of their improved physique, a richer, fuller, more agreeable life than their predecessors have enjoyed."[25] The idea of an American eugenic utopia emerged from statements like this and became a point of reference for later proponents. Over time, as eugenics permeated the personal behaviour and systems of government, society could then reach its potential.

How eugenicists envisioned the specific mechanisms for eugenic breeding and progress to occur varied significantly. In contrast to more benign and generalized language about eugenic utopias, an aggressive form of eugenics advocacy pushed for the forced quarantine, examination, sterilization, and/or elimination of those deemed unfit. Dr. Eugene Davenport (1856–1941) of the University of Illinois was one such proponent. He argued bluntly "that all the 'culls' or 'scalawags' of the human race should be taken before the courts, scientifically investigated, and if found unworthy, colonized and permitted to die off."[26] Extreme measures seemed appropriate to those especially panicked about America's acute problem with race suicide and its laggard status with regard to eugenic knowledge and policies overall. Although scientists varied in their fervour for eugenics and the specifics of implementing eugenic principles, their rhetoric in newspaper discussions consistently emphasized that eugenics presented a scientifically based set of corrections to problem groups in American society, such as the vast patient populations of the mental asylums, the white working-class populations of the mining and heavy industry cities, the hill colonies of Virginia with their alleged problems of mental retardation and physical disability rates, and the African American populations of the Deep South, among others.

The tension between notions of American exceptionalism and connection with transatlantic communities and social processes is apparent. In these early years of the eugenics movement, articles noted similarities in the effects of industrialization and urbanization on Europeans and Americans but also gestured to the ways that these same effects were perceived as heightened or worse in America. Writing for the *Evening Star* in Washington, DC, in 1906, John Elfreth Watkins (1852–1903) from the prominent Smithsonian Institution and Museums stressed that "blond immigrants and their descendants"—despite being perceived as the most prized immigrants in the United States—"cannot thrive in this country, save in the cloudy regions of the extreme northwestern corner." More generally, "every now and then we learn of some great man collapsing of nervous breakdown before forty-five under loads which Europeans seem to bear safely until sixty or sixty-five." And perhaps most damning, "Suicides, which are nearly always due to mental or nervous diseases, are increasing in the United States."[27] That large areas of the United States proved unhealthy for European immigrants and detrimental to those Americans expected to be both physically and mentally robust indicated the need for the measured and wide-reaching application of eugenics, and the movement's supporters had a ready supply of anecdotal evidence to support these assertions.

American eugenicists also participated in the transatlantic conversations throughout this period by contributing their own insights abroad. The middle-class norm among eugenicists also cut the other way, and the affluent upper class received a fair amount of scrutiny on both sides of the Atlantic. The primary accusation held that the wealthy—assumed in articles on eugenics to be men only—used their money and privilege to achieve marriages that may not have occurred if the only considerations for such unions were attractiveness, health, and love. Eugenicists were quick to point out that their principles did not preclude love or forming loving attachments. Freeing partnering from "the influences that do violence to love"—especially "the still more fatal influence of wealth and position and worldly convenience, which give a factitious value to persons who would never appear attractive partners in life were love and eugenic ideals left to go hand in hand"—was a particular concern for American and British eugenicists deeply concerned with the power and privilege of wealth.[28] The middle class served as the fulcrum for eugenic norms in the United States and Europe, with those classes above and below suspect by virtue of their social status.

Reverend Dr. Samuel George Smith (b. 1851?) of Minneapolis spoke at the 1912 Eugenics Congress in London, calling for attention to the ways that the wealthy and upper class could circumvent ideal eugenic practices. He speculated that "we may say they will not permit poor to breed, but how can we deal with those who defy society by wealth, social position, and power," and stated that excellence of the mind should be sought in the same way as—and even in cases of a lack of—physical excellence.[29] Smith's class critique likely played well to his European audience, but it also calls attention to a broader transatlantic concern with the growth and consolidation of wealth among a few that accompanied industrialization around the turn of the century. Also speaking to the relation between eugenics and class, John C. Hudson (1919–96), superintendent to the education committee of the borough of Hornsey, England, praised what he saw as the increased possibility for social mobility in American society, and in the city of Chicago's education system specifically: "As, for example, every boy who goes to the public school in the states has the possibility of becoming president someday. The greatest ambition of a boy in the older countries of Europe can only rise to the height of following some occupation like that of his father, uncle, or of some relative."[30]

The potential for improvement and belief in progress underpinned many early accounts and discussions of eugenics in American newspapers. The convergence of innovations in animal and plant science with medical and neuropsychiatric diagnostics and treatment concerns, a decline in the birth rate in many areas of Europe and the United States, increased immigration, and changing social relationships linked to mass industrialization and urbanization in the Progressive Era opened space for the eugenics movement to assert itself. In cobbling together a set of approaches and principles based in part on contemporary scientific research on heredity, early eugenicists presented a vision, albeit still vague, of a progressive science and related social program. As Stern describes, "the coalescence of organized eugenics movements required the convergence of the competing and complementary hypotheses in plant and animal biology that gave rise to modern genetics."[31] While scientists worked to solve the puzzle of human heredity, eugenicists speculated on how to apply eugenic principles to the general public. As will be discussed in the next section, education and regulation of marriage—and, to a lesser extent, parenting—seemed the optimal place for eugenicists to implement their notion of social change.

MARRIAGE, LEGISLATION, AND PUBLIC MENTAL HEALTH EDUCATION

American eugenicists, and among them many psychiatrists and mental health administrators, diverged greatly in their opinions on the optimal combination of formal and informal guidance to ensure public compliance with eugenic principles. While individual states passed marriage regulations and forced sterilization laws with the support of eugenics advocates, education programs and tests were devised as bottom-up methods for spreading eugenics knowledge and changing social norms. Keenly motivated to demonstrate the efficacy of the movement to their Northern Atlantic peers (see also chapter 2), American eugenicists pursued a wide range of approaches for shaping ideal couples and marriages. A key implication in much of the discourse was that the drunkards, the feeble-minded, and other undesirable people were by and large men. It could be that degeneracy in men was seen as more debilitating to society than degeneracy in women and so sparked more discussion of how to decrease the prevalence of these unfit groups. Many eugenicists argued that a primary way to ensure that degenerate men did not reproduce was to educate women in choosing better husbands. This sense of choice, as I will later discuss, was greatly limited by women's lack of financial and political power, but it is interesting to note that the early discourse on eugenics did not explicitly describe women as prone to the moral and physical degeneration or deficiencies so often noted in men. The recurring fear expressed in the media was that women would marry degenerate men, which would then increase the chances for below-average offspring and further regress the race.

Rhetoric on marriage, and the increasing discussions of the role of eugenics in this social institution, particularly resonated with the public because of long-standing concern over who should marry and which pairings would be most beneficial to society. Fear of undesirable pairings caused by young people's misplaced affections and lack of education on "proper" matches quickly found a platform in turn-of-the-century eugenics discourse. Specifically, proponents claimed that human nature and emotions deterred and harmed the selection process at the individual level. At the same time, eugenicists were trained to evaluate and identify appropriate matches based on observable physical and behavioural traits and therefore had a duty to communicate to the public the benefits of and need for eugenic-based couplings to ameliorate the risk of poor matches. An article in the *New York Times* emphasized how a "eugenicist only puts more care and more intelligence in the selection of his life mate," because of the eugenicist's greater knowledge in the desirable traits for a mate. Eugenic societies, as Weingart argues, sought to "take decisions about reproduction out of the hands of individuals, with their irrational considerations under the influence of passion, and leave only the satisfaction of their sexual needs to themselves."[32] Eugenicists, informed by their keen insights into human heredity, saw themselves as experts in recognizing optimal couples.

Jurisdiction over who was to wield the power to influence and regulate marriage was a tricky subject. The emergent position of eugenics meant that its proponents had to avoid alienating large constituencies of Americans and institutions that could be useful in the future. As Thomas Leonard argues, "Progressive Era eugenics opposed laissez-faire values, by substituting an objective, expert determination of the social good for a subjective, individual determination of the social good. Individuals could not be relied upon to promote the social good of better heredity, but experts could."[33] Beyond this, however, is the fact that eugenicists themselves varied widely in their visions of how eugenic principles could best be applied to American society. Eugenicists carefully positioned themselves in relation to other groups with vested interest in the institution of marriage. Dr. H. W. Anderson (b. 1901?), president of the California State Eugenics Association, adamantly argued that "legitimate eugenics has no quarrel with the church, with marriage.... Its mission is to take society as it finds it and improve upon it, and, in every legitimate way, labor to produce a better race of human beings."[34] Statements like this demonstrated some eugenicists' apprehension about appearing too socially radical and thereby limiting the appeal of the movement. The institution of marriage demanded wary respect from a number of eugenicists, who were generally careful about framing their rhetoric to accommodate traditional views.

Eugenics rhetoric placed a significant burden on women as the arbiters of good marriages that would lead to "quality" children but foresaw the intervention in marriages of poorer stock and guidance of the eugenics movement along the way. In several articles, eugenicists argued that greater social freedom for women, achieved in large part as a result of women's suffrage, to choose healthy and loving marriages (hopefully with eugenic principles in mind). La Reine Helen Baker (b. 1882) was one of those who agreed with the sentiment that women would achieve greater control over their lives through suffrage—and that it had implications for the eugenics movement. An outspoken attendee of the 1910 National Woman Suffrage Association convention, Baker declared that "it is quality we want in children, not quantity. Woman suffrage will produce better children, for it will produce better thinking."[35] Baker's statement interpreted declining birth rates from a different perspective: her position focused on a broader definition of female autonomy than that of the previously discussed group of eugenicists, which, according to Baker, linked women's suffrage to women's education to high quality eugenic marriages to a small number of "better" children. Her response to race suicide emphasized increasing the quality of women's and children's lives rather than increasing family size. Women, to Baker's mind, should hold the power to enact eugenic principles—they merely needed additional knowledge to do so correctly. Baker thus joined a circle of very ardent women supporters of eugenics in the United States.

Writing for the *San Francisco Call* in 1913, Dr. Edward C. Spitzka (1852–1914) claimed, "The more that women are emancipated the fewer marriages there will be for financial reasons, women being today the greater offenders in this respect. The universal establishment of the real love marriage would be a boon to the human race."[36] Spitzka's words connected female autonomy, love, and marriage into a surprisingly feminist and altogether eugenic vision of society. His inclusion of "financial reasons" hints at the common distrust of money as a primary motivator for marriage. While it was not uncommon for wealthy women to be pursued for their dowry and money, eugenics discourse emphasized a seeming problem of weak wealthy men obtaining good marriages and having children based on their social position alone.[37] The significance of "real love" bonds, in relation to scientific hereditary knowledge, varied from contemporary eugenicist to eugenicist, yet overall it opened a place in the discourse for women's action and choice as integral to visions of a eugenic society.

Despite uncertainty over who should be invested with the power to form couples for marriage, there was general agreement that marriage and reproduction should be regulated in three main ways: through strict legislation, with public education, and by social pressure. Of the three approaches typically described, legal regulation of marriage was seen by eugenicists as a more immediate and practical solution than the other two. This piecemeal approach did little for the kind of broad societal change eugenicists wished to see, but it did present evidence to European peers that the United States was making serious efforts to reform society with eugenics. Further, as Benjamin Witt (b. 1860) wrote in 1915, progressive reformers wanted to "bring the United States abreast of Germany and other European countries in the matter of remedial legislation," largely connecting with similar "progressivist" tendencies in Germany and central Europe at the time (see chapter 7 on the historical case of Kurt Goldstein).[38] Eugenics-based laws, then, served as a measure to inhibit race suicide while bringing the United States closer in line with its transatlantic peers.

Forms of marriage legislation varied greatly. Dr. G. Frank Lydston (1858–1923), a criminal anthropologist and psychologist, argued that all degenerates—the "criminal, epileptic, insane and drunken"—should be prevented from marrying unless they first submitted to sterilization.[39] He believed that barring degenerates from marriage took precedence over broader marriage legislation, because of the perceived immediate danger posed by those groups. Indiana's sterilization law (1907), Michigan's neurologically inspired prohibition of marriage for epileptics (1913), and Nebraska's prohibition of marriage for first cousins (1915) exemplified this mindset. Fear of how undesirable social behaviours, psychological traits, and illnesses could be passed from generation to generation helped push such laws into force.

Some eugenicists saw legal regulations of marriage as stepping stones in eugenic progress. Dr. Henry Maudsley (1835–1918), a British eugenicist, expressed doubt in the efficacy of doctors and laws in actually shaping and restricting marriage to the most ideal couples. Reviewing the approaches taken by several northern US states, he was of the opinion that "the legal restrictions upon marriage proposed by the homeopathic physicians to the Legislatures of Nebraska, Colorado, and Michigan would be negligible even should they be fixed in the statute books."[40] While perhaps overlooking the extent to which marriage laws could be interpreted and implemented at the local level, Maudsley's views do emphasize the ways that laws regulating marriage were structurally contained to small geographic areas and lacked any sense of systematic consistency. Archibald Primrose (1847–1927), Earl of Rosebery and former British prime minister, stated in a 1908 speech to the Society for Comparative Legislation in London that the most fortunate states were those that "achieved development by the individual efforts of its citizens as little as possible supported or guided by legislation."[41] He mentioned the Michigan and Nebraska laws specifically, noting that while "people might be inclined to smile" at them, they could be the start of a long-term social change in the country. European observers were likely those who would "smile" at the American laws, as Primrose implied. The newspaper article that mentioned his speech the recently passed laws in Michigan and Nebraska as indicative of growing support for eugenics in the United States and mused that "time might show that the Michigan enactment was of great value."[42] These comments only suggested the potential merit of such legislation, and in the context of the article, the opinions on eugenics were relegated to a small paragraph at the end of the article.

Keller likewise saw legal regulations as only the beginning for eugenics. More crucially, the Yale professor said,

> The conviction that such and such unions are evil must be brought home to the masses, if at all, not by the microscope or the statistical table, but by actual, tangible misfortune, and on the large scale. This alone will cause them to distrust their accepted "ways," and to tolerate the thought of other ways. There must at least be personal suffering to be compared with the weal of others; or, since this is a social matter, there must at least be a comparison of the destinies of societies practicing, respectively, good and bad systems of man-breeding.[43]

This idea of changing the public's mind socially through education, peer pressure, competition, and negative experiences, in addition to formal legislation, struck a balance between those who advocated for strict top-down regulation and those who argued for education and gradual adoption of eugenic principles on an individual level.

A society-based, education-driven effort to reform and regulate marriage garnered the most support. Alexander Graham Bell (1847–1922), inventor of the telephone, was highly regarded in the American eugenics community and among those opposed to legislative measures for marriage. Instead, he appealed to the idea that American society wished to produce the finest progeny and that this desire alone would shape marriage and breeding practice for the nation. He also believed that through public education, and a clear explanation of the dangers of the combination of certain groups in marriage, "mere dissemination of that knowledge would of itself tend to promote desirable and prevent undesirable unions of the sexes."[44] Bell's language reflects both the progressive desire to reform society and an uncertainty toward the appropriate measures needed to achieve finer offspring.

Suggestion and education, rather than law, was put forward as the appropriate way to affect marriage choices and ensure proper breeding. Optional medical tests and certificates of eugenic health were also proposed as indicators of individual adherence to eugenic principles, to signal that a person was of ideal health and reproductive ability. "Such certificates," explained biological psychologist Havelock Ellis (1859–1939), "would imply an inquiry and examination into the hereditary influences dominating or conditioning the constitution, health, intelligence and character of the individual. . . . The possession of such a certificate would involve a superiority to the average in all these respects. No one would be compelled to offer himself for such examination, just as no one is compelled to seek a university degree." These "patents of natural nobility" would, to Ellis's mind, serve to validate people who may not have the backing of wealth or privileged social status in many areas of their lives, including marriage, jobs, or any situation that would involve personal evaluation.[45] This evaluative approach accompanied by some kind of award or certification suffused events like the better-baby contests or psychological IQ tests prevalent after World War I, which offered people validation of their supposed fitness in relation to their peer groups and society at large. As demonstrated by the examples above, while the shape and scope of eugenics-oriented legislation was still heavily contested among eugenicists in the media, it was largely agreed that even if such laws were enacted, public education and changes to social norms would result in the greatest long-term success in infusing eugenic principles into the behaviours and minds of Americans.

The American context for eugenics discourse prior to World War I is acutely apparent in an example from a 1913 edition of the *Day Book*, a Chicago publication. The feature element of page 4 was a large photograph of Eugenette Bolce (1913–1938), the "first baby born in England in accordance to the laws of eugenics." Her parentage points to the transatlantic reach of the eugenic movement: her father was "of Austrian descent, born in California" and her mother was English. The only other information about Eugenette included in the short article accompanying her picture was that "for a seven-month-old youngster Baby Bolce is displaying remarkable intelligence and already has a pronounced sense of humor. Since her birth she has been reared under the healthiest conditions."[46] The juxtaposition of Eugenette's photograph and story, which together take up over 80 percent of the entire page, with the only other article on page 4, titled "Negress Would Marry White," points to the particular social issues facing American eugenicists. The terse latter article reports that Blanche Shoemaker had begun legal proceedings to compel the local county clerk to issue her a marriage licence so she could marry a white man. County clerks' denial of marriage licences to interracial couples is a well-documented occurrence over the twentieth century as a de facto form of miscegenation law.[47] The contrast in this instance with the image of a "perfectly" conceived white marriage and child starkly highlights the limits implicit in eugenic rhetoric to the kinds of choices available to women related to marriage and childbirth.

Early eugenics discourse often focused on marriage as the key site for social change and implementation of eugenics knowledge and principles. While tension between formal legal regulations and socially based education continued, from 1900 to 1915 the emerging sense was that a combination of the two was needed to move toward an ideal society. Implementation is where the United States differentiated itself from Europe, primarily with the wide-ranging forms of marriage bans passed across the country. The diffuse nature of the eugenics movement and its efforts, coupled with the varied beliefs of the eugenicists and the sense that practical measures needed to be put in place quickly, resulted in a hodgepodge of regulations and ideas for education on eugenics and also its application in the field of public mental health across the country.

CONCLUSION

The earliest discussions of eugenics framed it within popular notions and established ideologies to make it acceptable to a general public. This discourse cast eugenics as a progressive, scientific solution to social issues, and scientists such as Burbank, Bell, and David Starr Jordan who advocated for various eugenic policies were portrayed as a vanguard in the fight against race suicide and the degeneration of the American people. Trading on well-established racialized views of social stratification, the pseudo-science of eugenics seemingly presented new evidence to reinforce systemic racism. Concerns over "proper" couplings opened space for eugenicists to argue for the precise selection, by eugenics experts, of the most desirable combinations of people to marry and have children along with a general (and often contradictory) set of parameters for ideal marriages and parenting environments.

The American eugenics community had the "acute hunger of the era's social reformers for international information."[48] Like other Progressive Era movements, the American eugenics movement found itself a latecomer to develop specific eugenic policy and stimulate scientific research when compared with the eugenics developments across the Atlantic. From 1900 to 1915, American eugenicists looked primarily to Britain, in part because of long-standing historical connections and also because it was the home of Galton and of the first concerted eugenics programs of study. After World War I, German eugenic science aligned more with the American community's goals, and both countries moved strongly toward more of a negative eugenic bent. Newspaper coverage of early eugenicists reveals a sense of urgency behind the rhetoric. The changes to the health of the race wrought by the "modern social organism"—namely, "the rapid intensification of market relations, the swelling great city populations, and the rising working class resentments from below"—caused considerable concern and calls for immediate action.[49] American progressives and eugenicists, taking up the metaphor of lagging behind in the race of progress with European states along with concerns about degeneracy and the deterioration of the public health situation, pushed for a wide range of eugenic solutions, both immediate (e.g., marriage bans) and long-term (e.g., public education of women on eugenic marriages).[50]

Newspapers as the main historical source for this study have enabled analysis of the early eugenics movement through the words of eugenicists, mental health–care physicians, and social reformers. Newspapers played an early and vital role in disseminating eugenic principles to the public and served to inform and reassure the public that eugenics was in line with both traditional belief systems and the new progressive movements. While the peak of eugenics in America can most easily be seen in the 1920s and 1930s, the fervour and support for such ideas in that period was not new. In fact, these early years of eugenic discourse laid a strong foundation in establishing the US eugenics movement as, simultaneously, part of a transatlantic conversation on ordering and regulating industrialized nation-states (see also chapters 2, 3, and 7) and a more localized response to the particular shape of American society during the Progressive Era. The numerous instances of forced sterilization legislation, the organization of eugenic institutions and associations nationwide, and the attention given eugenics in general after 1915 drew heavily upon the groundwork set by this early public discourse around mental and public health.

7

The "Eugenics Paradox"

Core Beliefs of Progressivism versus Relics of Medical Traditionalism—The Example of Kurt Goldstein

Frank W. Stahnisch

A discussion of well-known German-American neurologist, psychiatrist, and psychologist Kurt Goldstein (1878–1965) as a prime example of eugenic thought—highlighting the interrelated nature of eugenic issues in the United States, Europe, and Canada at the beginning of the twentieth century—is quite paradoxical in several ways. By many scholars, Goldstein is regarded as an impressive interdisciplinary researcher who made numerous and lasting contributions to the fields of clinical neurology, brain psychiatry, experimental psychology, medical rehabilitation, and philosophical anthropology—in both the German-speaking and North American communities, following his forced emigration to the United States in 1935. Goldstein attempted to combine the analytical approach of classical neurology with a new holistic theory of brain function, while also integrating the insights of the contemporary "Gestalt theory" developed among clinical and experimental psychologists. In his clinical departments at the Universities of Frankfurt am Main and Berlin, Goldstein had educated hundreds of medical and psychology students and residents not only in basic brain research and neuropathology but in broader psychoanalytic and clinicopathological methodologies as well, emphasizing the distinct need for a more humanistic attitude in future generations of medical doctors.[1]

SEVERAL EUGENICS PARADOXES

From the perspective of the history of eugenics, one might be quite astonished to find Goldstein an early representative of what later became a drastic and inhumane movement worldwide. This is particularly so given his major achievements in holist neurology just mentioned, but also because of his peculiar biography as a German-born physician-scientist with early eugenicist inclinations who later became a victim of the Nazi regime in Germany. After the seizure of power by the Nazi Party on January 30, 1933, Goldstein—who was perceived as a Jewish physician, psychoanalyst, and medical doctor with socialist inclinations—was forced to leave Germany the same year. As British historian and journalist John Cornwell has pointed out, Goldstein's holist neurology "was generally criticized by Nazi doctors for its 'negative features,'[2] which were described as 'liberalism, individualism, mechanistic-materialist thinking, Jewish-communist human ideology, lack of respect for the blood and soil, neglect of race and heredity, emphasis on individual organs and the undervaluing of soul and constitution.'"[3]

On April 6, 1933, GeStapo agents pulled Goldstein out of his medical practice at the academic City Hospital of Moabit in Berlin and threw him into the terrible city prison located in the General Pape-Strasse, where he was incarcerated and tortured for half a year.[4] Through the intervention of his student, and later wife, Dr. Eva Rothmann (1878–1960), he was freed: she was acquainted with Matthias Heinrich Goering (1893–1945), leader of a right-wing *voelkisch* movement of psychoanalysis and, more importantly, an elder cousin of the prime minister of Prussia, Hermann Goering (1893–1946).[5] Following this intervention, Goldstein was able to flee to Zurich, before he eventually found exile in Amsterdam for the next five years.[6]

Given Goldstein's biographical background, at first glance it appears more than paradoxical that this Jewish physician could already be a protagonist of "eugenics"—in its German terminology of *Rassenhygiene* (racial hygiene), with all its imminent infamous and sinister connotations—in 1913.[7] He is so well known and his work held in such high esteem by many physicians, scholars, intellectuals, and social workers worldwide[8]—having made numerous and lasting contributions to the communities of neurology, neurorehabilitation, experimental psychology, and psychosomatics, as well as holist philosophy—that this chapter may even appear as a somewhat hagioclastic undertaking, in which a significant "medical role model" is thrown from his pillar.[9] Methodologically, however, this is done to understand in retrospect how this "intellectual digression" became possible in the first place and to reconstruct the remnants and fragments of Goldstein's working biography. This historiographical process may help us to follow the transition from the person and work in "Goldstein I" to that of "Goldstein II"—his alter ego, who truly became the appraised advocate of the neurologically handicapped—after having assumed the directorship of the Frankfurt Institute for the Brain Injured in 1919, a position he held throughout most of the interwar period.[10]

The explanation for the *first paradox*—why Goldstein got interested in eugenics at all—which I will furnish after briefly introducing Goldstein's life and work, is one based on his socialist inclinations toward the early twentieth-century secularist ideal—in the North American tradition often the social-theological ideal—of the "New Man."[11] During his years of study and his residency period, this ideal became for Goldstein paired with nationalist and patriotic values, which was quite typical for many leading physicians, such as human geneticist Franz Josef Kallmann (1897–1965) and well-known neurosurgeon Ludwig Guttmann (1899–1980), assimilated Jews who were very appreciative of the bourgeois liberties offered by the Wilhelminian Empire since 1871 while often also sharing the expansivist politics of the German Kaiser.[12] As such, with respect to the pertinent issues of eugenic motivations and social intentions, even the humanist and socially motivated neurologist Goldstein exemplified a personal modernist and libertarian trait, intrinsically paired with patriotic values, that one could find mirrored in Canada—in the social philosophies and political views not only of a number of early feminist activists such as the "Famous Five" in Alberta, for example, but also in the writings on the relation of the healthy family to eugenics of future Saskatchewan premier Tommy Douglas (1904–86) in the early 1930s, in which he mentioned a system that would have required couples seeking to marry to be certified as morally fit.[13] Those deemed "subnormal" because of low intelligence, moral laxity, or venereal disease would have to be sent to state farms or camps while those judged mentally defective or incurably diseased would be sterilized, according to Douglas: "Sterilization of the mentally and physically defective has long been advocated, but only recently has it seeped into the public consciousness. . . . [S]terilization seems to meet the requirements of the situation most aptly. For while it gives protection to society, yet it deprives the defective of nothing except the privilege of bringing into the world children who only be a care to themselves and a charge to society."[14]

This was certainly not an isolated affair[15]—even though Canadian contextual factors clearly do apply and principal British and American influences in medical, political, and philosophical areas were much more pronounced in Canada than were German and European ones—yet it places the discussion about the political philosophy of eugenics in western Canada in the wider, international British, American, and German contexts, where it likewise needs to be addressed.[16] Other contemporaries—such as the well-known case of Swiss-German psychiatrist Ernst Ruedin (1874–1952), who displayed open socialist inclinations even in the 1920s—continued to promote their eugenics line of thought and laid the ground for the murderous context of the National Socialist health-care philosophy.[17] In considering Goldstein's 1913 book *On Eugenics* (*Ueber Rassenhygiene*) in its wider social and cultural context, I attempt here to untangle some medical and philosophical trends that were based on the opposition of social progressivism versus traditionalism in medicine, along with contemporary eugenics convictions as they emerged from the context of medical modernity during the historical time period.[18]

The *second paradox* concerns eugenics theorizing versus medical holism and social philosophy. At face value, of course, it is inconsistent to see eugenics approaches (such as separation, sexual segregation, marriage rules, and forced sterilization) as associated or even integrated with medical holism and social philosophy ideals. In hindsight, then, how was it possible for Goldstein to theoretically align the assumptions of this dreadful development with the implications of his own neurological approach? Along with such eugenics considerations, there are also systematic reasons why Goldstein's neurology can be seen as an adequate example to study the marginalization and persecution of the field through protagonists of Nazi medicine and racial hygiene. In the new health and welfare programs in Nazi Germany, cultural and medico-legal views on the neurologically handicapped and mentally ill—first in Germany and later also in Austria and the recently occupied countries—saw an unfortunate evolution of applied eugenics programs comprising family counselling of parents, marriage laws, and eventually forced sterilization regulations (see also chapter 8, by Paul J. Weindling, on the wider implications of the central

European eugenics programs and the compensation legacy for victims of coerced sterilization).[19] This further created the background for a transformation of the public mental health system in which psychiatric and neurological patients became the prime targets of racial hygienists and applied eugenicists. The transformation of the health care system through the influences by Nazi philosophies were additionally substantiated by a growing enthusiasm for racial hygiene, forced sterilization, and, later, euthanasia programs for children and the mentally ill. What is crucial to my narrative here is the active expulsion of what the Nazis saw as "Jewish medicine and science," which included particular areas of psychiatry and neurology along with psychoanalysis, medical sexology (*Sexualwissenschaft*), and socialist public health.[20]

The *third paradox* regards Goldstein's own becoming a victim of the wider racial-anthropological regimes (in their medical, political, and also social dimensions through the threatening of his own Jewish family), while he had himself not anticipated the scope and radicalism of the "political philosophy" of National Socialism.[21] On the other hand, this appears to have been the reason that Douglas gave up his eugenics inclinations around 1936, after having visited the Third Reich and seen some of the drastic effects and reverberations that the Nazi racial and sterilization laws had had on contemporary German society.[22] With new therapeutic approaches arising, and eventually Goldstein's and his wife's forced migration to New York City, the traces of his own early embrace of eugenics regulations were lost, as was most of Goldstein's overarching holistic medical approach and social theorizing.[23]

At least in terms of these three paradoxes, a new look at Goldstein's earlier work and international story can help us to understand similar paradoxes in the Canadian context of eugenics as well as the discussions and quarrels within the neurological and psychiatric communities on both sides of the Atlantic in a new light. An open dispute about the "eugenics question" was apparently more pronounced in the United States than it was in Canada, particularly in the Canadian medical professional communities.[24] However, before looking at each of these three paradoxes in turn, I will first outline some biographical details of Goldstein's life and career, why he was so important for the international neurological and psychiatric community, and why it is necessary to look at his embrace of *Rassenhygiene* in different ways.

> A pseudo-social organization may be compared with an organism in disease, and we may speak of such a society [in which the normal relations are no longer sustained] as sick. Normal society means a type of organization through which the fullest possible actualization on the part of all individuals is assured. . . . If we acknowledge and utilize social organization as an instrument by means of which all individuals may actualize themselves to an optimal degree, then a genuine social life becomes possible. Only under these conditions is a social organization capable of doing justice to every individual; only this makes it a real organization and secures its duration. . . . Only in this way can we discover the concrete causes of failure in a given situation and the appropriate ways to correct the failure.[25]

This excerpt from Goldstein's "William James lectures," which the German émigré neurologist gave at Harvard University between 1937 and 1938, is indicative of his new apprehension of the direction and future destiny of modern Western societies in the wake of the Second World War.[26] As much as it represents his own experiences as a Jewish refugee in Switzerland, Holland, and finally the United States, it can also be seen as an embodiment of his early views as a rehabilitation specialist in neurology and psychiatry.[27] The lectures, held during Goldstein's own exile in the United States, conveyed his broad social ideas and holistic approaches to medicine and psychology—after all, he had been invited by émigré-educator Robert Ulrich (1905–66?) and experimental psychologist Arno David Gurewitsch (1902–74) to Harvard's Department of Education to talk about his neurological and psychological experiences with brain-injured patients after the First World War.[28] The lectures are likewise a testimony of his concern with general social and political issues, in that the neurologist should take an active stance as both a citizen and a professional whose role in early "public health" considerations was a pivotal one.[29]

It should be emphasized here, for the sake of the argument, that this direction was evident in Goldstein's theorizing right from the beginning, even though the preconditions of his medical philosophy had changed quite visibly over time.[30] Goldstein's biography and the course of his innovative clinical research work passed through a number of distinctive

Figure 7.1 Kurt Goldstein. International Neurological Congress, 1949. Portrait no. 1, HMD [History of Medicine Division] Prints & Photos, Digital Collections, National Library of Medicine, Bethesda, MD. Photograph courtesy of National Library of Medicine.

phases, including, for example, his succession of Ludwig Edinger (1855–1918) as the director of the Frankfurt Neurological Institute in 1918 and the onset of his pioneering work with head-injured World War I soldiers.[31] When Goldstein later accepted the directorship of the neurological clinic at the Krankenhaus Moabit (City Hospital of Berlin at Moabit), in 1930, he organized the network of his groups of collaborators, contributors, and discussants in Frankfurt and Berlin—such as Max Wertheimer (1880–1943), Wolfgang Koehler (1887–1967), and Kurt Lewin (1890–1947)—according to his new understanding of interdisciplinary neurology.[32]

Goldstein's biography is altogether far from typical: Born into a Jewish mercantile family in the German province of Lower Silesia, he was educated at the integrative Jewish (Junior) High School, before entering the Humanistische Gymnasium in Breslau (see Figure 7.1). It seems quite important for the understanding of his early eugenics inclinations that in his youth and during his years in school he saw himself as a secular Jew for whom Jewishness was "rather a fate than a mission."[33] Given his broad interests in the humanities and his love for music and literature, he first decided to study philosophy at the University of Heidelberg. Yet because of strong pressure from his father—a landowner in the Kattowitz district and successful merchant in the Silesian logging industry—Goldstein switched to the study of medicine at the University of Breslau, where he graduated as an MD in 1903. Already with his doctoral thesis, conducted in the psychiatric clinic of Carl Wernicke (1848–1905)—one of the most renowned psychiatric and neurological diagnosticians (particularly of speech and language problems and the aphasias) at that time—Goldstein's interests were set. Adding to his theoretical preoccupation with neurology and psychiatry, further philosophical inspirations moved into his medical work "through the back door"; cultural philosopher Ernst Cassirer (1874–1945), who later fled Germany for England, Sweden, and the United States, became his cousin and exerted a strong influence on him, specifically regarding Cassirer's analysis of the cultural context of scientific thought and the interplay of "form" and "function" that he had analyzed in physics, biology, and the arts.[34]

More details of Goldstein's further training and early medical career will be described in quite some detail in the next part of this chapter, and the relation of his work to his eugenicist inclinations will also be addressed there. It is more imperative here to summarize several of the major achievements and fundamental contributions for which he became so well known in Europe as well as later in North America. Edinger, an eminent neuroanatomist and neurologist, was particularly aware of Goldstein's pioneering work on the aphasias and language disorders resulting from brain injuries.[35] By offering Goldstein the directorship of the Institute for Research into the Effects of Brain Lesions (*Institut fuer die Erforschung der Folgeerscheinungen von Hirnverletzungen*) affiliated with the Frankfurt Neurological Institute, he helped to provide the latter's research program with excellent working conditions and thereby foster his important work with soldiers with head injuries.[36] The institute was a clinical subdivision of the Neurological Institute, which in 1914, shortly before the outbreak of the war, was annexed to the newly established, bourgeois University of Frankfurt am Main, and it was here that Goldstein joined the experimental psychologist Adhémar Gelb (1887–1936), who became his closest collaborator for many years.[37] The work performed between 1918 and 1930 by Goldstein and his interdisciplinary group at the Institute for Research into the Effects of Brain Lesions is a particularly good example of a closer study of the cultural exchanges and interrelations between neurology and the postwar Weimar Republic through integration of philosophy, social psychiatry, and neuroscientific innovations into the program of "holist neurology."[38] It would, however, be a mistake to regard it as part of the then-mainstream research tradition, as it displayed ambiguities even within contemporary neuropathological views:

> At that time [mental diseases] were considered the expression of abnormal brain conditions. The study of the nervous system was taken for granted, and I [Goldstein] became attracted by professors who were occupied with studies in this field: the anatomist, Professor [Edward Albrecht] Schaper [b. 1875], who was interested in the embryonic development of the nervous system; the famous psychiatrist, Professor Karl Wernicke, who tried to understand the symptoms of the patients psychologically and to combine this understanding with the findings on their brains; and Professor Ludwig Edinger, who laid the foundations of comparative anatomy of the nervous system.[39]

Due to organizational changes in the institute and emerging anti-Semitic undertones in the medical faculty of the University of Frankfurt, Goldstein decided in 1930 to leave for Berlin, where he accepted the directorship of the clinic for neurology at the Charité teaching hospital of Moabit, in Berlin, which was soon to become an important centre of clinical neuroscientific research.[40] Here, Goldstein established a multidisciplinary research and patient care model that incorporated integrative services of neurology, clinical psychology, neuropathology, and brain histological research on the basis of a considerable group of assistants, collaborators, and contributors.[41] However, with the passing of the Nazi Law on the Re-establishment of a Professional Civil Service on April 7, 1933, Goldstein officially lost his academic position. The law made it so that all state officials understood as being of non-Aryan descent had to be dismissed from office. Nazi ideology deemed it unacceptable for Jews to teach "Aryans," so university professors, teachers, and doctors in the public health service lost their primary positions, and the law cut deeply into the existing culture of science and medicine of Weimar Germany.[42] It was only after his flight to and refuge in the Netherlands that Goldstein could finalize his seminal publication, *Der Aufbau des Organismus. Einfuehrung in die Biologie unter besonderer Beruecksichtigung der Erfahrungen an kranken Menschen* (The Organism: A Holistic Approach to Biology Derived from Pathological Data in Man), for which he would become so well known, with the help of the American Rockefeller Foundation.[43]

In 1935, Goldstein left the Netherlands for New York, where he continued his clinical work as a neurologist in private practice and lectured at Columbia University until the end of the war. Together with other German émigrés—including social philosophers Max Horkheimer (1895–1973) and Erich Fromm (1900–80)—he even pursued sociopsychology research on the "authoritarian character" at the New School of Social Research, until his death in 1965.[44] Starting in 1938, Goldstein—already sixty years of age—tried to re-establish a fruitful intellectual exchange, with his cousin, Cassirer; his new postdoctoral fellow, the experimental psychologist Martin Scheerer (1900–61); Cambridge education scholar Robert Ulrich; and phenomenologist Aron Gurwitsch (1901–73); however, this work only gained minor ground in physical therapy and rehabilitative psychology. Being forced to practice medicine for his living and the survival of his family, Goldstein toured and lectured at diverse places, while stretching his research interests increasingly into psychology and sociology.[45] This is reflected in a description by Harvard psychologist Marianne Simmel

(1923–2010), who met Goldstein in 1942 and judged that the forced migration had ruined Goldstein's career as a clinical neurologist.[46] As she stated, he did not find the right scientific culture he was looking for, and thus he never seemed to feel at home. Or, as his friend Ulrich cunningly summarized while reflecting on Goldstein's Harvard lectures, "[Americans] wondered suspiciously about his many-sided interests, which extended from medical research to psychology and philosophy. What was he really, they asked: a physician, a psychologist or a philosopher?"[47]

JEWISH ASSIMILATION, PERSONAL SOCIALIZATION, AND THERAPEUTIC NIHILISM VERSUS NEUROLOGICAL OPTIMISM

As far as we now know—and this is fairly in line with the biographies of many assimilated Jewish physicians of the later Wilhelminian Empire (Goldstein's long-time mentor Edinger and the clinical neurologist Frederic Henry Lewy [1885–1950] are also good examples)[48]—at the beginning of his medical studies Goldstein had applied for a parallel military education as a reserve officer (in the medical corps) with the Breslau Garrison.[49] It appears that, particularly from this socializational context, Goldstein developed quite a positive view of the military as a central element of the "organism of the nation," an integral "training school for the nation," and an "instrument that channels the struggle of the nations" (as he later used to call it).[50] The military figures centrally in his 1913 book *On Eugenics* as well, where he writes,

> One cannot underestimate the advantages of the military service. It is beyond doubt, for example, that a considerable number of men will be greatly supported by the military, both mentally and physically. Particularly, the education in social discipline and physical exercises is a remedy against the general nervousness of our times and is also of a great advantage.... Another question, which is harder to answer, is that of whether war is assuming a selective role in the general competition among the nations, which would lead to the survival of the fitter races [*Rassen*] over the unfit races? [Alfred] Ploetz writes for example that war is the best means to secure the white races from being flooded by other races, so that they may further expand and secure their general survival for all times.[51]

These emphatic and enthusiastic views of the military and its social role in the Wilhelminian Empire were rather common among many assimilated Jews in the German civil service, economic circles, and the higher-education sector, a circumstance that influential German historian Fritz K. Ringer (1934–2006) analyzed thoroughly in his book *The Decline of the German Mandarins: The German Academic Community, 1890–1933*, based on available social-historical statistical data: "Higher officials, academics, doctors and clergymen still accounted for 40 per cent of the [German officer] corps, while landowners and officers declined in representation. In the meantime, a full secondary education had actually increased in importance as a criterion of entry into the military profession; . . . 65 per cent of them held graduate certificates in 1912."[52]

Comprising nearly 16 percent of all university instructors, Jewish doctors and professors were by far overrepresented in institutions of higher learning in the first two decades of the twentieth century (given their 1 percent proportion in the general population).[53] Often enough, academics of Jewish origin thereby needed to prove their value to the wider German society against prevailing anti-Semitic prejudices of university and physician colleagues, many of whom were members of the nationalistic pan-German league and fervent supporters of the military and of imperial naval expansion (so-called *Flottenprofessoren*).[54] In part, these steps in the assimilation of Jewish doctors and professors can be understood as concessions to the academic ideology at the time, yet they were also an element of Goldstein's own medico-psychiatric theorizing:

> In a fundamental racial-anthropological sense, we may identify the aim of this [social] development as the emergence of the best race, whichever this will be in the end. It is evident that it is the plan of each race and each nation to survive in the struggle of the fittest. Yet with the demise of its sovereignty, many of the national values would be lost which, beyond doubt, comprise a major part of its potential to sustain the living conditions of each individual and nation as a whole.[55]

To further understand and contextualize the explicitly social-Darwinist undertones of "the survival of the fittest" in these writings, it is very important to note that Goldstein had done his medical rotations as an intern (*Klinischer Assistent*) not only in Berlin for one year (after Theodor Ziehen

[1862–1950] had assumed the directorship of the Department of Psychiatry at the Charité) but—what is very important for the discussion of Goldstein's eugenics inclinations—for another year in southern Germany with the most ardent supporter of psychiatric eugenics, Alfred Erich Hoche (1865–1943), as chief of the psychiatric department at the University of Freiburg.[56] Between 1906 and the outbreak of World War I, Goldstein completed his residency there before moving to the University of Koenigsberg in East Prussia, where he graduated for a second time with a *Habilitation* thesis in neurology. Most of his writing of the thesis manuscript, however, seems to have been done in the psychiatric department of the University of Freiburg im Breisgau. Apart from his endorsement and advocacy of eugenics in the psychiatric community of the German-speaking countries, Hoche had also become infamous as a major opponent of Sigmund Freud's (1856–1940) psychoanalysis, which he rebutted primarily on brain psychiatric and somaticist grounds based largely on the brain psychiatric approach of his mentor Wilhelm Griesinger (1817–68), in Berlin.[57]

Hoche is known particularly for his drastic postwar views on eugenics and the forced sterilization of the mentally and physically disabled.[58] At the time that Goldstein entered his clinic, however, Hoche was already teaching eugenics theory to medical students and he interacted with an international network of eugenicists around the Swiss psychiatrist Auguste Forel (1848–1931).[59] This is apparent, for example, in his 1903 treatise *Die Grenzen der geistigen Gesundheit* (The boundaries of mental health); in *Zur Frage der Zeugnisunfaehigkeit der geistig anormalen Personen* (On the question of bearing testimony in mentally abnormal persons), co-written with Austrian lawyer August Finger (1858–1935); and in "Konstitutionelle Psychopathien" (Constitutional psychopathies), Hoche's contribution in the seminal *Lehrbuch der Psychiatrie* (Texbook of psychiatry), which Hoche co-edited with eminent psychiatrist Otto Binswanger (1852–1929) from the University of Jena and other colleagues.[60]

The respective sections in Goldstein's book *On Eugenics* reveal subject titles and content very similar to those in related publications of Hoche's writings, such as "Die Koerperlichen und Geistigen Faehigkeiten der Bevoelkerung" (The physical and mental abilities of the population); "Das Erziehungsproblem—Herabgesetzte Zeugungsfaehigkeit bei den Geisteskrankheiten" (The educational problem—On the decreased capability to bear witness in the mentally ill); and "Die so genannte nervoese

Entartung—Geisteskrankheit" (On nervous degeneration—Mental illness).[61] Regarding Goldstein's writing in the book, in various respects it shows a very standardized and abstract narrative, featuring many reasons for the rhetoric used—especially when discussing the ethical views that are put forward: "one should not threaten the lives of the mentally ill"—and standard psychiatric tropes of the time.[62] It is very likely that Hoche even had a direct influence on the writing process, perhaps editing passages of the book itself; many of the contemporary *Ordinarius* professors often substantially rewrote the theses they supervised.[63] However, this hypothesis would have to be corroborated, though it is unlikely that any documentation or correspondence with Goldstein after his move to Koenigsberg (today Kaliningrad, in Russia) can still be found, as most of the material in the University Archives of Koenigsberg was lost in the destruction of the Second World War.[64]

After the First World War, with its countless casualties and nearly three million mutilated soldiers, Hoche become notorious for his collaborative work with law professor, and later provost of the University of Leipzig, Karl Binding (1841–1920), in which both explored and sanctioned negative eugenics approaches to what they called the problem of "bodily and mental degeneration."[65] For psychiatrists and neurologists this was an ongoing research problem since the beginning of the century, when various members of the Deutsche Gesellschaft fuer Nervenheilkunde (German Society for the Nerve Sciences)—including psychiatrists, neurologists, and pathologists such as Hoche, Ruedin, Emil Kraepelin (1856–1926), and Oswald Bumke (1877–1950)—entered into a debate about an assumed increase in "functional nervous disorders."[66] Relations between psychiatrists and eugenicists were common at that time and are represented in Kraepelin's article "On Degeneration" ("*Zur Entartungsfrage*") published in 1908, only three years after the Nordic group Gesellschaft fuer Rassenhygiene (Society for Racial Hygiene) had been founded in Munich.[67] The implication was a major shift in concern away from the social origins of disease as affecting the individual and toward a primarily biologistic perspective that envisaged the "collective culture" or "folk body" (*Volkskoerper*).[68]

In "On Degeneration," Kraepelin also identified a number of medically relevant phenomena in modern society to be addressed by psychiatrists: an increased frequency of insanity, a higher suicide rate, greater numbers of epileptics and drug addicts, and a decline in the general birth rate.[69] He especially emphasized the roles played by alcohol and syphilis, as agents toxic to the "germ plasma"—these themes also feature in one-third of the whole text in Goldstein's book *On Eugenics*.[70] In this regard, as pointed out by Kraepelin's colleagues Hoche and Ruedin, what could have been more devastating than the Great War, with its millions of casualties "negatively selected" from the germ line?[71] In a way, both had taken up Kraepelin's legacy after the First World War: Ruedin as director of the Demographic Study Unit (*Demographische Abteilung*) at the leading and globally renowned German Research Institute for Psychiatry;[72] and Hoche by explicitly formulating a psychopathology- and neurology-based degeneration thesis, founded on dubious statistical data and fostered by the views of "therapeutic killing"—that is, an assumption that medical remedies were available to decrease the number of the mentally disabled. This position was also shared by Ruedin, when he euphemistically wrote of "below-average material which the softened process of elimination [*gemilderte Ausmerze*] leaves behind in the arena of humanitarian activity."[73]

In response to what they saw as the Darwinian process of "natural selection" being decelerated or even stopped in postwar Germany, Ruedin and Hoche launched severe polemics against the social welfare programs of the Weimar Republic.[74] In a Kraepelinian vein, the social welfare programs appeared as highly problematic and unwarranted expenditures because they secured the longevity of populations regarded as "of low value" and thus negatively contributed to the deterioration of the "germ plasm," such as through increasing substance abuse and alcoholism.[75] During the Weimar Republic this view emanated as a battle credo of the far right, and early Nazi doctors began to marginalize psychiatric and neurological research because it addressed degenerate patients, or "conditions of hereditary or early childhood degeneration of the brain," as Hoche and Binding formulated in their infamous 1920 pamphlet *On the Liberation of the Annihilation of Life Not Worth Living*:

> For the non-physician, it must be pointed out that conditions of 'mental death' have to be faced in [this] group, [further] in the dementia-associated changes of the brain, in conditions that lay people call the softening of the brain, in dementia paralytica, . . . juvenile dementia praecox—in which a great number of patients reaches most advanced states of imbecility—and in the gross morphological changes of the brain.[76]

Along with the emergence of racial hygiene as a respected scientific discipline came a parallel view of the mentally ill and mentally defective in purely economic terms as a national burden.[77] In their influential work, Binding and Hoche felt that those with severe mental retardation were without a sense of the value of life and put an enormous strain on the gross national income. Binding and Hoche believed that the elimination of such individuals could be construed as a "humane" and "acceptable" gesture.[78] Later, on the eve of the Second World War, as has been well investigated in historical scholarship, mechanisms put into place for an active euthanasia program targeted first mentally and physically disabled children and then the mentally ill and somatically handicapped adults. Registrations were reviewed by an advisory committee called the Committee for the Scientific Treatment of Severe Genetically Determined Illness and were selected and transported to the appropriate institutions.[79] Eventually, the same committee, which based its policies largely on the Binding and Hoche treatise, received authorization from Adolf Hitler (1889–1945) to administer an adult euthanasia program under the supervision of physician Victor Brack (1904–48).[80]

In a similar form, though of course with a different political and medical direction, Goldstein's early functional anatomical interests became interwoven with the cultural discourses of "degeneration" and "exhaustion" in *On Eugenics*.[81] On the one hand, Goldstein described here his models and theories of brain functioning coupled with deeper clinical insights into intelligence, cognition, and emotional functions, though these ultimately proved to be among the fixed ideas of the period—following his training mentor Hoche—being scientifically questionable and regretfully promulgated alongside racist discourses and imprecise, speculative talk of degeneration and neurodegeneration. On the other hand, the book is hence highly revealing of the culture of the late Wilhelminian Empire on the eve of World War I.[82] It contextualizes neurological practice even though the state of contemporary knowledge was quite demanding:

> The reality of intellect, of self-determination, which even in its most primitive form represents essential characteristics of man, dooms to failure any breeding experiment of the usual type. However, if the relation of hereditary conditions aims not at specific characteristics but aspires to meliorate the human race by eliminating the unfit individuals, such endeavour presupposes a thorough knowledge of

> the significance of individual peculiarities for human natures. And who would venture any decision in this respect at the present state of research![83]

This strongly indicates that even the great holistic neurologist had paid tribute to the demands of contemporary social discourses on "weeding out the unfit" and "mobilizing" the bodies of the German people, on the cusp of the "Great War." At the same time, Goldstein's early embrace of eugenics—even if we subtract the influences of Hoche's mentorship—can also be read as a concession to limited therapeutic options and neurological nihilism at a time when institutionalization, physical therapy, and electrophysiological applications were the only options for treating psychiatric and neurological patients.[84] Goldstein was quite explicit about this when he discussed sterilization of the mentally ill in relation to the passing in 1907 of sexual sterilization legislation in the state of Indiana: "Following the judgement of a committee of experts and members of the administration an improvement of the mental health condition of the patient cannot be anticipated. In order to prevent offspring from the patient, an operation should be performed, which is the most secure and effective [method]."[85]

CONCLUSION

Rarely has the scholarship on eugenics history explored the fact that German-American émigré neurologist and rehabilitation specialist Kurt Goldstein had profoundly embraced eugenicist and racial-anthropological ideals, as found in his concise publication *On Eugenics* from 1913.[86] In this early work, Goldstein pondered, for example, the interdependencies of structural brain anomalies that have clinical neurological symptoms. With respect to *On Eugenics*, the argumentation becomes somewhat interwoven with elements from the "degeneration" and "exhaustion" discourse, which displays major cultural characteristics of Weimar medicine and science.[87] Among some of his other claims, Goldstein stated that "the relationship of hereditary conditions" points "not at specific characteristics, but aspires to meliorate the human race by eliminating the unfit individuals."[88] With similar biologistic—and in many respects militaristic—formal rhetoric, he came to side with many ardent racial anthropologists and medical philosophers, as they embraced notions of the "hardening of the people's body" or the "cleansing of the nation's health system of useless patients."[89]

At the end of this chapter, we have now come full circle. Beginning with Goldstein's socialization in the multicultural and open city of Breslau during the last decades of the German Empire, and having seen the emergence of his early interests in philosophy, medicine, and psychiatry, we see the *first paradox*: how this outstanding interdisciplinary scholar on brain injuries as well as the rehabilitation of psychic and motor disorders could become so drawn to the introduction and advocacy of strong and negative eugenic measures in the area of psychiatry.[90] In particular, Goldstein's enthusiasm for the military—being an officer of the reserve himself—as a "character and nation building school" proved pivotal. His early enthusiasm for the military can thus be interpreted as a vital part of his own assimilation process into Wilhelminian society along with the larger process of en-culturing (*kulturelle Einbindung*) the bourgeois Jewry in Imperial Germany—which also led Goldstein to employ militaristic language and war metaphors in the context of social-Darwinist theorizing.[91] Yet despite his early turn toward these nationalistic stances and ideologies, along with the rather direct influences of Hoche, his medical superior at the University of Freiburg and the central eugenics advocate in German psychiatry, there is another major element—as a *second paradox*—that combined Goldstein's progressivism with the restrictive and drastic promotion of eugenics, as psychiatry faced the effects of therapeutic nihilism and hopelessness in the first two decades of the twentieth century, both in central Europe and in North America.[92] This chapter has contextualized eugenics in German neuropsychiatry and wider psychological science, showing how more vigorous eugenic programs were abetted by emergent conceptualizations of brain structure and mental processes at work in the historical period and intellectual milieu under consideration.

Though much of this explanation would have to be based on the rather implicit statements that Goldstein made throughout *On Eugenics*, a change of direction nevertheless becomes noticeable with regard to his involvement with the partly successful treatment of the war injured by his multidisciplinary team at the Frankfurt Institute of Neurology after the First World War.[93] The respective approaches to physiological experimentation, clinical psychology, and early rehabilitation could flourish only in the particular cultural milieu of the liberal city of Frankfurt am Main.[94]

In Frankfurt we see a contrast to the university settings in the cities of Breslau and Freiburg—the cities in which Goldstein's eugenic thinking originated—with their garrisons, while the pressures of forced migration in Nazi Germany eventually came to destroy the Goldstein group's enormous neurological, rehabilitational, and social medical potential.[95]

Figure 7.2 Kurt Goldstein and Martin Scheerer re-established an experimental laboratory for neurology and psychology at the Montefiore teaching hospital in the Bronx, New York. National Library of Medicine, Digital Collections, Bethesda, MD.

The outcome of the reconstruction efforts undertaken by Goldstein at Columbia University and the academic Montefiore Hospital in the Bronx, New York (see Figure 7.2), in no way resembled the interdisciplinary research program that Goldstein had headed in Frankfurt and Berlin in Germany.[96] Moreover, the North American reception of the work occurred almost solely in specialized rehabilitation communities, with aphasiologists Gordon Allport (1897–1967) and Gardner Murphy (1895–1979), or with psychologists Abraham Maslow (1908–70) and Carl Rogers (1902–87).[97] As psychologist Hans-Lukas Teuber later recalled, "The incredibly rapid development of our field in the 50's and 60's [*sic*] of this century was bound to make Goldstein into an historical figure, seemingly before his time, but history has a curious way of reaching into the present and of replaying half-forgotten themes in the future."[98]

The narrative of this chapter does not attempt to relativize Goldstein's holistic and humanist neurological theory; nevertheless, it seeks to emphasize the important overlap of core social progressivist beliefs and relics of medical traditionalism shared by many psychiatrists, social medical physicians, public health activists, and racial hygienists of the 1910s and 1920s in the German-speaking countries and also in the United States.[99] This second "paradox of eugenics"—as I have used the term above—haunted many social progressivists of that period. Many of these individualists shared eugenics ideals and were supportive of counselling, sexual segregation, and sterilization means. However, prominent scientists and intellectuals, such as Goldstein after his emigration to North America or Canadian social and health-care politician Tommy Douglas, eventually overthrew and discarded their earlier beliefs.[100] To the contrary, psychiatrists such as Ruedin completely endorsed eugenics and paved the way for the infamous medical context in Nazi Germany, while Ruedin's own development could be traced from being politically a socialist in the 1910s and 1920s to becoming a National Socialist during the 1930s.[101] Ruedin frankly called for the sterilization of so-called *Ballastexistenzen* (ballast lives) and prided himself not only on running the most extensive research program on psychiatric epidemiology at the time—based on the largest mental health database in the world, on which later applied eugenics programs could draw—but also for being one of the designated commentators on the Law for the Prevention of Hereditarily Diseased Offspring, together with West Prussian physician Arthur Guett (1891–1949) and Halle lawyer Falk Ruttke (1894–1955).[102]

In considering Goldstein's book *On Eugenics* in its wider social and cultural context, similar Canadian examples come into focus as well—Douglas's position, for instance, or that of the "Famous Five."[103] It is apparent that all of these intellectuals held very strong beliefs about social progressivism and reformism, which became paired with a parallel belief in technological utopias to reach these goals. More conservative—in the sense of psychological and psychiatric traditionalism—was the approach of John M. MacEachran (1878–1971), psychologist and chair of the Alberta Eugenics Board, whose promotion of biostatistics, advocacy for forced sterilization, and application of racist ideology could in many ways be compared with the position of Ruedin, the protagonist of psychiatric epidemiology and racial anthropology. This chapter has emphasized the ways in which eugenics discourse influenced psychiatric education and governmental policy as well as social attitudes through sterilization conceptions and research practices that are addressed in the introduction to this volume (see also chapter 1 on MacEachran and eugenics in Alberta).

Though many were rather indirect—through participation at international meetings, in the reading of international journals such as the *Eugenics Review*, and mediated through the American reception of forced sterilization—there were also more direct exchanges that brought Canadian eugenics advocates close to their German counterparts.[104] MacEachran, as an Ontario-born psychologist, had the distinction of being the only Canadian student of German experimental psychologist Wilhelm Wundt (1832–1920). While in Europe in 1909, MacEachran developed a hybrid interest in both philosophy and psychology while also subject to Wundt's discussions, in his *Grundzuege der physiologischen Psychologie*, of Galton's views on the inheritability of mental traits.[105] In addition, one Canadian neuroscientist came to study at Ruedin's German Institute for Psychiatric Research in Munich: Ardrey W. Downs (1913–66), later head of the University of Alberta's Department of Physiology and Pharmacology and outspoken critic of eastern European immigration to Canada, visited the German institute for one year, in 1928, to learn neuropharmacological techniques. Downs continued to publish papers on the biological basis of eugenics in relation to his major field, the autonomous nervous system control of bodily glands.[106]

Nevertheless, despite the rise of Nazism in central Europe and the massive application of negative eugenics measures resulting in the dreadful mass murder of tens of thousands of mentally handicapped,[107] Goldstein himself remained understandably silent on the issue of eugenics after the end of World War I and embraced the early neurorehabilitation approach along with teaching self-adaptive skills to patients. He thus took a turn to the new therapeutic options to compensate for lost functions—whether mental or physical—as these became available through the interdisciplinary clinical work of his research group.[108] While in the 1920s Goldstein had not anticipated the inhumane and murderous scope of the "political philosophy" of National Socialism—which is often portrayed as having changed Douglas's personal views on eugenics after a 1936 visit to the Third Reich—he later became a victim of the very same nationalist and racist ideologies that had accompanied German eugenics thought early on, ideologies that he had once deeply embraced himself and that now forced him to leave the site of his prolific neurological and rehabilitational work, in his home country, while being barely able to save his own life after the GeStapo entered his patient clinic in Berlin.

8

Too Little, Too Late

Compensation for Victims of Coerced Sterilization

Paul J. Weindling

During the twentieth century, perhaps a million, perhaps more, involuntary sterilizations were forcibly performed as a medically and psychiatrically justified "solution" for a range of inherited illnesses and behaviours. A second wave of coercive sterilizations then came about as a birth control measure. Medical professionals carried out these operations in violation of basic human rights and for reasons that were medically and demographically dubious. At the outset, there was considerable confidence in such modern surgical or radiological solutions to the presumed economic and genetic burden of the sick, disabled, and socially deviant on the healthy, and in the elimination of pathogenic genes from the gene pool. The criminality of coerced sterilization was slow to be recognized even after the Nuremberg trial prosecutions for the medical crimes under German National Socialism. The problem was simply that the German authorities declined to accept the criminality of the Nazi-era sterilizations. It was only in the 1980s that this criminality began to be accepted, opening the way to questions of compensation. Yet compensation, let alone the right to a compensatory pension, has been slow in being realized—so that many victims died before receiving even recognition of the injustice of the violation to their bodily integrity. In addition, in Germany as elsewhere, documents have been difficult to access and collections have been destroyed, making it challenging to render medical and state authorities accountable. Different countries and provinces adopted differing procedures, and compensation has been piecemeal and paltry.

ORIGINS

Turning to the origins of coerced sterilization, we find the coincidence of a new surgical technique and rationale for its large-scale imposition. The belief in cleansing the genetic stream of the nation or race was an overriding incentive. Tubal sterilization through the method of vasectomy was a surgical technique pioneered in 1890 and then used by Albert J. Ochsner (1858–1925) for so-called degenerates.[1] Another technique increasingly considered for sterilization was X-rays, newly discovered by Wilhelm Conrad Roentgen (1845–1923) in 1895 in Wurzburg, Germany, and by the time of the First World War proven to have sterilizing effects. Soon after 1900 came calls for sterilization of chronic alcoholics and other bearers of hereditary degenerative traits. Eugenicists rapidly saw how sterilization could be used to prevent the proliferation of unwanted progeny. They put themselves in the position of medical guardians of the nation and race and assumed powers over the capacity to father and bear children.

The rediscovery of the Mendelian laws of heredity around 1900 meant German biologists and doctors adapted the traditional pedigree to show "racial poisons" carried by both male and female lines—often by construing oversimplified monogenetic Mendelian inheritance sequels and charts (see also chapter 2). This broadened the potential carriers of pathogenic genes. Since the Dresden International Hygiene Exhibition of 1911, vivid representations of hereditary illness using pictograms and symbols were used to communicate genetic risks to a wider public. Charts using symbols and pictorial representations of statistics functioned as propaganda in exhibits on hereditary threats to racial health and on a shrinking population. These drew public attention to schizophrenics, the so-called "schizoid," and epileptics (all deemed to be indicators of mental subnormality), who were to be identified, as well as the healthy "carriers." The intensifying barrage of propaganda claimed that all of these mentally ill and hidden carriers posed risks to hereditary health. The apparently healthy were deemed carriers of recessive genes for schizophrenia and other mental disorders. Eugenicists attempted to raise the spectre of a severe threat to collective racial health so as to justify wide-ranging genetic screening of the population, especially prior to marriage, as well as a colossal program of sterilization.[2]

Among the protagonists of sterilization for alcoholics was the pioneer of psychiatric eugenics, Ernst Ruedin (1874–1952), who claimed from

1916 that schizophrenia was inherited on a Mendelian basis.[3] Swiss-born, Ruedin was influenced by Alfred Ploetz (1860–1940), whose first wife was Ruedin's sister. Ploetz was the founder of the Gesellschaft fuer Rassenhygiene (Society for Racial Hygiene) in 1905 (which was the first eugenics society), while its designation as the German Society for Racial Hygiene was later added in 1910.[4] Ploetz advocated some form of what he called "chromosomal engineering" as (again, in his jargon) a "humane" form of eugenics.[5] Rather than measures based fully in scientific evidence, the faith in sterilization was more a utopian expectation than any objectively proven technique of diminishing what was called the "genetic burden" on society. Ruedin had originally proposed sterilization as a means of combatting the hereditary effects of alcoholism in 1903. In 1916, he published a ground-breaking paper applying Mendelian genetics to what was known as "dementia praecox" or "schizophrenia."[6] He pioneered large-scale "genealogical-demographic" or hereditary studies into the genetics of schizophrenia and other conditions at the German Institute for Psychiatry, founded in 1917 in Munich by the psychiatrist Emil Kraepelin (1856–1926) and, from 1924, affiliated as a Kaiser Wilhelm Institute. Ruedin advocated systematic screening of populations over generations for psychiatric and physical diseases and defects. The German Research Institute for Psychiatry provided increased opportunities for research on patterns of inheritance.

NAZI STERILIZATION

Ruedin remained a dedicated advocate of sterilization. He was largely responsible for the medical scope of the compulsory German sterilization legislation rapidly drafted after the Nazi takeover. The new Nazi ministerial director of the Prussian Medical Department, Dr. Arthur Julius Guett (1891–1949), wanted all sterilization records centrally archived and available to researchers.[7] This research element was also distinctive in Germany. Following the scientific conviction that psychiatric illness was genetically caused, persons designated schizophrenics became the largest group among those compulsorily sterilized. German sterilizations under National Socialism occurred on a larger scale than anywhere else in Europe or North America. Indeed, while sterilization in Germany increased, North American rates were diminishing (see table 8.1). Ultimately, roughly 65,000 sterilizations were performed in the United States and approximately

3,500 in Canada, according to the existing literature to date.[8] The United Kingdom saw very few sterilizations—six are known to have taken place in Leicester, of blind children. Sterilization legislation was proposed there initially, but it was rejected by the House of Commons in July 1931.

Table 8.1 Overview on global sterilization programs and subsequent compensation claims

Country	Date of Sterilizations	Estimate Numbers of Persons	Compensation	Amount	Apology
USA – 33 states	1907-83	65000	No	Some apologies by state governors. Uniquely in North Carolina with application deadline of summer 2014: $20,000 US dollars (~ 18340 Euros)	Virginia 2002
Switzerland	1928-85	3600 Zurich	No	1999 refused	
Canada – Alberta	1928-72	ca. 1920	Yes	Individual claims by litigation against the provincial administration	
Canada – British Columbia	????	????	No	No	
Denmark	1929/35-1967	11000			
Finland	1930-ca. 70	1460			
Norway	1934-77	40000			
Germany – Vasectomy, X-ray sterilization for a few older women	1934-45	375000	Yes, but no full apology 16000 claimants	1980 – 5000 Deutsch Mark (~ 2556 Euros) 1990 – additional monthly social security allowance 2011 extended to children of euthanasia victims	Partial apology and suspension of law
Sweden	1935-75	63000	1999 - ca. 200 applicants	175,000 Swedish Kronas (~ 16588 Euros)	
Estonia	1936 (1 April 1937 in force) -Oct 1940 1941-45	41 (no data from 1939)			No

Country	Date of Sterilizations	Estimate Numbers of Persons	Compensation	Amount	Apology
Germany – mixed-race children	1937	385	In theory yes, as sterilization was "illegal". Not known if compensated. Video testimonies exist in Shoah Foundation		No
Austria (annexed by Germany)	1938-45	ca. 6000	1945-95 — occasional under victims of Nazism law (*Opfer-fürsorgegesetz*). 1995 National-fonds – yes, but not as a special category		No specific apology by the Austrian Medical Association
Latvia	1938	63			No
Iceland	1938				
Germany and Auschwitz – Xray sterilizations, and experimental injections	1942-44	ca. 900	1951-1965 1998-2004	1951 – ca. 1000 to 3000 Deutsche Mark (~ 12000 Euros) Today ca. 12000 Euro 1998-04 – ca. 7900 Euro	2012 apology by German Medical Association
Japan	1941-45/ 1949-70	435/ 14000			
Kenya – Mau Mau prisoner castrations by the British	ca. 1952-61		Legal action in progress since 2012		No
Hungarian Roma					
Czech/Slovak Roma	1973-2001		2008 rejected		
India	1975-77		No		
Peru	1995-2000	331,600 women, 25,590 men (source: Wikipedia)	No		
Uzbekistan	continuing	?	No		

Source: Table designed by Paul J. Weindling, based on information from Kathrin Braun and Svea Luise Herrmann (2011): The Long Shadow of Biopolitical Rationality: Coming to Terms with Nazi-Sterilization Policy in Germany (or not) and Paul J. Weindling, *Victims and Survivors of Nazi Human Experiments: Science and Suffering in the Holocaust* (London, Eng.: Bloomsbury, 2015).

The German law of 1933 was influenced by legislation in California, where the numbers of sterilizations were the highest in North America at around 10,000, but also by prior legislation in Denmark in 1929, the Swiss canton of Vaud in 1928, and Finland in 1930.[9] The Nazi law was modelled on Prussian draft legislation of 1932 but added the element of compulsion that characterized earlier American (and especially Californian) legislation since 1907 in Indiana. The German law reflected Nazi enthusiasm for a biological "solution" to social problems and for purifying the race.

In July 1933, the newly instituted Nazi state passed legislation for compulsory sterilization of the sick and disabled. Between 1934 and 1945, roughly 350,000 persons were forcibly sterilized in Germany and Nazi-annexed Austria. In addition, there were approximately 1,000 sterilizations in the so-called Reichsgau Sudetenland (annexed from Czechoslovakia).[10] Sterilizations also took place in the annexed former free city of Danzig and the eastern Baltic Memel peninsula. Questions arose regarding sterilization of the unfit in the German-annexed Warthegau area of western Poland and of repatriated ethnic Germans.[11] It can also be argued that sterilization was a key stage on the "slippery slope" to the mass killings of psychiatric and neurological patients. Sterilization could be imposed as a condition for discharge from a psychiatric hospital. What is clear is that as the rate of sterilizations in Nazi Germany diminished in 1940, that of killing psychiatric patients increased. In the case of Nazi-annexed Austria from March 1938, the number of sterilizations was proportionately lower, but euthanasia killings were at a high level.[12] Regional variations existed: compulsory sterilizations occurred at a high rate in the North German port city of Hamburg but were proportionately lower in the northern Bavarian region of Franconia, which was both Protestant in terms of its heritage and enthusiastically Nazi.[13] For both sterilization and euthanasia, the diagnosis of schizophrenia was a major cause for falling victim to the procedures.[14] The original sterilization law passed in July 1933 was aimed at a range of conditions believed to be inherited. These conditions included epilepsy, inherited (as opposed to acquired) blindness, and inherited deafness, and a link to feeble-mindedness was assumed. This posed questions as to how to distinguish supposedly inherited from acquired conditions (similar diagnostic categories were also applied in Alberta's eugenics program, as chapters 1 and 4 demonstrate).

The Scandinavian and Baltic countries enforced sterilization in parallel with Germany: following the Danish precedent, Norway legislated sterilization in 1934, Sweden in 1935, and Estonia in 1936. Overall, one can see a pattern of support for sterilization in Protestant countries. The German law imposed sterilization on presumed hereditary schizophrenics, the so-called "feeble-minded," sufferers of Huntington's chorea or muscular dystrophy, persons deemed to be hereditarily blind or deaf (creating the necessity of distinguishing between acquired and congenital blindness and deafness), so-called "mental defectives," and chronic alcoholics. Tribunals of two doctors and a lawyer decreed sterilization irrespective of the patient's wishes. A person could appeal to a higher tribunal, but this was typically unsuccessful. The Nazi onslaught on civil law removed the legal basis for the inviolability of a citizen's body, thereby undermining protection against vicarious experimentation. The medically unfit were increasingly vulnerable to invasive sterilization, as racial hygiene posited the need to cleanse the German hereditary stream as it flowed from generation to generation—these developments need to be understood in terms of emotive propaganda. The sterilization law was extended by Nazi legislation, to include castration of criminals and homosexuals from November 1933. By 1945 over two hundred "genetic health courts" had mandated the forced sterilization of over 400,000 persons. Most sterilizations under the 1933 law were carried out prior to 1940. Gerhard Wagner (1888–1939), leader of the Nazi Physicians' League, opposed the sterilization law as insufficiently racial, and the outbreak of the war saw a shift to the forced killing of the mentally ill and disabled, with an estimated 220,000 victims. Ruedin saw eugenics and euthanasia as a research opportunity for studies of "idiocy" at the Heidelberg Psychiatric Institute, where a group of around fifty children were exhaustively studied and then their brains were dissected.[15]

Most sterilizations were surgical. Men underwent vasectomy, involving the cutting of sperm ducts. Castration was also possible, at times inflicted on homosexuals. Female sterilization was more complex and had a higher rate of fatalities: the recommended method was to sever the oviducts or

Fallopian tubes. From 1935 X-ray sterilizations were permitted for older women. X-ray sterilization of Jews was trialled at Auschwitz during 1943, so as to produce a sterile workforce that could be worked to death. The Nazi slave labour force underwent sporadic forced sterilization and forced abortion.[16]

POSTWAR GERMANY

At the end of the war, the sterilization legislative and administrative machinery was only partially dismantled. Issues of compensation and care for victims were neglected. Given that the Allies were directly involved in Germany, both as regards war crimes measures and in denazifying German public health, the Allied responses to sterilization can be seen as illustrative of the extent that Nazism had damaged demands for negative eugenic measures, and for eugenics in general. A question arises: Did the Allies regard sterilization as an act of Nazi criminality or accept it as a legitimate component of public health and reproductive medicine? After the war, surgical reversal of sterilization was not offered by the German medical profession or state authorities. Allied efforts to prosecute doctors involved with sterilization were unsuccessful.[17] Compensation in terms of a single 5,000 DM payment was granted only from 1980, and a monthly pension supplement of 300 DM (now approximately 1,200 euros) was approved. A full apology to the victims by the German state has yet to be made, although there have been a series of partial gestures. Compensation for victims of sterilization can be characterized as late and limited. After World War II, some German victim organizations requested that victims be operated on for "re-fertilization" to restore the capacity to have children. These demands were ignored by German medical officials. In fact, the reversal of sterilization would have had good chances of success in cases of vasectomy. It would have provided the most effective form of redress. The German medical profession did not (until 2012) accept responsibility for sterilization as a medical measure, thereby effectively endorsing the Nazi coercive sterilization.[18]

The Federal German authorities drew a distinction between routine sterilization, for which there was no compensation, and experimental operations, notably at Auschwitz. From 1949 the United Nations pressed for compensation for victims of medical experimentation. On July 26,

1951, the Federal Republic's observer informed the UN in New York City that West Germany would compensate all victims—not as an act of the Bundestag (Parliament) and thus subject to democratic scrutiny, but as an administrative declaration. This was possible under a decree by German Chancellor Adenauer in 1951 that victims of medical experiments should be supported.[19] In practice, it meant single lump-sum compensation on a varying scale. In Block 10 at Auschwitz, gynecologist and hormone researcher Carl Clauberg (1898–1957) sterilized several hundred Dutch, Greek, and French Jewish women by means of experimental injections of a fluid designed to seal the Fallopian tubes. The formaldehyde-based fluid was often extremely painful. Clauberg also conducted sterilizations at the end of the war in the Ravensbrueck concentration camp. The Federal German authorities tried to argue that these sterilizations were routine, to avoid paying compensation, but this argument was based on Clauberg having persuaded Heinrich Himmler (1900–45) that his technique was already established. Victims of such experimental sterilizations received single lump-sum compensation rather than a pension. The compensation was calculated on the basis of loss of earnings, so if a victim had a prosperous husband, she was paid nothing.[20]

The second group of those forcibly sterilized to be compensated were the mainly Polish and Greek male victims of X-ray sterilization. Most had then had one or two testicles removed so that the doctor in charge, a certain Horst Schumann (1906–83), could evaluate the effects of different X-ray doses. The Federal German authorities paid relatively low rates of compensation for such injuries. The Auschwitz surgical registers indicate at least 137 such victims. X-ray sterilization by Schumann at Auschwitz was mentioned at the International Military Tribunal at Nuremberg. One Polish victim gave eloquent testimony in court at the Nuremberg Doctors Trials held from December 1946 to August 1947.[21] Historian Aleksandra Loewenau has been reconstructing the experience of this victim group.[22] As we know from studies of the fate of eugenicists—notably Ruedin, Fritz Lenz (1887–1976), and Otmar von Verschuer (1896–1969)[23]—at the end of the war any comprehensive program to purge German medicine of its racial element was realized only very partially.[24] Remarkably, the Kaiser Wilhelm Institute for Anthropology was allowed to continue in the American sector of Berlin until 1948.[25] The geneticist Hans Nachtsheim (1890–1979) remained in office negotiating at various times with the Soviets and the

Americans; Verschuer, who had left Berlin in February 1945 with part of the Kaiser Wilhelm Institute for Anthropology's equipment, attempted to secure an academic post, and Lenz was re-employed at the major British scientific centre of Goettingen in West Germany.[26]

The American war crimes authorities received information from an agent code-named "Bruno." On the basis of his information, a report, titled *Report on Sterilisation in Germany and Occupied Countries* had been written that was forwarded to the Americans by the UN War Crimes Commission; its Czechoslovak representative had received it through a Czechoslovak minister. As it turned out, "Bruno" was Dr. Theo Lang (1898–1957), who at the time was senior medical officer at the Kantonale Heil- und Pflegeanstalt Herisau (County Hospital) in Switzerland. Lang had worked at the German Research Institute for Psychiatry until 1941 and had been one of the founders of the Nazi Physicians' League, done research on the genetic basis of homosexuality and had been a close associate of Ruedin. Lang now gave information on the political and SS affiliations of eugenicists, particularly those in Munich. The Americans referred to his "'Black List' of National Socialist criminals,"[27] which pointed out that a group of Ruedin's assistants had been involved not only in X-ray sterilization and euthanasia but also in the assassination of the Austrian chancellor Engelbert Dollfuss (1892–1934). In a series of Swiss newspaper articles Lang suggested that Ruedin's assistants were primarily SS doctors.[28] The KWI (then known as the DFA) for Psychiatry continued although Ruedin was arrested by the Americans and subjected to searching interrogation. In September 1945, Ruedin submitted a memorandum to US authorities outlining his contacts with leading Nazis concerning racial policy and psychiatry. His memorandum played up his tensions with the SS (the Nazi Defence Corps), while conveniently masking the fact that euthanasia was outside the sphere of competence of the SS—ultimately to cast himself in a better light. On June 16, 1946, eminent scientist Max Planck (1858–1947) even petitioned for Ruedin's release, depicting him as a scientist devoid of political intentions.

Lang's accusations were countered in a deposition to Rector Georg Hohmann (1880–1970) of the University of Munich on August 24, 1946. Lang was depicted as a grudge-bearing former SA General who in 1940 was excluded from Ruedin's institute. After the war, Ruedin and his assistant Bruno Schulz (1892–1942) argued that this preeminent Nazi psychiatrist was an opponent of both the SS and euthanasia, as stated in a deposition to the denazification tribunal on May 9, 1949. This overlooked Ruedin's joint project with the eminent psychiatrist Carl Schneider (1891–1946) of brain research on euthanasia victims in Heidelberg, carried out by Julius Deussen (1906–74), who had been Ruedin's assistant.[29] A victim of forced sterilization and Lang gave evidence in December 1949. In the end, Ruedin was not prosecuted but was apprehended for a considerable period through the pursuit of the Counter Intelligence Corps by the Americans. He was deemed a *Mitlaeufer* (follower) and ordered by the denazification tribunal to pay costs of 37,500 DM. Ruedin's detention showed that sterilization measures were regarded as an area of potential criminality.

Neurologist and medical intelligence officer Leo Alexander (1905–85) compiled a Combined Intelligence Operations Services report titled *Public Mental Health Practices in Germany: Sterilization and Execution of Patients Suffering from Nervous or Mental Disease, August 1945*.[30] Alexander here linked sterilization and euthanasia. He returned to his native Germany as medical expert for the prosecution at the Nuremberg trial of twenty physicians and three SS administrators. Certainly, for the Allied prosecution there was no inherent criminality in their previous eugenics programs. Alexander, the chief medical expert for the prosecution, had been a signatory of the American Neurological Society declaration of 1936 on human sterilization. This committee argued for a medically more rigorous eugenic approach to forced sterilization.[31] Between 1945 and 1947, Alexander changed from regarding the Germans under investigation as former colleagues who could provide potentially valuable medical information on wartime research to viewing them in pathological terms as mentally deranged criminals.

In November 1946, the American prosecutors at Nuremberg collected details of drugs used for procreation and sterilization as well as of doctors involved in sterilization.[32] A Staff Evidence Analysis included twenty-six letters from individuals sterilized as a result of verdicts by the hereditary health court for, for example, the remark by a sixteen-year-old girl—"What comes after the Third Reich—the fourth"—or for being part Jewish.[33] As the trial was being prepared, numerous victims of sterilization and racial policy wrote in. One case personally investigated by Alexander was that of a Holocaust survivor named Chaim Balicky, born February 28, 1920, at Dzialaszyoi, Kielce, now at a displaced persons' camp at Konstanz. Balicky spoke to Alexander about his experiences in Auschwitz and Dachau, where he was sterilized and castrated. On November 22, 1946, he provided the office of the Chief of Counsel for War Crimes with a deposition including eleven photos. Alexander noted Balicky's traits:

> Emotionally this man was deeply hurt and humiliated by his mutilation. He has not yet been able to tell even his own sisters about it. Although all this happened through no fault of his own, he feels deeply ashamed about his castration. He is afraid that his increasing gain of weight and loss of male characteristics are bound to ultimately give him away for the wreck which he has become. He feels that he has no future and has nothing to live for and has had no real life so far, and nothing to really live for ahead of him. At times his thought and emotions overcome him, and he begins to cry when talking about what has happened to him.
>
> When he heard over the radio that the people responsible for the German medical atrocities are going to be tried, he decided that it was his duty to come here and to testify although he is afraid that, esp. if his name is printed in newspapers, his sisters might find out about his condition that way. However, he feels that it is his duty to be helpful in bringing those responsible for the atrocities, to which he and others have been subjected, to justice.
>
> It appears that he is one of 100 young Jewish boys who were castrated for no reason other than to confirm the fact that they had been sterilised by sufficient X-ray radiation as if X-ray burns which resulted from a fifteen-minute exposure were not enough to prove that point. A great many of his fellow sufferers have in the meantime developed cancer of the irradiated skin. While his skin is severely indurated no evidence of cancer is yet discernible.[34]

The Allied zonal administration found that sterilization was problematic. War crimes prosecutions in the Soviet zone took as their legal basis the notion of crimes against humanity. From November 12 to 14, 1946, a trial of the deputy chair of the National Socialist hereditary health tribunal took place at the court in Schwerin in the Soviet Occupied Zone in East Germany. Indicted were the director of the health office, a medical officer, a member of the sterilization tribunal, and a medical director of a local hospital. Seven doctors were prosecuted for sterilization as a "crime against humanity."[35] The matter was by no means clear cut; after the initial convictions, the sentences were reduced or quashed by a higher court, and the case dragged on.

In the Western Zones, there was a noted lobby—including the public health expert Hans Harmsen (1899–1989), the geneticist Hans Nachtsheim, and the psychiatrist Karl Ludwig Bonhoeffer (1868–1948)—urging a new sterilization law, using the Weimar legislative proposals as a model. There were renewed calls for sterilization in the context of the family policy of the West German government under chancellor Konrad Adenauer (1876–1967). The initial ardour for prosecuting the perpetrators of sterilization and associated research in Nazi Germany dissipated rapidly.

GERMAN COMPENSATION COMPLEXITIES

Compensation for victims of medical experiments was first instituted in 1951.[36] At first, the German Federal Finance Ministry provided small amounts to the male victims of X-ray sterilization. A further phase of compensation came with funds provided by Germany to be administered on a devolved basis by the governments of victims' countries. In contrast to the Federal German allocation, the French tribunal awarded X-ray sterilization victims the highest rate of compensation. The United Nations (UN) had already ratified declarations on genocide and human rights, in 1948, and the UN's human rights division secured compensation for victims of Nazi human experiments.[37] Women's organizations took up the case of the need for compensation for women victims of the experiments, with particular attention paid to the victims of Ravensbrueck sulphonamide experiments and Clauberg's inter-uterine sterilization experiments. The UN's section on women kept a watchful eye on the issue.[38] The French survivors' organization *Association nationale des anciennes déportées et internées de la Résistance* had a number of women activists working on this issue. Victims had widely dispersed after the war and many nationalities were involved. The UN Commission on the Status of Women adopted at its fourth session in 1950 a resolution calling attention to the plight of women survivors of concentration camps who were subjected to medical experiments. The Economic and Social Council examined the report from the commission and stated that the UN would lend its support to negotiations between the Allied High Commission and the Federal German Government for compensation legislation in Germany for these victims. To this end, the Economic and Social Council adopted resolution 305 (XI) on July 14, 1950. The UN Secretary-General was asked to consider, with the competent authorities and institutions, the means for alleviating the plight of survivors of concentration camps who were victims of the so-called scientific experiments.

While the German authorities could award up to 25,000 DM (ca. 96,000 Euros today), most victims—especially sterilization victims—received a single payment of 3,000 DM (ca. 12,000 Euros today) or less. The UN wanted to compensate pain and suffering, but the Germans insisted on narrower criteria: medical damage to health and loss of earning capacity. This meant that victims of X-ray sterilization received only minimal compensation. Herein lay a bone of contention. Victims wrote about their state of mind and nerves, but this had no effect on the Federal Finance Ministry, which fixated on the earnings issue. Also, women deemed by the German authorities to be "housewives" were further disadvantaged. Victims felt that single, lump-sum payments were of little value. By August 1952, victims were already complaining about the meagre amounts. The UN's lawyers felt let down and undermined by German bureaucracy. Victims also felt let down. Many victims of compulsory sterilization found that as claimants they did not fit the available categories. One was an Austrian socialist who had left Nazi-occupied Austria for safety in the Netherlands but, after German occupation, was sterilized in Amsterdam.[39]

The four Allied occupying powers responded differently to sterilization, suspending the operations of the law. Only the Soviets abolished the law, on January 8, 1946, declaring it to be a crime against humanity and attempting to prosecute its perpetrators.[40] But even in the Soviet zone opinions were divided. Berlin psychiatrist Karl Bonhoeffer, at the Charité, argued that the sterilization law was medical rather than racial. In the Western Occupied Zones the situation remained complex. The British kept the law as valid but did not put it to actual use: this was out of a sense that it would allow victims to make claims for abuses. A renewed campaign for a sterilization law by Harmsen and Nachtsheim in the late 1950s and early 1960s, reflecting a strong alliance of sterilization advocates, aimed to keep sterilization as a eugenic measure in medical hands. In the Federal Republic of Germany during the same period, the 1933 sterilization law was viewed not as a Nazi law but as something comparable to US, Canadian, and Scandinavian laws. It therefore remained on the statute books but was not actively in operation. The League of Persons Damaged by "Euthanasia" and Compulsory Sterilization (*Bund der "Euthanasie"–Geschaedigten und Zwangssterilisierten*, or *BEZ*) was founded only in 1987. It has since campaigned for a full repeal of the law and a full apology: both aims have only partially been realized.

German victims of sterilization could from 1953 *attempt* to claim compensation under a general law for compensation of Nazi victims. This had certain advantages in that a lifelong monthly pension was provided. At first it was open to non-German residents but was rapidly changed to exclude them. All sorts of reasons for refusing any award were given. The first hardship compensation fund specifically for sterilized persons was established by the German Federal minister of finance in 1980, enabling victims of coercive sterilization to receive a one-off payment of 5,000 DM. Since 1988 victims could claim a regular monthly pension of 100 DM (today raised to 120 Euros after the introduction of the Euro in 1999, which is more than twice the amount of the original pension—excluding currency inflation). In September 2014 only 364 victims were claiming this pension.[41] But it has not been just a matter of financial compensation. Victims of sterilization campaigned to be acknowledged as "victims of Nazi persecution," in order to be included under the Federal German compensation law for Nazi victims. Victims campaigned for the annulment of the Nazi sterilization law. Their success was limited. The law has never been formally abolished. Only the rulings of the heredity courts were declared to be a Nazi injustice in 1988. Finally, in 2007, the Bundestag declared that the Nazi sterilization law of July 1933 was not constitutionally valid. By December 31, 2007, sterilization victims had submitted 3,696 applications for compensation. Of these, 2,100 were rejected—meaning that of the approximately 350,000 Nazi sterilization victims, fewer than 1 percent of cases were compensated. In 2011 compensation was extended to children of "euthanasia" victims. Clearly the compensation came late, and few were compensated. Moreover, the German situation remains unsatisfactory because of the lack of full acknowledgment that sterilization was a Nazi injustice.[42]

A later round of compensation payments became possible between 1998 and 2004. The German Foundation for Memory, Responsibility and the Future (*Stiftung Erinnerung, Verantwortung und Zukunft*) was founded primarily to compensate forced labourers with funds from industry and the state in Germany. Because of class actions against German pharmaceutical firms, the foundation provided compensation for victims who could make a "plausible" case as victims of what were called "other personal injuries."[43] This allowed non-German victims to make claims; however, given that sterilization victims in Auschwitz were exclusively Jewish, it made only a marginal difference. One Jewish victim went public denouncing the initial payment for lifelong sterilization as an insult and as humiliating.[44] Other claims were challenged because locations such as Dachau and Majdanek were not known as locations of experimental sterilizations. Claims brought by the The League of Persons Damaged by "Euthanasia" and Compulsory Sterilization (BEZ) were for the most part rejected.

INTERNATIONAL FAILURES

The German and central European case can be put into a wider international perspective. In comparison, coerced sterilization continued in Sweden until the mid-1960s, but the law there was finally repealed only in 2012. The Canadian province of Alberta repealed its 1928 Sexual Sterilization Act only in 1972. Coerced sterilization found an echo in population control programs fuelled by the ideology of a global population explosion in the Cold War period. Certain Indian states have been the targets of programs that were nominally voluntary yet in practice have involved high levels of coercion. China's one-child policy remains the most notorious biopolitical project. Social and ethnic minorities such as Indigenous peoples and the Nordic Sami (formerly known as Lapps) have also been vulnerable to sterilization. However, global population thinking has become less intervention-oriented since the late 1960s, and vasectomy has become an accepted form of voluntary contraception in the West. From the 1980s onwards, it has been increasingly realized, female education and career opportunities and rising prosperity resulted in many couples choosing to have one or two children or to remain childless. Disability rights campaigners have extended the positive acceptance of the variety of physical and mental states. The biological notion of schizophrenia was questioned by radical psychiatrists, and from the 1970s, medications have been found to be more effective than earlier in the management of mental disorders. Few countries have provided compensation apart from Sweden.[45] In the United States, only North Carolina has done so, for persons still alive to make a claim, and of the two Canadian provinces where sterilizations took place based on provincial law, compensation claims have succeeded only in the Alberta courts. In contrast, Austria has not had a specific scheme but has provided compensation under its generic Nazi Victims Law (*Opferfuersorgegesetz*) rather than specifically for sterilization victims. Switzerland decided not to compensate, despite the lobbying for it, and this appears to be the case also for Denmark, Sweden, and Norway. In any case, one can ask, what sum of money could possibly compensate for the loss of reproductive autonomy?

A major defect in all compensation schemes is that the authorities generally assess official documentation without taking into account doctors who simply went ahead to sterilize. An important study of an obstetric clinic in Finland found a large number of sterilizations in the clinic's records for which authorization under the law had not been obtained.[46] In Switzerland there were cantons where sterilizations were carried out without any legislative framework.[47] Much of the debate on sterilization as a Nazi war crime was first shaped and then marginalized by the onset of the Cold War. Alexander, the neurologist, saw sterilization and euthanasia as manifestations of totalitarianism. In 1949 he commented, "The killing center is the *education ad absurdum* of all health planning based only on rational principles and economy and not on humane compassion and divine law."[48] Indeed, he warned that "euthanasia and the belief in utility posed severe dangers to American medicine."[49] The abuses concerning sterilization were inadequately addressed in the postwar period. For the most part, sterilization as a Nazi measure escaped scrutiny. It initially looked as though a serious effort might be made to mount a case against the German eugenicists, but this effort had dissipated by 1948.

In conclusion, the best redress was—where possible—operative re-fertilization. The medical and psychiatric neglect of victims meant that the medical profession effectively condoned the mass sterilizations. Where there was financial compensation, the delivery has been lamentably late, and the low sums hardly compensate for childlessness for those who would have wished to have children. One consequence is unfortunately that the uptake of the compensation program was and is by only a fairly small proportion of the original victims. Delays have meant victims have died—and by definition there cannot be heirs.

9

Commentary One

Marc Workman

Throughout this volume, contributors have described shocking violations of the rights of people with disabilities: compulsory sterilization, scientific experimentation, institutionalization, and euthanasia. The most deplorable of these actions primarily took place prior to the emergence of the disability rights movement in Canada in the 1970s.[1] It is no coincidence that such atrocities occurred during a time when disabled people were largely voiceless.

For decades now, people with disabilities have fought to influence both government policy and public attitudes toward disability. As a result, important legislative protections have been adopted, such as the Charter of Rights and Freedoms, the Canadian Human Rights Act, and, more recently, the United Nations Convention on the Rights of Persons with Disabilities. Although significant progress has been achieved, disabled Canadians are still worse off when it comes to educational achievements, participation in the labour force, and income relative to those without disabilities.[2] Moreover, harmful attitudes about disability continue to be demonstrated through discriminatory immigration policy and negative perceptions of parents with disabilities. By providing a disability rights perspective in this commentary, I hope to illuminate some of the attitudes about disability that were behind past eugenic initiatives and that continue to persist today. Additionally, this consideration of disability advocacy will highlight the importance of collective action for those living with disabilities.

DISABILITY RIGHTS IN CANADA

The concept of human rights has been a powerful force in the disability rights movement in Canada. In fact, as Henderikus J. Stam and Ashley Barlow observe in chapter 1, the primary justification for repealing Alberta's Sexual Sterilization Act was that it violated fundamental human rights. Since its own inception, the disability rights movement has fought to expand human rights protections for Canadians with disabilities. The disability rights movement in Canada goes back to the 1970s and the founding of the Coalition of Provincial Organizations of the Handicapped (COPOH), later known as the Council of Canadians with Disabilities.[3] Certainly, there were organizations established earlier that advocated to improve the lives of people with disabilities—including the Canadian Federation of the Blind, the War Amps, and the Canadian Paraplegic Association, today known as Spinal Cord Injury Canada—but these predecessor organizations tended to focus on a specific impairment (e.g., blindness) or a particular subset of disabled people (e.g., war wounded).[4] It was not until COPOH that a national organization, comprising primarily disabled people themselves, fighting on behalf of all Canadians with disabilities, was established.

HUMAN RIGHTS LEGISLATION IN CANADA

One of the most important victories in the early years of the Canadian disability rights movement was in successfully persuading the Liberal government in the early 1980s to include mental and physical disability as a protected status in the Canadian Charter of Rights and Freedoms.[5] Those familiar with the Charter may not realize that the initial draft of section 15 (the equality clause) made no mention of disability. An arguably more significant deficiency was that the first draft offered an exhaustive—rather than illustrative—list of protected groups, which, if adopted as initially written, would have meant that only those groups that were listed would have been guaranteed equality under the Charter. Thanks to significant pressure from the disability community, along with lobbying by other equality-seeking groups, the version of the Charter that was adopted included disability as a protected group and made the list of protected groups illustrative.[6]

The importance of making the list illustrative rather than exhaustive has been demonstrated in numerous legal cases, including *Vriend v. Alberta* in 1998.[7] In its decision in this case, the Supreme Court of Canada read sexual orientation into the Charter as a characteristic analogous to those that were enumerated in section 15. In other words, even though the Charter does not explicitly mention sexual orientation in section 15, this characteristic is similar enough to the characteristics that are listed so as to receive the same sorts of protections and guarantees as the groups mentioned. Additional grounds that the court has determined to be analogous are marital status and citizenship. The result has been that millions of Canadians have been guaranteed constitutional protection from discrimination who otherwise would not have.[8]

Notably, disability was the only class to be added to the Charter between the initial draft and the version that was ultimately adopted, which indicates the extraordinary work on the part of disability advocates.[9] Because disability was included as a protected ground, Canadians with disabilities have been able to challenge government policies across Canada that discriminate on the basis of disability. One such case was *Eldridge v. British Columbia*, which ultimately made it to the Supreme Court.[10] In its decision, the court found that the policy of the British Columbia government, which failed to provide sign language interpretation to deaf citizens who were attempting to access the health-care system, was a violation of section 15 of the Charter. What makes the *Eldridge* case so significant is the court's recognition that respecting a citizen's right to equality will sometimes require that governments—and those operating on behalf of governments—take extra steps to ensure that benefits of the law are equally available to all. The court found:

> Adverse effects discrimination is especially relevant in the case of disability. In the present case, the adverse effects suffered by deaf persons stem not from the imposition of a burden not faced by the mainstream population, but rather from a failure to ensure that deaf persons benefit equally from a service offered to everyone.

> Once it is accepted that effective communication is an indispensable component of the delivery of a medical service, it is much more difficult to assert that the failure to ensure that deaf persons communicate effectively with their health care providers is not discriminatory.[11]

This decision makes clear that a provincial government cannot avoid violating the Charter by claiming that it is treating citizens with and without disabilities the same. If a benefit of the law is not equally available to someone as a result of her disability, then the government will have to take certain steps—what is often called "reasonable accommodation"—to enable that person to access the benefit.

Despite the importance of securing protection from discrimination in the Charter and in human rights statutes across the country, there are limitations to how much progress can be achieved under these laws. First off, they are in essence reactive. Human rights legislation does not require governments or businesses to proactively identify accessibility barriers and systematically remove them. Instead, once a person experiences discrimination, they can file a complaint or launch a lawsuit—assuming, that is, they have the resources, financial and otherwise, to embark on a process that often takes several years and can be very expensive.[12] Moreover, if they are successful in a complaint against Company A, there is no guarantee that Company B, which offers a similar service, will offer the accommodation without also having to be taken through the human rights process. In other words, barriers must often be removed one at a time. For these reasons, beginning in the mid-1990s, many in the Canadian disability rights movement began to turn their attention to comprehensive accessibility legislation to supplement the human rights protections that had already been won.[13]

ACCESSIBILITY LEGISLATION IN CANADA

Although the United States had enacted the Americans with Disabilities Act of 1990 (ADA), it was not until 2005 that Canada adopted the first example of this type of legislation, the Ontarians with Disabilities Act (ODA).[14] Disability advocates denounced the ODA, however, primarily because compliance was voluntary. Without proper enforcement, the advocates argued, the legislation would be meaningless. Following adoption of the ODA, disability rights advocates in the province—led by David Lepofsky, chair of the Ontarians with Disabilities Act Committee—continued to press the government to enact strong and effective disability legislation. In 2005, their work was rewarded when the Ontario government passed the Accessibility for Ontarians with Disabilities Act (AODA).[15]

What distinguishes accessibility legislation like the AODA from human rights legislation like the Charter is that while the latter is reactive, the former is decidedly proactive. Like the ADA before it, the AODA relies on accessibility standards. It requires the Ontario government to work with the disability and business communities to develop standards across a range of areas—transportation, customer service, public spaces, and others—that outline exactly what is needed to make the province fully accessible to Ontarians with disabilities. Ideally, under this approach, a disabled Ontarian no longer has to wait until they experience discrimination and then end up in an arduous human rights complaint process; instead, the standards are agreed to by all from the outset, and the government simply needs to enforce them. Unfortunately, due to a lack of enforcement, the AODA also has not fully lived up to its promise.[16]

Since Ontario's enactment of the AODA, similar legislation has been adopted in Manitoba and Nova Scotia, and the Government of Canada had introduced federal accessibility legislation with The Accessible Canada Act (Bill C-81), which garnered unanimous support in the House of Commons in May of 2019.[17] It is important to note that all of the legislative victories highlighted above were the result of concerted and sustained efforts from the disability rights movement in Canada. These types of changes do not happen without significant efforts to bring the government and the public on side.

DISABILITY TODAY

It has been nearly forty years since the Charter was adopted in 1982 and more than thirty years since section 15 (the equality clause) came into effect.[18] More than twenty years have passed since the *Eldridge* decision, and the AODA has been in place since 2005. It is worth considering how

Canadians with disabilities are currently faring from a socioeconomic perspective.

According to Statistics Canada's 2012 Canadian Survey on Disability, nearly twice as many people without disabilities have a bachelor-level diploma or degree compared to those with disabilities (27 percent compared to 14 percent).[19] Not surprisingly, a similar imbalance also exists in employment outcomes. Just under half (47 percent) of working-age people with disabilities are employed, compared with 74 percent of the population without disabilities. This disparity in employment prospects results in a significant income gap. The results of the 2010 National Household Survey showed that the median income for working-age people with disabilities was $10,000 less than those without disabilities ($21,420 compared to $31,160).[20] These statistics demonstrate that the fight for equality and inclusion is not yet over. The disability community continues to push for social change with a view toward closing the persistent gaps between those with and without disabilities.

IMMIGRATION AND DISABILITY

One long-standing issue that the disability community has attempted to resolve is what is perceived to be a discriminatory immigration policy in Canada.[21] Immigration policy played several key roles in the eugenics movement. Nearly every chapter in this volume refers to immigration policy and its relationship to eugenics. Both Diana Mansell and Mikkel Dack outline the evidence suggesting that a primary reason for passage of the Sexual Sterilization Act in Alberta was a belief that the province was being overrun by immigrants from central and eastern Europe. Although Dack goes on to argue that this fear of immigration cannot adequately explain why the act was expanded in 1937, it is clear from reading this volume that in many instances eugenicists and their supporters throughout Canada and the United States were motivated by prejudice against immigrants and that immigration policy was used as a tool to prevent the "unfit" from entering their respective countries and multiplying.

Today's immigration policy no longer entails the racially motivated discrimination that it did during the height of the eugenics movement; however, many in the Canadian disability rights movement believe that the existing policy continues to discriminate against those with disabilities.[22]

Section 38(1)(c) of the Immigration and Refugee Protection Act states that a foreign national is inadmissible on health grounds if their health condition "might reasonably be expected to cause excessive demand on health or social services."[23] According to Immigration, Refugees and Citizenship Canada, approximately one thousand applicants for permanent or temporary residence are ruled inadmissible for medical reasons each year.[24]

For many years, disability advocates have argued that this clause enables blanket discrimination against people with disabilities wishing to immigrate to Canada.[25] Advocates have been calling for its repeal and, in December 2017, were joined by the House of Commons Standing Committee on Citizenship and Immigration, which recommended the full repeal of section 38(1)(c). Canada's immigration minister, Ahmed Hussen, inaugurated a threefold increase of the cost threshold—that is considered excessive—which took effect on June 1, 2018, meaning that approximately 75 percent of those people with disabilities or chronic health conditions previously rejected on medical grounds will no longer be deemed inadmissible.[26] The government is expected to completely abolish section 38(1)(c) at a future date. Although disability advocates continue to call for a full repeal of the clause in question, the government's action demonstrates steady progress in the disability rights movement in Canada.

PARENTING AND DISABILITY

As noted throughout this volume, one of the primary aims of eugenic practices such as sterilization was to prevent people with disabilities from passing on their "defects" to future generations. Less remarked upon, though, is the fact that these policies were often enacted to prevent people with disabilities from becoming parents at all—whether the children would inherit the disability or not. Section 6(1) of the Sexual Sterilization Act, for example, identifies two conditions according to which a compulsory sterilization could be ordered:

> If . . . the Board is unanimously of the opinion that the exercise of the power of procreation by that person (a) would result in the transmission of any mental disability or deficiency to his progeny, or (b) involves the risk of mental injury either to such person or his progeny, the Board may in writing direct such surgical operation

for the sexual sterilization of that person as may be specified in the written direction.[27]

The first condition refers to transmission from one generation to another, but the second does not. Moreover, the second condition refers to mental injury to the person being considered for sterilization, which implies that the second condition is not related to transmission. Finally, the act allowed for compulsory sterilization of individuals labelled "mental defectives," which was defined as "any person in whom there is a condition of arrested or incomplete development of mind existing before the age of eighteen years, whether arising from inherent causes or induced by disease or injury."[28] Taken together, these parts of the act indicate that although a primary concern may have been transmission of what were considered undesirable conditions, sterilization could be ordered even in cases where transmission was not possible, as in the case of someone whose condition was the result of disease or injury.

In chapter 2, Douglas Wahlsten demonstrates that the scientific evidence available at the height of the Alberta eugenics program actually undermined the approach adopted by the Alberta Eugenics Board. The science of genetics—even as it was understood at the time—indicated that sterilizing people at the levels undertaken by the province would have had an insignificant influence on the average IQ of the general population. Even more disturbing, Wahlsten is able to point out that the evidence available at the time would have shown that a more significant influence on IQ could have been achieved by implementing initiatives to improve social conditions for precisely those sorts of individuals who ended up being sterilized.

As noted above, however, what motivated eugenicists was not just the fear that "defects" would be passed on; many also had concerns about the ability or inability of people with disabling traits to adequately parent their offspring. As Stam and Barlow note in chapter 1, even as late as the 1970s, advocates lobbied the Alberta government to reintroduce eugenics legislation, arguing that "people certified to be mentally unfit to become parents should have their reproductive capabilities curtailed."[29] A key element of this argument is that it applies whether or not transmission of a condition will take place. From an additional disability studies perspective, one can state that disabled parents still face the default assumption that they will be unfit parents. It is only after disabled parents prove that they are capable that they are permitted to be parents in Western societies, as the mental hygiene and social medical counselling programs of the 1920s, in particular, have claimed.[30] It is important to keep this development in mind, as these sorts of attitudes are alive and well today. Parents with a variety of disabilities regularly face questions about their fitness to parent. All too often, parents with disabilities are presumed to be unfit and are expected to prove otherwise to friends and family, the general public, and government officials.[31]

In one heartbreaking case, negative presumptions about a disabled couple's ability to care for their child had terrible consequences. Erika Johnson and Blake Sinnett are a blind couple in the United States whose baby was removed from their custody shortly after Johnson gave birth in 2010.[32] A nurse observed Johnson experiencing some difficulty breast-feeding—not an unusual experience for a new mother—only this time, rather than offering additional support to the new parents, the nurse wrote on the chart: "The child is without proper custody, support, or care due to both of [the] parents being blind, and they do not have specialized training to assist them."[33] Harkening back to Diana Mansell's chapter, we observe here again the power a nurse can have in these situations. As a result of the nurse's observation, the Missouri Department of Social Services removed the baby from the parents' custody. It was not until fifty-seven days later—following a significant outcry from blind people, including blind parents—that a judge ordered that the baby be returned to the parents.[34] Unfortunately, cases similar to this one are not unusual, particularly for parents with developmental disabilities.

CONCLUSION

What I have tried to highlight in this commentary is the extent to which the disability rights movement has influenced government policy and public attitudes about disability in Canada. Major legislative and legal achievements have occurred since the 1970s and continue to take place. People with disabilities experienced deplorable treatment throughout the twentieth century—largely resulting from the eugenic beliefs and practices examined and detailed in this book. Unfortunately, even with the significant progress that has been made in legislatures and courts, socioeconomic indicators continue to show serious gaps between those with and those without disabilities. The types of attitudes that motivated eugenicists—that disability is an individual problem, that disabled people are an economic burden, that the world would be better off without disability—are very much alive and well today. These attitudes are reflected in contemporary discussions of immigration policy or parenting with a disability, as I have highlighted, but also in debates about prenatal genetic testing and assisted suicide. The contributions in this volume are important to the disability rights movement, as they provide a valuable historical context to the fight for equality taking place today. At the same time, consideration of the contemporary experience of people with disabilities can illuminate the study of the eugenics movement by uncovering some of the deeper motivations and attitudes about disability—beliefs that persist today and continue to shape the lives and experience of those living with disabilities.

IO

Commentary Two

Gregor Wolbring

Throughout history, people as individuals and as collectives have been judged regarding their abilities, whether physical or mental ones, with often negative, disabling consequences for the targeted individual or groups of people. The focus of this book is the practice of eugenics as a social movement toward "improving" human hereditable physical, mental, and other abilities while influencing the judgment of individuals' and groups' abilities—or disabling consequences, for that matter. This commentary chapter will examine several of the chapters through a lens of disability and ability studies.

WHAT IS DISABILITY STUDIES?

Disability studies is an interdisciplinary or multidisciplinary academic discipline that investigates the social situations that disabled people face. The discipline appeared rather late, in the 1970s, within the domain of other scholarly disciplines harnessing central human rights agendas, such as Marxist, feminist, and postcolonial studies and critiques. Ever since, disability studies has thereby challenged "the view of disability as an individual deficit or defect that can be remedied solely through medical intervention or rehabilitation by 'experts' and other service providers. Rather, a program in Disability Studies should explore models and theories that examine social, political, cultural, and economic factors that define disability and help determine personal and collective responses to difference."[1] According to Dan Goodley, twentieth-century disability studies was associated with establishing the factors that led to the structural, economic, and cultural exclusion of people with (so-called) sensory, physical, and cognitive impairments.[2] One of disability studies' main foci is the investigation and critique of ableism. The disabled people rights movement had already coined the term "ableism" in the 1970s, in order to question species-typical, normative physical, mental, neuro-, or cognitive ability expectations (see, for example, deaf culture and neurodiversity discourses) and the ability privileges (e.g., the ability to work, to gain education, to be part of society, to have a social identity, to be seen as a citizen) that normally come with species-typical physical, mental, neuro-, or cognitive abilities.[3] Furthermore, the negative consequences have been highlighted, which emerged through disableism that one experiences if one does not fulfill species-typical physical, mental, neuro- or cognitive ability expectations.[4] Indeed, as I have suggested elsewhere, "many disabled people perceive themselves in a cultural identity war with the so called non-disabled people where their self-identity understanding of being ability diverse and ability variant, as being a culture and not being ability deviant and ability deficient, is rejected by many."[5]

DISABILITY STUDIES AND EUGENICS

According to its founder, Francis Galton (1822–1911), eugenics is a theory and movement that emphasizes the "investigation under which men of a high type are produced," which should cover all kinds of abilities that aimed to "bring as many influences as can be reasonably employed, to cause the useful classes in the community to contribute *more* than their proportion to the next generation."[6] Disabled people form one group that has been a target of mostly negative eugenic practices (as a type of prevention of something undesirable), such as sterilization and prenatal and pre-implantation diagnostics aiming to prevent the birth of humans seen as impaired. In Germany, for example, the Reich Association of the Blind had published jurist Rudolf Kraemer's (1885–1945) pamphlet *Kritik der Eugenik: Vom Standpunkt des Betroffenen* (Critique of eugenics: From the standpoint of one affected by it) since April 1933.[7] The book formed the only well-founded critique of eugenics written up to that time by a disabled person. Kraemer's project was to unmask the ideological nature of eugenic conceptions of inferiority. He warned against the forthcoming Nazi sterilization law and predicted that euthanasia of "useless" persons was a logical consequence of eugenic thinking as a whole.[8] Also, he critiqued eugenicists for exaggerating the cost of caring for the impaired, for viewing impaired people as necessarily suffering, and for overemphasizing the importance of productive labour and military fitness.[9] Kraemer's views hint at a fundamental position that there was more to ableism than covered through disability studies.

WHAT IS ABILITY STUDIES?

Ability studies was introduced in 2008 as a field to investigate how ability expectations ("want stage") and ableism hierarchies and preferences ("need stage") come to pass, as well as the impact of such hierarchies and preferences on multiple subject formations, social relationships, and lived experiences based on diverse ability expectations.[10] My 2008 article, entitled: "Why NBIC [Nanotechnology, Biotechnology, Information Technology and Cognitive Science]? Why Human Performance Enhancement?," exemplified how sexism and racism have been justified through specific narratives, in which one powerful group decided that certain abilities were essential and that other groups lacked these "essential abilities."[11] In the case of sexism, the ability expectation of male rationality and the labelling of women as irrational was and still is used as an ability expectation of human cognition.

ABILITY STUDIES AND EUGENICS

Given Galton's early vision of eugenics, negative eugenics was often instrumental in targeting the poor and other groups seen as physically or mentally impaired. It was also used to justify racism, anti-Semitism, and other negative-isms targeting other groups. Positive eugenics was achieved by encouraging those with desirable traits to continue to reproduce (see, for example, the Nazi *Lebensborn* program).[12] In the future, positive eugenics might be achieved through a synthesis of desired genomes (synthetic biology) in combination with the prospect of the artificial womb. Eugenic thinking could then be applied to enhance humans beyond the normal, through for example somatic and germ line genetic enhancement. Indeed, in recent years the debate around genetic modifications has intensified under the term of "gene editing," and through these discussions the debate has been pushed to accept enhancement directions as well. The debate has seen many supporters among ethicists and not much explicit criticism, as is evidenced by the 2015 International Summit on Gene Editing (see also the foreword by Guel A. Russell).[13] The only prerequisite would be that these interventions give an advantage beyond the normal enhancement over the physiological functioning of others and that this advantage be durable and benefit the genetic stock.

In chapter 1, Henderikus J. Stam and Ashley Barlow write about John M. MacEachran (1873–1947) and eugenics in Alberta. This chapter reflects on the discourse around MacEachran, who was an influential and highly decorated academic as well as the chair of the Alberta Eugenics Board (AEB) from 1929 to 1964. From a disability studies perspective it is of interest to know how eugenicists became involved in the negative treatment of people labelled as "ability-impaired" today. There were many contemporary academics like MacEachran: for example, Margaret Thompson (1920–2014), a member of the AEB from 1960 to 1962, the former president of the Genetics Society of Canada, and a member of the Order of Canada. She fervently defended the sterilization practice in Alberta during the lawsuit brought by Leilani Muir against the Alberta government in the 1990s, saying that "some causes of mental defectiveness are hereditary and when the eugenics board was created there was a real danger of passing on those causes because contraceptive choices were limited. Today, people at risk of inheriting or passing on a defect to their children have the pill and other contraceptives available. They can seek genetic counselling before a child is born and can abort a child likely to be defective."[14] Thompson mentioned health and medical professionals in many of her publications, in which she dealt with genetic connivance—such as genetic "carrier detection" and physician-induced "termination of pregnancy"—within wider eugenic practices.[15]

Many put forward that people should not be judged on their eugenic history. Cases in point include, for example, the "famous five"—progressive women who stand in high regard in Canada for their fight for women's rights despite their connections to the eugenics movement.[16] In the case of geneticist Thompson, however, she was still defending the practice of forced sterilization as late as 1995, when it had become widely critiqued in Canadian society, but she faced no consequences for her views. From a disability studies perspective, the lack of consequences for the deeds of eugenic protagonists is quite troubling. That the eugenic leaders met with no negative sanctions might be one reason why public education—at least in Alberta—largely ignores the breadth and scope of Canada's eugenic past. At least, I assume it is not taught, given that nearly all students taking my first year "Introduction to Disability Studies" (CORE 205) course at the University of Calgary as part of their Bachelor of Community Rehabilitation degree had never heard the term "eugenics" at high school. It is apparent that people are often not aware of the eugenic background of prominent public figures such as Margaret Sanger (1879–1966), the founder of the Planned Parenthood movement, or Woodrow Wilson (1856–1924), the twenty-eighth president of the United States.[17]

However, the lack of investigation into eugenic pasts is not only linked to people covered through disability studies. Paul Weindling's chapter, "Too Little, Too Late: Compensation for Victims of Coerced Sterilization," also describes the reluctance to prosecute. As Weindling suggests, "the criminality of coerced sterilization was slow to be recognized even after the Nuremberg trial prosecutions for the medical crimes under German National Socialism. The problem was simply that the German authorities declined to accept the criminality of the Nazi-era sterilizations."

In chapter 2, "The Consequences of Eugenic Sterilization in Alberta," Douglas Wahlsten discusses the issue of science's sales pitches and the uses of science as a tool to justify social policies. Disability studies pursues a long-standing narrative of questioning many of the claims used to sell eugenic practices—claims that have often been ignored in the wider scientific and public literature. Let me here also discuss chapters 4 and 6 through the lens of media responsibility, a topic that is also approached from both disability studies and ability studies angles. Mikkel Dack's contribution, entitled "The Alberta Eugenics Movement and the 1937 Amendment to the Sexual Sterilization Act," highlights the unique situation in which

Alberta increased its eugenic actions virtually unopposed by government officials, health administrators, and the general public in the province when the practice had been largely discredited in other countries. Dack identifies four reasons for this phenomenon: (1) that Alberta experienced a mass influx of immigrants, resulting in growing fears that "inferior stocks" were polluting the local community, (2) that the general public had been unaware of the sterilization laws themselves, since such legislation had been confined to conversations and debates by politicians and health administrators, (3) that the public was unaware of the racial eugenics programs in Nazi Germany, the discrediting of hereditary science, and the decline of eugenics movements throughout North America, and finally (4) that there were widespread popular beliefs that eugenics legislation would improve the economic conditions of the province and that sexual sterilization helped reducing frivolous government spending.

If these four points were really valid, one could make the argument that the media had either missed their obligation to support charitable initiatives or that they formed an active part of the problem. Diffusion of knowledge through printed media was seen as an essential part of the fabric of society that enabled social participation.[18] In the 1936 case of *Grosjean v. American Press Co.*, the US Supreme Court emphasized the important role of newspapers and magazines in informing the public regarding national affairs.[19] If the four points above were correct, then this suggests that social participation is highly limited, because the media did not inform the public accurately on national affairs such as the actual danger posed by immigrants, if any. Media violated their responsibility to sustain political freedom and stable social order.[20] The four points further suggest that the stable order supported by contemporary societies was that of the powerful. The media have thereby helped to set the discussion agenda and created the boundaries within which debates have taken place.[21] Further, if the four points were correct, one needs to say that the media set boundaries biased toward the powerful. This conclusion as to the problematic role of the media is also reflected in chapter 6, "'New Fashioned with Respect to the Human Race': American Eugenics in the Media at the Turn of the Twentieth Century" by Celeste Tường Vy Sharpe, who argues that the American print media discourse on eugenics from 1900 to 1915 blended established nineteenth-century preoccupations with racial taxonomies and reproductive control. During the Progressive Era, ideas of social control and collectivism thus situated eugenics as a response to old and new social and political problems alike.

From a disability studies perspective the role of the media is important not only during the historic past but to modern societies today. Many investigations by disability studies scholars have provided evidence for a negative and one-sided coverage of disabled people. Article 8 of the UN Convention on the Rights of Persons with Disabilities posits that state parties undertake to adopt immediate, effective, and appropriate measures to combat stereotypes, prejudices, and harmful practices relating to persons with disabilities, including those based on sex and age, in all areas of life. In addition, the "Convention requires States to take steps to encourage all organs of the media to portray persons with disabilities in a manner consistent with the purpose of the Convention (art. 8 (2) (c))" because of "the important role that the media play in both reflecting and influencing public opinion."[22]

"IS IT ALL HISTORY?"

As stated earlier in this chapter, eugenics is not just a historical phenomenon but a contemporary and future one as well. What changes are the scientific and technological methods deployed to fulfill eugenic goals. Many of the problems intrinsic to the historical eugenics discourse are still evident and pertinent today. Disabled people are still often portrayed in very negative ways, and just as Kraemer's *Kritik der Eugenik* was ignored, so for the most part are those who question the negative narrative around disabled people today. Various groups of immigrants were and still are seen in a negative way and feel disempowerment and social neglect (as, for example, mentioned in Diana Mansell's chapter, "The Involvement of Nurses in the Eugenics Program in Alberta, 1920–1940"). Marc Workman includes in his commentary a section related to immigration and disabled people, outlining the still unresolved problem of immigrating as a disabled person to Canada (see chapter 9)—a problem profoundly questioned by the disability rights movement in Canada. The views of health professionals were and still are important in discussions around disabled people and eugenic practices in their broader scope, as I have outlined here. Mansell in chapter 3 outlines the role of nurses and other health professionals in promoting eugenics from 1920 to 1940 and Erna

Kurbegović in chapter 5 also describes the role of medical professionals in promoting eugenic practices. Yet it is well documented that health professionals today, including nurses, often have negative views of disabled people, and of course, health and medical professionals are often involved in the discourses and practices around genetic-testing programs today.[23]

People quite often are not aware of the contemporary reality of eugenic practices and future potential eugenic practices (see, for example, in the human enhancement discourse),[24] nor do many know the history of eugenics. This history is essential for the understanding of current discussions and debates about recent "newgenic" developments in the biomedical and sociobiological discourse.

CONCLUSION

Lessons from the History of Eugenics

Frank W. Stahnisch and Erna Kurbegović

The relationship between eugenics, psychiatry, and mental health has always been a very complex and problematic one. In fact, since the emergence of modern eugenic thought in the latter half of the nineteenth century, asylum superintendents, clinical psychiatrists, psychologists, and biological anthropologists have been at the forefront of applying eugenics concepts, protocols, and legislation to medical practice in Western health-care systems at large.[1] This is particularly so when taking into account the new social movements and progressive reform plans that emerged in the early 1900s, often as a reflex to larger economic and technological changes in most Western societies at the *fin de siècle*.[2] Growing industrialization of more and more European countries as well as Canadian provinces and American states, an increasing trend toward urbanization, and the settlement of populations in larger metropolises gave rise to increasing social anxieties and situations of unrest.[3] Similarly, increasing social conflicts between the proletarian and bourgeois classes and the visible demands of women and individuals from religious and racial minority populations to receive democratic political rights for their general participation in societal, economic, and health-care discourses were widely discussed in Western societies.[4] This led to the development of new and often large-scale programs in psychiatric genetics and public mental health activities that were inspired by racial and social hierarchical ideas.[5]

As German medical historian Volker Roelcke has pointed out, the tendency in psychiatry and biomedical research to include eugenics and racial elements was a largely international development, which took root in several if not most Western industrialized countries at the beginning of the twentieth century.[6] This development has, furthermore, been characterized by Austrian historian Philipp Blom as "the vertigo years," particularly in European and North American societies.[7] As the individual chapters in this volume show, the history of eugenics in western Canada in its foundational theoretical direction, form of application, and involvement of health-care personnel (such as psychiatrists, nurses, teachers, and public health administrators)[8] was not too different from the general developments in medicine, psychiatry, and the neurosciences in other countries of the Western world. Diana Mansell, for example, in her pivotal and instructive contribution to this collection, shows how a focus on the role played by other health-care professionals, such as nurses and nursing assistants, can widen the traditional perspective on eugenic programs in Canada and North America in general (see chapter 3, "The Involvement of Nurses in the Eugenics Program in Alberta, 1920–1940").

This volume on eugenics and psychiatry is concerned primarily with Canadian and transatlantic perspectives from 1905 to 1972. It has endeavoured to explore the intersections of and borders between the topic areas of eugenics history, mental health policies, and prevailing scientific and social views in contemporary psychiatry and health care, by explicitly setting the historical development of eugenics in western Canada in its comparative cultural contexts.[9] Certainly, we do not wish to ignore the existence of local differences on the level of the execution of eugenics measures, the specific types of legislation used, or—as for the field of psychiatry—the nature of the involvement of psychiatrists and other health-care workers in the "therapeutic" and "preventive" medical and social programs used during the first half of the twentieth century (see Appendix).[10] As applied and theoretical knowledge became further integrated into political spheres, social and psychological considerations within neurology and mental health disciplines also appeared increasingly relevant. In fact, neurological and psychiatric sciences had been involved in the *biopolitical discourses* between the 1900s and the 1970s.[11] This was most notably so in discussions on eugenics and racial hygiene in the Western industrialized world, where particular research assumptions of the nineteenth century—regarding substance abuse, neurodegenerative diseases, and inherited mental illnesses—influenced the biopolitical discourses of the first half of the century that followed.[12]

From a historiographical point of view, the social context regarding psychiatry and mental health issues—particularly, the triad of white supremacy, immigration biases, and persecution of Indigenous populations—played a large and unique role in the course of eugenics-oriented social and health-care programs in western Canada.[13] This was the case in, above all, the Prairie provinces of Manitoba, Saskatchewan, and Alberta after they joined Confederation in 1870, 1905, and 1905, respectively.[14] The social context is further visible in the case of Nazi eugenics between 1933 and 1945, with its wide intrusion of German society, politics, and the health-care system, which also prompted Tommy Douglas (1904–87) to reflect on his early advocacy for eugenics from the standpoint of being a social progressivist and close to the religious Social Gospel movement.[15] This is pointed out in depth by Henderikus J. Stam and Ashley Barlow (chapter 1), Mikkel Dack (chapter 4), and Erna Kurbegović (chapter 5). These authors show that western Canadian eugenics developed largely as a means to incorporate social and cultural notions of well-meaning and technocratic progressivism into provincial politics and public health programs. And while often overlooked in historical treatises on eugenics, this trend toward "social progressivism" is quite visible in western Canada and pervades most of the chapters assembled here. Western Canadian eugenics was at once a minute reflection of international eugenics (see Appendix) and at the same time had certain historically unique features, with its origins in agricultural unions, clandestine processes run through a relatively small group of experts, and the centrality of the Alberta Eugenics Board, for instance (Appendix). A special case for psychiatry and eugenics (for reasons of disciplinary hierarchies in medicine, the inheritable nature of many pathologies and conditions in psychiatry, and urges toward professional autonomy, among others) can certainly be made, since the overall concerns of all eugenicists squared front and centre with unease and anxieties about the mentally ill, alcoholics, and people with neurodegenerative disorders. At the same time, psychiatrists and neurologists were strongly involved in the eugenics movement at the time.

While some sociologists and anthropologists might think these are new phenomena, we hope that the chapters on the relationship of eugenics and psychiatry assembled in this book will shed light on the same "modernist" tendencies at work in driving the eugenics programs during the 1920s and 1930s. The analysis and categorization of the problems, players, and institutions in the contemporary eugenics movements—along with the case studies, theoretical and empirical pieces, and comparative approaches—enable such a perspective here. In line with research pursued by a group of Canadian and international historians and interdisciplinary scholars assembled in the Archives on Eugenics in Western Canada initiative,[16] the primary focus of this book is on the history of eugenics developments in Alberta, Manitoba, and British Columbia. These historical developments have been linked to their international contexts, particularly the dimensions of psychiatry, neuroscience, and psychological medicine.

Important similarities and differences to the medical communities in other countries could be identified vis-à-vis their reception of eugenic thought and practices, views that highlight the vast scope with which medical doctors and health-care professionals became active in influencing eugenics legislation in different jurisdictions. Scientific, political, and professional interests instigated psychologists, psychiatrists, and other physicians to collaborate in mutual research programs for policy initiatives and political programs. In an age in which concise pathological and genetic knowledge about diseases of the mind and the brain was largely lacking, intrinsic conceptual assumptions from eugenics and racial hygiene came to foster the scientific and clinical approaches in somatic psychiatry and psychological mental health, both in Europe and North America. Through international training exchanges and incorporation of diagnostic and therapeutic repertoires from Europe and the United States, Canada's health-care system, especially in the western provinces, was increasingly affected by contemporary international medical and biological trends.[17]

LOOKING BACK

Previous scholarship on the relation between eugenics and psychiatry provided essential and critical perspectives on eugenics history in western

Canada and its international contexts.[18] Historians have pointed in particular to the heterogeneous levels, agency groups, and legislative and policy principles in many Canadian provinces (see, for example, chapter 1 in this volume). This volume contributes to this work by drawing scholarly attention to the place of psychiatry, public mental health, and the brain sciences in the history of eugenics.[19] Since the early decades of the twentieth century, clinical neurologists, psychiatrists, and superintendents of mental asylums were for the most part inclined to receive the medical and social propositions of the new eugenic and racial hygienic tradition, first in Britain and Europe, then in the United States and Canada.[20] Such sentiments were largely fuelled by bourgeois anxieties about racial and nervous degeneration, which increased during and after the First World War and became prominent in many Western countries.[21] The last decades of the nineteenth century had already witnessed an overall medicalization of the cultural discourse, as Joachim Radkau's *Das Zeitalter der Nervositaet* (The age of nervousness) has suggested, describing a historical phase in which the clinical disciplines of neurology and psychiatry were in constant debates and struggles over professional identity and autonomy from their mother discipline of internal medicine.[22] Many social and medical historians and scholars have reinterpreted the very phenomena of "eugenics" and "racial hygiene" in terms of a popular cultural trope since the last decades of the nineteenth century.[23] It must be noted, however, that this reflected not only psychiatrists' professional assumptions, but also opinions prevalent among middle- and upper-class populations on both sides of the Atlantic that held that "cultural degeneration" had rapidly ensued.[24] A stronger concern for the individual body resulted in widespread medical reconfigurations, programs to sustain public health, and new cultural conceptions of psychiatric illness (often referred to as inherited feeble-mindedness).[25] Irrespective of the somatic or psychic pole of this spectrum, the specific medical reconfigurations took place in a general framework of eugenic theorizing.[26] This further translated into shifting social frontiers between right-wing and left-wing political camps, when the eugenics movement brought to light the anxieties and concerns shared by social traditionalists and progressivists regarding the cost-effectiveness of state-run mental asylums and institutions in the first decades of the twentieth century.[27]

This volume also traces the changing societal emphases on research, along with the new concepts in neurology and psychiatry, during the first half of the twentieth century. Political conflicts, the increasing popularity of the eugenics movement, and economic influences reframed interdisciplinary neurological, psychiatric, and psychological work within the context of mental health care and public health, along with tighter political control mechanisms.[28] This becomes increasingly apparent when focusing on international relationships between Germany and the United States or Britain and Canada.[29]

The work in eugenics and breeding that, for example, German racial anthropologist Alfred Ploetz (1860–1940) pursued as a temporary émigré physician in America was, like that of many of his reformist colleagues and friends, deeply rooted in late nineteenth-century sanitary and hygiene movements.[30] Both Ploetz—the doyen of German eugenic thought—and the experimental biologist Charles B. Davenport (1866–1944)—the leader of America's human breeding movement and later head of the Eugenics Record Office of Cold Spring Harbor—held beliefs in Nordic superiority, which formed the centrepiece of their ideology.[31] Indeed, Davenport developed strong professional relations with German racial hygienists such as Ploetz and the physician Fritz Lenz (1887–1976), who was invited by leading American eugenicists to describe the status of "Eugenics in Germany" for the *Journal of Heredity* in 1924.[32] In this article, Lenz explicitly emphasized common intellectual ground between white Western Anglo-Saxon and German-speaking eugenicists. He openly referred back to Ploetz, who had "noted in particular that the Anglo-Saxons of America would be left behind, unless they developed a policy that would change the relative proportions of the populations."[33] Germans understood the problem all too well, since they anticipated soon being in a similar situation—with respect to what they understood as the detrimental effects of the "Rhineland bastards," the perceived increase of the Jewish population, and above all the "Slavic takeover" of the eastern German lands. Lenz also discussed what he saw as the devastating effects of the First World War.

Although Canadian, American, British, Scandinavian, and German eugenics thus all contained unique elements, there was a lot of common ground between those "national styles" of eugenic thought.[34] The British eugenics movement had been largely moulded by Francis Galton (1822–1911) and Karl Pearson (1857–1936) before it was transferred to the United States and Canada; in North America, the movement was particularly driven by Davenport, who kept close contacts with German leaders of the racial hygiene movement.[35] He was also well aware of psychiatrist Ernst Ruedin's (1874–1952) massive research program on psychiatric genetics and epidemiology in Munich and later Germany at large.[36] Likewise, subsequent generations of eugenic supporters came from widely diverse political perspectives, but they all shared the belief that effects of modernization and civilization endangered the human species as in contexts of armed conflict. Nevertheless, these eugenic thinkers assumed that modern society could be improved through the "betterment" of the people's stocks and the marginalization of the feeble-minded, the physically unfit, and the morally corrupt through planned restrictions on the reproduction of "inferior grades of humanity."[37]

Research-minded German brain psychiatrists of the late nineteenth century, such as anatomist and histologist Alois Alzheimer (1864–1915) in Frankfurt am Main and Munich—who worked as a colleague of the doyen of modern clinical psychopathology, Emil Kraepelin (1856–1926), at the Psychiatry Clinic of the University of Munich, who helped shape the modern field of psychiatry and mental health on an international scale—promoted the view that basic research into early neurodegenerative diseases (*hereditaere Degeneration des Gehirns*) should first be advanced before specific actions were taken. Later, psychiatrists like the eugenicists Alfred Erich Hoche (1865–1943) and Ruedin saw little advantage in such experimental basic research of human hereditary conditions. They rather favoured statistical and clinical "phenotype" data banking and meta-analyses to track the biological and psychological traits of the feeble-minded and mentally ill.[38] The engagement of psychiatrists in public health discussions of eugenics measures also developed into a strategy of bolstering professional recognition and the renown of their own discipline. Many psychiatrists and brain researchers, including Auguste Forel (1848–1931) and Constantin von Monakow (1853–1930) in Switzerland and Ruedin in Germany, had been instrumental in this regard as they developed a much bigger picture of their discipline as an all-encompassing social-medical program in which eugenics had a major role to play.[39] Eugenic thought thus became an important discursive tool that served clinical psychiatry well in establishing its own professional identity vis-à-vis the biological and medical sciences, and it also extended a strong influence on the next generation of young psychiatrists and neurologists such as Kurt Goldstein (1878–1965), described in chapter 7. Moreover, the boundary between the political right and left was increasingly challenged during the first decades of the twentieth century, since the eugenics movement cut across social traditionalism and progressivism in both wider public discourses and the context of mental hygiene from the 1880s to the 1930s.[40]

A special case—in terms of both the rather late establishment of sterilization laws and the drastic means promoted through the negative eugenics legislation and medical measures taken in the Nazi euthanasia program—presented the development of eugenics in the German-speaking countries. While the unstable governments of the Weimar Republic had often introduced positive eugenics–oriented policies to their health and social programs, it was only during the Nazi period that Germany enacted more racial and eugenics laws than the United States and Canada.[41] Nazi Germany further launched large-scale eugenics research programs, in supporting, for example, the Division for Inheritance Statistics at the German Research Institute for Psychiatry and multiple large science programs at the Berlin Kaiser Wilhelm Institute (KWI) for Anthropology and Human Genetics and the KWI for Brain Research.[42] These programs sought to gather large-scale databases of all Germans diagnosed with inheritable psychiatric and neurological disorders and diseases.

The increasing politicization of the reorganization process of the sciences since the 1910s can be seen in, for example, the continuing creation of working groups at the national German Research Council (DFG) throughout the 1930s, which formed important networks and collaborative relationships between researchers and clinicians from all over Germany.[43] One such group was the Arbeitsgemeinschaft II for Racial Hygiene and Racial Politics. Representatives from all major neuroscience and biological psychiatric institutions took part in the proceedings of this specific working group. Its tasks were meticulously laid out in the founding policy paper, which included programs for public education, basic brain research, clinical psychiatric investigations, postgraduate training, research into sterilization practices, demographic statistics, and patient and family counselling.[44] Members of the advisory committee of the Arbeitsgemeinschaft II met on February 22, 1930; among them were Berlin racial anthropologist Eugen Fischer (1874–1967); the director of the KWI for Brain Research, Oskar Vogt (1870–1959); the surgeon and *Preussischer Geheimrat* (Prussian privy councillor) August Bier (1861–1949); Munich psychiatrist and eugenicist Ruedin; the Freiburg military pathologist

Ludwig Aschoff (1866–1942); Munich public hygienist Friedrich von Mueller (1858–1941); the racial hygienist Ludwig Schmidt-Kehl (1891–1941) from Wuerzburg; venereal hygienist Ernst von Duering (1858–1944); the president of the Kaiser Wilhelm Society, Friedrich Glum (1891–1974); and the racial anthropologist Liam Roiste (1882–1959) from the Reichsgesundheitsamt (National public health office) in Berlin.[45]

The organizational network and multiple funding activities were not limited to the self-declared racial anthropologists, who made use of the enormous funding opportunities that were offered through the Arbeitsgemeinschaft II, as historians of psychiatry Matthias M. Weber and Volker Roelcke have shown.[46] Conversely, Ruedin, the director of the demographic division at the Deutsche Forschungsanstalt (DFA) for Psychiatry, wrote to the minister of state, Friedrich Schmidt-Ott (1860–1956), on January 16, 1930, detailing the future effects of his research on the new public tasks "of counting and *identifying the mentally ill and handicapped* as well as the respective disease prevalence in the individual regions of Germany" [italics added].[47] Yet credulous brain researchers also shared the values and promoted the ideals of the new German Research Council (Deutsche Forschungsgemeinschaft, DFG), as did Vogt, a human cortex researcher and the director of the KWI for Brain Research in Berlin-Buch. In a letter to the DFG president, Friedrich Schmidt-Ott, on December 2, 1930, Vogt tried to position the emerging brain research activities as a valuable contribution to the major science programs in public health and racial hygiene and helped to move them into DFG's institutional awareness.[48] As in many other negotiations with major funding agencies, Vogt promoted his collaborators and offered research aid through the associates in his institutes. In order to support the *Gemeinschaftsaufgaben* (community responsibilities), which the DFG had singled out as primary areas for its research support, Vogt also advocated for the scientific promises of the new interdisciplinary makeup of his own institute and underlined the huge progress that had been made in the institute since its inception as the small Neurobiological Laboratory in Berlin in Germany.[49]

All of these scholars advocated the position that it was insufficient to consider scientific achievements of clinicians and experimental research teams in isolation from their technological, economic, and cultural environments. Instead, they demanded analyzing such experimental systems as intertwined with political discourses and technological innovations during different historical epochs. The fruitful sociotechnical research conditions also attracted many international postgraduate students and visiting researchers for training in psychiatry and neurology. With financial support from the Rockefeller Foundation for the Munich DFA for Psychiatry, for example, North American students, fellows, and visiting professors flocked again to Munich and other centres of interest after the war.[50] The individual funding program of the Rockefeller Foundation, in return, enabled numerous German neuroscientists to work on the other side of the Atlantic. There, they introduced scientific practices, which were subsequently "enriched" with utilitarian ideals as well as eugenic perspectives that loomed large in the American medical communities.[51]

These political alignments resulted in a differentiation of psychiatric and neurological research activities that became supplemented with psychopathological, anthropometrical, and genetic counselling programs.[52] The Rockefeller Foundation, for instance, defended its continued funding on the basis of the involvement of individual recipients and their distinct research programs. Ruedin, however, always found ways to channel parts of this financial support into the DFA's general endowment, thus securing its contribution to the demographic department's program on psychiatric eugenics and public mental health.[53] Frequently, the Rockefeller Foundation's funding activities added up to quite substantial amounts, due to the concentration of well-supported psychiatrists in the big Reich cities. As such, its continuing support of brain research centres and eugenic psychiatric projects in places such as Munich, Berlin, Breslau, and Wuerzburg can be seen as a direct expression of its own preoccupation with sustaining the research exchanges and training conditions of North American investigators in German laboratories and hospital wards. The director of the foundation's Division of Medical Education, Alan Gregg (1890–1957), kept a working diary from the 1910s; it shows the extent to which relations with German psychiatrists continued throughout the Weimar Republic and even in the National Socialist period. This collaborative development was particularly based on genetics and social epidemiological research and training programs in psychiatry.[54] Several chapters in this volume (e.g., chapters 4 and 6) thus resonate with the public perceptions and media portrayals of the pro-nativist conceptions and biopolitical programs from the 1920s to the 1940s, which must be understood as an important background discourse and development that brought eugenic ideals from the delineated scientific and expert circles to the social masses and literally to the streets of Europe and North America.[55]

The cultural and biological contexts of "eugenics" had an important complementary influence on the field of neuroscience, because many diseases of the brain were understood as inherited. It is interesting to see that a great number of physicians in the eugenics movements had previously worked in social medicine and psychiatry.[56] For them, neurology and psychiatry became "in the true sense of the word a healing medical discipline," because the therapeutic repertoire—electrotherapy, surgery, pharmacotherapy, and physical therapy—were still very limited at the time.[57] These social and technological trends developed into a multidisciplinary albeit murderous field in the context of Nazi medicine, where the healing of the sick and the extinction of the weak coincided with barbarous endeavours of health professionals and medical and neuroscientific researchers. Hence, the state and development of medicine and public health in the Third Reich cannot be regarded as mere contingencies. Moreover, the idea that medical knowledge was intrinsically in conflict with ethical values may not be unique to this period.[58] The narrative has served here to answer some of the questions that arise through the conundrums posed by the Nuremberg trials, from 1945 to 1947: namely, the effect of *prima facie* absent ethical rules for scientific and medical aberrations during the first decades of the twentieth century (see also chapter 8). This absence eventually made it necessary to treat Nazi atrocities legally as "war crimes" rather than as medical misconduct.[59]

There are many adherents to the thesis that "science thrives only under democracy and that democracy in turn benefits from values implicit in the free pursuit of science" and one could even see it as a well-entrenched view in the Anglophone research literature.[60] One such example, Robert N. Proctor's work *Racial Hygiene: Medicine under the Nazis*, is very fitting, with regard to both recent developments in the biomedical sciences and respective scholarship in science and technology studies.[61]

LOOKING AHEAD

Researching the history of eugenics in relation to psychiatry and mental health also offers us important insights into many ongoing debates in sociobiology, political philosophy, and anthropology regarding reproductive rights and modern biopolitics in North America and elsewhere. As the final two academic commentary chapters—which were individually solicited from specialists in the field of disability policy and disability studies—have shown, disability studies and disability policy still deal with the socially problematic long-term effects of eugenic legacies and preserved legislation. The findings of the two commentary chapters strengthen the argumentation in this edited collection through highlighting the plurality of recent scholarly debate. They focus on eugenics' thrust to actively set parental and women's reproductive choice and agency in the same philosophical and moral context as eugenics. They also stress that eugenics as state policy differed substantially from active decision-making by parents about whether to terminate their own pregnancy, since the former was about state-sponsored efforts at societal manipulation. At the same time, this line of thinking speaks to emerging theoretical and social debates about the relationship between early to mid-twentieth-century eugenics and modern-day reproductive technologies. For some disability scholars, *in utero* diagnoses of trisomy 21, for example, fall on the same philosophical plane as early twentieth-century psychiatric assertions of feeble-mindedness and idiocy. Linking these two ideas is part of what disability theorist Rosemarie Garland-Thomson calls a broader "eugenic logic."[62] Along these lines, the commentaries note that eugenics was based on widespread beliefs that "idiocy" and "feeble-mindedness" needed to be weeded out of society for the good of society and, further, that the state and its agents had a duty and a responsibility to make this happen. They also suggest that parents' choice to terminate pregnancies based on knowledge of disabilities in the fetus amounts to the same thing; that is, it is reflective of a society that does not value disability, that sees disability as a "misfortune," as "regrettable" and "limiting." This, of course, raises difficult questions about how societies value or potentially do not value human life. Who decides what lives are valuable? And who plays an active role in determining how to promote valuable lives and curb (or terminate) so-called valueless lives?

While Canada and the United States witnessed new "social reform movements" during the twentieth century in areas such as public health and psychiatry, they also saw the rise of eugenics in its first decades—the separation of "abnormal" populations from the "normal" and the commencement of drastic and often inhumane public mental health measures. Specifically, in the public mental health sector, the Canadian provinces of Alberta, British Columbia, and Saskatchewan experimented with different levels of forced sterilization, institutionalization, and segregation, by also looking at the "therapeutic consequences" of an eugenics program (see Appendix). To emphasize the case of Saskatchewan here further, attention can be drawn to the work and contributions of historian Erika Dyck, at the University of Saskatchewan, who established that the relationship between psychiatry and the legacies of eugenics was not one of an organized eugenics program in that province. Her argument has been, rather, that an unorganized and non-policy-based eugenics situation and movement existed in Saskatchewan. It did not allow too strong of a connection to be made between eugenics and psychiatry—other than the comparable cases of Alberta and Manitoba (which are both addressed in our volume, particularly in chapters 2, 3, 4, and 5)—as also depicted in Dyck's publication, co-authored with Alex Deighton, titled *Managing Madness*, on the Weyburn Mental Hospital in Saskatchewan.[63]

The Sexual Sterilization Act, enacted in Alberta in 1928, legalized coerced sterilization of the mentally ill and "morally deficient." It was a radical piece of legislation that marked a stark change in psychiatric care programs and in the extent to which the mentally ill were perceived as patients or even as a threat to society. In response, official legislation also impinged on medical practice in psychiatric institutions, such as the asylums at Ponoka and the Michener Centre in Red Deer, and became likewise informed by the physicians' knowledge and practices that shaped governmental and public views considerably.[64] In this volume, historians, philosophers, psychologists, sociologists, and disability scholars have discussed the knowledge basis and sociocultural background in the public mental health sector from the 1920s to the 1970s. In particular, questions were raised and answered about the contemporary factors that brought the eugenics movement, psychologists, psychiatrists, and other physicians together in their respective eugenics endeavours. The chapters explored the intrinsic conceptual assumptions that fostered biological and somatic views in psychiatry about mental illness, following the brain-psychiatric assumptions of leading figures (such as diagnostician and clinical researcher Emil Kraepelin) and their North American counterparts, by drawing attention to Canada's health-care system—which was affected by the same international discussions as in the United States, Britain, and Europe—and by shedding light on the impact of brain psychiatry and developments in the neurological sciences within the context of socioeconomic developments shortly before or during the first half of the twentieth century.

Eugenic discourses at the turn of the twentieth century had remarkably widespread appeal not only to medical doctors, biological, and social scientists. In this context, eugenics programs promised a biological redefinition of human morality and particularly of the modern soul. This prospect likewise accounted for the fact that professional psychiatrists were attracted to the specific implications of eugenic thought for questions of diagnosis and psychiatric treatment.[65] Quite frankly, biological scientists, psychiatrists, and social philosophers were not the only ones to have been influenced by ideas projecting an "improvement of the race" or the "breeding of social elites."

Taken together, the historical and recent considerations regarding the development of the eugenics movement and its specific influences on the field of psychiatry and neurology in Alberta and beyond offer us the opportunity to recognize how holistic neurologists developed views of degeneration and eugenics in line with the public demands and cultural discourses of the time. Far from being restricted to the transformation in neurological and psychiatric laboratories, the integrative character of the sociotechnical concepts of "neurodegeneration," "mental illness," and "hereditary nervous diseases" were strongly reflected in brain researchers' discourses of the time. Their *hinge character*—comprising both a researcher's assumptions about societal issues and deliberate strategies to meet wider public demands—emerged in the contemporary psychiatric and neurological conferences in North America and Europe alike.[66] In the middle of World War I, physicians, mental health nurses, and other health-care providers emphasized that the problem of degenerative psychiatric and neurological conditions was just a reflection of the phenomena of modern cultural degeneration. It slowly but steadily crept into the behaviours, value systems, and therapeutic approaches not only of medical doctors, but also of public health nurses and nursing aids, as Mansell shows in chapter 3. Interestingly, after the First World War ended, clinical neurologists diagnosed fewer instances of "civil" degenerative diseases. These developments were all part of a transformation of the research fields of eugenics and psychiatry, which led to altered views about hereditary diseases, human behaviour, and mental health concerns.

This book complements the existing literature and provides an original understanding as to the intersections between eugenics programs in western Canada and international developments and influences. In addition, it brings the psychiatric and mental health angle into the history of eugenics, which has largely been marginalized in Canadian historiography. The editors intended to contribute a new perspective on the history of eugenics in Canada, by encouraging the contributors to apply an international and thematically, as well as geographically, comparative lens. In his ground-breaking work *The Wellborn Science: Eugenics in Germany, France, Brazil, and Russia*, Mark Adams stresses the importance of a comparative approach in understanding the history of eugenics.[67] While it is important to study eugenics in the local, regional, or national contexts, a comparative approach allows for the emergence of broader patterns that might not be evident in single case reports and complements the international picture of a sociobiological movement in significant global scope.

This volume may further serve as a backdrop for further research on the history of eugenics in Canada and North America. In adding to recent scholarship particularly on eugenics issues regarding the involvement of families, the contributions of communities, and analyses of the legal aspects of eugenics programs in Canada and the United States, this volume also offers a perspective that takes into account the psychiatric, mental health, and neurological dimensions of eugenics movements internationally. Eugenics was steadfastly a transnational phenomenon, where exchanges of ideas took place among different communities and societies. For example, while Canada actively received physicians from Britain to staff its hospitals and asylums, many prominent eugenicists in North America also connected with their counterparts on the Continent, in countries such as Germany, Austria, and Switzerland.[68]

Among the main scholarly intentions and goals of this book, as we seek to emphasize here again in our conclusion, was to complement the received view that eugenics was a general science and practice for the improvement of the human species through selective mating of people with desirable inheritable traits. Eugenics held particular importance and meaning for psychiatrists, mental health administrators, and care workers, as the individual chapters in this edited collection show from specific western Canadian and international angles. In our narrative, we connect the individual historical perspectives assembled here with contemporary discussions about disability and human rights. An important intersection piece in this respect is chapter 8, on compensation claims, by Paul J. Weindling, which as a chronological contribution bridges the historical case studies and also offers a perspective on the global longer-term social, legal, and political effects of eugenics programs and movements in their respective psychiatric and mental health contexts. Yet, the compensation claims that Weindling investigates were subject to German and Austrian restitution laws—with the last ones expiring in the 1980s—which rather stirred the discussion toward historical (not contemporary) questions of cover-up and defensive juridical practices at the time.

Finally, ongoing debates over who has control over reproductive rights can be fundamentally understood and also deeply related to the heterogeneous developments in the historical relationship between eugenics and psychiatry. Technological advances have basically allowed modern citizens to be more selective, to decide voluntarily against handicapped and disabled children, and, in the latest turn of "newgenics," to opt even for the genetic manipulation of particular character and biological traits through the prospects and "brave new worlds" of current bioengineering technologies.[69] The history of eugenics allows for important insights into longer-term scientific research, medical ethics developments, and current reproductive policies and practices. It highlights the need to create awareness that such positive and well-meaning historical ways of thinking are in fact similar to those that have "re-emerged" in the recent fields of newgenics and "euthenics" during the past two decades.

The history of eugenics in western Canada thus provides us with important insights into longer-term scientific research, medical ethics developments, and current reproductive policies and practices, which cannot be dissociated from their wider international psychiatric and mental health implications.

APPENDIX

SEXUAL STERILIZATION.

FOUR YEARS EXPERIENCE IN ALBERTA.

By C. A. Baragar, B.A., M.D.C.M., Geo. A. Davidson, M.D., M.R. C.P. London, W. J. McAlister, M.D. C.M., and D. L. McCullough, B.A., M.B.B.CH., D.P.M. London.

Human sterilization is not by any means new. Ever since surgery became antiseptic and aseptic, operations such as oophorectomies, hysterectomies, salpingectomies, castrations and prostatectomies have frequently been performed of which sterilization was one of the results, though not usually the main result or even a desired result. Sterilization for eugenical purposes, notwithstanding its tremendous significance, is of relatively recent origin, though it is reported that in Switzerland sterilization has been practiced in selected mental cases for many years as a matter of course.

In the United States sexual sterilization has been legalized in certain states since 1907. According to Landman in 1932 30 states of the union had sterilization laws on their books and of these in 27 the statutes were held as valid. In 23 of the 30 states sterilization operations have been performed varying from 9 in Washington to 7548 in California.

With respect to the British Commonwealth of Nations, Alberta is the pioneer in legislation of this character, and to the Honorable George Hoadley and a group of active supporters—chiefly organizations of women—must be given the credit for the vision and courage that has placed this statute on the books of the province. This statute, known

---

This article originally appeared in the *American Journal of Psychiatry* 91 (1935): 897–923. It is reprinted here with selected tables with permission from the *American Journal of Psychiatry*

as the Sexual Sterilization Act, being Chapter 37 of the Statutes of the Province, was assented to March 21, 1928. It is brief and simplicity itself. Therein lie many of its merits. In some respects it may be thought not to have gone far enough, but as a first statute, for its educational value and for its simplicity, it is indeed admirable.

The operation of the act is under the direction of a specially named board of four well-known residents of Alberta. Prof. J.M. MacEachran, head of the Department of Philosophy of the University of Alberta, is chairman Dr. E.L. Pope, professor of medicine, Dr. E.G. Mason, and Mrs. Jean H. Field, constitute its membership. All, by reason of past experience and wide humanitarian interests, are particularly well qualified to understandingly and sympathetically adjudicate upon the cases presented to them. The Board is the sole authority having power to sanction the operation for eugenical sterilization, and names the hospital and surgeon for each operation. It meets quarterly and if necessary in each of five or more different centers in the province.

The act provides for the sexual sterilization of certain inmates of mental hospitals whom it is proposed to discharge if the Board is unanimously of the opinion that this may safely be done providing the danger of transmission of the disability to progeny were eliminated. Under "mental hospitals" are included not only the provincial institutions for mental disease and defect, but also special wards in certain general hospitals. Thus suitable cases for whom there is no accommodation in one of the mental hospitals, or whose admission is not yet expedient may be presented to the Board.

The classes of persons coming within the scope of the act are:

> Patients who are convalescent from a psychosis.
> Patients sufficiently improved from a psychosis to justify discharge with or without supervision.
> Patients who though unimproved might be cared for outside an institution.
> Mental defectives of all grades whose discharge from institutional care might be reasonably considered were the danger of reproduction removed.

By virtue of Section 6 of the act the operation cannot be performed unless the patient has consented thereto; or, in the case of patients considered by the Board to be mentally incompetent to give consent, the husband or wife; or, if unmarried, the parent or guardian has consented thereto; or, where there is no parent or guardian resident in the province, the Minister of Health has consented thereto.

Safeguards against abuse of the law are ensured not only by the provisons of the act itself, but also by the procedure adopted by the Board.

> Consent is necessary.
> All authority rests with a board composed of persons of high repute.
> Application to the Board for the sexual sterilization of a patient is made by a responsible medical officer, a psychiatrist in the Public Health Service, and his recommendation must be supported by at least one other psychiatrist, also in the public service.
> A concise but comprehensive summary of each case must be submitted to the Board setting forth the facts with respect to family and personal history, physical and mental state, and with the reasons for recommending sterilization.
> The patient is presented in person to the Board and examined by the medical members.
> Both surgeon and hospital act only when they receive the written authority of the Board for the operation.

With respect to discharge while many of the convalescent patients operated on would have been discharged in any event whether sterilized or not, notwithstanding the risk of procreation, the fact that procreation is no longer possible has facilitated discharge. Many cases, however, especially mental defectives, have been discharged who would not otherwise have been discharged.

While no special operation is prescribed in the act a vasectomy of the male and a salpingectomy in the female are the operations invariably performed. At times at the request of the parents or with consent the appendix has been removed and pathological conditions have been dealt with. In one case at the request of the parents a double oophorectomy was done in addition to the salpingectomy. The patient was a deteriorated paralytic epileptic girl with hypererotic tendencies.

As to immediate surgical results there have been no fatalities and no serious complications. In two or three cases there have been stitch abscesses and in one case a protracted convalescence.

The operation when performed on a female in reasonably good physical health, while a serious one like all laparotomies, in reality entails less risk than childbirth itself. In the male it is, of course, a minor operation and need not incapacitate the patient for more than a very few days.

With few exceptions there have been no complaints following the operation. One man complained of a variable dragging sensation of the testes afterwards, but it does not seem to have caused him any loss of time. Two women—both neurotic—complained of menstrual disturbances, in one case developing a year or more after the operation and in the other associated with numerous other complaints of a functional nature. These were not considered by the examining physician as related in any way to the operation.

One schizophrenic patient operated on during an improved interval relapsed into the former catatonic state following the operation.

One girl, a defective with a slowly developing schizophrenic reaction, was sterilized. Her psychosis continued to develop and later she had to be admitted to a mental hospital. As she had shown tendencies to promiscuity the operation was a very desirable precautionary measure.

Another patient, a high-grade defective who had made a very unsatisfactory moral, social and economic adjustment complained that she had lost her womanhood and expressed the idea that as the Eugenics Board had directed the operation the government should support her.

A social worker thought she noted a tendency in a number of the female patients to gain in weight and in a general feeling of well being.

Not sufficient time has elapsed to ascertain definitely whether there have been any effects whatever with respect to potency, sex desire and sex satisfaction. Certainly no complaints or adverse reports have been received from any of the patients, 31.9 per cent of whom were married. Judging from the California reports none of importance need be expected. In their experience the great majority of both males and females experienced no change whatever, in a few there was a slight increase in libido and satisfaction, and in a rare case a slight decrease. Undoubtedly in married females the removal of all fear of pregnancy may have the psychological effect in some cases of heightening satisfaction.

NOTES ON CASES PRESENTED.

As stated above the statute was assented to March 21, 1928. On May 10, 1929, the first operation—a vasectomy—was performed, and the second—a salpingectomy—on December 9, 1929. Since then the work has been steadily increasing as shown below:

Year.	Cases presented and passed.		Operations performed.	
1929	4		3	
1930	42		36	
1931	88		64	
1932	63		49	
1933	91		54	
	——	288	——	206
1934 (to June 15)	126		55	
	——	414	——	261

This report, however, covers only the cases presented or operated on up to December 31, 1933.

Of the 288 cases 87 were males and 201 females. Of these 48 males and 158 females—a total of 206—have been operated on. Of the 288, 150, or 52.1 per cent, were presented from the Provincial Mental Hospital, two from the Provincial Mental Institute (an institution caring mainly for chronic patients), 33, or 18.4 per cent, from the Provincial Training School, and 12 from the psychopathic ward, a total from these institutions of 217, or 75.4 per cent. Seventy-one, or 24.7per cent, have been presented through the three mental health clinics at Edmonton, Calgary and Lethbridge.

Of the 206 operations 98, or 47.6 per cent, have been performed in the University Hospital, Edmonton; 56, or 27.2 per cent, in the Calgary General Hospital, Calgary; 24, or 11.8 per cent, in the Municipal Hospital, Red Deer; 14, or 6.8 per cent, in the Galt Hospital, Lethbridge; and 14, or 6.8 per cent, in the recently organized surgical center at the Provincial Mental Hospital, Ponoka.

The ages of patients varied from 12 to 45, but as might be expected nearly 77 per cent are under 30 years of age, that is early in the reproductive period; and the largest group—30.2 per cent—fall within the half decade—16 to 20. (Table A1)

Of the 288 patients, 87 were males (30.2 per cent) and 201 females (69.8 per cent), 190, or 66 per cent, were single; 92, or 31.9 per cent, were married; two were widowed and four separated or divorced. (Table A1)

At least 189, or 65.6 per cent, had never got beyond public school, and of these 19, or 6.6 per cent, were so low in intelligence that they were incapable of any public school work. With respect to race and nationality the attention of the Board has been pretty evenly applied.

It is noteworthy that only 14.2 per cent of the 288 patients were regarded as self-supporting, and 24 per cent as potentially self-supporting, 34 per cent partially self-supporting and 27.8 per cent were dependent. Of these some were dependent by reason of their immaturity chronologically, and some by reason of their low intelligence rating.

In the matter of diagnostic classification 156, or 54.2 per cent, were defective. (Table A2) To this defect were in many cases added other problems such as sexual delinquency and other behavior problems, epilepsy and congenital syphilis. If one adds to these the 36 cases of mental deficiency with psychosis the total of those diagnosed as mental defectives with or without other complications amounts to 192, or 66.7 per cent, just two-thirds of the total. Formal psychometrics on those cases in which such a step was indicated or possible revealed that according to these tests 205 (71.2 per cent) of all cases were defectives with intelligence quotients of 75 or less. Of the 205 about two-thirds were morons and hence in the socially more difficult class, and one-third in the imbecile group, while six patients (2 per cent) were in the idiot group. It is noteworthy that at least one of these idiots as well as several with intelligence quotients below 30 had had illegitimate children.

On the other hand, 123, or 42.7 per cent, were or had been psychotic, the manic-depressive and schizophrenic cases especially of the catatonic group predominating. The future of the defective is in general more easily predicted than of the psychotic and hence a larger proportion of defectives presented to the Board have been operated on.

Of the 288 cases passed by the Board conditionally or unconditionally 206 (71.5 per cent) had been operated on by December 31, 1933. Various reasons, such as refusal or withdrawal of consent, consent not yet obtained, patient pregnant or not recovered, accounted for the fact that the operation had not yet been done in the other 82 cases. (Table A3) In 18 of the 82, consent was subsequently obtained, and the operation performed in the early months of 1934. Refusal, withdrawal or cancellation of consent account for failure to have the operation performed in 39 cases, or 47.6 per cent, of the 82. There is a greater reluctance on the part of males than of females to seek or submit to operation.

A consideration in some detail of the sexually moral reactions and childbearing records of the 201 female patients brings out in sharp relief some of the most cogent reasons for sterilization. Of these patients 122 were single and 79 were married. Of the single women 22 were regarded as having been promiscuous, 45 had had one or more illicit sexual experiences described throughout the report as irregularities though not apparently promiscuous, nine were doubtful in this respect and only 46, or 37.7 per cent, had clear moral records. It is to be remembered that the majority of these patients were defective and the rest had had mental breakdowns, and hence their conduct was to be interpreted as a symptom of impaired ability to make a social adjustment, and of lack of judgment and inhibition. Of these 122 single women 40, or 32.8 per cent, had given birth to 58 children, an average of 1.45 children each. Of the 40 unmarried mothers 27 had had one child each, 11 two children each, one three children and one six illegitimate children. The ages of the 82 nulliparous single women varied from 12 to 30 with an average of 20.9 years. The ages of the 40 unmarried mothers varied from 15 to 38 with an average of 22.7 years, hence the reproductive life of both groups had only just commenced.

Of the 79 married women (including widowed, separated and divorced) there was a history of promiscuity in 10 and of irregularity in 11, while in 56 the records were clear. Here again, however, with an unsatisfactory moral record in 29.1 per cent of cases the evidence of lowered power of social adjustment is clear.

Of these 79 patients 75, or 94.9 per cent, had borne a total of 300 children, an average of four children each. Of these children 28 (9.3 per cent) were illegitimate. Eleven mothers had one child each, 12 two, 15 three, 10 four, 13 five, 5 six, 2 eight, 2 nine, 4 ten and 1 eleven children.

Adding these 28 illegitimate children to the previous 58 gives us a total of 86 unwanted homeless children, or 24 per cent of the 358 children born to the 115 of the 201 female patients.

The ages of the 75 married multipara varied from 18 to 41 with an average of 30.9. The ages of· the other four married women varied from 25 to 30 with an average of 28.2 years. This group was, therefore, in general in the middle of the child bearing period of life.

As mentioned above the great majority of the single females were defectives (73.8 per cent), or if one includes mental defectives with psychosis, 86.1 per cent. While not so large a percentage of married women belonged to this group, of the 201, married and single, 135, or 67.2 per cent, belonged to the diagnostic groups of mental deficiency with and without psychosis, and hence to a great extent their inability to make a satisfactory social adjustment. In support of this is the fact that of the 86 illegitimate children 79, or 91.9 per cent, were born to this group of defective women.

There was a definite history of venereal disease in 15, and a probable history of it in seven—a total of 22 (10.9 per cent) of the female cases.

In parenthesis one may add that definite information about their 358 children would be of great value and interest. A limited social service personnel, great distances, the expense and the newness of the work have all prevented obtaining much in that respect. Considering the average age of the mothers, the average age of the children must be low, and as a matter of fact many are only infants. It is, therefore, utterly impossible to guess at the incidence of future psychoses among them or even to any extent at their mental developments. Of 281 (78.5 per cent) little or nothing is known, 20 (5.6 per cent) are dead, 9 (2.5 per cent) are weak physically, 20 (5.6 per cent) are at present normal and 28 (7.8 per cent) are known to be defective—certainly a large percentage even if all the rest were normal. We can only guess at what proportion of the 281 are defective or doomed to a mental breakdown later on. It may not be large, and it may not be small, but certainly it will be above the average.

The question will surely be asked, what of the moral conduct of those patients who have been operated on? One operative case of the doubtful group drifted into questionable habits after discharge, due, it is thought, to the influence of her sister. One of the irregular group, a defective who had had two illegitimate children, became promiscuous after discharge. These have both been readmitted. Four of the promiscuous group have, it is feared, returned to their former ways. But these are few indeed as compared with the number of pre-admission moral problem cases.

The situation is summarized well in, Fig. 19-6 [not reproduced], where it will be seen that of the 158 operative cases 98 (62.0 per cent) had been discharged and were making a good moral adjustment when last reported as against 71 (44.9 per cent) before admission; and only 2 (1.3 per cent) and 4 (2. 5 per cent) were causing worry on account of doubtful and questionable promiscuous behavior after discharge as compared with 11 doubtful (6.9 per cent), 49 (31 per cent) irregular, and 27 (17.7 per cent) promiscuous before. There were in institutions at the end of 1933 47, or 29.7 per cent.

This very reassuring improvement is doubtless due in part if not to a great extent to the effect of institutional training and to the follow-up contacts, though these contacts are admittedly inadequate. But of one thing we are convinced, sterilization does not lead to increased immorality.

A word about the moral reactions of the male patients. Information in this respect is inadequate, and the problem is not after all so important socially as in the case of the female sex. 47.1 per cent had previously good moral records which compares favorably with the 44.9 per cent of the female patients. 20.5 per cent had been doubtful, 23 per cent irregular and 9.2 per cent promiscuous. We have assembled no information about their children. The great majority of the men were, of course, single. There was a history of venereal disease in only seven cases.

In passing it is interesting to report that in two cases—one male and one female—sterilization has had the effect of keeping together a family that would inevitably have been broken up through separation. In two other cases sterilization has certainly prevented further mental breakdowns, and in the case of one mentally defective woman making a very satisfactory adjustment under the circumstances it enabled her to continue to do so.

Another interesting fact is that six patients who were operated on subsequently married. They were all females—morons except one, an imbecile, with I.Q.'s varying from 45 to 64. Two are making a very satisfactory adjustment according to last reports, due it is thought to the training they had received in the Provincial Training School; two a fair adjustment; one (I.Q. 45) rather a poor adjustment, on relief since marriage; and one very soon drifted away from home and back into her former unsatisfactory mode of living. She had been one of the promiscuous group.

A few observations are necessary with respect to one aspect of the study of these cases that is exceedingly important from a eugenics standpoint, and that is the evidence of morbid heredity As shown in Fig. 22-7 [not reproduced], in 16 per cent of the cases there was evidence of insanity; in 2.1 per cent of epilepsy; in 9 per cent of alcoholism; in 15.6 per cent mental deficiency and in 18 per cent other evidence of neuropsychopathic disturbances. Altogether in 60.8 per cent of the cases there was evidence of a mental morbidity, a taint if you like, in the family, and a further study of the detail will show more convincingly how overwhelmingly significant these facts are. In many of the families there was a multiplicity of significant historical facts.

The nature of the problems dealt with and the appropriateness of procedure adopted may very well be illustrated by the citation of four specimen cases which are not by any means unique:

(a) *Male*: 27, married, a defective (M.A. 8 years, I.Q. 50), psychotic attacks, shiftless, delinquent. Father and mother both psychotic and in mental hospital. Sister psychotic. Wife—a defective, M.A. 6 years 10 months, I.Q. 45, repeatedly in hospital. Only child a defective and in the Provincial Training School.

(b) *Male*: 30, single, a defective (M.A. 10 years 3 months, I.Q. 64), promiscuous. Father was insane and in hospital; one brother insane; one brother suicided; several brothers defective.

(c) *Female*: 17, single, a defective (M.A. 8 years 10 months, I.Q. 55), promiscuous, venereal disease. Father and paternal uncle alcoholic; paternal uncle a drug addict. Mother and maternal grandmother psychotic, suicided. Brothers—one retarded; one deserted wife and five children. Sisters—one retarded; one died status epilepticus; one has six illegitimate children and has venereal disease.

(d) *Female*: 35, married, borderline defective and psychoneurotic and physically weak. Maternal grandmother insane. Husband a defective with irritable spells. Children—four defective (two deaf and dumb as well), one a physical weakling, and one only apparently normal.

GENERAL REMARKS.

So much for the cases in detail. From a study of them certain general conclusions may be drawn. First, there are two great psychiatric problems involved—problems more or less closely interwoven and yet distinct. They are the problems of mental deficiency on the one hand, and of mental disease on the other. Associated with these problems, especially mental deficiency, and frequently arising out of them are those very grave problems of social maladjustment—moral, antisocial, economic—and of unmarried motherhood and illegitimacy.

Of the two mental deficiency is socially the more serious for here by reason of the mental defect we find individuals more or less incapable of profiting by ordinary systems of training, often incapable of making a satisfactory economic adjustment especially as parents, lacking in the discretion and inhibitions that enable individuals to conform properly to the requirements of the social group and yet reacting in a primitive and unacceptable manner to the urge of fundamental emotions, unduly prolific both within and without marriage and prone to pass on to posterity their own defects and to bring into the world children doubly handicapped by both heritage and early environment. Clearly they should not be permitted to assume the burdens nor the responsibilities of parenthood. And yet again by reason of their defect neither prohibition, supervision nor ordinary preventive measures are likely to prove effective. Sterilization is for them the only rational, the only logical procedure.

As for mental disease the situation is somewhat different. Not only is there the risk or tendency to pass on to posterity the predisposition to psychosis, instability or defect, there is the environmental effect of broken homes, of the frequent deprivation for children of at least one parent or of the undesirable presence in the home of a mentally diseased person. In the case of females who have had a breakdown there is the menace to continued good mental health that the stress that child bearing and rearing impose. Certainly the person who has had a mental breakdown should have the right to exemption from assuming or increasing the burden of parenthood and without sacrificing altogether the right to a normal married life.

In addition, as child welfare officials know, there is the growing and understandable disinclination on the part of prospective foster parents to accept a child with a bad family history whether of insanity or of defect.

To us these appear unanswerable reasons in favor of sterilization in properly selected cases.

In cases of mental disease rarely does the physician fail to advise against marriage if marriage means parenthood, and yet marriage might under some circumstances be permitted if there were no such risk. Ordinary measures of contraception consistent with normal married life are, even for intelligent people, notoriously unreliable. Where prevention of conception is so important sterilization is the only logical and absolutely dependable procedure especially where it involves no appreciable risk for the male and for the female less risk than childbirth. As previously suggested rarely does a man or woman hesitate to sacrifice not only procreative power, but even the essential organs of reproduction when necessary for the sake of physical health, and rarely under the circumstances does the surgeon hesitate to operate. The mental health of the individual and of the race are fully as important and especially so when weighed against the sacrifice of mere procreative ability alone. The question of mental health is one of great significance; it is in many respects a matter of life or death for the race.

Apart from an unfortunate and thoughtless tendency in some quarters not excluding our own profession to treat sexual sterilization with levity its great importance is becoming more and more widely recognized. There have been no criticisms of this work in Alberta and it is progressing steadily and smoothly. This is perhaps largely due to the composition of the Board, and to the great care exercised in the selection and preparation of cases, and also to the fact that invariably every effort is made to secure the intelligent cooperation of the patient or responsible guardian. Among those in this province who are carrying social welfare responsibilities, and have daily to deal in a practical way with the problems involved there is a steadily growing faith in sterilization as an effective and reasonable method of bringing about at least a partial solution, recognizing of course that neither sterilization nor any other one procedure will prove a complete cure. Sterilization does not, of course, take the place of hospital treatment in the case of patients with mental disease, nor does it make any the less necessary the very essential training carried out by institutions for the mentally subnormal. Neither does it make less desirable the very important contact work and supervision carried on by the corps of social workers in any adequate mental health program. Though a wise provision sterilization as a policy is one that should be put into practice with the utmost care and deliberation and without expecting too rapid progress especially during the early stages, and until public opinion has become fully appraised. of its undoubted wisdom and practicability.

In the mental institutions of Canada there are now some 35,000 patients. It is probable that there are as many more, chiefly defectives, outside or in other institutions, many of them constituting serious social problems. Medical science through its achievements is performing miracles in the preservation of life, but is doing little or nothing to counteract the growing menace that these great problems constitute, and which are probably actually aggravated by these very achievements. Many of the mentally and physically unfit are now being preserved for parenthood who would in the old days have perished in the struggle for existence. And yet sexual sterilization, rationally applied, in selected cases offers within limits an effective means of dealing with these growing problems, and this without effect on the personal health or liberty of the individual. Thus may be taken at least one step toward racial improvement.

The greatness of a country depends not so much upon the numbers of its people as upon the high mental and physical standards of its citizenship.

SUMMARY.

1. The Sexual Sterilization Act of Alberta was assented to March 21, 1928.
2. Up to the end of 1933, 288 cases—87 males and 201 females—had been passed by the Eugenics Board, and are dealt with in this report. Of these 206—48 males and 158 females—had at that time been operated on.
3. These operations—a vasectomy or salpingectomy—have been followed by no serious sequelæ.
4. No complaints have been received as to any change in libido or sex satisfaction, and none are expected.
5. Of the 288 cases 156, or 54.2 per cent, were diagnosed as mentally defective; 36, or 12.5 per cent, as mental deficiency with psychosis and 87, or 30.2 per cent, as otherwise psychotic and 9, or 3.1 per cent, as borderline cases including one with an exceedingly bad family history though otherwise normal.
6. Social problems, such as immorality, illegitimacy, delinquency, dependence, partial or complete, were prominent features in many of the histories.
7. Contrary to frequently expressed fears there is at present no evidence that sterilization will lead to promiscuity or a lowering of moral standards.
8. On the other hand, the treatment and training of patients and the maintenance of an adequate follow up system are still essential.

9. Facts indicating an hereditary taint or predisposition, in many cases to a startling extent, were found in 60.8 per cent of cases.
10. Sexual sterilization is undoubtedly a logical and acceptable method of coping with the great problems of mental disease and defect and their associated problems and should in properly selected and safeguarded cases be as readily resorted to as similar operations for physical disease.

TABLE A1.

Age Groups, Sex, and Civil State of all Patients Presented and Approved by the Eugenics Board, 1929–1933.

Ages	Single		Married		Widowed		Divorced Separated		Total	
	M	F	M	F	M	F	M	F	M	F
11–15	8	20	..	..	..	..	..	..	8	20
16–20	25	58	..	4	..	..	..	..	25	62
21–25	14	30	2	17	..	..	..	2	16	49
26–30	12	8	4	15	1	..	..	1	17	24
31–35	8	3	3	21	..	1	..	1	11	26
36–40	1	3	3	16	..	..	..	..	4	19
41–45	..	..	5	1	..	..	..	..	5	1
46–50	..	..	1	..	..	..	...	..	1	..
Total	68	122	18	74	1	1	..	4	87	201
Percentages	78.2	60.7	20.7	36.8	1.1	0.5	..	2.0	30.2	69.8

Note: The married group includes two common law wives.

TABLE A2.

DIAGNOSTIC CLASSIFICATION OF CASES PRESENTED TO EUGENICS BOARD, 1929–1933.

	Numbers								
	Operation								
	Yes			No			Total		
	M	F	T	M	F	T	M	F	T
Mental deficiency	15	31	46	7	3	10	22	34	56
Mental deficiency with delinquency or behavior problem	6	12	18	9	..	9	15	12	27
Mental deficiency with sex delinquency	2	58	60	..	4	4	2	62	64
Mental deficiency with epilepsy	1	8	9	..	..	..	1	8	9
Totals – mental deficiency	24	109	133	16	7	23	40	116	156
Mental deficiency with psychosis	9	11	20	8	8	16	17	19	36
Psychosis–schizophrenia	5	19	24	12	16	28	17	35	52
Psychosis–manic depressive	5	6	11	1	8	9	6	14	20
Psychosis–with somatic disease, etc.	1	5	6	..	2	2	1	7	8
Psychosis–with epilepsy	..	2	2	..	2	2	..	4	4
G. P. I.	..	2	2	1	..	1	1	2	3
Totals – psychoses	20	45	65	22	36	58	42	81	123
Neurosyphilis	1	..	1	..	..	..	1	..	1
Epilepsy	1	..	1	1	..	1	2	..	2
Psychopathic personality	..	2	2	..	..	...	..	2	2
Psychoneuroses	1	2	3	..	..	..	1	2	3
Normal with marked heredity	1	..	1	..	..	..	1	..	1
Totals – not psychotic or defective	4	4	8	1	..	1	5	4	9
Grand totals	48	158	206	39	43	82	87	201	288
Percentages	23.6	76.7	100	47.6	52.4	100	30.2	69.8	100

[1] Percentages refer to proportions of cases operated on or not in each diagnostic group.

[2] Refers to proportion of cases in each of the columns.

Percentages								
Operation								
Yes[1]			No[1]			Total[2]		
M	F	Total	M	F	Total	M	F	Total
68.2	91.2	82.1	31.8	8.8	17.9	25.3	16.9	19.4
40.0	100.0	66.7	60.0	...	33.3	17.2	6.0	9.4
100.0	93.5	93.8	...	6.5	6.3	2.3	30.8	22.2
100.0	100.0	100.0	...	...	...	1.1	4.0	3.2
60.0	94.0	85.3	40.0	6.0	14.7	46.0	57.7	54.2
52.9	57.9	55.6	47.1	42.1	44.4	19.5	9.5	12.5
29.4	54.3	46.2	70.6	45.7	53.8	19.5	17.4	18.1
83.3	42.9	55.0	16.7	57.1	45.0	6.9	7.0	6.9
100.0	71.4	75.0	...	28.6	25.0	1.1	3.5	2.8
...	50.0	50.0	...	50.0	50.0	...	2.0	1.4
...	100.0	66.7	100.0	..	33.3	1.1	1.0	1.0
47.6	55.6	52.8	52.6	44.4	47.2	48.3	40.3	42.7
100.0	...	100.0	...	...	...	1.1	...	0.3
50.0	...	50.0	50.0	...	50.0	2.3	...	0.7
...	100.0	100.0	...	...	...	...	1.0	0.7
100.0	100.0	100.0	...	...	...	1.1	1.0	1.0
100.0	...	100.0	...	...	...	1.1	...	0.3
80.0	100.0	88.9	20.0	...	11.1	5.7	2.0	3.1
55.2	78.6	71.5	44.8	21.4	28.5	100.0	100.0	100.0

TABLE A3.

Reasons for Operation Not Having Been Performed on the 82 of the 288 Cases Presented to the Board, 1929–1933.

Reasons	M	F	T	Percentage
Consent refused--parents or guardians	4	5	9	11.0
Consent refused--patient	16	11	27	32.9
Consent cancelled by Board on objection, patient's lawyer	..	1	1	1.2
Consent withdrawn	..	2	2	2.4
Total difficulties over consent	**20**	**19**	**39**	**47.6**
Operation deferred at parent's request	..	1	1	1.2
Awaiting consent	4	1	5	6.1
Awaiting consent, subsequently obtained, operation performed, 1934	9	9	18	22.0
Operation deferred on account of transfer to the Provincial Mental Hospital, Ponoka	1	..	1	1.2
Still Psychotic	3	10	13	15.9
Patient pregnant	..	1	1	1.2
Total number of operations still probable	**17**	**22**	**39**	**47.6**
Permanent institutional case	2	1	3	3.7
Died	..	1	1	1.2
Total number of operations cancelled for reasons given	**2**	**2**	**4**	**4.9**
Total	39	43	82	

TABLE A4.

FEMALE CASES–MORAL REACTIONS ACCORDING TO DIAGNOSIS, 1929–1933.

Diagnosis	Good		Doubtful		Irregular		Promiscuous		Total		
	S	M	S	M	S	M	S	M	S	M	
Mental deficiency											
Moron	15	7	6	..	14	2	14	5	49	14	63
Imbecile	13	1	1	..	19	1	5	2	38	4	42
Idiot	2	..	..	..	1	..	..	..	3	..	3
	30	8	7	..	34	3	19	7	90	18	108
Mental deficiency with psychosis	2	6	1	..	2	3	3	2	8	11	19
Mental deficiency with epilepsy	5	..	..	..	2	..	..	1	7	1	8
Psychosis–with epilepsy	..	2	..	1	1	..	..	..	1	3	4
Psychosis–manic-depressive	1	12	..	..	..	1	..	..	1	13	14
Psychosis–schizophrenia	8	20	..	..	4	3	..	..	12	23	35
Psychosis–with somatic disease	..	6	1	..	..	..	..	..	1	6	7
G. P. I.	..	..	..	1	1	..	..	..	1	1	2
Psychopathic personality	..	..	..	..	1	1	..	..	1	1	2
Psychoneurosis	..	2	..	..	..	..	..	..	..	2	2
Total	46	56	9	2	45	11	22	10	122	79	201
	102		11		56		32				
Percentages	37.7	70.9	7.4	2.5	36.9	13.8	18.0	12.7	60.7	39.3	
Total percentage	50.7		5.4		27.8		15.9		100		

M—Includes married, widowed, separated and divorced.

NOTES

FOREWORD

1. National Academy of Sciences, *International Summit on Human Gene Editing: A Global Discussion–Meeting in Brief, December 1–3, 2015*, 6–7. Washington, DC: National Academy of Sciences of the United States of America, 2016. https://www.ncbi.nlm.nih.gov/books/NBK343651/.
2. David Baltimore, opening remarks, quoted in National Academy of Sciences, *International Summit on Human Gene Editing*, 6.
3. Guel A. Russell, "Eugenics: A Paradigm for the Future?," in *The Proceedings of the 22nd Annual History of Medicine Days Conference at the University of Calgary, Alberta, Canada*, ed. Aleksandra Loewenau, William J. Pratt, and Frank W. Stahnisch (Newcastle upon Tyne: Cambridge Scholars Publishing, 2013), 114–48.
4. Francis Galton, *Hereditary Genius: An Inquiry into Its Laws and Consequences* (London: Macmillan, 1869), 28; Galton, "The Possible Improvement of the Human Breed under the Existing Conditions of Law and Sentiment (1905)," in *Essays in Eugenics*, ed. Eugenics Education Society (London: Eugenics Education Society, 1905), 1–34, esp. 1.
5. Daniel Kevles, *In the Name of Eugenics* (Cambridge, MA: Harvard University Press, 1985), 5–6.
6. Henry J. Muller, "The Dominance of Economics over Eugenics," in *A Decade of Progress in Eugenics: Scientific Papers of the Third International Congress of Eugenics* (Baltimore: William & Wilkins, 1933), 142–44.
7. Muller, "Dominance of Economics," 144–45.
8. Jan A. Inglis and John R. Inglis, eds. *Davenport's Dream: 21st Century Reflections on Heredity and Eugenics* (Cold Spring Harbor, NY: Cold Spring Laboratory Press, 2008), 15–16. Includes a reprint of Charles Davenport's *Heredity in Relation to Eugenics* (1911).
9. Kevles, *In the Name of Eugenics*, 3–4.
10. Stephen J. Gould, *The Mismeasure of Man*, rev ed. (New York: Norton, 1996), 10.
11. Gould, *Mismeasure of Man*, 10.
12. Gould, *Mismeasure of Man*, 24–25.

13. See in Michael Shermer, *The Moral Arc* (New York: Henry Holt, 2015), 3.

PROLOGUE

1. Robert A. Wilson, *The Eugenic Mind Project* (Cambridge, MA: MIT Press, 2018); Wilson, "Eugenic Thinking," *Philosophy, Theory, and Practice in Biology* 10, no. 12 (2018): 1–8; Wilson, "Eugenics Never Went Away," *Aeon Magazine*, June 5, 2018, https://aeon.co/essays/eugenics-today-where-eugenic-sterilisation-continues-now; Wilson, "Contemporary Forms of Eugenics," *eLS Wiley Online*, September 15, 2018, https://doi.org/10.1002/9780470015902.a0027075; Wilson, "The Role of Oral History in Surviving a Eugenic Past," in *Beyond Testimony and Trauma: Oral History in the Aftermath of Mass Violence*, ed. Steven High (Vancouver: University of British Columbia Press, 2015), 119–38; Robert A. Wilson and Joshua St. Pierre, "Eugenics and Disability," in *Rethinking Disability: World Perspectives in Culture and Society*, ed. Patrick Devlieger, Beatriz Miranda-Galarza, Steven E. Brown, and Megan Strickfaden (Antwerp: Garant, 2016), 93–112; and Matthew J. Barker and Robert A. Wilson, "Well-Being, Disability, and Choosing Children," *Mind* 128, no. 510 (2019): 305–28.
2. Daniel Kevles, *In the Name of Eugenics* (Cambridge, MA: Harvard University Press, 1985); Paul Lombardo, *Three Generations, No Imbeciles: Eugenics, the Supreme Court, and Buck v. Bell* (Baltimore: Johns Hopkins University Press, 2008).
3. Alison Bashford and Philippa Levine, eds., *The Oxford Handbook of the History of Eugenics* (Oxford: Oxford University Press, 2010); Gregor Wolbring, ed., "What Sorts of People Should There Be?," special issue, *International Journal of Disability, Community, and Rehabilitation* 12, no. 2 (2013); Erika Dyck, ed., "The History of Eugenics Revisited," special issue, *Canadian Bulletin of Medical History* 31, no. 1 (2014); Paul Lombardo, ed., *A Century of Eugenics in America: From the Indiana Experiment to the Human Genome Era* (Bloomington: Indiana University Press, 2011); Randell Hansen and Desmond King, *Sterilized by the State: Eugenics, Race, and the Population Scare in Twentieth-Century North America* (New York: Cambridge University Press, 2013); Jane Harris-Zsovan, *Eugenics and the Firewall: Why Alberta's UFA/Social Credit Legacy Matters to 21st Century Canadians* (Winnipeg: J. Gordon Shillingford, 2010); Erika Dyck, *Facing Eugenics: Reproduction, Sterilization, and the Politics of Choice* (Toronto: University of Toronto Press, 2013); Kevin Begos, Danielle Deaver, John Railey, and Scott Sexton, *Against Their Will: North Carolina's Sterilization Program and the Campaign for Reparations*

(Apalachicola, FL: Gray Oak Books, 2012); Leilani Muir, *A Whisper Past: Childless after Eugenic Sterilization in Alberta* (Victoria, BC: Friesen Press, 2014); Wilson, "Role of Oral History," 119–38. See also the Eugenics Archives website, http://eugenicsarchive.ca/.

4. Mohammed Abouelleil Rashed, "In Defense of Madness: The Problem of Disability," *Journal of Medicine and Philosophy* 44, no. 2 (2019): 150–74.
5. Gunnar Broberg and Nils Roll-Hansen, eds., *Eugenics and the Welfare State: Norway, Sweden, Denmark, and Finland* (East Lansing: Michigan State University Press, 2005).
6. Carolyn Frohmader, *Dehumanised: The Forced Sterilisation of Women and Girls with Disabilities in Australia*, Women with Disabilities Australia (WWDA) submission to the Senate Inquiry into the Involuntary or Coerced Sterilisation of People with Disabilities in Australia (Rosny Park, Tasmania, March 2013), http://wwda.org.au/wp-content/uploads/2013/12/WWDA_Sub_SenateInquiry_Sterilisation_March2013.pdf; Australia, Parliament, Senate, Community Affairs References Committee, *Involuntary or Coerced Sterilisation of People with Disabilities in Australia* (Canberra, 2013), https://www.aph.gov.au/Parliamentary_Business/Committees/Senate/Community_Affairs/Involuntary_Sterilisation/First_Report; Corey G. Johnson, "Female Inmates Sterilized in California Prisons without Approval," Reveal, Center for Investigative Reporting, July 7, 2013, https://www.revealnews.org/article/female-inmates-sterilized-in-california-prisons-without-approval/.
7. Henry H. Goddard, *The Kallikak Family: A Study in the Heredity of Feeble-Mindedness* (New York: Macmillan, 1913); Lennard J. Davis, *Enforcing Normalcy: Disability, Deafness, and the Body* (New York: Verso, 1995).
8. Robert A. Wilson, "Eugenic Traits," Eugenics Archives, April 28, 2014, http://eugenicsarchive.ca/database/documents/535eeb757095aa0000000221. For a more developed discussion, see also Wilson, *Eugenic Mind Project*, chap. 3.
9. Marsha Saxton, "Why Members of the Disability Community Oppose Prenatal Diagnoses and Selective Abortion," in *Prenatal Testing and Disability Rights*, ed. Erik Parens and Adrienne Asch (Washington, DC: Georgetown University Press, 2000), 147–64; Adrienne Asch, "Why I Haven't Changed My Mind about Prenatal Diagnosis: Reflections and Reminders," in Parens and Asch, *Prenatal Testing and Disability Rights*, 234–58; Asch, "Disability Equality and Prenatal Testing: Contradictory or Compatible?," *Florida State University Law Review* 30 (2003): 315–42. See also Angus McLaren and Arlene Tigar McLaren, *The Bedroom and the State: The Changing Practices and Politics of Contraception and Abortion in Canada, 1880–1980* (Toronto: McClelland & Stewart, 1997).

10. Rosemarie Garland-Thomson, "The Case for Conserving Disability," *Journal of Bioethical Inquiry* 9, no. 3 (2012): 339–55.
11. "Our Stories," Eugenics Archives, http://eugenicsarchive.ca/discover/our-stories; Jordan Miller, Nicola Fairbrother, and Rob Wilson, dirs., *Surviving Eugenics* (Vancouver: Moving Images Distribution, 2015), DVD, online at http://eugenicsarchive.ca/film/.
12. James I. Charlton, *Nothing about Us without Us: Disability Oppression and Empowerment* (Berkeley: University of California Press, 1998).
13. Wilson, "Eugenic Traits"; Wilson, *Eugenic Mind Project*, chap. 3; Theresa R. Richardson, *The Century of the Child: The Mental Hygiene Movement and Social Policy in the United States and Canada* (New York: State University of New York Press, 1989).
14. Robert A. Wilson, "Psychology," Eugenics Archives, December 1, 2014, http://eugenicsarchive.ca/database/documents/547ce966d7dacd0147000002; Aida Roige, "Intelligence and IQ Testing," Eugenics Archives, April 19, 2014, http://eugenicsarchive.ca/database/documents/535eecb77095aa000000023a.
15. Lionel Penrose, *The Biology of Mental Defect* (London: Sidgwick and Jackson, 1949); Nikolas S. Rose, *The Psychological Complex: Psychology, Politics and Society in England, 1869–1939* (London: Routledge, 1985); Kevles, *In the Name of Eugenics*.
16. See also Michael Hagner, *Homo cerebralis. Der Wandel vom Seelenorgan zum Gehirn* (Frankfurt am Main, Germany: Insel, 2000).
17. Emil Kraepelin, "Psychiatric Observations on Contemporary Issues" (1919), trans. Eric J. Engstrom, *History of Psychiatry* 3, no. 2 (1992): 256–69.
18. Natalie Ball, "Le Vann, Leonard J.," Eugenics Archives, n.d., http://eugenicsarchive.ca/database/documents/512fa4b134c5399e2c00000d; Muir, *A Whisper Past*.
19. Serife Tekin and Robyn Bluhm, eds., *The Bloomsbury Companion to Philosophy of Psychiatry* (London: Bloomsbury, 2019); Natalia Washington, "Contextualism as a Solution to Paternalism in Psychiatric Practice," *Philosophy, Psychiatry, & Psychology* 25, no. 4 (2018): 235–43; Washington, "Culturally Unbound: Cross-Cultural Cognitive Diversity and the Science of Psychopathology," *Philosophy, Psychiatry, & Psychology* 23, no. 2 (2016): 165–79.

INTRODUCTION

1. Frank W. Stahnisch and Fred Weizmann, "Eugenics and Psychiatry—Analyzing the Origin, Application, and Perception of Early Forced Sterilization Programs from a Medical History Viewpoint," in *ISHN and*

Cheiron, ed. University of Calgary (Calgary, AB: University of Calgary, 2011), www.ucalgary.ca/ISHN_ Cheiron/node/39.

2. See the Eugenics Archives website, a project of the Living Archives on Eugenics Research Group, at http://eugenicsarchive.ca.
3. Frank W. Stahnisch, "Eugenics and Psychiatry—Analyzing the Origin, Application and Perception of Early Forced Sterilization Programs from a Medical History Viewpoint," *Journal of the History of the Neurosciences* 21, no. 1 (2012): 97–98.
4. Eric Hobsbawm, *The Age of Extremes: The Short Twentieth Century, 1914–1991* (London: Michel Joseph, 1994).
5. See also Joachim Radkau, *Das Zeitalter der Nervositaet. Deutschland zwischen Bismarck und Hitler* (Munich: Fink Verlag, 1998), 9–15.
6. Ian Robert Dowbiggin, *Keeping America Sane: Psychiatry and Eugenics in the United States and Canada, 1880–1940* (Ithaca, NY: Cornell University Press, 2003), 23–69.
7. Frank W. Stahnisch, "The Early Eugenics Movement and Emerging Professional Psychiatry: Conceptual Transfers and Personal Relationships between Germany and North America, 1880s to 1930s," *Canadian Bulletin of Medical History* 31, no. 1 (2014): 17–40.
8. See, for example, Christian Promitzer, Sevasti Trubeta, and Marius Turda, *Health, Hygiene, and Eugenics in Southeastern Europe to 1945* (Budapest: Central European University Press, 2010).
9. Frans G. I. Jennekens, "A Short History of the Notion of Neurodegenerative Disease," *Journal of the History of the Neurosciences* 23, no. 1 (2014): 85–94.
10. Rolf Winau, "Menschenzuechtung—Utopien und ethische Bewertung," in *Machbarkeitsphantasien*, ed. Alfred Schaefer and Michael Wimmer (Berlin: Reimer Verlag, 2002), 55–65; Susan Lanzoni, "Diagnosing Modernity: Mania and Authenticity in the Existential Genre," *Configurations* 12, no. 2 (2004): 107–31.
11. In 1883, Galton coined the term "eugenics" and described it as "the study of agencies under social control that may improve or impair the racial qualities of future generations, either physically or mentally." Francis Galton, *Inquiries into Human Faculty and Its Development* (London: Macmillan, 1883), 30.
12. Angus McLaren, *Our Own Master Race: Eugenics in Canada, 1885–1945* (Toronto: McClelland & Stewart, 1990), 15.
13. The term "unfit" was used to describe a variety of individuals and groups, including the mentally disabled, the physically disabled, new immigrants, the poor, and criminals, among others. McLaren, *Our Own Master Race*, 16.
14. James E. Moran and David Wright, eds., *Mental Health and Canadian Society* (Montréal and Kingston: McGill-Queen's University Press, 2008).

15. Byron M. Unkauf, "The Sterilization of the Mental Defective," *The University of Manitoba Medical Journal* 5/6, no. 1 (1933–35): 46. See also chapter 5 in this volume.
16. Volker Roelcke, "Die Etablierung der psychiatrischen Genetik in Deutschland, Grossbritannien und den USA, ca. 1910–1960. Zur untrennbaren Geschichte von Eugenik und Humangenetik," *Acta Historica Leopoldina* 48, no. 2 (2007): 173–90; Peter Hoff and Matthias M. Weber, "Sozialdarwinismus und die Psychiatrie im Nationalsozialismus," *Der Nervenarzt* 11, no. 10 (2002): 1017–18.
17. Maren Lorenz, "Proto-Eugenic Thought and Breeding Utopias in the United States before 1870," *Bulletin of the German Historical Institute* 43, no. 1 (2008): 67–90.
18. Michael Haines and Richard H. Steckel, eds., *A Population History of North America* (Cambridge: Cambridge University Press, 2000), 81–91.
19. Redpath Library: Special Collections and Journal Collections; McGill University, Montréal, Sessional Papers. Select Standing Committee on Law Amendments re: Mental Deficiency. G8250 (1933).
20. McLaren, *Our Own Master Race*, 97–100.
21. Erna Kurbegović, "The Influence of the Manitoba Mental Hygiene Survey, 1918," *Western Humanities Review* 69, no. 3 (2016): 311.
22. See McLaren, *Our Own Master Race*, 31.
23. Collection on Immigration to Canada, Bibliothèque et Archives nationales du Québec, Montréal.
24. McLaren, *Our Own Master Race*, 47.
25. Amy Samson, "Eugenics in the Community: United Farm Women of Alberta, Public Health Nursing, Teaching, Social Work, and Sexual Sterilization in Alberta, 1928–1972" (PhD diss., University of Saskatchewan, 2014), 33.
26. McLaren, *Our Own Master Race*, 55.
27. Ian Robert Dowbiggin, *The Quest for Mental Health: A Tale of Science, Medicine, Scandal, Sorrow, and Mass Society* (Cambridge: Cambridge University Press, 2011), 102.
28. McLaren, *Our Own Master Race*; Ian Dowbiggin, *The Sterilization Movement and Global Fertility in the Twentieth Century* (Oxford: Oxford University Press, 2008); Erika Dyck, *Facing Eugenics: Reproduction, Sterilization, and the Politics of Choice* (Toronto: University of Toronto Press, 2013).
29. McLaren, *Our Own Master Race*.
30. Richard Cairney, "'Democracy Was Never Intended for Degenerates': Alberta's Flirtation with Eugenics Comes Back to Haunt It," *Canadian Medical Association Journal* 155, no. 7 (1997): 789.

31. Ian Dowbiggin, *Sterilization Movement and Global Fertility in the Twentieth Century* (Oxford: Oxford University Press, 2008); Angus McLaren, *Reproduction by Design: Sex, Robots, Trees, and Test-Tube Babies in Interwar Britain* (Chicago: University of Chicago Press, 2012).
32. Jana Grekul, "Sterilization in Alberta, 1928 to 1972: Gender Matters," *Canadian Review of Sociology* 45, no. 3 (2008): 247–66. See also Jana Grekul, Harvey Krahn, and David Odynak, "Sterilizing the 'Feeble Minded': Eugenics in Alberta, Canada 1929–72," *Journal of Historical Sociology* 17, no. 4 (2004): 358–84.
33. Geertje Boschma, "A Family Point of View: Negotiating Asylum Care in Alberta, 1905–1930," *Canadian Bulletin of Medical History* 25, no. 2 (2008): 367–89.
34. Michael Gauvreau and Olivier Hubert, eds., *The Churches and Social Order in Nineteenth and Twentieth Century Canada* (Montréal and Kingston: McGill-Queen's University Press, 2006).
35. Sebastien Normandin, "Eugenics, McGill and the Catholic Church in Montréal and Québec, 1890–1942," *Canadian Bulletin of Medical History* 15, no. 1 (1998): 59–86.
36. See Donald J. Dietrich, "Catholic Theologians in Hitler's Reich: Adaptation and Critique," *Journal of Church and State* 29, no. 1 (1987): 19–45; Donald J. Dietrich, "Catholic Eugenics in Germany, 1920–1945: Hermann Muckermann, S.J. and Joseph Mayer," *Journal of Church and State* 34, no. 3 (1992): 575–600.
37. See Erika Dyck and Alex Deighton, *Managing Madness: Weyburn Mental Hospital and the Transformation of Psychiatric Care in Canada* (Winnipeg: University of Manitoba Press, 2017); Deighton, "The Nature of Eugenic Thought and Limits of Eugenic Practice in Interwar Saskatchewan," in *Eugenics at the Edges of Empire: New Zealand, Australia, Canada, and South Africa*, ed. Diane B. Paul, Hamish G. Spencer, and John Stenhouse (Cham, NY: Palgrave Macmillan, 2018), 63–84; Dyck, *Facing Eugenics*; Karolina Kowalewski and Yasmin Mayne, "The Translation of Eugenic Ideology into Public Health Policy: The Case of Alberta and Saskatchewan," in *The Proceedings of the 18th Annual History of Medicine Days Conference 2009*, ed. Lisa Peterman, Kerry Sun, and Frank W. Stahnisch (Newcastle upon Tyne: Cambridge Scholars Publishing, 2012), 53–74.
38. Alex Deighton, "Saskatchewan," Eugenics Archives, March 26, 2015, http://eugenicsarchive.ca/discover/world/551482b25eff8d344d000001.
39. Deighton, "Nature of Eugenic Thought," 66.
40. Dyck and Deighton, *Managing Madness*, 73.
41. Deighton, "Nature of Eugenic Thought."

42. Jaclyn Duffin, "The Guru and the Godfather: Henry Sigerist, Hugh MacLean, and the Politics of Health Care Reform in 1940s Canada," *Canadian Bulletin of Medical History* 9, no. 2 (1992): 191–218.
43. Duffin, "Guru and Godfather."
44. Deighton, "Saskatchewan."
45. Mental Defectives Act, R.S.S. 1930, c. 196, sections 1–2.
46. Deighton, "Nature of Eugenic Thought," 77.
47. Deighton, "Nature of Eugenic Thought," 67–70.
48. Deighton, "Nature of Eugenic Thought," 78.
49. See Yvonne Boyer and Judith Bartlett, "External Review: Tubal Ligation in the Saskatoon Health Region: The Lived Experience of Aboriginal Women" (unpublished paper, Saskatoon, July 27, 2017), https://www.saskatoonhealthregion.ca/DocumentsInternal/Tubal_Ligation_intheSaskatoonHealthRegion_the_Lived_Experience_of_Aboriginal_Women_BoyerandBartlett_July_22_2017.pdf.
50. Carolyn Strange and Jennifer A. Stephen, "Eugenics in Canada: A Checkered History, 1850s–1990s," in *The Oxford Handbook of the History of Eugenics*, ed. Alison Bashford and Philippa Levine (Oxford: Oxford University Press, 2010), 527–38.
51. Naomi Nind, "Solving an 'Appalling' Problem: Social Reformers and the Campaign for the Alberta Sexual Sterilization Act, 1928," *Alberta Law Review* 38, no. 4 (2000): 536–62.
52. See also Amy Samson, "Eugenics in the Community: Gendered Professions and Eugenic Sterilization in Alberta, 1928–1972," *Canadian Bulletin of Medical History* 31, no. 1 (2014): 143–63.
53. MacEachran, interview by Myers.
54. Ian Robert Dowbiggin, *Keeping America Sane: Psychiatry and Eugenics in the United States and Canada, 1880–1940* (Ithaca, NY: Cornell University Press, 2003), 100. The first American state to pass a sterilization law was Indiana (1907), followed by California, Washington, and Connecticut (all 1909).
55. Deighton, "Nature of Eugenic Thought," 63–82.
56. This is quite visible from the historical information available in the Provincial Archives of Alberta's Department of Public Health Fond (acc. no. 86.36 (~RPC 85/230 – 11-30-5-Z 517), 1935), where early on all available reports and publications related to the forced sterilization program were collected and assembled, together with other "noteworthy" social and medical information related to the public health mandate of the province. See, for example, Charles A. Baragar, Georges A. Davidson, William J. McAlister, and David L. McCulloch, "Sexual Sterilization: Four Years Experience in Alberta," *American Journal of Psychiatry* 91 (1935): 897–923 (see Appendix).

57. On the abolishment of the act, and the Leilani Muir trial (1995–96) that followed, see Douglas Wahlsten, "Leilani Muir versus the Philosopher King: Eugenics on Trial in Alberta," *Genetica* 99, no. 1 (1997): 185–98; Leilani Muir, *A Whisper Past: Childless after Eugenic Sterilization in Alberta* (Victoria, BC: Friesen Press, 2014).
58. See Kowalewski and Mayne, "Translation of Eugenic Ideology."
59. Jana Grekul, Harvey Krahn, and Dave Odynak, "Sterilizing the 'Feeble-Minded': Eugenics in Alberta, Canada, 1929–1972," *Journal of Historical Sociology* 17, no. 4 (2004): 358–84.
60. See also Grekul, *Sterilization in Alberta*, 247–66.
61. Grekul, Krahn, and Odynak, "Sterilizing the 'Feeble-Minded,'" 361.
62. McLaren, *Our Own Master Race*, 168.
63. See Kowalewski and Mayne, "Translation of Eugenic Ideology."
64. McLaren, *Our Own Master Race*, 127–-45.
65. Amanda Oliveira, "The Coming and Going of Eugenics in Alberta: A Discarded History, 1928 to 1972," (MA thesis, Lakehead University, 2016), 62.
66. See for example, Dominique Marshall, *The Social Origins of the Welfare State: Quebec Families, Compulsory Education, and Family Allowances, 1940–1955* (Waterloo, ON: Wilfrid Laurier University Press, 2006).
67. See McLaren, *Our Own Master Race*, 55.
68. See, for example, Neal Ross Holtan, "The Eitels and Their Hospital," *Minnesota Medicine* 36 (2003): 52–54; David Gibson, "Involuntary Sterilization of the Mentally Retarded: A Western Canadian Phenomenon," *Canadian Psychiatric Association Journal* 19, no. 1 (1974): 59–63.
69. Bénédict Augustin Morel, *Traité des dégénérescences physique, et intellectuelles et morales de l'espèce humaine et de ces causes qui produisent ces variétiés maladives*, 2 vols. (Paris: Baillière, 1857/58).
70. Constantin von Monakow and Raoul Mourge, "Introduction biologique à l'étude de la neurologie et de la psychopathologie," *Zeitschrift fuer Psychologie* 115, no. 4 (1928): 403–10.
71. Erwin H. Ackerknecht, *A Short History of Psychiatry* (New York: Hafner, 1968), 70.
72. Hermann Oppenheim, *Die traumatischen Neurosen nach den in der Nervenklinik der Charité in den letzten 5 Jahren gesammelten Beobachtungen* (Berlin: Hirschwald, 1889).
73. Joachim Radkau, *Das Zeitalter der Nervositaet*. Deutschland zwischen Bismarck und Hitler. Munich: Fink Verlag, 1998, 9–15.
74. Axel Karenberg, "Klinische Neurologie in Deutschland bis zum Ersten Weltkrieg—die Begruender des Faches und der Fachgesellschaft," in *100*

Jahre Deutsche Gesellschaft fuer Neurologie, ed. Detlef Koempf (Berlin: Deutsche Gesellschaft fuer Neurologie, 2007), 20–29.

75. Heinz-Peter Schmiedebach, "The Public's View of Neurasthenia in Germany—Looking for a New Rhythm of Life," in *Cultures of Neurasthenia: From Beard to the First World War*, ed. Marijke Gijswijt-Hofstra and Roy Porter (Amsterdam: Rodopi, 2001), 219–38; Wolfgang U. Eckart, "'Die wachsende Nervositaet unserer Zeit'—Medizin und Kultur im Fin de siècle am Beispiel der Modekrankheit Neurasthenie," in *Psychiatrie um die Jahrhundertwende*, ed. Fritz Reimer (Heilbronn, Germany: Weinsberger Kolloquium, 1994), 9–38; Hans-Georg Hofer, "War Neurosis and Viennese Psychiatry in World War One," in *Uncovered Fields: Perspectives in First World War Studies*, ed. Jenny Macleod and Pierre Purseigle (Amsterdam: Amsterdam University Press, 2004), 243–60.
76. Wilhelm Erb, *Ueber die wachsende Nervositaet unserer Zeit. Akademische Rede zum Geburtsfeste des hoechstseligen Grossherzogs Karl Friedrich am 22. November 1893 beim Vortrage des Jahresberichts und der Verkuendigung der akademischen Preise gehalten* (Heidelberg: Universitaetsreden, 1893), 1; translated by Frank W. Stahnisch.
77. Joachim Radkau, "The Neurasthenic Experience in Imperial Germany: Expeditions into Patient Records and Side-Looks upon General History," in Gijswijt-Hofstra and Porter, *Cultures of Neurasthenia*, 199–217.
78. Alois Alzheimer, "Ist die Einrichtung einer psychiatrischen Abteilung im Reichsgesundheitsamt erstrebenswert?," *Zeitschrift fuer die gesamte Neurologie und Psychiatrie* 6, no. 2 (1911): 242–46; Auguste Forel, *Hygiene der Nerven und des Geistes im Gesunden und kranken Zustande* (Stuttgart: E. Moritz, 1905); Peter Zuerner, "Von der Hirnanatomie zur Eugenik. Die Suche nach den biologischen Ursachen der Geisteskrankheiten. Eine Untersuchung am Beispiel des Werkes von August Forel, (1848–1931)" (Med. diss., University of Mainz, 1983).
79. See also Radkau, *Das Zeitalter der Nervositaet*, 9–15.
80. Johannes Hendrikus Burgers, "Max Nordau, Madison Grant, and Racialized Theories of Ideology," *Journal of the History of Ideas* 72, no. 1 (2011): 119–40.
81. Volker Roelcke, "Electrified Nerves, Degenerated Bodies: Medical Discourses in Neurasthenia in Germany, ca. 1990–1914," in Gijswijt-Hofstra and Porter, *Cultures of Neurasthenia*, 177–97; William H. Tucker, *The Funding of Scientific Racism: Wickliffe Draper and the Pioneer Fund* (Urbana: University of Illinois Press, 2002), 32–47.
82. Roelcke, "Electrified Nerves."
83. Stefan Kuehl, *The Nazi Connection: Eugenics, American Racism, and German National Socialism* (New York: Oxford University Press, 1994), 6.

84. Angelique Richardson, *Love and Eugenics in the Late Nineteenth Century: Rational Reproduction and the New Woman* (Oxford: Oxford University Press, 2003).
85. Garland E. Allen, "The Ideology of Elimination: American and German Eugenics, 1900–1945," in *Medicine and Medical Ethics in Nazi Germany: Origins, Practices, Legacies*, ed. Francis R. Nicosia and Jonathan Huener (New York: Berghahn Books, 2002), 19.
86. Dowbiggin, *Keeping America Sane*, 77.
87. André Dupras, "Public Attitudes towards the Sterilization of Handicapped People," in *Sterilization and Mental Handicap: Proceedings of a Symposium Sponsored by the National Institute on Mental Retardation and the Ontario Association for the Mentally Retarded*, ed. Mental Institute on Mental Retardation, Ontario Association for the Mentally Retarded (Downsview, ON: National Institute on Mental Retardation, 1980), 65.
88. Robert N. Proctor, *Racial Hygiene: Medicine under the Nazis* (Cambridge, MA: Harvard University Press, 1988), 145–48.
89. Henry Friedlander, *Origins of Nazi Genocide: From Euthanasia to the Final Solution* (Chapel Hill: University of North Carolina, 1995), 26.
90. Proctor, *Racial Hygiene*, 131.
91. Kuehl, *Nazi Connection*, 20.
92. Dowbiggin, *Keeping America Sane*, 36.
93. Oswald Bumke, *Ueber Nervoese Entartung* (Berlin: Julius Springer, 1912).
94. See also Michael Hau, *The Cult of Health and Beauty in Germany: A Social History, 1890–1930* (Chicago: Chicago University Press, 2003), 120–24.
95. [Sender of letter] to former Kaiser Wilhelm Society, July 20, 1928, Personal File Ruedin, Historical Archive of the Max-Planck-Society, Div. I, Rep. IA, Library of the Max Planck Institute for the History of Science, Berlin.
96. See also Graham Baker, "Eugenics and Migration: A Case Study of Salvation Army Literature about Canada and Britain, c.1890–1930," *Canadian Bulletin of Medical History* 31, no. 1 (2014): 77–98.
97. Kuehl, *Nazi Connection*, 123.
98. Matthias M. Weber, "Die Deutsche Forschungsanstalt fuer Psychiatrie," in *75 Jahre Max-Planck-Institut fuer Psychiatrie*, ed. Max-Planck-Gesellschaft (Munich: Max Planck Gesellschaft, 1992), 11–33.
99. See also Ruth Leys and Rand B. Evans, *Defining American Psychology: The Correspondence between Adolf Meyer and Edward Bradford Titchener* (Baltimore: Johns Hopkins University Press, 1990); Susan D. Lamb, "Pathologist of the Mind: Adolf Meyer, Psychobiology and the Phipps Psychiatric Clinic at the Johns Hopkins Hospital, 1908–1917" (PhD diss., Johns Hopkins University, 2010).

100. Theodore M. Brown, "Friendship and Philanthropy: Henry Severest, Alan Gregg and the Rockefeller Foundation," in *Making Medical History: The Life and Time of Henry E. Sigerist*, ed. Elizabeth Fee and Theodore M. Brown (Baltimore: Johns Hopkins University Press, 1997), 288–312.
101. Emigré psychiatrist Adolph Meyer also ranked high on Alan Gregg's (1890–1957) influential research support list of US and Canadian brain science. See Dr. Gregg's List, American Association of Neurology, n. d. 1936 RG1C15:2, Department of Neurology and Psychiatry, Series 2, n. p.
102. Frank W. Stahnisch, "Flexible Antworten—Offene Fragen: Zu den Foerderungsstrategien der Rockefellerstiftung fuer die deutsche Hirnforschung im Nationalsozialismus," *Journal fuer Neurologie, Neurochirurgie und Psychiatrie* 12, no. 2 (2011): 56–62.
103. Edwin R. Embrée (1883–1950), diary entry, November 10, 1922, Rockefeller Archive Center. For the wider institutional and organizational research context, see Frank W. Stahnisch, *A New Field in Mind: A History of Interdisciplinarity in the Early Brain Sciences* (Montréal and Kingston: McGill-Queen's University Press, 2019), 368n64.
104. Alexander von Schwerin, *Experimentalisierung des Menschen: Der Genetiker Hans Nachtsheim und die Erbpathologie, 1920–1945* (Goettingen: Wallstein, 2000); Matthias M. Weber, "Harnack-Prinzip oder Fuehrerprinzip? Erbbiologie unter Ernst Ruedin an der Deutschen Forschungsanstalt fuer Psychiatrie (Kaiser-Wilhelm-Institut) in Muenchen," in *Die Kaiser-Wilhelm-Max-Planck-Gesellschaft und ihre Institute*, ed. Bernhard vom Brocke and Hubert Laitko (Berlin: de Gruyter, 1996), 412.
105. McLaren, *Our Own Master Race*, 119.
106. Grekul, Krahn, and Odynak, "Sterilizing the 'Feeble-Minded,'" 362.
107. McLaren, *Our Own Master Race*, 40–85.
108. Tommy C. Douglas, *The Making of a Socialist: The Recollections of T. C. Douglas*, ed. Lewis Thomas (Edmonton: University of Alberta Press, 1984), 108.
109. See, for example, Canadian Society for the Protection of Science and Learning file, RG95-1. box 540, and Passenger Lists: Halifax, 1865–1935, RG76, Library and Archives Canada, Ottawa.
110. McLaren, *Our Own Master Race*, 168.
111. See "Editorial," *Washington Post*, January 7, 1936, 1; "Editorial," *Washington Post*, January 23, 1936, 4; and "Editorial," *New York Times*, January 26, 1936, 8.
112. See, for example, Doug Owram, *Born at the Right Time: A History of the Baby-Boom Generation* (Toronto: University of Toronto Press, 1999).
113. Grekul, Krahn, and Odynak, "Sterilizing the 'feeble-minded,'" 371. For additional information on the Provincial Training School (Michener

Centre) see Claudia Malacrida, *A Special Hell: Institutional Life in Alberta's Eugenic Years* (Toronto: University of Toronto Press, 2015).

114. On the Prairie provinces of Canada, see Gerald Friesen, *The Canadian Prairies: A History* (Toronto: University of Toronto Press, 1987).
115. Gerald O'Brien, *Framing the Moron: The Social Construction of Feeble-Mindedness in the American Eugenic Era* (Manchester: Manchester University Press, 2013).
116. Dowbiggin, *Keeping America Sane*.
117. Susanne Klausen, "Rethinking Reproduction: New Approaches to the History of Sexuality, Gender, the Family, and Reproductive Control," *Journal of Contemporary History* 44, no. 1 (2009): 117–27.
118. Ute Deichmann, *Biologists under Hitler* (Cambridge, MA: Harvard University Press, 1996).
119. Donald H. Avery, *Reluctant Host: Canada's Response to Immigrant Workers, 1896–1994* (Toronto: McClelland & Stewart, 1995).
120. Geoffrey Bilson, "'Muscles and Health': Health and the Canadian Immigrant," in *Health, Disease and Medicine*, ed. Charles G. Roland (Toronto: University of Toronto Press, 1984), 398–411.
121. Cecily Devereux, *Growing a Race: Nellie L. McClung and the Fiction of Eugenic Feminism* (Montréal and Kingston: McGill-Queen's University Press, 2006).
122. Francis Galton, *Essays in Eugenics* (London: Eugenics Education Society, 1909), 35.
123. Alan F. J. Artibise, *Winnipeg: A Social History of Urban Growth, 1874–1914* (Montréal and Kingston: McGill-Queen's University Press, 1975).
124. Frank W. Stahnisch, "Von der Kriegsneurologie zur Psychotherapie – Kurt Goldstein (1878–1965) Ansaetze zur fruehen Form der Gruppenanalyse," *Gruppenpsychotherapie und Gruppendynamik – Zeitschrift zur Theorie und Praxis der Gruppenanalyse* 50, no. 2 (2014): 136–55.
125. Marius Turda, *Modernism and Eugenics* (London: Palgrave Macmillan, 2010); Marius Turda and Paul Weindling, eds., *Blood and Homeland: Eugenics and Racial Nationalism in Central and Southeast Europe, 1900–1940* (Budapest: Central European University Press, 2006).
126. George Canguilhem, *The Normal and the Pathological*, trans. Carolyn R. Fawcett (New York: Zone Books, 1989).
127. See also Johanna Schoen, *Choice and Coercion: Birth Control, Sterilization, and Abortion in Public Health and Welfare* (Chapel Hill: University of North Carolina Press, 2005).

CHAPTER 1

1 The authors thank Robert Lampard for his comments on an earlier version of this chapter.

2 The occasional article that focuses on MacEachran never provides more than the most basic information about his life that can be readily gleaned online; see for example, Korbla Puplampu, "Knowledge, Power, and Social Policy: John M. MacEachran and Alberta's 1928 Sexual Sterilization Act," *Alberta Journal of Educational Research* 54, no. 1 (2008): 129–46.

3 Doug Wahlsten notes that Timothy Christian (the author of an important legal study of eugenics in Alberta: Timothy Christian and Burke Barker, "The Mentally Ill and Human Rights in Alberta: A Study of the Alberta Sexual Sterilization Act" (Edmonton: University of Alberta. Faculty of Law, 1973) informed him that MacEachran burned his personal papers prior to his death. See Wahlsten, "The Eugenics of John M. MacEachran Warrants Revocation of Honours," *History and Philosophy of Psychology Bulletin* 10, no. 1 (1998): 22–25.

4 Natalie Ball, "MacEachran, John," Eugenics Archives, n.d., http://eugenicsarchive.ca/database/documents/512fa14834c5399e2c000006.

5 For further expansion of this discussion at the University of Alberta see Wahlsten, "Eugenics of John M. MacEachran"; Wahlsten, "Leilani Muir versus the Philosopher King: Eugenics on Trial in Alberta," *Genetica* 99, no. 1 (1997): 185–98; and David Kahane, David Sharp, and Martin Tweedale, "Report of the MacEachran Subcommittee" (Department of Philosophy, University of Alberta, April 1998), https://s3.amazonaws.com/bmcmahen/maceachran_report.pdf.

6 Kelley Torrance, "The Sterilization of History," *Alberta Report* 24, no. 47 (1997): 32–33; Ric Dolphin, "Honours Shelved for Professor Linked to Eugenics," *Edmonton Journal*, October 17, 1997, A1. The scholarships given in his name no longer appear to exist (e.g., the MacEachran Gold Medal in Philosophy, the MacEachran Humanities Prize). However, a scholarship given each year in his wife's name (the Elizabeth Russell MacEachran Scholarship) can still be found in University of Alberta scholarship listings.

7 Two laudatory versions were written by Thomas Nelson prior to the public discussions that followed the Leilani Muir lawsuit of 1995. Nelson, "John A. [*sic*] MacEachran," *Western Psychologist* 3 (1972): 51–62; Nelson, "Psychology at Alberta," in *History of Academic Psychology in Canada*, ed. Mary Wright and C. Roger Myers (Toronto: C. J. Hogrefe, 1982), 192–219. The relevant context of MacEachran's life (particularly the history of the province of Alberta and the University of Alberta) will not be covered here except for those issues

that are directly relevant. For background, see Howard Palmer and Tamara Palmer, *Alberta: A New History* (Edmonton: Hurtig, 1990); and Walter H. Johns, *A History of the University of Alberta, 1908–1969* (Edmonton: University of Alberta Press, 1981).

8 John MacEachran, interview by C. Roger Myers, 1970, 25-17, Canadian Psychological Association fonds, MG 28 I 161, Library and Archives Canada.

9 Robert Douglas Gidney and Wyn P. J. Millar, "The Salaries of Teachers in English Canada 1900–1940: A Reappraisal," *Historical Studies in Education* 22, no. 1 (2010): 1–38; Gidney and Millar, *How Schools Worked: Public Education in English Canada, 1900–1940* (Montréal and Kingston: McGill-Queen's University Press, 2012).

10 In MacEachran's article "Twenty-Five Years of Philosophical Speculation" he states that he entered Queen's University in 1888. However, this is likely a typographical error because this would have made him only eleven years old when he began his university education. It is much more likely that he entered Queen's in 1898. MacEachran, "Twenty-Five Years of Philosophical Speculation," in *These Twenty-Five Years: A Symposium*, ed. William Hardy Alexander, Edmund Kemper Broadus, Francis John Lewis, and John M. MacEachran (Toronto: Macmillan, 1933), 79–113.

11 See also his evaluation of John Watson in MacEachran, "John Watson," in *Some Great Men of Queen's*, ed. Robert Charles Wallace (Toronto: Ryerson University, 1941), 22–50.

12 Charles Tolman, *John Watson of Queen's* (unpublished manuscript, Kingston, ON, 1999).

13 Leslie Armour and Elizabeth Trott, *The Faces of Reason: An Essay on Philosophy and Culture in English Canada; 1850–1959* (Waterloo, ON: Wilfrid Laurier University Press, 1981).

14 Queen's University Archives was unable to locate a copy.

15 John M. MacEachran, "A Dream of Olympus" (paper presented to the Faculty Club at the University of Alberta, Edmonton, October 23, 1932), John MacEachran fonds, acc. no. 71-217, University of Alberta Archives, Edmonton.

16 This was not an unusual choice; most of the early psychologists who initiated laboratory studies in psychology in North America in the latter decades of the nineteenth century had obtained doctorates in Germany. Ludy T. Benjamin, Maureen Durkin, Michelle Link, Marilyn Vestal, and Jill Acord, "Wundt's American Doctoral Students," *American Psychologist* 47, no. 2 (1992): 123–31.

17 Nelson, "John A. MacEachran."

18 Benjamin et al., "Wundt's American Doctoral Students." The steady stream of foreign students working with Wundt slowed considerably after 1900,

in part because of the number of universities in North America offering doctoral degrees in psychology. In addition, an advanced degree from a German university no longer appeared to offer an automatic advantage to American students, at least in securing employment. Furthermore, as is well known, Wundt began work on his *Voelkerpsychologie* in 1900.

19 John MacEachran, *Pragmatismus: Inaugural-dissertation zur Erlangung der Doktorwuerde der hohen philosophischen Fakultaet* (Leipzig: Druck von G. Kreysing, 1910).

20 MacEachran, interview by Myers.

21 MacEachran, interview by Myers.

22 William James, *Pragmatism: A New Name for Some Old Ways of Thinking* (New York: Longmans, Green and Company, 1907).

23 Nelson, "Psychology at Alberta"; MacEachran, interview by Myers.

24 MacEachran, *Pragmatismus*, 79.

25 Later he refers to James's pragmatism as a "very delectable mess of pottage, which had a way of steaming up and boiling over in brilliant literary outbursts of great freshness and rare fragrance. Yet while its particular flavoring proved very appetising to a rising generation of young and vigorous thinkers, it afforded no regulation diet for their diverse tastes." MacEachran, "Twenty-Five Years," 101.

26 MacEachran, "Twenty-Five Years."

27 MacEachran, "Twenty-Five Years," 101.

28 "Population History," 1878–2016, City of Edmonton website, https://www.edmonton.ca/city_government/facts_figures/population-history.aspx.

29 The future prime minister of Canada, John Diefenbaker (1895–1979) served in this battalion in 1916 and 1917. *Dictionary of Canadian Biography*, s. v. "Diefenbaker, John George," by Denis Smith, accessed April 19, 2018, http://www.biographi.ca/en/bio/diefenbaker_john_george_20E.html.

30 Ellen Schoek, *I Was There: A Century of Stories about the University of Alberta, 1906–2006* (Edmonton: University of Alberta Press, 2006). MacEachran was not the only recipient of an unusual offer. Edmund Kemper Broadus (1876–1936), the first English professor, was at Harvard (where he was completing his PhD) and said, "On a day in June, 1908, the president of a university not yet in being, in a province which I had never heard of, in a country which I had never visited, came to Harvard and offered me the professorship of English. The offer sounded like midsummer madness. I think that what I accepted was, not the position or the salary, but the man." *Dictionary of Canadian Biography*, s. v. "Broadus, Edmund Kemper," by Ernest George Mardon and Austin Mardon in collaboration with Elizabeth Hulse, http://www.biographi.ca/en/bio/broadus_edmund_kemper_16E.html.

31 Nelson, "John A. MacEachran."
32 Johns, *History of the University of Alberta*.
33 Douglas A. Smith, "Development of the Department of Psychology, University of Alberta: 1909–1963," typescript, 1975, UAA-2006-163, Department of Psychology collection, University of Alberta Archives, Research & Collections Resource Facility, Edmonton.
34 Nelson, "Psychology at Alberta," 195.
35 John MacEachran, *An Outline of Modern Philosophy* (Edmonton: University of Alberta Archives, n.d.).
36 Johns, *History of the University of Alberta*.
37 In 1938, he also wrote the first draft of the constitution of the Canadian Psychological Association. He was clearly viewed as an *éminence grise* among Canadian psychologists, and the correspondence about the founding of the new association indicates the respect accorded him. See Canadian Psychology Association fonds, accession number 1986-0317, 17–9, National Library and Archives of Canada, Ottawa, Ontario.
38 See, for example, Dyck, *Facing Eugenics*; Jana Grekul, "The Social Construction of the Feebleminded Threat: Implementation of the Sexual Sterilization Act in Alberta, 1929–1972" (PhD diss., University of Alberta, 2002); Malacrida, *Special Hell*; Angus McLaren, *Our Own Master Race: Eugenics in Canada, 1885–1945* (Toronto: McClelland & Stewart, 1990); Carolyn Strange and Jennifer A. Stephen, "Eugenics in Canada: A Checkered History, 1850s–1990s," in *The Oxford Handbook of the History of Eugenics*, ed. Alison Bashford and Philippa Levine (Oxford: Oxford University Press, 2010), 527–38.
39 Ian H. Clarke, "Public Provisions for the Mentally Ill in Alberta, 1907–1936" (master's thesis, University of Calgary, 1973).
40 Sexual Sterilization Act, S.A. 1928, c. 37, 117.
41 Sexual Sterilization Act Amendment Act, S.A. 1937, c. 47, 181.
42 E. Mary Frost, "Sterilization in Alberta: A Summary of the Cases Presented to the Eugenics Board for the Province of Alberta from 1929–1941" (master's thesis, University of Alberta, 1942).
43 Wahlsten, "Leilani Muir."
44 Sexual Sterilization Repeal Act, S.A. 1972, c. 87.
45 Dyck, *Facing Eugenics*; Wahlsten, "Leilani Muir."
46 Alberta, Legislative Assembly, *Hansard*, 17th Leg., 1st Sess., No. 58-37 (May 31, 1972) at 3945, http://www.assembly.ab.ca/Documents/isysquery/07e597c6-b4af-430c-b5e6-c7a7cf8a7b09/1/doc/.
47 David King, interview, April 20, 2018.

48 Anon. quoted in John Schmidt, "Agricultural Alberta," *Calgary Herald*, March 26, 1969, 8.

49 Along with a review of the Common Property Act (an affront to Hutterite communities), the Sexual Sterilization Act was an impediment to the Bill of Rights (King, interview). The Women of Unifarm was a group created when the province's major agricultural organizations merged in 1970. However, it carried forward the ideology that was so long part of the United Farm Women of Alberta that had preceded it. See Carol Jacques, *Unifarm: A Story of Conflict and Change* (Calgary: University of Calgary Press, 2001).

50 Muir v. Alberta (1996), 132 DLR (4th) 695, http://canlii.ca/t/1p6lq; see also Wahlsten, "Leilani Muir."

51 It should be noted that on March 9, 1998, the provincial government of the day—a Progressive Conservative government led by then premier Ralph Klein (1942–2013)—introduced legislation to limit compensation to victims of sexual sterilization. Klein intended to use the "notwithstanding clause" in the Charter of Rights and Freedoms to bypass any damages the courts might award to the sexually sterilized. The bill was withdrawn the next day following outrage from the public. See Sandra Martin, "Ralph Klein, 70: The Man Who Ruled Alberta," *Globe and Mail*, March 29, 2013, https://www.theglobeandmail.com/news/national/ralph-klein-70-the-man-who-ruled-alberta/article10569210/.

52 These include Dyck, *Facing Eugenics*; Malacrida, *Special Hell*; Grekul, "Social Construction"; Amy Kaler, *Baby Trouble in the Last Best West: Making New People in Alberta, 1905–1939* (Toronto: University of Toronto Press, 2017); and Robert A. Wilson, *The Eugenic Mind Project* (Cambridge, MA: MIT Press 2018). See also Erna Kurbegović, "Eugenics in Comparative Perspective: Explaining Manitoba and Alberta's Divergence on Eugenics Policy, 1910 to the 1930s" (PhD diss., University of Calgary, 2019).

53 C. Roger Myers, interview by Thomas Nelson, Canadian Psychology Association fonds, accession number 1986-0317, 26–33, National Library and Archives of Canada, Ottawa.

54 Heather Pringle, "Alberta Barren," *Saturday Night*, June 1997, 35. Pringle does not say why she makes this strong claim. Certainly, no one who had known MacEachran ever described him as a "bull terrier."

55 Douglas A. Smith, "Development of the Department of Psychology, University of Alberta: 1909–1963," typescript, 1975, UAA-2006-163, Department of Psychology collection, University of Alberta Archives, Research & Collections Resource Facility, Edmonton.

56 "Notice of Return: Return asked for by Mr. [Leonidas Alcidas] Giroux respecting members of the Sexual Sterilization Act Board," 1932, acc. no. 70.414, box 31, item 1173, Provincial Archives of Alberta.

57 Both William R. N. ("Buck") Blair (1929–2006) and David Gibson (1926–2006), faculty in the Department of Psychology at the University of Calgary, were members of the AEB in its final years. However, there were no attempts to revisit this at the University of Calgary, possibly because there are no scholarships, rooms, or other honours still associated with Blair or Gibson and their participation was for one year each. Furthermore, Blair distinguished himself as the author of the well-known report on the Alberta Mental Health Study, otherwise known as the "Blair Report," in which he called for an overhaul of the Sexual Sterilization Act—although not its repeal. Blair, *Mental Health in Alberta: A Report on the Alberta Mental Health Study, 1968*, vol. 1 (Edmonton: Human Resources Research and Development Executive Council, Government of Alberta, 1969). For the names of all board members from 1929 to 1972, see Grekul, "Social Construction," 102.

58 "Reports of Societies," *British Medical Journal* 3868 (February 23, 1935), 378.

59 Reports of Societies, 379.

60 McLaren, *Our Own Master Race*.

61 See, for example, Pringle, "Alberta Barren"; and Grekul, "Social Construction."

62 Grekul, "Social Construction," 103.

63 The brevity led to some very unusual cases, such as that of the fifty-eight-year-old man who was sterilized and whose record indicated "he has made homosexual attempts on his brother." The patient granted no permissions, and no IQ test was performed. This man had been hospitalized for the better part of a decade and was not likely to be released.

64 Eugenics Board Minutes, June 14, 1945, GR0008.0004F, Provincial Archives of Alberta.

65 The case discussed here is more striking because of the pleas contained in the letter. But the minutes contain others like it, such as a case that was summarily dismissed on January 23, 1941, from a woman, by then married, who had written to the Edmonton clinic asking for a reversal of her sterilization. The minutes only indicate "the board directed that [she] be advised that so far as it is concerned there is no way in which it can act further in the matter." Eugenics Board Minutes, January 23, 1941, GR0008.0004F, Provincial Archives of Alberta.

66 MacEachran, "Crime and Punishment: Address to the United Farm Women's Association of Alberta," reprint, *Press Bulletin*, May 6, 1932, 3.

67 See, for example, the discussion of "guardians of the race" in Erin Moss, Henderikus J. Stam, and Diane Kattevilder, "From Suffrage to Sterilization: Eugenics and the Women's Movement in 20th Century Alberta," *Canadian Psychology* 54, no. 1 (2013): 105–14; and Wendy Kline, *Building a Better Race: Gender, Sexuality and Eugenics from the Turn of the Century to the Baby Boom* (Berkeley: University of California Press, 2001).

68 Ironically, he also argues that "we should be very careful to make sure that we are not depending too much upon legislation to raise and protect our moral standards." MacEachran, "Crime and Punishment," 3.

69 John M. MacEachran. *State Prisons: Radio Talk*, December 1931, acc. no. 71-217, item 8, box 1, University of Alberta Archives; MacEachran, "Criminals Are Not Reformed by Brutality or Inhumanity," *Mental Health* 7 (1932): 9–14.

70 MacEachran, "Twenty-Five Years," 89.

71 MacEachran, "Twenty-Five Years," 97.

72 MacEachran, "Twenty-Five Years," 113.

73 John MacEachran, "A Philosopher Looks at Mental Hygiene," *Mental Hygiene* 16 (1932): 101.

74 Plato, *Charmides*, 156d6–157a3.

75 MacEachran, "Philosopher Looks," 113–14.

76 MacEachran, "Philosopher Looks," 119.

77 Shortly thereafter, German doctors began euthanizing the mentally handicapped and the mentally ill as well as the criminally insane. Robert J. Lifton, *The Nazi Doctors* (New York: Basic Books, 1986) (see also Paul J. Weindling in chapter 8).

78 See Lifton, *Nazi Doctors*.

79 It should be noted that in other jurisdictions in North America, sterilizations also continued unabated after World War II, indeed, sometimes with greater enthusiasm. North Carolina, for example, began a new campaign after the end of the war. Kevin Begos, "The American Eugenics Movement after World War II (Part 1 of 3)," *Indy Week*, May 18, 2011, https://indyweek.com/news/american-eugenics-movement-world-war-ii-part-1-3/.

80 Sterilization did not cease with the formal closing of the eugenics program. There are still cases before the courts of illegal and unwanted sterilizations that have been performed routinely, especially on women from First Nations in Canada. See "Class-Action Lawyer Told of 2 Coerced Sterilizations of Indigenous Women in Manitoba," *CBC News*, November 14, 2018, https://www.cbc.ca/news/canada/manitoba/manitoba-indigenous-women-forced-sterilization-lawsuit-1.4904421; and Kristy Kirkup, "Examine 'Monstrous' Allegations of Forced Sterilization of Indigenous Women: NDP," *CBC News*,

January 8, 2019, https://www.cbc.ca/news/politics/sterilization-indigenous-allegations-forced-1.4911837.

CHAPTER 2

1 Muir v. Alberta (1996), 132 D.L.R. (4th) 695, Viet J, http://canlii.ca/t/1p6lq; M. Sadava and T. Arnold, "Sterilization Victim Receives Personal Apology from Klein," *Edmonton Journal*, February 20, 1997, A4.
2 See, further, Amy Dyrbye and Caroline Lyster, "Alberta Repeals the Sexual Sterilization Act," Eugenics Archives, n.d., http://eugenicsarchive.ca/discover/timeline/517310e2eed5c60000000032.
3 Patricia Sealy and Paul C. Whitehead, "Forty Years of Deinstitutionalization of Psychiatric Services in Canada: An Empirical Assessment," *Canadian Journal of Psychiatry* 49, no. 4 (2004): 249–257.
4 A similar exercise is included in a recent publication by the author of this chapter. See Douglas Wahlsten, *Genes, Brain Function, and Behavior: What Genes Do, How They Malfunction, and Ways to Repair Damage* (New York: Elsevier, 2019).
5 Douglas Wahlsten, "Single-Gene Influences on Brain and Behavior," *Annual Review of Psychology* 50, no. 6 (1999): 599–624; Wahlsten, "The Theory of Biological Intelligence: History and a Critical Appraisal," in *The General Factor of Intelligence: How General Is It?*, ed. Robert Sternberg and Elena Grigorenko (Mahwah, NJ: Erlbaum, 2002), 245–77.
6 See Douglas Wahlsten, "Leilani Muir versus the Philosopher King: Eugenics on Trial in Alberta," *Genetica* 99, no. 1 (1997): 185–98; Leilani Muir, *A Whisper Past: Childless after Eugenic Sterilization in Alberta* (Victoria, BC: Friesen Press, 2014).
7 Douglas Wahlsten, *Report on Eugenic Sterilization in Alberta from 1950 to 1968* (June 15, 1999) (Edmonton, AB: Department of Psychology, University of Alberta, 1999), 22–25.
8 Wendy Kline, "Sterilization," Eugenics Archives, September 14, 2013, http://eugenicsarchive.ca/discover/encyclopedia/5233e4e35c2ec500000000e0.
9 James Tabery, "Genetics," Eugenics Archives, April 29, 2014, http://eugenicsarchive.ca/discover/encyclopedia/535eec197095aa000000022c.
10 Natalie Ball, "Galton, Sir Francis," Eugenics Archives, n.d., http://eugenicsarchive.ca/database/documents/518c1ed54d7d6e0000000002.
11 Peter J. Bowler, *Evolution: The History of an Idea* (Berkeley: University of California Press, 2003).

12 Galton, *Hereditary Genius: An Inquiry into Its Laws and Consequences* (London: Macmillan, 1869), 157.

13 Galton, *Inquiries into Human Faculty and Its Development* (London: Macmillan, 1883), 17.

14 Mendel, "Versuche ueber Pflanzenhybriden," *Verhandlungen des naturforschenden Vereines in Bruenn* 4, no. 1 (1866): 3–47; Ulrich Kutschera and Niklas Karl J. Ulrich, "The Modern Theory of Biological Evolution: An Expanded Synthesis," *Naturwissenschaften* 91, no. 2 (2004): 255–76.

15 A[lfred] Sturtevant, *A History of Genetics* (New York: Harper & Row, 1965), 58–116.

16 University of Alberta, Course Calendars, multiple years: 1917–24, 1950–51, 1955–56, 1960–61, 1965–66. University of Alberta Archives, Research & Collections Resource Facility, Edmonton.

17 Thomas Hunt Morgan, "The Mechanism and Laws of Heredity," in *The Foundations of Experimental Psychology*, ed. Carl Murchison (Worcester, MA: Clark University Press, 1929), 1–44.

18 Ernest Brown Babcock, *Genetics in Relation to Agriculture* (New York: McGraw-Hill, 1918).

19 John M. MacEachran, "Crime and Punishment: Address to the United Farm Women's Association of Alberta," reprint, *Press Bulletin*, May 6, 1932, 1–4; Hilda Pocock, "Eugenics Propaganda," *Eugenics Review* 30, no. 1 (1938): 77; Russell C. Wallace, "The Quality of the Human Stock," *Canadian Medical Association Journal* 31, no. 4 (1934): 427–30.

20 Jay L. Lush, *Animal Breeding Plans* (Ames: Iowa State College Press, 1945); Altenburg, *Genetics* (New York: Henry Holt, 1945).

21 It thereby relied on Alfred Binet and Théodore Simon, *The Development of Intelligence in Children (The Binet-Simon Scale)*, trans. by Elizabeth S. Kite (Vineland, NJ: The Training School at Vineland, 1916).

22 Lester D. Crow and Alice Crow, *Educational Psychology* (New York: American Book Co., 1948); Anne Anastasi, *Differential Psychology*, 3rd ed. (New York: Macmillan, 1958); Arthur I. Gates, Arthur T. Jersild, Thomas R. McConnell, and R[obert] C. Challman, *Educational Psychology* (New York: Macmillan, 1948).

23 George D. Stoddard, *The Meaning of Intelligence* (New York: Macmillan, 1945); Lewis Madison Terman and Maud E. Merrill, *Measuring Intelligence: A Guide to the Administration of the New Revised Stanford-Binet Tests of Intelligence* (Boston: Houghton Mifflin, 1937); David Wechsler, *The Measurement of Adult Intelligence*, 3rd ed. (Baltimore: Williams & Wilkins, 1944).

24 Joseph McVicker-Hunt, *Intelligence and Experience* (New York: Ronald Press, 1961).

25 Anne Anastasi, *Psychological Testing* (New York: Macmillan, 1954).

26 Luke Kersten, "Alberta Passes Sexual Sterilization Act," Eugenics Archives, n.d., http://eugenicsarchives.ca/discover/timeline/5172e81ceed5c6000000001d.

27 Mental Defectives Act, R.S.A. 1955, c. 199, s. 2(a).

28 Sexual Sterilization Act, R.S.A. 1955, c. 194, s. 4(1).

29 Sexual Sterilization Act, R.S.A. 1955, c. 194, s. 6(1).

30 Lionel Penrose, *The Biology of Mental Defect* (London: Sidgwick and Jackson, 1949); Anastasi, *Psychological Testing*, 378–79; Wechsler, *Measurement of Adult Intelligence*, 31.

31 Claudia Malacrida, *A Special Hell: Institutional Life in Alberta's Eugenic Years* (Toronto: University of Toronto Press, 2015), 204.

32 Howard Gardner, "Who Owns Intelligence?," *Atlantic Monthly*, February 1999, 67–76; Robert J. Sternberg, "How Intelligent Is Intelligence Testing?," *Scientific American* 9, no. 1 (1999): 12–17.

33 Allan Chase, *The Legacy of Malthus: The Social Costs of the New Scientific Racism* (New York: Knopf, 1977).

34 Alfred Binet, *Modern Ideas about Children* (1909), trans. Suzanne Heisler (1975; Albi, France: Les Presses de l'Atelier Graphique Saint-Jean, 1984).

35 Binet, *Modern Ideas*, 105.

36 Chase, *Legacy of Malthus*, 232–38; Stephen J. Gould, *Mismeasure of Man*, rev. ed. (New York: Norton, 1996).

37 Lewis M. Terman and Maude Merville, *The Measurement of Intelligence* (Boston: Houghton Mifflin, 1916).

38 Terman and Merrill, *Measuring Intelligence*, 4.

39 Wechsler, *Measurement of Adult Intelligence*, 3.

40 Wechsler, *Measurement of Adult Intelligence*, 3.

41 Stoddard, *Meaning of Intelligence*, 3.

42 McVicker-Hunt, *Intelligence and Experience*, 5, 11.

43 David Gibson, "Involuntary Sterilization of the Mentally Retarded: A Western Canadian Phenomenon," *Canadian Psychiatric Association Journal* 19, no. 1 (1974): 59–63;Eugenics Board Minutes Collection, Eugenics Board Minutes series, 1939–41, no. GR0008.0004F, "Transcript Excerpts from the Examination for Discovery." Provincial Archives of Alberta, Edmonton.

44 Edgar Altenburg, *Genetics* (New York: Henry Holt, 1945), 437–38.

45 Gates et al., *Educational Psychology*.

46 [Stanley Charles Tremayne] Clarke, Verner R. Nyberg, and [Walter H.] Worth, *Technical Report on Edmonton Grade III Achievement 1956–1977 Comparisons* (Edmonton: Alberta Advisory Committee on Educational Studies, 1978).

47 Crow and Crow, *Educational Psychology*; Gates et al., *Educational Psychology*; Penrose, *Biology of Mental Defect*; Terman and Merrill, *Measuring Intelligence*; Wechsler, *Measurement of Adult Intelligence*; Wechsler, *The Measurement of Adult Intelligence*, 4th ed. (Baltimore: Williams & Wilkins, 1958); Anastasi, *Differential Psychology*.

48 Transcript Excerpts from the Examination for Discovery by [Graham] Thomson, 55 and 311, questioned by Mr. [Allan] Garber, undated, 2–286; questioned by Garber, Oct–22, 1998, 293–544; questioned by Garber, June–14, 15, and 16, 1997, Eugenics Board Minutes Collection, Provincial Archives of Alberta, Edmonton.

49 Penrose, *Biology of Mental Defect*, 119–21.

50 David Wechsler, *The Measurement of Adult Intelligence* (Baltimore, MA: Williams & Wilkins, 1939; reprint Baltimore: Williams & Wilkins, 1958), 55. Citations henceforth refer to the reprint edition.

51 Government of Alberta, *Annual Report of the Department of Public Health* (Edmonton: J. W. Jeffrey King's Printer, 1955), 24.

52 Government of Alberta, *1955 Annual Report*, 25.

53 Government of Alberta, Department of Education, *Annual Report of the Division of Mental Health* (Edmonton, 1955), 75–122, esp. 126.

54 Penrose, *Biology of Mental Defect*, 125.

55 Gibson, *Transcript Excerpts from the Examination for Discovery*, 428–429.

56 Stoddard, *Meaning of Intelligence*; Anastasi, *Differential Psychology*, 378–79.

57 David Wechsler, *Measurement of Adult Intelligence*, 47.

58 Florence L. Goodenough, "The Measurement of Mental Growth in Childhood," in *Manual of Child Psychology*, ed. Leonard Carmichael (New York: Wiley, 1954), 459–91.

59 Thomas James Reid, "A Survey of the Language Achievement of Alberta School Children in Relation to Bilingualism, Sex, and Intelligence" (MEd thesis, University of Alberta, 1954), 67.

60 Goodenough, "Measurement of Mental Growth," 486.

61 Timothy Christian, *The Mentally Ill and Human Rights in Alberta: A Study of the Alberta Sexual Sterilization Act*. Edmonton, AB: University of Alberta with the Assistance of Professor Burke Barker of the Faculty of Law, 1973. Wallace, "Quality of the Human Stock"; Douglas Wahlsten, "The Malleability of Intelligence Is Not Constrained by Heritability," in *Intelligence, Genes, and Success: Scientists Respond to the Bell Curve*, ed. Bernie Devlin, Stephen E. Fienberg, Daniel P. Resnick, and Kathryn Roeder (New York: Copernicus, 1974), 71–87.

62 Government of Alberta, Health Survey Committee, *A Survey of Alberta's Health* (Edmonton: Department of Public Health, 1950).

63 Government of Alberta, Department of Public Health, *Annual Report of the Bureau of Vital Statistics* (Edmonton, 1959), 188; Thomson, *Transcript Excerpts from the Examination for Discovery*, 128–129.

64 Wahlsten, "Single-Gene Influences," 601–3.

65 Garland E. Allen, "Eugenics and Modern Biology: Critiques of Eugenics, 1910–1945," *Annals of Human Genetics* 75, no. 3 (2011): 314–25.

66 F. Clarke Fraser, "Medical Genetics in Pediatrics," *Journal of Pediatrics* 44, no. 1 (1954): 85–103; Penrose, *Biology of Mental Defect*, 75; Sheldon C. Reed, *Counseling in Medical Genetics* (Philadelphia: Saunders, 1955), 84.

67 Reed, *Counseling in Medical Genetics*; Hubert C. Soltan, ed., *Medical Genetics in Canada: Evolution of a Hybrid Discipline: Essays on the Early History* (London: University of Western Ontario, 1992).

68 Robert J. Bridges and Neil Bradbury, "Cystic Fibrosis, Cystic Fibrosis Transmembrane Conductance Regulator and Drugs: Insights from Cellular Trafficking," *Handbook of Experimental Pharmacology* 103, no. 1 (2018): 1–41.

69 Tom Strachan and Andrew Reid, *Human Molecular Genetics* (Philadelphia and London: Garland Science, 2010), 345–80.

70 Morgan, "Mechanism and Laws."

71 See also Douglas Wahlsten, "The Intelligence of Heritability," *Canadian Psychology* 35, no. 2 (1994): 244–58.

72 Kersten, "Alberta Passes Sexual Sterilization Act."

73 Lancelot Hogben, *Nature and Nurture* (London: Williams & Norgate, 1933), 65.

74 Lush, *Animal Breeding Plans*, 126.

75 Lush, *Animal Breeding Plans*, 126.

76 John Burdon Sanderson Haldane, *Heredity and Politics* (London: Allen & Unwin, 1938), 79.

77 Only recently has it become possible to identify pre-symptomatic carriers of Huntington's disease using DNA methods. See also Kathleen L. Poston and David Eidelberg, "Network Biomarkers for the Diagnosis and Treatment of Movement Disorders," *Neurobiological Diseases* 35, no. 1 (2009): 141–47.

78 Douglas Wahlsten, "The Hunt for Gene Effects Pertinent to Behavioral Traits and Psychiatric Disorders: From Mouse to Human," *Developmental Psychobiology* 54, no. 5 (2013): 475–92.

79 See Lush, *Animal Breeding Plans*, chaps. 8, 12, 13; and Douglas S. Falconer, *Introduction to Quantitative Genetics* (Edinburgh: Oliver and Boyd, 1960).

80 Government of Alberta, Department of Education, *Fiftieth Annual Report* (Edmonton, 1955).

81 See Bernard Devlin, Michael Daniels, and Kathryn Roeder, "The Heritability of IQ," *Nature* 388, no. 4 (1997): 468–70; Gilbert Gottlieb, Douglas Wahlsten, and Robert Lickliter, "The Significance of Biology for Human Development:

A Developmental Psychobiological Systems View," in *Handbook of Child Psychology*, vol. 1, *Theoretical Models of Human Development*, ed. Richard M. Lerner, 5th ed. (New York: Wiley, 1997), 233–73; Peter Schoenemann, "On Models and Muddles of Heritability," *Genetica* 99, no. 1 (1997): 97–108; and Wahlsten, "Intelligence of Heritability."

82 John Fuller and W. Robert Thompson, *Behavior Genetics* (New York: Wiley, 1960), 110.

83 Devlin, Daniels, and Roeder, "Heritability of IQ."

84 William H. Coull, "A Normative Survey of Reading Achievement of Alberta Children in Relation to Intelligence, Sex, Bilingualism, and Grade Placement" (MEd thesis, University of Alberta, 1957), 37.

85 Government of Alberta, Department of Education, *Fiftieth Annual Report*.

86 Penrose, *Biology of Mental Defect*, 6.

87 See also Wahlsten, "Intelligence of Heritability."

88 Stoddard, *Meaning of Intelligence*, 69.

89 Stoddard, *Meaning of Intelligence*; Harold Jones, "The Environment and Mental Development," in *Manual of Child Psychology*, ed. Leonard Carmichael (New York: Wiley, 1954), 631–96; Anastasi, *Differential Psychology*; McVicker-Hunt, *Intelligence and Experience*.

90 Thomas Hardy Leahey, *A History of Modern Psychology* (Upper Saddle River, NJ: Prentice Hall, 2001), 334–50.

91 Read D. Tuddenham, "Soldier Intelligence in World Wars I and II," *American Psychologist* 3, no. 1 (1948): 54–56.

92 Lewis M. Terman and Maud A. Merrill, *Stanford-Binet Intelligence Scale: Manual for the Third Revision Form L-M* (Boston: Houghton Mifflin, 1960).

93 Raymond Bernard Cattell, "Is National Intelligence Declining?," *Eugenics Review* 28, no. 1 (1936–37): 181–203.

94 Raymond Bernard Cattell, "The Fate of National Intelligence: Test of a Thirteen-Year Prediction," *Eugenics Review* 42, no. 3 (1950): 136–48.

95 Stoddard, *Meaning of Intelligence*; Reid, "Survey of the Language Achievement"; Anastasi, *Differential Psychology*.

96 Bradford J. Rennie, *The Rise of Agrarian Democracy: The United Farmers and Farm Women of Alberta, 1909–1921* (Toronto: University of Toronto Press, 2000), 244.

97 Stoddard, *Meaning of Intelligence*, 72; Anastasi, *Differential Psychology*, 378–79.

98 Marie Skodak and Harold M. Skeels, "A Final Follow-Up Study of One Hundred Adopted Children," *Journal of Genetic Psychology* 75, no. 1 (1949): 85–125.

99 McVicker-Hunt, *Intelligence and Experience*, 12–13.

100 Douglas Wahlsten, *Genes, Brain Function, and Behavior: What Genes Do, How They Malfunction, and Ways to Repair Damage* (London, UK: Elsevier, 2019), 178–180.
101 Gottlieb, Wahlsten, and Lickliter, "Significance of Biology."
102 John R. Flynn, "Massive IQ Gains in 14 Nations: What IQ Tests Really Measure," *Psychological Bulletin* 101, no. 2 (1987): 171–91.
103 Randall Hansen and Desmond King, *Sterilized by the State: Eugenics, Race, and the Population Scare in Twentieth Century North America* (New York: Cambridge University Press, 2013).
104 Gerald Robertson, at Muir trial, June 26, 1995, cited in Muir, *A Whisper Past*, 136.
105 IQ Test Comparisons from the Leilani Muir Case, 1957 to 1989; in: Muir, *A Whisper Past*, 208–09.
106 Personal file of Ilsa Anderchuk (pseudonym), created July 8, 1949, Willow Creek RCMP, Eugenics Board Minutes, Provincial Archives of Alberta.
107 Quoted in Erika Dyck, *Facing Eugenics: Reproduction, Sterilization, and the Politics of Choice* (Toronto: University of Toronto Press, 2013), 3.
108 Alexandra Stern, *Telling Genes: The Story of Genetic Counseling in America* (Baltimore: Johns Hopkins University Press, 2012).

CHAPTER 3

1 See, for example, Karolina Kowalewski and Yasmin Mayne, "The Translation of Eugenic Ideology into Public Health Policy: The Case of Alberta and Saskatchewan," in *The Proceedings of the 18th Annual History of Medicine Days Conference* 2009, ed. Lisa Peterman, Kerry Sun, and Frank W. Stahnisch (Newcastle upon Tyne: Cambridge Scholars Publishing, 2012), 53–74.
2 Clarence B. Farrar, "Editorial," *Canadian Public Health Journal* 22, no. 1 (1931): 92–93.
3 Kowalewski and Mayne, "Translation of Eugenic Ideology," 53.
4 Kowalewski and Mayne, "Translation of Eugenic Ideology," 54.
5 See Glynis Whiting, dir., *The Sterilization of Leilani Muir* (Edmonton: National Film Board of Canada, 1996).
6 Farrar, "Editorial," 92–93.
7 See also Erika Dyck, *Facing Eugenics: Reproduction, Sterilization, and the Politics of Choice* (Toronto: University of Toronto Press, 2013), 39–41.
8 Patricia Dantonio, "Histories of Nursing: The Power and the Possibilities," *Nursing Outlook* 58, no. 2 (2010): 208.
9 "Editorial," *Edmonton Journal*, March 1, 1996, 1.

10 Viet J. quoted in Whiting, *The Sterilization of Leilani Muir*.

11 "Editorial," *Edmonton Journal*, January 26, 1996, 1. Alberta was not alone in adopting a policy of eugenics. Many European countries were being criticized in the press for taking a similar position to that taken by the Alberta government in 1928. See Barbara Amiel, "Sweden's Shameful Eugenics Policies," *Maclean's*, September 8, 1997, 13; "Scandals over Sterilization," *Maclean's*, September 8, 1997, 42; *Edmonton Journal*, August 29, 1997, A15, and *Edmonton Journal*, September 5, 1997, A18.

12 Statutes of Alberta. 18 George V, 1928, 117.

13 "Editorial," *Edmonton Journal*, January 29, 1996, n. p.

14 For example, Christopher Maggs, "A History of Nursing: A History of Caring?," *Journal of Advanced Nursing* 22, no. 6 (1996): 630–35; and Janet C. Ross-Kerr, *Prepared to Care* (Edmonton: University of Alberta Press, 1998).

15 Quoted in Whiting, *The Sterilization of Leilani Muir*.

16 See Thomas Olson, "Laying Claim to Caring: Nursing and the Language of Training, 1915–1917," *Nursing Outlook* 41, no. 2 (1993): 68–72.

17 On the role of physicians in relation to women and women patients, see Wendy Mitchinson, *The Nature of Their Bodies: Women and Their Doctors in Victorian Canada* (Toronto: University of Toronto Press, 1991).

18 Ian Stewart, "Commandeering Time: The Ideological Status of Time in the Social Darwinism of Herbert Spencer," *Australian Journal of Politics and History* 57, no. 4 (2011): 389–402.

19 Francis Galton, *Essays in Eugenics* (London: Eugenics Education Society, 1909), 35–36.

20 Carol Lee Bacchi, "Race Regeneration and Social Purity: A Study of the Social Attitudes of Canada's English-Speaking Suffragists," in *Readings in Canadian History: Post-Confederation*, ed. R. Douglas Francis and Donald B. Smith (Toronto: Holt, Rinehart, and Winston, 1986), 309. See also Birgit Kirkebaek, "Da de andssvage blev farlige" [When the Mentally Deficient Became Dangerous]. (PhD diss, Forlaget Socpol, Copenhagen, Denmark, 1993).

21 Bacchi, "Race Regeneration and Social Purity," 310.

22 Marianna Valverde, *The Age of Light, Soap, and Water: Moral Reform in English Canada, 1885–1925* (Toronto: McClelland & Stewart, 2008), 93.

23 Kowalewski and Mayne, "Translation of Eugenic Ideology," 56.

24 Kowalewski and Mayne, "Translation of Eugenic Ideology," 56.

25 Kowalewski and Mayne, "Translation of Eugenic Ideology," 57.

26 Ian Robert Dowbiggin, "'Keeping This Young Country Sane': C. K. Clarke, Immigration Restriction, and Canadian Psychiatry, 1890–1925," *Canadian Historical Review* 76, no. 4 (1995): 598–627.

27 Charles C. Roland, *Clarence Meredith Hincks: Mental Health Crusader* (Toronto: Oxford University Press, 1990).
28 Dyck, *Facing Eugenics*, 39–41.
29 David MacLennan, "Beyond the Asylum: Professionalization and the Mental Hygiene Movement in Canada, 1914–1928," *Canadian Bulletin of Medical History* 4, no. 1 (1987): 7–23, esp. 15.
30 Angus McLaren, *Our Own Master Race: Eugenics in Canada, 1885–1945* (Toronto: McClelland & Stewart, 1990), 93.
31 For a full examination of these developments, see Terry L. Chapman, "Early Eugenics Movements in Western Canada," *Alberta History* 25, no. 1 (1977): 13–14.
32 Dyck, *Facing Eugenics*, 6–7.
33 Bradford Rennie, *The Rise of Agrarian Democracy: The United Farmers and Farm Women of Alberta, 1909–1921* (Toronto: University of Toronto Press, 2000), 31.
34 Rennie, *Rise of Agrarian Democracy*, 31.
35 Rennie, *Rise of Agrarian Democracy*, 31.
36 United Farm Women of Alberta (UFWA) Papers, M1749, file 44, Glenbow Archives, Calgary.
37 Carol Lee Bacchi, *Liberation Deferred? The Ideas of the English-Canadian Suffragists 1877–1918* (Toronto: University of Toronto Press, 1983), 319.
38 Dyck, *Facing Eugenics*, 51.
39 Dyck, *Facing Eugenics*, 52.
40 Dyck, *Facing Eugenics*, 52–3.
41 UFWA Papers, Glenbow Archives, Calgary.
42 Howard Palmer and Tamara Palmer, *Alberta: A New History* (Edmonton: Hurtig, 1990), 212.
43 Mary Myskiw, "The Influence of the Alberta Association of Registered Nurses on Health Care Policy from 1916 to 1950" (master's thesis, University of Alberta, 1992), 75–76.
44 Myskiw, "Influence of the Alberta Association of Registered Nurses," 71, 86.
45 Myskiw, "Influence of the Alberta Association of Registered Nurses," 88.
46 Sharon Richardson, "Political Women, Professional Nurses and the Creation of Alberta's District Nursing Service, 1919–1925," *Nursing History Review* 6, no. 1 (1998): 44.
47 Myskiw, "Influence of the Alberta Association of Registered Nurses," 90.
48 Richardson, "Political Women," 35–36.
49 Richardson, "Political Women," 39.
50 Richardson, "Political Women," 44.
51 Richardson, "Political Women," 45.

52 Ina J. Bramadat and Marion I. Saydak, "Nursing on the Canadian Prairies, 1900–1930: Effects of Immigration," *Nursing History Review* 1, no. 1 (1993): 106.

53 Bramadat and Saydak, "Nursing on the Canadian Prairies," 107.

54 Public Health Nursing Division, *Public Health Nursing in Manitoba 1916–1936* (Winnipeg: Department of Health and Public Welfare, 1936), 6.

55 Bramadat and Saydak, "Nursing on the Canadian Prairies," 110.

56 Bramadat and Saydak, "Nursing on the Canadian Prairies," 110.

57 Dyck, *Facing Eugenics*, 45.

58 Elizabeth C. Koester, "An Evil Hitherto Unchecked: Eugenics and the 1917 Ontario Royal Commission on the Care and Control of the Mentally Defective and Feebleminded," *Canadian Bulletin of Medical History* 33, no. 1 (2016): 59–81.

59 Koester, "An Evil Hitherto Unchecked," 69.

60 Amy Samson, "Eugenics in the Community: United Farm Women of Alberta, Public Health Nursing, Teaching, Social Work, and Sexual Sterilization in Alberta, 1928–1972" (PhD diss., University of Saskatchewan, 2014).

61 Unpublished manuscript by Robert Barritt, *History of United Farm Women*, 1934, 34, M1749, File 45, Glenbow Archives, Calgary.

62 See Ian M. Clarke quoted in K. Randall MacLean and Ethel T. Kibblewhite, "Sexual Sterilization in Alberta," *Canadian Public Health Journal* 28, no. 5 (1937): 587–90.

63 Quoted in Whiting, *The Sterilization of Leilani Muir*.

64 Georgina Taylor, "Ground for Common Action: Violet McNaughton's Agrarian Feminism and the Origins of the Farm Women's Movement in Canada" (PhD diss., Carleton University, 1997).

65 "Immigration Report" by UFWA, Fifteenth Annual Convention, 1929, M1749, File 44, Glenbow Archives, Calgary.

66 Eugenics Board of Alberta report, by the secretary of the UFWA, *Eighteenth Convention*, 1929, 42–45, M1749, File 44, Glenbow Archives, Calgary.

67 Jana Grekul, Harvey Krahn, and Dave Odynak, "Sterilizing the 'Feeble-Minded': Eugenics in Alberta, Canada, 1929–1972," *Journal of Historical Sociology* 17, no. 4 (2004): 363.

68 Grekul, Krahn, and Odynak, "Sterilizing the 'Feeble-Minded,'" 362.

69 Tim Christian, "The Mentally Ill and Human Rights in Alberta: A Study of the Alberta Sexual Sterilization Act" (University of Alberta with the assistance of Professor W. M. Barker of the Faculty of Law, 1974), 132.

70 Dyck, *Facing Eugenics*, 72.

71 Department of Public Health annual report, by Department of Public Health,1937, Department of Public Health fond. Accession no. 86.36, RPC

87/230, Provincial Archives of Alberta, Edmonton; Eugenics Board of Alberta report, by the secretary of the UFWA, *Eighteenth Convention*, 1929, 78, M1749, File 44, Glenbow Archives, Calgary.

72 McLaren, *Our Own Master Race*, 216n64.

73 Leslie Bell, "Nurses and Their Attitude towards Sex," *Canadian Nurse* 24, no. 10 (1928): 515–28, esp. 525.

74 James C. Whorton, "The Solitary Vice: The Superstition that Masturbation Could Cause Mental Illness," *Western Journal of Medicine* 175, no. 1 (2001): 66–68.

75 Elizabeth W. Odell, "Eliminating the Unfit from the School of Nursing," *Canadian Nurse* 11, no. 12 (1929): 723–24.

76 Mary Millman, "Special Classes as a Factor in Health," *Canadian Public Health Journal* 21, no. 3 (1930): 355–57; Marion Lindeburgh, "The Educational Objective of Public Health Nursing," *Canadian Public Health Journal* 23, no. 3 (1932): 327–30; Lindeburgh, "Why Canada is Healthier …," *Canadian Public Health Journal* 30, no. 1 (1939): 11.

77 Farrar, "Editorial," 93.

78 "A True Story," *Canadian Nurse* 11, no. 10 (1929): 629. For further discussion of this topic, see McLaren, *Our Own Master Race*; and Valverde, *Age of Light*.

79 E. Wayne MacKinnon, "Wide-Awake," *Canadian Nurse* 6, no. 5 (1925): 247–48.

80 Adelaide M. Plumptre, "Caught Napping," *Canadian Nurse* 6, no. 1 (1925): 5–8.

81 Bramadat and Saydak, "Nursing on the Canadian Prairies."

82 Tony Cashman, *Heritage of Service: The History of Nursing in Alberta* (Edmonton: Alberta Association of Registered Nurses, 1966), 127, 150, 159, 163.

83 Barritt, *History of United Farm Women*, 5–7.

84 UFWA Eighteenth Annual Convention report, by the secretary of the UFWA, *Eighteenth Convention*, 1929, 45, M1749, File 44, Glenbow Archives, Calgary.

85 For further discussion, see Ian M. Clarke quoted in MacLean and Kibblewhite, "Sexual Sterilization in Alberta."

86 Kitchener-based businessman Alvin Ratz Kaufman (1885–1975), a self-proclaimed eugenicist, hired women from across Canada to promote the use of birth control packages that he distributed through the philanthropy of his Parents' Information Bureau. See McLaren, *Our Own Master Race*, 77; and Catherine Annau, "Eager Eugenicists: A Reappraisal of the Birth Control Society in Hamilton," *Histoire Sociale / Social History* 27, no. 53 (1995): 111–33.

87 Linda Revie, "More Than Just Boots! The Eugenic and Commercial Concerns behind A. R. Kaufman's Birth Controlling Activities," *Canadian Bulletin of Medical History* 23, no. 1 (2006): 119–43.

88 Anne Hammill's (b. 1914?) papers are in author's possession, as well as an audiotaped interview conducted by Patty White in Calgary (1984).
89 Papers by Anne Hammill, Diana Mansell, Calgary, Alberta, Canada.
90 Interview with Patty White, 1984, Diana Mansell, Calgary, Alberta, Canada.
91 Annau, "Eager Eugenicists," 116–19.
92 Hard evidence is virtually unobtainable due to non-inclusion in relevant primary and secondary sources.
93 Dyck, *Facing Eugenics*, 79.
94 Dyck, *Facing Eugenics*, 79.
95 Dyck, *Facing Eugenics*, 80.
96 Annual Reports of Public Health (Edmonton; Province of Alberta), J. W. Jeffrey, King's Printer, 1940 (printed copy), Department of Public Health fond. Accession no. 86.36, RPC 87/230, Provincial Archives of Alberta, Edmonton.
97 *Edmonton Journal*, December 14, 1995, 1.
98 Hilde Steppe, "Historical Research in Nursing," *13th Meeting of the Workgroup of European Nurse Researchers for National Representatives, September 1990*, 312.
99 Steppe, "Historical Research in Nursing," 308.
100 Steppe, "Historical Research in Nursing," 314.
101 Quoted in Cashman, *Heritage of Service*, 167.
102 Cashman, *Heritage of Service*, 168.
103 Oral history interviews with retired nurses and instructors previously employed at the Alberta Hospitals located in Edmonton and Ponoka, August, 1996, Diana Mansell, Calgary.
104 Olson, "Laying Claim to Caring."
105 Dyck, *Facing Eugenics*, 228–29.
106 Alvin Finkel, *Social Policy and Practice in Canada* (Waterloo, ON: Wilfrid Laurier University Press, 2006).
107 Judy Coburn, "I See and Am Silent: A Short History of Nursing in Ontario," in *Health and Canadian Society: Sociological Perspectives*, ed. Janice Acton, Penny Goldsmith, and Bonnie Shepherd (Toronto: Fitzhenry & Whiteside, 1981), 129.

CHAPTER 4

1 Stefan Kuehl, *The Nazi Connection: Eugenics, American Racism, and German National Socialism* (New York: Oxford University Press, 1994), 6. Positive eugenics includes the encouragement of procreation by individuals and groups who are viewed as possessing desirable characteristics and genes

(e.g., financial and political stimuli, in vitro fertilization, egg transplanting and cloning). Negative eugenics involves discouraging and decreasing procreation by individuals and groups who are viewed as having inferior or undesirable characteristics and genes (e.g., coercive or medically indicated abortions, sterilization, methods of family planning).

2 Ian Robert Dowbiggin, *Keeping America Sane: Psychiatry and Eugenics in the United States and Canada, 1880–1940* (Ithaca, NY: Cornell University Press, 2003), 77.

3 Kuehl, *Nazi Connection*, 17.

4 Garland E. Allen, "The Ideology of Elimination: American and German Eugenics, 1900–1945," in *Medicine and Medical Ethics in Nazi Germany: Origins, Practices, Legacies*, ed. Francis R. Nicosia and Jonathan Huener (New York: Berghahn Books, 2002), 19.

5 André Dupras, "Public Attitudes towards the Sterilization of Handicapped People," in *Sterilization and Mental Handicap: Proceedings of a Symposium Sponsored by the National Institute on Mental Retardation and the Ontario Association for the Mentally Retarded*, ed. Mental Institute on Mental Retardation, Ontario Association for the Mentally Retarded (Downsview, ON: National Institute on Mental Retardation, 1980), 65.

6 Robert N. Proctor, *Racial Hygiene: Medicine under the Nazis* (Cambridge, MA: Harvard University Press, 1980), 145, 148. The Weimar government established "counselling centers" that advocated for marriage based on principals of racial hygiene, and physicians and geneticists during this period were the first to recommend that all citizens carry "health passes" and that "racial offices" be established.

7 Henry Friedlander, *Origins of Nazi Genocide: From Euthanasia to the Final Solution* (Chapel Hill: University of North Carolina, 1995), 26.

8 Proctor, *Racial Hygiene*, 131.

9 Dowbiggin, *Keeping America Sane*, xiii.

10 Kuehl, *Nazi Connection*, 20. A number of private organizations, such as the Rockefeller Foundation and the Carnegie Foundation, financed eugenics research in Germany between 1920 and 1934.

11 Dowbiggin, *Keeping America Sane*, 36.

12 The western provinces in Canada were geographically closer to the United States than to Ontario and as a result were strongly influenced by American political and cultural trends in the 1920s.

13 Jana Grekul, Harvey Krahn, and Dave Odynak, "Sterilizing the 'Feeble-Minded': Eugenics in Alberta, Canada, 1929–1972," *Journal of Historical Sociology* 17, no. 4 (2004): 362; Angus McLaren, *Our Own Master Race: Eugenics in Canada, 1885–1945* (Toronto: McClelland & Stewart, 1990), 99.

14 Grekul, Krahn, and Odynak, "Sterilizing the 'Feeble-Minded,'" 362. Among the members of the UFWA who advocated for sterilization legislation was Nellie McClung (1873–1951), the well-known Canadian feminist, social activist, and politician. Other groups active in the pro-sterilization campaign were the Women's Christian Temperance Movement Union and the Alberta Department of Public Health. On the role of women suffragists in the Alberta eugenics movement, see Erin Moss, Henderikus J. Stam, and Diane Kattevilder, "From Suffrage to Sterilization: Eugenics and the Women's Movement in 20th Century Alberta," *Canadian Psychology* 54, no. 1 (2013): 105–14.

15 McLaren, *Our Own Master Race*, 100. The existing literature does not address the question of who exactly in the Legislative Assembly objected to the original Sexual Sterilization Act and on what grounds.

16 The act was passed despite advice from the British House of Lords on the illegality of such a measure.

17 Jana Grekul, "A Well-Oiled Machine: Alberta's Eugenics Program, 1928–1972," *Alberta History* 59, no. 1 (2011): 16. Sterilization operations in Alberta hospitals consisted of vasectomies, salpingectomies (tubal ligation), orchiectomies (removal of testes), oophorectomies (removal of the ovaries), and sometimes hysterectomies. On sterilization procedures, see Mary E. Frost, "Sterilization in Alberta: A Summary of the Cases Presented to the Eugenics Board for the Province of Alberta from 1929 to 1941" (master's thesis, University of Alberta, 1942). For a "genetic critique" of eugenic science and Alberta's sterilization legislation, see Kennedy G. McWhirter and Judy Weijer, "The Alberta Sterilization Act: A Genetic Critique," *University of Toronto Law Journal* 19, no. 3 (1969): 424–31.

18 Timothy Caulfield and Gerald Robertson, "Eugenic Policies in Alberta: From the Systematic to the Systemic?," *Alberta Law Review* 35, no. 1 (1996): 61.

19 Grekul, Krahn, and Odynak, "Sterilizing the 'Feeble-Minded,'" 366–75. Of the cases presented to the AEB, 54 percent were women (in 1931 only 45 percent of Alberta's population was female), 19 percent were eastern European (although they represented 17 percent of the province's population), and 6 percent were Indigenous (who accounted for only 2 percent of the population). On gender differences and the overrepresentation of women, see Jana Grekul, "Sterilization in Alberta, 1928 to 1972: Gender Matters," *Canadian Review of Sociology* 45, no. 3 (2008): 247–66.

20 Allen, "Ideology of Elimination," 34.

21 Sheila Faith Weiss, "The Race Hygiene Movement in Germany," *Osiris*, 2nd ser., 3, no. 1 (1987): 193–236.

22 Kuehl, *Nazi Connection*, 82.

23 Antoine d'Eschambault, *Eugenical Sterilization* (Winnipeg: Canadian Publishers, 1937), 74.

24 D'Eschambault, *Eugenical Sterilization*, 19.

25 Grekul, Krahn, and Odynak, "Sterilizing the 'Feeble-Minded,'" 376.

26 Although sterilization operations became increasingly unpopular in the years following the Second World War, the eugenics movement was already being severely discredited by a new generation of doctors and social advocates as early as the mid-1930s.

27 Timothy J. Christian, "Mentally Ill and Human Rights in Alberta: A Study of the Alberta Sterilization Act" (honours thesis, University of Alberta, 1974), 25.

28 Christian, "Mentally Ill and Human Rights," 28.

29 *Edmonton Bulletin*, April 1, 1937, n. p.

30 Sexual Sterilization Act Amendment Act, S.A. 1937, c. 47. The 1937 Amendment made virtually every inmate of Alberta mental institutions vulnerable to forced sterilization. The Amendment also made castration permissible.

31 The 1942 Amendment, which also lacks scholarly study, permitted the sterilization of individuals suffering from epilepsy and Huntington's disease. On the abolishment of the act and the Leilani Muir trial (1995–96) that followed, see Douglas Wahlsten, "Leilani Muir versus the Philosopher King: Eugenics on Trial in Alberta," Genetica 99, no. 1 (1997): 185–98.

32 Studies have been conducted by a number of historians, sociologists, psychologists, and administrators at the University of Alberta, including Timothy Caulfield, Gerald Robertson, Douglas Wahlsten, Jana Grekul, Harvey Krahn, David Odynak, and Terry Chapman, as well as prominent gender historian Angus McLaren. For a list of publications on Alberta's sexual sterilization program, see Grekul, "Sterilization in Alberta."

33 University of Alberta law professor Gerald Robertson has argued that legalized sterilization in the late 1920s and early 1930s was likely in step with the public mood at the time. See Richard Cairney, "'Democracy Was Never Intended for Degenerates': Alberta's Flirtation with Eugenics Comes Back to Haunt It," *Canadian Medical Association Journal* 155, no. 7 (1997): 789.

34 The only other Canadian province to pass an involuntary sterilization law was British Columbia, which did so in 1933; however, considerably fewer sterilization operations were performed there. See Richard Foulkes, "British Columbia Mental Health Services: Historical Perspective to 1961," *Canadian Medical Association Journal* 85, no. 6 (1961): 649–55.

35 Terry L. Chapman, "Early Eugenic Movements in Western Canada," *Alberta History* 25, no. 1 (1977): 9.

36 Dowbiggin, *Keeping America Sane*, 141. The 1869 Immigration Act was highly discriminatory, favouring British, American, Scandinavian, and Protestant immigrants over southern and eastern Europeans and Catholics. See Ellen Keith, "'Human Wreckage from Foreign Lands': A Study of the Ethnic Victims of the Alberta Sterilization Act," *Constellations* 2, no. 2 (2011): 81–89.

37 McLaren, *Our Own Master Race*, 47.

38 Christian, *Mentally Ill and Human Rights*, 5.

39 Chapman, "Early Eugenic Movements," 9; Valerie Knowles, *Strangers at Our Gates: Canadian Immigration and Immigration Policy, 1540–1990* (Toronto: Dundurn Press, 1992).

40 Chapman, "Early Eugenic Movements," 13.

41 Christian, *Mentally Ill and Human Rights*, 8.

42 Ninette Kelley and Michael Trebilcock, *The Making of the Mosaic: A History of Canadian Immigration Policy* (Toronto: University of Toronto Press, 1998), 216.

43 The most famous of these policies were order-in-council PC 695, passed in 1931, that essentially ended Canada's sixty-year open-door policy on immigration.

44 Statistics Canada, "Immigrant Arrivals in Canada, 1892 to 1946," *Canada Yearbook* (Ottawa: Government of Canada, 1947).

45 Kelley and Trebilcock, *Making of the Mosaic*, 227; see also Barbara Roberts, *Whence They Came: Deportation from Canada, 1900–1935* (Ottawa: University of Ottawa Press, 1988).

46 Statistics Canada, "Destinations of Immigrants into Canada, by Provinces, Calendar Years 1929 to 1936," *Canada Yearbook* (Ottawa: Government of Canada, 1937).

47 Statistics Canada, "Destinations."

48 Statistics Canada, "Nationalities of Immigrants, Calendar Years 1931 to 1935," *Canada Year Book* (Ottawa, 1937). Only 20 percent of immigrants who entered Alberta in the mid-1930s were from eastern Europe, or approximately two hundred per year.

49 Christian, *Mentally Ill and Human Rights.*

50 "Immigration Activities Will Be Curbed," *Edmonton Journal*, March 7, 1929, 1.

51 "Editorial," *Calgary Daily Herald*, September 11, 1930, 8; *Calgary Daily Herald*, September 8, 1930, 4.

52 "Sterilization Bill Passes Third Reading," *Edmonton Bulletin*, March 7, 1928, 1.

53 "Editorial," *Edmonton Bulletin*, March 26, 1927, 1.

54 "Editorial," *Edmonton Bulletin*, December 9, 1935, 2.

55 "Sterilization Board Given Wide Powers," *Calgary Daily Herald*, April 1, 1937, 4. Many other newspapers published articles and editorials on Alberta's

sterilization law, including the *Montréal Gazette* (February 7, 1934, p. 3) and the *Buckingham Post* (March 12, 1937, p. 5).

56 Letitia Fairfield, *The Case against Sterilization*, pamphlet (London, ON: Catholic Truth Society, 1934); Helen MacMurchy, *Sterilization? Birth Control? A Book for Family Welfare and Safety* (Toronto: Macmillan, 1934); d'Eschambault, *Eugenical Sterilization*, 69. D'Eschambault argued that the science of eugenics was based on "dubious theories" and that Alberta's Sexual Sterilization Act resembled eugenics laws in Nazi Germany.

57 McLaren, *Our Own Master Race*, 10.

58 "Whither Germany?," editorial, *Edmonton Journal*, July 16, 1933, 4. The other German legislation and programs included the Law for the Restoration of the Professional Civil Service, passed on April 7, 1933; the Jewish boycott of April 1, 1933; and the "25 points of the Nazi program."

59 "Nazis Bar Jews from Citizenship," *Calgary Daily Herald*, September 16, 1935, 1; "New Laws Persecute German Jews," *Calgary Daily Herald*, September 16, 1935, 2.

60 "Nazis Bar Jews," 1; "New Laws Persecute German Jews," 2.

61 Bruce Kidd, "Canadian Opposition to the 1936 Olympics in Germany," *Sport in Society* 16, no. 4 (2013): 432.

62 McLaren, *Our Own Master Race*, 166; Tommy C. Douglas, *The Making of a Socialist: The Recollections of T.C. Douglas*, ed. Lewis Thomas (Edmonton: University of Alberta Press, 1984), 108.

63 "Against Sterilization," originally published in the *New York Times*, January 26, 1936, 8.

64 "Sterilization Forced upon Her," *Washington Post*, January 7, 1936, 1; "Woman Is Saved from Sterilization," *Washington Post*, January 23, 1936, 4.

65 McLaren, *Our Own Master Race*, 119.

66 Grekul, Krahn, and Odynak, "Sterilizing the 'Feeble-Minded,'" 362.

67 Quoted in McLaren, *Our Own Master Race*, 119.

68 Christian, *Mentally Ill and Human Rights*, 7. Hincks was also general director of the Canadian National Committee on Mental Hygiene.

69 Christian, *Mentally Ill and Human Rights*, 8.

70 Christian, *Mentally Ill and Human Rights*, 28.

71 Haudley quoted in Caulfield and Robertson, "Eugenic Policies in Alberta," 62.

72 Haudley quoted in Caulfield and Robertson, "Eugenic Policies in Alberta," 63.

73 *Medicine Hat News*, February 24, 1928.

74 Christian, *Mentally Ill and Human Rights*, 23.

75 Christian, *Mentally Ill and Human Rights*, 11.

76 Christian, *Mentally Ill and Human Rights*, 9.

77 See Deborah C. Park, "From the Case Files: Reconstructing a History of Involuntary Sterilization," *Disability and Society* 13, no. 3 (1998): 317–42; and Wahlsten, "Leilani Muir."

78 Park, "From the Case Files"; Wahlsten, "Leilani Muir."

79 This is a common assumption: that the support for sterilization from key individuals and organizations reflected the opinions of the Alberta population at large. See Park, "From the Case Files," 318.

80 Further research is needed on the definition and diagnosis of "mental deficiency" in Alberta during the 1930s, as is more detailed knowledge regarding the overrepresentation of specific ethnic groups in sterilization procedures.

81 On the Catholic Church in the province, see Sheila Ross, "'For God and Canada': The Early Years of the Catholic Women's League in Alberta," *Historical Studies* 62, no. 1 (1996): 89–108; see also Erna Kurbegović, "Eugenics in Comparative Perspective: Explaining Manitoba and Alberta's Divergence on Eugenics Policy, 1910s to the 1930s" (PhD diss., University of Calgary, 2019).

82 Jana Grekul has asked many of these questions in her work and has spent considerable time studying the 1937 Amendment and the longevity of Alberta's sterilization practices. See Grekul, "Sterilization in Alberta"; and "A Well-Oiled Machine." Recent publications on Alberta's history of sterilization include Robert A. Wilson, "The Role of Oral History in Surviving a Eugenic Past," in *Beyond Testimony and Trauma: Oral History in the Aftermath of Mass Violence*, ed. Steven High (Vancouver: University of British Columbia Press, 2015), 119–38; and Ericka Dyck, *Facing the History of Eugenics: Reproduction, Sterilization and the Politics of Choice in 20th Century Alberta* (Toronto: University of Toronto Press, 2013).

CHAPTER 5

1 "Editorial," *Journals of the Legislative Assembly of Manitoba: Nineteenth Legislative Assembly* (1933), 20, Manitoba Legislative Library Collection, Winnipeg.

2 "Editorial," *Journals of the Legislative Assembly of Manitoba: Nineteenth Legislative Assembly* (1933), 198-199, Manitoba Legislative Library Collection, Winnipeg.

3 See, for example, Timothy Christian, "The Mentally Ill and Human Rights in Alberta: Study of the Alberta Sexual Sterilization Act" (honours thesis, University of Alberta, 1974); Erin Moss, Henderikus J. Stam, and Diane Kattevilder, "From Suffrage to Sterilization: Eugenics and the Women's

Movement in 20th Century Alberta," *Canadian Psychology* 54, no. 1 (2013): 105–14.

4 See, for example, Terry L. Chapman, "Early Eugenics Movement in Western Canada," *Alberta History* 25, no. 1 (1977): 9–18; Angus McLaren, *Our Own Master Race: Eugenics in Canada, 1885–1945* (Toronto: McClelland & Stewart, 1990); Moss, Stam, and Kattevilder, "From Suffrage to Sterilization"; and Sheila Gibbons, "'Our Power to Remodel Civilization': The Development of Eugenic Feminism in Alberta, 1909–1921," *Canadian Bulletin of Medical History* 31, no. 1 (2014): 123–42.

5 For a discussion of eugenics in Alberta in the postwar period, see Douglas Wahlsten, "Leilani Muir versus the Philosopher King: Eugenics on Trial in Alberta," *Genetica* 99, no. 1 (1997): 185–98; Jana Grekul, Harvey Krahn, and Dave Odynak, "Sterilizing the 'Feeble-Minded': Eugenics in Alberta, Canada, 1929–1972," *Journal of Historical Sociology* 17, no. 4 (2004): 358–84; Jana Grekul, "Sterilization in Alberta, 1928 to 1972: Gender Matters," *Canadian Review of Sociology* 45, no. 3 (2008): 247–66; and Amy Samson, "Eugenics in the Community: Gendered Professions and Eugenic Sterilization in Alberta, 1928–1972," *Canadian Bulletin of Medical History* 31, no. 1 (2014): 143–63. On reproductive rights and reproductive technologies, see Ian Dowbiggin, *The Sterilization Movement and Global Fertility in the Twentieth Century* (Oxford: Oxford University Press, 2008); and Erika Dyck, *Facing Eugenics: Reproduction, Sterilization, and the Politics of Choice* (Toronto: University of Toronto Press, 2013).

6 For further reading, see Charles Darwin, *On the Origin of Species by Means of Natural Selection, Or the Preservation of Favoured Races in the Struggle for Life* (London: J. Murray, 1859).

7 Philippa Levine and Alison Bashford, "Introduction: Eugenics and the Modern World," in *The Oxford Handbook of the History of Eugenics*, eds. Alison Bashford and Philippa Levine (Oxford: Oxford University Press, 2010), 4.

8 Diane B. Paul, *Controlling Human Heredity, 1865 to the Present* (Atlantic Highlands, NJ: Humanities Press, 1995).

9 Francis Galton, *Inquiries into Human Faculty and Its Development* (London: Macmillan, 1883), 17.

10 See, for example, Paul, *Controlling Human Heredity.*

11 See Marius Turda, *Modernism and Eugenics* (London: Palgrave Macmillan, 2010), 7.

12 See Karolina Kowalewski and Yasmin Mayne, "The Translation of Eugenic Ideology into Public Health Policy: The Case of Alberta and Saskatchewan," in *The Proceedings of the 18th Annual History of Medicine Days Conference 2009*,

ed. Lisa Peterman, Kerry Sun, and Frank W. Stahnisch (Newcastle upon Tyne: Cambridge Scholars Publishing, 2012), 53–74.

13 Ian Robert Dowbiggin, *Keeping America Sane: Psychiatry and Eugenics in the United States and Canada, 1880-1940* (Ithaca: University of Cornell Press, 1997), 170–171.

14 Erna Kurbegović, "The Influence of the Manitoba Mental Hygiene Survey, 1918," *Western Humanities Review* 69, no. 3 (2016): 298.

15 Kurbegović, "The Influence of the Manitoba Mental Hygiene Survey, 1918," 298.

16 Canadian National Committee for Mental Hygiene (CNCMH), "Manitoba Survey," Winnipeg, October 1918.

17 McLaren, *Our Own Master Race*, 99.

18 Grekul, Krahn, and Odynak, "Sterilizing the 'Feeble-Minded,'" 361–62.

19 "Editorial," *Journals of the Legislative Assembly of Manitoba: Nineteenth Legislative Assembly* (1933), 20, Manitoba Legislative Library Collection, Winnipeg, Manitoba, Canada.

20 Byron M. Unkauf, "The Sterilization of the Mental Defective," *University of Manitoba Medical Journal* 5/6, no. 1 (1933–35): 46.

21 Alvin Mathers, "Report on the Prevention of Mental Disorders," 1925, 8, Premier's Office Files, G541, Health Programme, 1925–26, Government and Private Sector Archives, Archives of Manitoba, Winnipeg (hereafter, GPSA).

22 David MacLennan, "Beyond the Asylum: Professionalization and the Mental Hygiene Movement in Canada, 1914–1928," *Canadian Bulletin of Medical History* 4, no. 1 (1987): 19.

23 MacLennan, "Beyond the Asylum," 19; Elizabeth Lunbeck, *The Psychiatric Persuasion: Knowledge, Gender, and Power in Modern America* (Princeton, NJ: Princeton University Press 1995), 63.

24 Kurbegović, "Manitoba Mental Hygiene Survey," 302-3; "Mental Deficiency Measure Effective in Province since June 1," *Winnipeg Free Press*, June 7, 1933.

25 CNCMH, "Manitoba Survey," 10.

26 "Report on the Prevention of Mental Disorders," 11, GPSA.

27 Thomas G. B. Caunt, "Some Facts Concerning Mental Disease," *University of Manitoba Medical Journal* 3/4, no. 2 (1931–33): 119.

28 Caunt, "Some Facts," 119.

29 Unkauf, "Sterilization of the Mental Defective," 27.

30 Gerald Friesen, *The Canadian Prairies: A History* (Toronto: University of Toronto Press, 1987), 403.

31 *Winnipeg Tribune*, March 11, 1933.

32 "Sterilization of the Mental Defective," 46.

33 McLaren, *Our Own Master Race*, 97–98.

34 "New Defectives Bill Passes Law Amendments Body," *Winnipeg Free Press*, February 23, 1933.
35 "Sterilization," *Northwest Review*, March 4, 1933.
36 McLaren, *Our Own Master Race*, 98.
37 "Bill Sponsored by Hoey in Legislature Meeting Opposition," *Winnipeg Free Press*, February 23, 1933.
38 Alexandra Minna Stern, *Eugenic Nation: Faults and Frontiers of Better Breeding in Modern America* (Berkeley: University of California Press, 2005), 83.
39 Philip R. Reilly, "Eugenics and Involuntary Sterilization: 1907–2015," *Annual Review of Genomics and Human Genetics* 16, no. 3 (2015): 356.
40 Wendy Klein, *Building a Better Race: Gender, Sexuality, and Eugenics from the Turn of the Century to the Baby Boom* (Berkeley: University of California Press, 2005), 31.
41 McLaren, *Our Own Master Race*, 104.
42 See also Erna Kurbegović, "Eugenics in Comparative Perspective: Explaining Manitoba and Alberta's Divergence on Eugenics Policy" (PhD diss., University of Calgary, 2019).
43 See Sebastien Normandin, "Eugenics, McGill, and the Catholic Church in Montréal and Québec: 1890–1942," *Canadian Bulletin of Medical History* 15, no. 1 (1998): 59–86.
44 Erika Dyck, "Sterilization and Birth Control in the Shadow of Eugenics: Married Middle-Class Women in Alberta, 1930-1960s," *Canadian Bulletin of Medical History* 31, no. 4 (2014): 173–78.
45 See, for example, Sharon M. Leon, *An Image of God: The Catholic Struggle with Eugenics* (Chicago: University of Chicago Press, 2013); Christine Rosen, *Preaching Eugenics: Religious Leaders and the American Eugenics Movement* (Oxford: Oxford University Press, 2004); John M. Bozeman, "Eugenics and the Clergy in the Early Twentieth Century United States," *Journal of American Culture* 27, no. 4 (2004): 422–31; and Sharon M. Leon, "'Hopelessly Entangled in Nordic Pre-suppositions': Catholic Participation in the American Eugenics Society in the 1920s," *Journal of the History of Medicine and Allied Sciences* 59, no. 1 (2004): 3–49.
46 Rosen, *Preaching Eugenics*, 139–45.
47 Rosen, *Preaching Eugenics*, 140.
48 Nancy Leys Stepan, *"The Hour of Eugenics": Race, Gender, and Nation in Latin America* (Ithaca, NY: Cornell University Press, 1991), 112.
49 Leon, *Image of God*, 14.
50 See also McLaren, *Our Own Master Race*, 154–57; Rosen, *Preaching Eugenics*, 142.

51 Sean Springer, "Eugenics in Ontario: Reconsidering Catholicism, the Culture of Government, and Post War Eugenics in the Canadian Historiography" (MA thesis, Trent University, 2012), 66.

52 Pius XI, *Casti connubii*, encyclical letter (December 31, 1930), sec. 68, 70, Vatican website, http://www.vatican.va/holy_father/pi-us_xi/encyclicals/documents/hf_p-xi_enc_31121930_casti-connubii_en.html.

53 Leon, *Image of God*, 89.

54 *Winnipeg Tribune*, March 8, 1933.

55 "The British Medical Association and the Prevention of Mental Deficiency," *Mental Welfare* 6 (1925): 11–13, esp. 13.

56 Reverend W.L. Jubinville to Premier Bracken, February 24, 1933, Premier's Office Files, G601, Sterilization Bill, GPSA.

57 Garland E. Allen, "Eugenics and Modern Biology: Critiques of Eugenics, 1910–1945," *Annals of Human Genetics* 75, no. 3 (2011): 322.

58 Leon, *Image of God*, 76–77.

59 F. Faure to Premier Bracken, February 27, 1933, Premier's Office Files, G601, Sterilization Bill, GPSA.

60 *Winnipeg Tribune*, March 21, 1933.

61 J. H. Daignault to Premier Bracken, February 25, 1933, Premier's Office Files, G601, Sterilization Bill, GPSA.

62 Rev. Antoine d'Eschambault to Premier John Bracken, March 31, 1933, Premier's Office Files, G601, Sterilization Bill, GPSA.

63 "Manitoba Legislature Condemns Sterilization of Mental Defectives," *Catholic Register*, March 20, 1933.

64 John Kendle, *John Bracken: A Political Biography* (Toronto: University of Toronto Press, 1979), 41–42.

65 "Bill Sponsored by Hoey."

66 "Bill Sponsored by Hoey."

67 "Fight against Sterilization Is to Be Resumed," *Winnipeg Free Press*, April 21, 1933.

68 "Fight against Sterilization."

69 "Sterilization Clause Passed by Committee," *Winnipeg Tribune*, April 22, 1933.

70 "Sterilization Clause Passed by Committee."

71 Allen, "Eugenics and Modern Biology," 317–18.

72 "Sterilization Clause Passed by Committee."

73 "Sterilization Clause Passed by Committee."

74 "Sterilization Clause Passed by Committee."

75 "Sterilization Clause Passed by Committite."

76 "Editorial," *Journals of the Legislative Assembly*, 198–199; "Sterilization Proposals Are Killed by House," *Winnipeg Tribune*, May 4, 1933.

CHAPTER 6

1. "Folk Ways and Eugenics," *New York Times*, August 14, 1908.
2. Daniel E. Bender, *American Abyss: Savagery and Civilization in the Age of Industry* (Ithaca, NY: Cornell University Press, 2009), 8–9.
3. "Folk Ways and Eugenics," 6.
4. Galton, *Essays in Eugenics* (London: Eugenics Education Society, 1909), 35; Alexandra Minna Stern, *Eugenic Nation: Faults and Frontiers of Better Breeding in Modern America* (Berkeley: University of California Press, 2005), 11.
5. My research for this chapter was conducted primarily between 2011–2014 and thus reflects the eugenics scholarship available at the time.
6. Wendy Kline, "Eugenics in the United States," in *The Oxford Handbook of the History of Eugenics*, ed. Alison Bashford and Philippa Levin (Oxford: Oxford University Press, 2010), 511–22.
7. Allen, "The Ideology of Elimination: American and German Eugenics, 1900–1945," in *Medicine and Medical Ethics in Nazi Germany: Origins, Practices, Legacies*, ed. Francis R. Nicosia and Jonathan Huener (New York: Berghahn Books, 2002), 13–39; Edwin Black, *War against the Weak: Eugenics and America's Campaign to Create a Master Race* (New York: Four Walls Eight Windows, 2003).
8. Stern, *Eugenic Nation*, 6.
9. Nathaniel Deutsch, *Inventing America's "Worst" Family; Eugenics, Islam and the Fall and Rise of The Tribe of Ishmael* (Berkeley: University of California Press, 2009), 19–41.
10. Edward J. Larson, *Sex, Race, and Science: Eugenics in the Deep South* (Baltimore: Johns Hopkins University Press, 1995).
11. Marouf Arif Hasian, *The Rhetoric of Eugenics in Anglo-American Thought* (Atlanta: University of Georgia Press, 1996), 23–4.
12. Daniel T. Rodgers, *Atlantic Crossings: Social Politics in a Progressive Age* (Cambridge, MA: Belknap Press of Harvard University Press, 1998).
13. Stefan Kuehl, *The Nazi Connection: Eugenics, American Racism, and German National Socialism* (Oxford: Oxford University Press, 2001).
14. Stern, *Eugenic Nation*, 47.
15. Black, *War against the Weak*, 30.
16. Amory C. Stevens, "Perfect Men and Women," *Blue Grass Blade* 15 (November 18, 1906): 1.
17. Alexandra Minna Stern, "'We Cannot Make a Silk Purse Out of a Sow's Ear': Eugenics in the Hoosier Heartland," *Indiana Magazine of History* 103, no. 1 (2007): 20.
18. "Perfect Men and Women," 1.

19. Peter Weingart, "Eugenics—Medical or Social Science?," *Science in Context* 8, no. 2 (1995): 201.
20. "Science to Make Men and Women Better," *Washington Post*, May 18, 1906, 2. Sharon M. Leon and Christine Rosen and have done excellent work in examining some of the religious communities' reactions to eugenics, in both support and opposition. Leon, *An Image of God: The Catholic Struggle with Eugenics* (Chicago: University of Chicago Press, 2013); Rosen, *Preaching Eugenics: Religious Leaders and the American Eugenics Movement* (Oxford: Oxford University Press, 2004).
21. Allen, "Ideology of Elimination," 17.
22. "Folk Ways and Eugenics," 6.
23. "Improve Human Race," *Washington Post*, October 28, 1906, 13.
24. "Improved Quality of Humans Sought," *Los Angeles Times*, October 31, 1906, 12.
25. *Blue Grass Blade*, November 18, 1906, 1.
26. Eugene Davenport, "To Weed Out Human Race," *Washington Post*, January 30, 1909, 6.
27. John Elfreth Watkins, "Quest of Superman," *Evening Star*, November 10, 1906, 13.
28. "Lovemaking," *Boston Daily Globe*, September 2, 1906.
29. "Whom Would You Choose as Father?" *Washington Times*, July 29, 1912, 14.
30. John C. Hudson, "The School System of Chicago," *Chicago Daily Tribune*, July 17, 1905, 14.
31. Stern, *Eugenic Nation*, 14.
32. Weingart, "Eugenics," 199.
33. Thomas C. Leonard, "American Economic Reform in the Progressive Era: Its Foundational Beliefs and Their Relation to Eugenics," *History of Political Economy* 41, no. 1 (2009): 136.
34. "Eugenics Head Takes Prof. Larkin to Task," *San Francisco Call*, September 15, 1907.
35. "Child Quality Not Quantity," *Toronto Daily Star*, April 14, 1910, 3.
36. Edward C. Spitzka, "Health First and Matrimony Afterward," *San Francisco Call*, May 18, 1913, 1.
37. Thanks to Jeri Wieringa for pointing me to an 1897 George du Maurier (1834–96) cartoon depicting a man, who had married a homely woman for her money, interacting with an old flame. Money clearly played a role in forging many marriages and did so in a variety of ways. The eugenics discourse's focus on degenerate or ideal men, then, framed much of the language about the perceived dangers of suboptimal wealthy men using their privilege to attract women into marriage. George Du Maurier, *English Society* (New York: Harper and Brothers, 1897).

38. Benjamin Witt quoted in Rodgers, *Atlantic Crossings*, 74.
39. "Quest of a Standard," *New-York Daily Tribune*, April 25, 1909, 3.
40. "Selective Environment," *New York Times*, October 2, 1905, 3.
41. "Rosebery on Eugenics," *New York Times*, July 5, 1908, C2.
42. "Rosebery on Eugenics."
43. "A Perfect Race of Men," *New York Times*, September 27, 1908, SM8.
44. "Close Divorce Doors If Any Children," *New York Times*, January 30, 1908, 2.
45. "Lovemaking," SM7.
46. "First Eugenic Baby Born in England," *Day Book*, October 29, 1913, 4.
47. Peggy Pascoe analyzes in great detail the numerous ways that local officials willfully interpreted marriage laws and denied marriage licenses to interracial couples over the nineteenth and twentieth centuries. Peggy Pascoe, *What Comes Naturally: Miscegenation Law and the Making of Race in America* (Oxford: Oxford University Press, 2009). See also Mark Brilliant, *The Color of America Has Changed: How Racial Diversity Shaped Civil Rights Reform in California, 1941–1978* (Oxford: Oxford University Press, 2010).
48. Rodgers, *Atlantic Crossings*, 30.
49. Rodgers, *Atlantic Crossings*, 59.
50. Martin S. Pernick, "Eugenics and Public Health in American History," *American Journal of Public Health* 87, no. 11 (1997): 1767–72.

CHAPTER 7

1 Frank W. Stahnisch, "Von der Kriegsneurologie zur Psychotherapie—Kurt Goldstein (1878-1965) und die fruehen Ansaetze der Gruppenanalyse," *Gruppenpsychotherapie und Gruppendynamik* 50, no. 1 (2014): 146–65.

2 John Cornwell, *Hitler's Scientists: Science, War, and the Devil's Pact* (New York: Viking, 2003), 154.

3 Cornwell, *Hitler's Scientists*, 154.

4 Radio interview with Kurt Goldstein (Series on Forced-Migration of German-Jewish Intellectuals to North America) by Irmgard Bach, *Radio Bremen* (June, 1959), Radio Bremen, Bremen, Germany; see also Bach, M[ichelle] I[rmgard]. "Interview with Kurt Goldstein (June, 1959) in NYC." In *Auszug des Geistes. Bericht ueber eine Sendereihe*, edited by Lutz Besch, 93–114. Bremen, Germany: B. C. Hege, 1962.

5 Andreas Strippel, *NS-Volkstumspolitik und die Neuordnung Europas. Rassenpolitische Selektion der Einwandererzentralstelle des Chefs der Sicherheitspolizei und des SD (1939–1945)* (Paderborn, Germany: Ferdinand Schoeningh Verlag, 2011), 102-6.

6 Anne Harrington, "Kurt Goldstein's Neurology of Healing and Wholeness: A Weimar Story," in *Greater Than the Parts: Holism in Biomedicine, 1920–1950*, ed. George Weisz and Christopher Lawrence (New York: Oxford University Press, 1998), 24–45.

7 Kurt Bayertz, Juergen Kroll, and Peter Weingart, *Rasse, Blut und Gene. Geschichte der Eugenik und Rassenhygiene in Deutschland* (Frankfurt am Main: Suhrkamp, 1988), 424–38.

8 For example, see Yehuda Ben-Yishay and Leonard Diller, "Kurt Goldstein's Holistic Ideas—An Alternative, or Complementary, Approach to the Management of Traumatically Brain-Injured Individuals," *US Neurology* 4, no. 1 (2008): 79–80.

9 See Douglas Gairdner, "Reading for Pleasure: History Opened My Eyes!," *British Medical Journal* 284, no. 11 (1982): 1105–6.

10 Stephen Pow and Frank W. Stahnisch, "Kurt Goldstein (1878–1965)—Pioneer in Neurology," *Journal of Neurology* 261, no. 10 (2014): 1049–50.

11 Johannes Hendrikus Burgers, "Max Nordau, Madison Grant, and Racialized Theories of Ideology," *Journal of the History of Ideas* 72, no. 1 (2011): 119–40.

12 Franz Josef Kallmann, *The Genetics of Schizophrenia: A Study of Heredity and Reproduction in the Families of 1,087 Schizophrenics* (New York: J. J. Augustin, 1938); John D. Rainer, "Franz Kallmann's Views on Eugenics," *American Journal of Psychiatry* 146, no. 12 (1989): 1361–62; correspondence from Ludwig Guttmann concerning rescinding of license to practice medicine, learning English, and translated transcripts of documents, 1938–1939, PP/GUT/A.1/3, box.1, 6, Wellcome Library of the History of Medicine, London, United Kingdom. See also the following seminal works: Michael Kater, "Hitler's Early Doctors: Nazi Physicians in Pre-Depression Germany," *Journal of Modern History* 95, no. 1 (1987): 25–52; Fritz Ringer, *The Decline of the German Mandarins: The German Academic Community, 1890–1933* (Cambridge, MA: Harvard University Press, 1969), 14–80.

13 The "Famous Five," or "Alberta Five," were early feminist activists Emily Murphy (1868–1933), Irene Marryat Parlby (1868–1965), Nellie Mooney McClung (1873–1951), Louise Crummy McKinney (1868–1931), and Henrietta Muir Edwards (1849–1931). Erika Dyck, "Sterilization and Birth Control in the Shadow of Eugenics: Married, Middle-Class Women in Alberta, 1930s–1960s," *Canadian Bulletin of Medical History* 31, no. 1 (2014): 165–78; Tommy C. Douglas, *The Making of a Socialist: The Recollections of T. C. Douglas*, ed. Lewis Thomas (Edmonton: University of Alberta Press, 1984), 108.

14 Tommy C. Douglas, "The Problems of the Subnormal Family" (MA thesis, McMaster University, 1933), 25.

15 Although the neighbouring province of Saskatchewan—in which the revered Tommy Douglas became premier in 1944—saw continuous intellectual and partially public debate regarding a "program of eugenics," this must be seen as a "social movement" or a "cultural climate." Saskatchewan did not have any far-reaching eugenics program and was, in fact, surpassed by provinces such as British Columbia and Alberta, with their centralized provincial legislation, and even by medical system–based programs in Ontario and Nova Scotia. On the case of Saskatchewan, see, for example, Erika Dyck and Alex Deighton, *Managing Madness: Weyburn Mental Hospital and the Transformation of Psychiatric Care in Canada* (Winnipeg: University of Manitoba Press, 2017), 151–70; and Alex Deighton, "The Nature of Eugenic Thought and Limits of Eugenic Practice in Interwar Saskatchewan," in *Eugenics at the Edges of Empire: New Zealand, Australia, Canada and South Africa*, ed. Diana B. Paul, John Stenhouse, and Hamish G. Spencer (London: Palgrave Macmillan, 2018), 63–84.

16 See Stefan Kuehl, *The Nazi Connection: Eugenics, American Racism, and German National Socialism* (New York: Oxford University Press, 1994), 6.

17 Matthias M. Weber, *Ernst Ruedin: Eine kritische Biographie* (Berlin: Springer, 1993), 174–211.

18 Kurt Goldstein, *Ueber Rassenhygiene* (Berlin: Springer, 1913).

19 See, for example, Erwin Stransky, "Aus einem Gelehrtenleben um die Zeitenwende: Rueckschau, Ausblick, Gedanken," n. d., 318–19, collection of autographs, History of Medicine Library and Institute for the History of Medicine; Josephinum, Medical University of Vienna, Austria.

20 Paul Weindling, *John W. Thompson: Psychiatrist in the Shadow of the Holocaust* (Rochester, NY: University of Rochester Press, 2010), 3–10; Francis R. Nicosia and Jonathan Huener, eds., *Medicine and Medical Ethics in Nazi Germany: Origins, Practices, Legacies* (New York: Basic Books, 2002), 1–15.

21 Radio interview with Kurt Goldstein (Series on Forced-Migration of German-Jewish Intellectuals to North America) by Irmgard Bach, *Radio Bremen* (June, 1959), Radio Bremen, Bremen, Germany; see also Bach, M[ichelle] I[rmgard]. "Interview with Kurt Goldstein (June, 1959) in NYC." In *Auszug des Geistes. Bericht ueber eine Sendereihe*, edited by Lutz Besch, 93–114. Bremen, Germany: B. C. Hege, 1962.

22 Angus McLaren, *Our Own Master Race: Eugenics in Canada, 1885–1945* (Toronto: McClelland & Stewart, 1990), 166.

23 Robert Ulrich, "Kurt Goldstein," in *The Reach of Mind: Essays in Memory of Kurt Goldstein*, ed. Marianne L. Simmel (New York: Springer, 1968), 13–15.

24 Edwin Black, *War against the Weak: Eugenics and America's Campaign to Create a Master Race* (New York: Dialog, 2007), 261–62.

25 Kurt Goldstein, *Human Nature in the Light of Psychopathology* (Cambridge, MA: Harvard University Press, 1940), 222–23.

26 Mitchell G. Ash, "Scientific Changes in Germany 1933, 1945, 1990: Towards a Comparison," *Minerva* 37, no. 3 (1999): 329–54.

27 See Ben-Yishay and Diller, *Kurt Goldstein's Holistic Ideas*, 79–80.

28 At Harvard, the protagonist of holist neurology spoke mainly in front of an audience interested in general questions of clinical psychology, patient education, and rehabilitation, with only a few participants attending from the medical community. See also the assessment of MIT psychologist Hans-Lukas Teuber (1916–77), who helped to make Goldstein's Harvard visit possible, in Teuber, "Kurt Goldstein's Role in the Development of Neuropsychology," *Neuropsychologia* 4, no. 4 (1966): 299–310.

29 Kurt Goldstein, "Die Neuroregulation. Referat," *Verhandlungen der Deutschen Gesellschaft fuer Innere Medizin* 43, no. 1 (1931): 9–13; Kurt Goldstein, "Das psychophysische Problem in seiner Bedeutung fuer aerztliches Handeln," *Therapie der Gegenwart* 72, no. 1 (1931): 1–11; typescripts and lecture notes by Kurt Goldstein, 1938–1939, MS#0498, Box 14 and 15, Bib ID 4078817, Series II Lectures notes, Kurt Goldstein papers, 1900–1965, Rare Book & Manuscript Library. Columbia University, New York.

30 Gerhard Danzer, ed., *Vom Konkreten zum Abstrakten. Leben und Werk Kurt Goldsteins (1878–1965)* (Frankfurt am Main: Mabuse Verlag, 2006), 11–70.

31 Uta Noppeney, "Kurt Goldstein—A Philosophical Scientist," *Journal of the History of the Neurosciences* 10, no. 1 (2001): 67–78; Frank W. Stahnisch, "Ludwig Edinger (1855–1918)—Pioneer in Neurology," *Journal of Neurology* 255, no. 1 (2008): 147–48; "Petition to the Medical Faculty in Frankfurt am Main," n. d. 1919, Edinger Commission, 5–8, Senckenberg Library Frankfurt, Johann Wolfgang Goethe University, Frankfurt am Main, Germany.

32 Mitchell G. Ash, *Gestalt Psychology in German Culture, 1890–1967: Holism and the Quest for Objectivity* (Cambridge: Cambridge University Press, 1995), 325–404.

33 Goldstein quoted in Anne Harrington, *Reenchanted Science: Holism in German Culture from Wilhelm II to Hitler* (Princeton, NJ: Princeton University Press, 1996), 140–41. On Breslau at the time, see Till van Rahden, *Jews and Other Germans: Civil Society, Religious Diversity, and Urban Politics in Breslau, 1860–1925* (Madison: University of Wisconsin Press, 2008), 21–63.

34 Pow and Stahnisch, "Kurt Goldstein," 1049.

35 Ludwig Edinger, *The Anatomy of the Central Nervous System of Man and of Vertebrates in General*, trans. Winfield S. Hall, Philo Leon Holland, and Edward P. Carlton (Philadelphia: F. A. Davis, 1899); "Petition to the Medical Faculty in Frankfurt am Main," n. d. 1919, Edinger Commission,

1–2, Senckenberg Library Frankfurt, Johann Wolfgang Goethe University, Frankfurt am Main, Germany.

36 Frank W. Stahnisch and Thomas Hoffmann, "Kurt Goldstein and the Neurology of Movement during the Interwar Years—Physiological Experimentation, Clinical Psychology and Early Rehabilitation," in *Was bewegt uns? Menschen im Spannungsfeld zwischen Mobilitaet und Beschleunigung*, ed. Christian Hoffstadt, Franz Peschke, and Andreas Schulz-Buchta (Bochum, Germany: Projektverlag, 2010), 283–311.

37 Klaus J. Neumaerker and Andreas Joachim Bartsch, "Karl Kleist (1879–1960)—A Pioneer of Neuropsychiatry," *History of Psychiatry* 14, no. 4 (2003): 411–58; Kurt Goldstein, "Notes on the Development of My Concepts," in *Kurt Goldstein: Selected Papers/Ausgewaehlte Schriften*, edited by Aron Gurwitsch, Else M. Goldstein-Haudek, and William E. Haudek (The Hague: Martinus Nijhoff, 1971), 1–12; Richard Jung, "Ueber eine Nachuntersuchung des Falles Schn. von Goldstein und Gelb," *Psychiatrie, Neurologie und medizinische Psychologie* 1, no. 3 (1949): 353–62.

38 Goldstein, "Development of My Concepts," 5.

39 Goldstein, "Development of My Concepts," 5.

40 Michael Kuetemeyer and Ulrich Schultz, "Kurt Goldstein (1878–1965): Begruender einer psychosomatischen Neurologie?," in *Nicht misshandeln. Das Krankenhaus Moabit, 1920–1933. Ein Zentrum juedischer Aerzte in Berlin, 1933–1945. Verfolgung, Widerstand, Zerstoerung*, ed. Christian Pross and Rolf Winau (Berlin: Edition Hentrich, 1984), 133–39.

41 See, for example, Udo Benzenhoefer and Gerald Kreft, "Bemerkungen zur Frankfurter Zeit (1917–1933) des juedischen Neurologen und Psychiaters Walther Riese," *Schriftenreihe der Deutschen Gesellschaft fuer Geschichte der Nervenheilkunde* 3, no. 1 (1997): 31–40; or Thomas Plaenkers, eds., *Psychoanalyse in Frankfurt am Main. Zerstoerte Anfaenge. Wiederannaehrung. Entwicklungen* (Tuebingen, Germany: Niemeyer, 1996).

42 Michael I. Shevell, "Neurosciences in the Third Reich: From Ivory Tower to Death Camps," *Canadian Journal of Neurological Sciences* 26, no. 2 (1999): 132–38; Eric D. Weitz, *Weimar Germany: Promise and Tragedy* (Princeton: Princeton University Press, 2007).

43 Goldstein, Kurt. *Der Aufbau des Organismus: Einfuehrung in die Biologie unter besonderer Beruecksichtigung der Erfahrungen am kranken Menschen*, edited by Thomas Hoffman and Frank W. Stahnisch, 2nd ed. (Munich: Wilhelm Fink, 2014).

44 Walter Riese, "Kurt Goldstein: The Man and His Work," *The Reach of Mind: Essays in Memory of Kurt Goldstein*, ed. Marianne L. Simmel (New York: Springer, 1968), 17–29.

45 Frank W. Stahnisch, "German-Speaking Émigré-Neuroscientists in North America after 1933: Critical Reflections on Emigration-Induced Scientific Change," *Oesterreichische Zeitschrift fuer Geschichtswissenschaften (Vienna)* 21, no. 1 (2010): 36–68.

46 Marianne L. Simmel, "Kurt Goldstein 1878–1965," in *The Reach of Mind: Essays in Memory of Kurt Goldstein*, ed. Marianne L. Simmel (New York: Springer, 1968), 2–11.ron

47 Ulrich, "Kurt Goldstein," 15.

48 See Sulamit Volkov, "Jewish Scientists in Imperial Germany (Parts I and II)," *Aleph: Historical Studies in Science and Judaism* 1, no. 1 (2001): 1–36; Frederic Henry Lewy, "Historical Introduction: The Basal Ganglia and Their Diseases," *The Diseases of the Basal Ganglia*, edited by Research Publication of the Association for Research in Nervous and Mental Disease. Baltimore, MD: Johns Hopkins University Press, 1942, 1–20.

49 Wolfram Belz, "Kurt Goldstein (1878–1965)—Lebens- und zeitgeschichtliche Hintergruende," in Danzer, *Vom Konkreten zum Abstrakten*, 11–70.

50 Goldstein, *Ueber Rassenhygiene*, 1–3.

51 Goldstein, *Ueber Rassenhygiene*, 28–29; trans. Frank W. Stahnisch. Alfred Ploetz (1860–1940) was the racial hygienist who had the most profound influence on Adolf Hitler's writing of *Mein Kampf* (1925), his foundational book of National Socialism.

52 Ringer, *Decline of the German Mandarins*, 174–175.

53 Ringer, *Decline of the German Mandarins*, 136.

54 Michael Kater, *The Nazi Party: A Social Profile of Members and Leaders 1919–1945* (Cambridge: Cambridge University Press, 1983), 239.

55 Goldstein, *Ueber Rassenhygiene*, 94; trans. Frank W. Stahnisch.

56 Richard Weikart, "Darwinism and Death: Devaluing Human Life in Germany 1859–1920," *Journal of the History of Ideas* 63, no. 3 (2002): 323–44; Frank W. Stahnisch, "Psychiatrie und Hirnforschung: Zu den interstitiellen Uebergaengen des staedtischen Wissenschaftsraums im Labor der Berliner Metropole—Oskar und Cécile Vogt, Korbinian Brodmann, Kurt Goldstein," in *Psychiater und Zeitgeist. Zur Geschichte der Psychiatrie in Berlin*, ed. Hanfried Helmchen (Berlin: Pabst Science Publisher, 2008), 76–93.

57 Sigmund Freud, *Vorlesungen zur Einfuehrung in die Psychoanalyse und Neue Folge* (1916/17) [Vol. 1 of the series: Collected works of Sigmund Freud (*Studienausgabe*), edited by Mitscherlich, Alexander, Angela Richards, and James Stratchey] (Frankfurt am Main: S. Fischer, 1989), 282–95; Eric J. Engstrom, *Clinical Psychiatry in Imperial Germany: A History of Psychiatric Practice* (Ithaca, NY: Cornell University Press, 2003), 194–98; Frank W. Stahnisch, "Griesinger, Wilhelm (1817–1869)," in *Dictionary of Medical*

Biography, ed. William F. Bynum and Helen Bynum, vol. 2 (London: Greenwood, 2007), 582–83; Wilhelm Griesinger, *Mental Pathology and Therapeutics* (London: New Sydenham Society, 1867).

58 Karl Heinz Hafner and Rolf Winau, "'Die Freigabe der Vernichtung lebensunwerten Lebens': Eine Untersuchung zu der Schrift von Karl Binding und Alfred Hoche," *Medizinhistorisches Journal* 9, no. 2 (1974): 227–54.

59 Anton Leist, *Auguste Forel. Eugenik und Erinnerungskultur* (Zurich: Hochschulverlag, 2006), 31.

60 Hoche, *Die Grenzen der geistigen Gesundheit* (Halle, Germany: Marhold, 1903); Hoche and Finger, *Zur Frage der Zeugnisfaehigkeit geistig abnormer Personen* (Halle, Germany: Marhold, 1904); Hoche, "Konstitutionelle Psychopathien," in *Lehrbuch der Psychiatrie*, ed. Ernst Schultze, Alfred Hoche, Alexander Westphal, Rolf Wallenberg, Otto Binswanger, and Ernst Siemerling (Jena, Germany: Gustav Fischer, 1926), 290–321.

61 Goldstein, *Ueber Rassenhygiene*, 36, 69, 38.

62 Goldstein, *Ueber Rassenhygiene*, 70.

63 The scientific output published from each of these institutes was, in most cases, (co-)authored under the name of, or at least together with, the directing *Professor ordinarius*, so as to thank the chief of the institution for the laboratory and office space and for the academic positions themselves, which provided the basis for contemporary researchers to produce their scientific work. For example, see Frank W. Stahnisch, "'Der Rosenthal'sche Versuch' oder: Ueber den Ort produktiver Forschung—Zur Exkursion des physiologischen Experimentallabors von Isidor Rosenthal (1836–1915) von der Stadt aufs Land," *Sudhoffs Archiv. Zeitschrift fuer Wissenschaftsgeschichte* 94, no. 1 (2010): 1–30.

64 Peter Woerster, "Archive im Koenigsberger Gebiet nach 1945," *Zeitschrift fuer Ostmitteleuropaforschung* 39, no. 1 (1990): 85–92.

65 Karl Binding and Alfred Hoche, *Die Freigabe der Vernichtung lebensunwerten Lebens. Ihr Mass und ihre Form* (Leipzig: Verlag von Felix Meiner, 1920).

66 Ruth Kloocke, Heinz-Peter Schmiedebach, and Stefan Priebe, "Psychological Injury in the Two World Wars: Changing Concepts and Terms in German Psychiatry," *History of Psychiatry* 16, no. 1 (2005): 43–60.

67 Emil Kraepelin, "Zur Entartungsfrage," *Zentralblatt fuer Neurologie und Psychiatrie*, n. s., 31, no. 7 (1908): 745–51; Peter Emil Becker, *Zur Geschichte der Rassenhygiene. Wege ins Dritte Reich* (Stuttgart: Thieme, 1988), 61.

68 Becker, *Zur Geschichte der Rassenhygiene*, 32–41.

69 Kraepelin, "Zur Entartungsfrage," 745–48.

70 Goldstein, *Ueber Rassenhygiene*, 32–65.

71 Volker Roelcke, "Von Emil Kraepelin zu Ernst Ruedin: Die Deutsche Forschungsanstalt fuer Psychiatrie 1917–1945," *Schriftenreihe der Deutschen Gesellschaft fuer Psychiatrie* 2, no. 4 (1997): 419–35.

72 Volker Roelcke, "Psychiatric Research and Science Policy in Germany: The History of the Deutsche Forschungsanstalt fuer Psychiatrie," *History of Psychiatry* 11, no. 2 (2000): 235–58.

73 Ernst Ruedin, "Ueber den Zusammenhang zwischen Geisteskrankheit und Kultur," *Archiv fuer Rassen- und Gesellschaftsbiologie* 7, no. 1 (1910): 741; trans. Frank W. Stahnisch.

74 Detlev Peukert, *The Weimar Republic: The Crisis of Classical Modernity*, trans. Richard Deveson (New York: Hill and Wang, 1989).

75 See also Max Gruber and Emil Kraepelin, *Wandtafeln zur Alkoholfrage. Erlaeuterungen nebst den 10 verkleinerten Tafeln in mehrfachem Farbendruck* (Munich: Lehmann, 1911).

76 Binding and Hoche, *Die Freigabe*, 39; trans. Frank W. Stahnisch.

77 E. Fuller Torrey and Robert H. Yolken, "Psychiatric Genocide: Nazi Attempts to Eradicate Schizophrenia," *Schizophrenia Bulletin* 36, no. 1 (2010): 26–32.

78 Binding and Hoche, *Die Freigabe*, 1–6.

79 Goetz Aly, ed., *Aktion T4 1939–1945. Die "Euthanasie–Zentrale" in der Tiergartenstrasse* (Berlin: Edition Hentrich, 1987); Hans-Walther Schmuhl, *Hirnforschung und Krankenmord. Das Kaiser-Wilhelm-Institut fuer Hirnforschung 1937–1945* (Berlin: Max-Planck-Gesellschaft, 2000); memo, by general secretary Ernst Telschow (1889–1988), September 11, 1931, based on letters by Oscar Vogt to Gustav Krupp von Bohlen und Halbach (1870–1950), September 9, 1931; Oscar Vogt to John Campbell Merriam (1869–1945), February 10, 1932; Merriam to Vogt on May 26, 1932; and Vogt to Krupp von Bohlen und Halbach, September 19, 1932, II. Sect., Rep. 1 A, 39, Collection on the Kaiser Wilhelm Institute for Brain Research, Berlin-Buch and Max Planck Institute for Brain Research, Frankfurt am Main, Archive on the History of the Max Planck Society, Berlin (MPG Archive), Germany.

80 Paul Weindling, "From International to Zonal Trials: The Origins of the Nuremberg Medical Trial," *Holocaust Genocide Studies* 14, no. 3 (2000): 367–89.

81 Goldstein, *Ueber Rassenhygiene*, 32–34.

82 Hans-Walther Schmuhl and Volker Roelcke, eds., *"Heroische Therapien": Die deutsche Psychiatrie im internationalen Vergleich, 1918–1945* (Goettingen: Wallstein Verlag, 2013).

83 Goldstein, *Ueber Rassenhygiene*, 34; trans. Frank W. Stahnisch.

84 Jack Pressman, *Last Resort: Psychosurgery and the Limits of Medicine* (Cambridge: Cambridge University Press, 1998), 48–84.

85 Goldstein, *Ueber Rassenhygiene*, 62. See Alexandra Minna Stern, "Improving Hoosiers: Indiana and the Wide Scope of American Eugenics," *Indiana Magazine of History* 106, no. 2 (2010): 219–23.

86 A few noteworthy examples are Ash, *Gestalt Psychology*, 477; and Uwe Gerrens, *Medizinisches Ethos und theologische Kritik. Karl und Dietrich Bonhoeffer in der Auseinandersetzung um Zwangssterilisation und "Euthanasie" im Nationalsozialismus* (Munich: Oldenbourg, 1996), 47; however, they have not treated Goldstein's embracing of eugenics theory in the wider social and scientific context of the time.

87 Heinz-Peter Schmiedebach, "The Public's View of Neurasthenia in Germany—Looking for a New Rhythm of Life," in *Cultures of Neurasthenia: From Beard to the First World War*, ed. Marijke Gijswijt-Hofstra, and Roy Porter (Amsterdam: Rodopi, 2001), 219–38.

88 Goldstein, *Ueber Rassenhygiene*, 34–5.

89 See Ulrich Sieg, *Geist und Gewalt. Deutsche Philosophen zwischen Kaiserreich und Nationalsozialismus* (Munich: Carl Hanser, 2013), 103–32.

90 Frederick B. Churchill, "Regeneration, 1885–1901," in *A History of Regeneration Research: Milestones in the Evolution of a Science*, ed. Charles E. Dinsmore (Cambridge: Cambridge University Press, 1991), 113–32.

91 Richard Weikart, "The Origins of Social Darwinism in Germany, 1859–1895," *Journal of the History of Ideas* 54, no. 3 (1993): 469–88.

92 Edward Shorter, *A History of Psychiatry: From the Era of the Asylum to the Age of Prozac* (New York: John Wiley & Sons, 1997), 33–68.

93 Jason Crouthamel, "Invisible Traumas: Psychological Wounds, World War I and German Society, 1914–1945" (PhD diss., Indiana University, 2001).

94 Kurt Goldstein, *Die Behandlung, Fuersorge und Begutachtung der Hirnverletzten: Zugleich ein Beitrag zur Verwendung psychologischer Methoden in der Klinik* (Leipzig: F. C. W. Vogel, 1919); Goldstein, "Das psychophysische Problem."

95 Radio interview with Kurt Goldstein (Series on Forced-Migration of German-Jewish Intellectuals to North America) by Irmgard Bach, *Radio Bremen* (June, 1959), Radio Bremen, Bremen, Germany; see also Bach, M[ichelle] I[rmgard]. "Interview with Kurt Goldstein (June, 1959) in NYC." In *Auszug des Geistes. Bericht ueber eine Sendereihe*, edited by Lutz Besch, 93–114. Bremen, Germany: B. C. Hege, 1962.

96 Ulrich, "Kurt Goldstein," 15.

97 Gerald Goldstein, "Contributions of Kurt Goldstein to Neuropsychology," *Clinical Neuropsychology* 4, no. 1 (1990): 3–17; see also Kurt Goldstein, *Language and Language Disturbances: Aphasic Symptom Complexes and Their*

Significance for Medicine and Theory of Language (New York: Grune & Stratton, 1948).

98 Teuber, "Kurt Goldstein's Role."

99 See Robert N. Proctor, *Racial Hygiene: Medicine under the Nazis* (Cambridge, MA: Harvard University Press, 1988), 65–94.

100 Radio interview with Kurt Goldstein (Series on Forced-Migration of German-Jewish Intellectuals to North America) by Irmgard Bach, *Radio Bremen* (June, 1959), Radio Bremen, Bremen, Germany; see also Bach, M[ichelle] I[rmgard]. "Interview with Kurt Goldstein (June, 1959) in NYC." In *Auszug des Geistes. Bericht ueber eine Sendereihe*, edited by Lutz Besch, 93–114. Bremen, Germany: B. C. Hege, 1962; Michael I. Shevell, "A Canadian Paradox: Tommy Douglas and Eugenics," *Canadian Journal of Neurological Sciences* 39, no. 1 (2012): 35–39.

101 Joseph Jay and Norbert A. Wetzel, "Ernst Ruedin: Hitler's Racial Hygiene Mastermind," *Journal of the History of Biology* 46, no. 1 (2013): 1–30.

102 Ernst Ruedin, "Die Bedeutung der Eugenik und Genetik fuer die Psychische Hygiene," *Zeitschrift fuer psychische Hygiene* 3, no. 1 (1930): 133–47.

103 Sheila Gibbons, "'Our Power to Remodel Civilization': The Development of Eugenic Feminism in Alberta, 1909–1921," *Canadian Bulletin of Medical History* 31, no. 1 (2014): 123–42.

104 Deborah Barrett and Charles Kurzman, "Globalizing Social Movement Theory: The Case of Eugenics," *Theory and Society* 33, no. 5 (2004): 487–527; Ian Dowbiggin, *The Sterilization Movement and Global Fertility in the Twentieth Century* (Oxford: Oxford University Press, 2008), 32–35.

105 Solomon Diamond, "Buckle, Wundt, and Psychology's Use of History," *Isis* 75, no. 1 (1984): 143–52; Wilhelm Wundt, *Grundzuege der physiologischen Psychologie*, 3 vols. (Leipzig: W. Engelmann, 1859–62).

106 See David Zimmerman, "'Narrow Minded People': Canadian Universities and the Academic Refugee Crises, 1933–1941," *Canadian Historical Review* 88, no. 3 (2007): 298; collection on the Department of Physiology and Pharmacology, 1933, UAA-2012-044, University of Alberta Archives, Research & Collections Resource Facility, Edmonton.

107 Schmuhl, *Hirnforschung und Krankenmord*, 20–48.

108 Even the term "race" (*Rasse*) is only mentioned on five pages (pp. 375, 376, 377, 378, and 379) in his 1934 magnum opus, "The Organism." Here, Goldstein particularly calls for a "better proof" and definition of the reality (*Seinsweise*) of racial concepts, such as those of minor intelligence (*geringere Intelligenz*), in order to avoid any "inhumane deeds" (*alles Unmenschliche*), which could be associated with the medical and political pressures exerted on neurological and psychiatric patients. At this time, however, Goldstein

was all too aware of his expulsion from his own position and torture by the Gestapo during the previous year, before he sat down again to write his famous book and avoid any connection to his earlier eugenics theorizing from 1913. Hoffmann and Stahnisch, *Kurt Goldstein, Der Aufbau des Organismus*, 376–79.

CHAPTER 8

1 Elof Axel Carlson, "The Indiana Origins of Sterilization," in *A Century of Eugenics in America*, ed. Paul Lombardo (Bloomington: Indiana University Press, 2010), 18–20.

2 Andrew Scull, *Madness in Civilization: A Cultural History of Insanity* (Princeton: Princeton University Press, 2015), 290-321.

3 Paul Weindling, *Health, Race and German Politics between National Unification and Nazism, 1870–1945* (Cambridge: Cambridge University Press, 1989); Matthias M. Weber, "Ernst Ruedin, 1874–1952: A German Psychiatrist and Geneticist," *American Journal of Medical Genetics* 67, no. 4 (1996): 323–31.

4 Weindling, *Health, Race and German Politics*.

5 Alfred Ploetz, *Grundlinien einer Rassenhygiene*, vol. 1 (Berlin: Prognos, 1895).

6. Ernst Ruedin, *Zur Vererbung und Neuentstehung der Dementia Praecox*. (Berlin: Springer Verlag, 1916).

7 Paul Weindling, *Victims and Survivors of Nazi Human Experiments: Science and Suffering in the Holocaust* (London: Bloomsbury, 2014).

8 Stefan Kuehl, *The Nazi Connection: Eugenics, American Racism, and German National Socialism* (New York: Oxford University Press, 1997), 23–4.

9 Paul Ehrenstroem, "Eugenics and Public Health: Legal Sterilization of Mentally Ill in the Vaud Canton (Switzerland)," *History and Philosophy of the Life Sciences* 15, no. 2 (1993): 205–27.

10 Marek V. Simunek, "Making Infertile (Unfruchtbarmachung)/Sterilisations in the Reich District of Sudetenland During the Nazi Occupation, 1938–45: Overview," *Specialni pedagogika* 24, no. 1 (2014): 24–40.

11 Bjorn M. Felder and Paul Weindling, eds., *Baltic Eugenics: Bio-Politics, Race and Nation in Interwar Estonia, Latvia, and Lithuania 1918–1940* (Amsterdam: Rodopi, 2013).

12 Claudia Spring, *Zwischen Krieg und Euthanasie. Zwangssterilisation in Wien* (Vienna: Boehlau, 2009); Herwig Czech, *Erfassung, Selektion und "Ausmerze": Das Wiener Gesundheitsamt und die Umsetzung der nationalsozialistischen "Erbgesundheitspolitik" 1938 bis 1945* (Vienna: Deuticke, 2003).

13 Astrid Ley, *Zwangssterilisation und Aerzteschaft. Hintergruende und Ziele aerztlichen Handelns 1934–1945* (Frankfurt am Main: Campus, 2004); Angelika Ebbinghaus and Heidrun Kaupen-Haas, *Heilen und Vernichten im Mustergau Hamburg. Bevoelkerungs- und Gesundheitspolitik im Dritten Reich* (Marburg, Germany: Konkret Verlag, 1984).

14 Maike Rotzoll, Gerrit Hohendorf, Petra Fuchs, Paul Richter, Christoph Mundt, and Wolfgang Eckart, eds., *Die nationalsozialistische "Euthanasie" – Aktion "T 4" und ihre Opfer: Geschichte und ethische Konsequenzen fuer die Gegenwart*, (Paderborn: Ferdinand Schoeningh, 2010).

15 Christoph Mundt, Gerrit Hohendorf, and Maike Rotzoll, eds., *Psychiatrische Forschung und NS-Euthanasie, Beitraege zu einer Gedenkveranstaltung an der Psychiatrischen Universitaetsklinik Heidelberg* (Heidelberg: University of Heidelberg, 2001), 329–30.

16 Gabriele Czarnowski has reconstructed incidents of research on forced labourers and their fetuses in minute detail. Czarnowski, "Nationalsozialistische Frauenpolitik und Medizin: zum Zusammenhang von Zwangssterilisation und Sterilitaetsforschung am Beispiel des Koenigsberger Universitaetsgynaekologen Felix von Mikulicz-Radecki," in *Frauen und Faschismus in Europa. Der faschistische Koerper*, ed. Leonore Siegele-Wenschkewitz and Gerda Stuchlik (Pfaffenweiler, Germany: Centaurus, 1990), 90–113; Czarnowski, "'Die restlose Beherrschung dieser Materie.' Beziehungen zwischen Zwangssterilisation und gynaekologischer Sterilitaetsforschung im Nationalsozialismus," *Zeitschrift fuer Sexualforschung* 14, no. 2 (2001): 226–46.

17 Paul Weindling, *Nazi Medicine and the Nuremberg Trials: From Medical War Crimes to Informed Consent* (Basingstoke: Palgrave-Macmillan, 2004), 229-245.

18 Stephan Kolb, Paul Weindling, Volker Roelcke, and Horst Seithe, "Apologising for Nazi Medicine: A Constructive Starting Point," *Lancet* 380, no. 7 (2012): 722–23.

19 United Nations Office at Geneva, Switzerland (UNOG), SOA 407/02 Plight of Survivors of Concentration Camps Weis Note, February 15, 1951.

20 UNOG, SOA 417/3/01 for individual cases.

21 Weindling, *Nazi Medicine*.

22. Aleksandra Loewenau, "The Failure of the West German Judicial System in Serving Justice: The Case of Dr. Horst Schumann," *Wiener Klinische Wochenschrift* 18, no. 3 (2018):169–172.

23 Heiner Fangerau and Irmgard Mueller, "Das Standardwerk der Rassenhygiene von Erwin Baur, Eugen Fischer und Fritz Lenz im Urteil der Psychiatrie und Neurologie 1921–1940," *Der Nervenarzt* 73, no. 10 (2002):

1039–46; Hans-Peter Kroener, *Von der Rassenhygiene zur Humangenetik* (Stuttgart: Gustav Fischer, 1998).

24 Otmar von Verschuer, "Alfred Ploetz," *Der Erbarzt* 8, no. 6 (1940): 69–72.

25 Sheila Faith Weiss, Mark B. Adams, and Garland E. Allen, "Human Heredity and Politics: A Comparative Institutional Study of the Eugenics Record Office at Cold Spring Harbor (United States), the Kaiser Wilhelm Institute for Anthropology, Human Heredity and Eugenics (Germany) and the Maxim Gorky Medical Genetics Institute (USSR)," *Osiris* 20, no. 1 (2005): 232–62.

26 Weindling, *Health, Race and German Politics.*

27 Paul Weindling, *Nazi Medicine and the Nuremberg Trials. From Medical War Crimes to Informed Consent* (Basingstoke: Palgrave-Macmillan, 2004), 41.

28 Persons and Places File (Dossier File), Judge Advocate General, 1944–49, RG153, box 90, no. 125709-17, National Archives and Record Administration, Washington, DC, United States (hereafter, NARA).

29 Persons and Places File (Dossier File), Judge Advocate General, 1944–49, RG153, box 90, no. 125709-17, NARA.

30 Leo Alexander, *Public Mental Health Practices in Germany: Sterilization and Execution of Patients Suffering from Nervous or Mental Disease.* Combined Intelligence Operations Services, Item No. 24, File No. XXVIII-60, Aug. 1945, 1–173.

31 Committee of the American Neurological Association for the Investigation of Eugenical Sterilization (Abraham Myerson, James B. Ayer, Tracy J. Putnam, Clyde E. Keeler, and Leo Alexander), *Eugenical Sterilization: A Reorientation of the Problem* (New York: Macmillan, 1936).

32 USAR/JAG War Crimes Records Regarding Medical Experiments No. 125571-4 Straight to McHaney and Hardy, November 5, 1946, RG338, NARA.

33 USAR/JAG War Crimes Records Regarding Medical Experiments No. 127376-9, RG338, NARA.

34 Description of the wounds of the witness Chaim Balitzki, notes and reports of Leo Alexander, November 22, 1946, 63, 00641, ZSg 154/73, Bundesarchiv Koblenz, Germany.

35 Landesarchiv Mecklenburg Vorpommern, Schwerin, ZAST K 153 70/47 Bd. 1, 3 re sterilisation trial in Schwerin, Germany.

36 Stefanie Michaela Baumann, *Menschenversuche und Wiedergutmachung* (Munich: Oldenbourg, 2009).

37 Egon Schwelb, *Human Rights and the International Community* (Chicago: University of Chicago Press, 1964).

38 UNOG SOA 417/3/01 A Compensation for Injuries June 1, 1950, letter by Shamsee to Weis re Iwanska. Letter by George Brand (in the United

Kingdom) to E. Garcia-Sayan 10 August 1950, Possible Programme of Aid to Victims of Medical Atrocities cc to Mary Tennison-Woods, head of section on women, NY.

39 UNOG Case G/SO 262/2.

40 Paul Weindling, "Entschaedigung der Sterilisierungs- und Euthanasie-Opfer nach 1945," in *Toedliche Medizin im Nationalsozialismus. Von der Rassenhygiene zum Massenmord*, ed. Klaus-Dietmar Henke (Cologne: Boehlau, 2008), 31–46.

41 Antje von Windmann, "Ein Stigma, lebenslang," *Der Spiegel*, September 1, 2014.

42 Von Windmann, "Ein Stigma."

43 Paul Weindling, "Sonstige Personenschaeden—die Entschaedigungspraxis der Stiftung 'Erinnerung, Verantwortung und Zukunft,'" in *Die Entschaedigung von NS-Zwangsarbeit am Anfang des 21. Jahrhunderts*, ed. Constantin Goschler, vol. 2 (Goettingen: Wallstein Verlag, 2012), 197–225.

44 "Capping the Cost of Atrocity: Survivor of Nazi Experiments Says $8,000 Isn't Enough," *New York Times*, November 13, 2003.

45 Paul Weindling, "International Eugenics: Swedish Sterilization in Context," *Scandinavian Journal of History* 24, no. 1 (1999): 179–97.

46 Markku Mattila, *Kansamme parhaaksi: Rotuhygienia Suomessa vuoden 1935 sterilointilakiin asti* (Helsinki: Biblioteca Historica, 1999); Gunnar Broberg and Nils Roll-Hansen, eds., *Eugenics and the Welfare State: Norway, Sweden, Denmark, and Finland* (East Lansing: Michigan State University Press, 2004).

47 Imogen Foulkes, "The Trauma of Switzerland's Morality Detentions," *BBC News*, September 14, 2010, http://www.bbc.co.uk/news/mobile/world-europe-11295538; Thomas Huonker, *Anstaltseinweisungen, Kindswegnahmen, Eheverbote, Sterilisationen, Kastrationen. Fuersorge, Zwangsmassnahmen, "Eugenik" und Psychiatrie in Zuerich zwischen 1890 und 1970* (Zurich: Orell Fuessli Verlag, 2003); Hans Jakob Ritter, *Psychiatrie und Eugenik. Zur Auspraegung eugenischer Denk- und Handlungsmuster in der schweizerischen Psychiatrie 1850–1950* (Zurich: Chronos Verlag, 2009); Gisela Hauss and Beatrice Ziegler, "Sterilisationen bei Armen und Unmuendigen. Eine Untersuchung der Vormundschaftspraxis in den Staedten St. Gallen und Bern," in *Wie nationalsozialsozialistisch ist die Eugenik? What is National Socialist about Eugenics?*, ed. Regina Wecker, Sabine Braunschweig, Gabriela Imboden, Bernhard Kuechenhoff, and Hans Jakob Ritter (Vienna, Cologne, and Weimar, Germany: Internationale Debatten zur Geschichte der Eugenik im 20. Jahrhundert / International Debates on the History of Eugenics in the 20th Century, 2009), 75–91; Véronique Mottier and Laura von Mandach, eds., *Pflege, Stigmatisierung und Eugenik: Integration und Ausschluss in Medizin, Psychiatrie und Sozialhilfe* (Zurich: Seismo, 2007); Geneviève Heller, Gilles

Jeanmonod, and Jacques Gasser, eds., *Rejetées, rebelles, mal adaptées: Débats sur l'eugénisme—Pratiques de la stérilisation non volontaire en Suisse romande au XXe siècle* (Geneva: Georg Editeur, 2012).

48 Leo Alexander, "Medical Science under Dictatorship," *Lancet* 241, no. 2 (1949): 39–47, esp. 46.

49 Alexander, "Medical Science under Dictatorship," 47.

CHAPTER 9

1 ARCH Disability Law Centre, "A Brief History of Disability Rights in Canada" (unpublished PowerPoint presentation, ARCH Disability Law Centre, Toronto, October 21, 2013), http://www.archdisabilitylaw.ca/sites/all/files/history%20of%20disability%20rights%20-%20pp_0.ppt.

2 Arim Rubab, *A Profile of Persons with Disabilities among Canadians aged 15 Years or Older* (Ottawa: Statistics Canada, 2012), http://www.statcan.gc.ca/pub/89-654-x/89-654-x2015001-eng.pdf.

3 ARCH Disability Law Centre, "Brief History."

4 Mary Tremblay, "Lieutenant John Counsell and the Development of Medical Rehabilitation and Disability Policy in Canada," in *Disabled Veterans in History*, ed. David A. Gerber (Ann Arbor: University of Michigan Press, 2012), 322–46.

5 David Lepofsky, "The Long, Arduous Road to a Barrier-Free Ontario for People with Disabilities: The History of the Ontarians with Disabilities Act—The First Chapter," *National Journal of Constitutional Law* 15 (2004): 125–33.

6 Canadian Charter of Rights and Freedoms, s. 8, Part 1 of the Constitution Act, 1982, being Schedule B to the Canada Act 1982 (UK), 1982, c. 11.

7 Vriend v. Alberta (1998), 1 S.C.R. 493.

8 The Harvard Law Review Association, "Developments in the Law: The Law of Marriage and Family," *Harvard Law Review* 7 (2003): 1996–2122.

9 Lepofsky, "Long, Arduous Road," 128.

10 Eldridge v. British Columbia (Attorney General) (1997), 3 S.C.R. 624.

11 *Eldridge*, 3 S.C.R .

12 Pearl Eliadis, *Speaking Out on Human Rights: Debating Canada's Human Rights System* (Montréal and Kingston: McGill-Queen's University Press, 2014), 63–108.

13 Lepofsky, "Long, Arduous Road," 135.

14 Ontarians with Disabilities Act, 2001, S.O. 2001, c. 32.

15 Accessibility for Ontarians with Disabilities Act, 2005, S.O. 2005, c. 11.

16 AODA Alliance, *Report on the Enforcement of the Accessibility for Ontarians with Disabilities Act* (Ottawa: AODA Alliance, 2018), See also the related news release by the Grassroots Disability Coalitions, Ottawa, Ontario, 2018. https://www.aodaalliance.org/whats-new/news-release-grassroots-disability-coalitions-new-report-reveals-five-consecutive-years-of-rampant-violations-of-ontarios-disabilities-act-known-to-the-wynne-government-and-ineffective-provinci/; Michelle McQuigge, "Federal Government Passes Canada's First National Accessibility Legislation," *National Post*, May 30, 2019.

17 Michelle McQuigge, "What Will Canada's New Accessibility Law in 2018 Look Like?," *Toronto Star*, December 29, 2017.

18 Although the Canadian Charter of Rights and Freedoms was patriated in 1982, section 15 did not come into effect until 1985.

19 Rubab, *Profile of Persons with Disabilities*.

20 Rubab, *Profile of Persons with Disabilities*, 4.

21 "Immigration and People with Disabilities," Council of Canadians with Disabilities (CCD) website, http://www.ccdonline.ca/en/socialpolicy/immigration.

22 "Immigration and People with Disabilities," CCD website.

23 Immigration and Refugee Protection Act, S.C. 2001, c. 27.

24 Evaluation Division, Immigration, Refugees and Citizenship Canada (IRCC), "Immigration, Refugees and Citizenship Canada, Evaluation of the Health Screening and Notification Program, ref. no.: E8-2013, November, 2015, http://ow.ly/jkEE309RLK3.

25 See Catherine Dauvergne, "International Human Rights in Canadian Immigration Law—The Case of the Immigration and Refugee Board of Canada," *Indiana Journal of Global Legal Studies* 19 (2012): 305–26.

26 Theresa Wright, "After 40 Years, Federal Government Removes Barriers to Disabled Immigrants," *National Post*, April 16, 2018.

27 Sexual Sterilization Act, R.S.A. 1955, c. 194, s. 6(1).

28 Based on the Mental Deficiency Act (1927); see Anselm Eldergill, *Mental Health Review Tribunal – Law and Practice* (London, Dublin, and Hong Kong: Sweet & Maxwell, 1997), 72.

29 Quoted in John Schmidt, "Agricultural Alberta," *Calgary Herald*, March 27, 1931, 61.

30 Rosemarie Garland-Thomson, "The Case for Conserving Disability," *Journal of Bioethical Inquiry* 9, no. 3 (2012): 339–55.

31 Kerry Abrams and R. Kent Piacenti, "Immigration's Family Values," *Virginia Law Journal* 100, no. 7 (2014): 629–709.

32 Susan Donaldson James, "Baby Sent to Foster Care for 57 Days Because Parents Are Blind," *ABC News*, July 28, 2010, http://abcnews.go.com/Health/missouri-takes-baby-blind-parents/story?id=11263491.

33 Eric Schultz, "Blind Independence Couple Gets Newborn Back after 57 Days," KSHB Kansas City, July 21, 2010.

34 James, "Baby Sent to Foster Care."

CHAPTER 10

1 "What is Disability Studies," Society for Disability Studies website, <https://disstudies.org/index.php/about-sds/what-is-disability-studies/>, accessed on January 11, 2020.

2 Dan Goodley, "Dis/entangling Critical Disability Studies," *Disability & Society* 28, no. 6 (2012): 631–44.

3 *Encyclopedia of Disability*, ed. Gary L. Albrecht (Newbury Park, CA: Sage, 2006), s.v. "ableism"; Gregor Wolbring, "Ability Privilege: A Needed Addition to Privilege Studies," *Journal for Critical Animal Studies* 12, no. 1 (2014): 118–41.

4 Gregor Wolbring, "Expanding Ableism: Taking Down the Ghettoization of Impact of Disability Studies Scholars," *Societies* 2, no. 1 (2012): 75–83.

5 Gregor Wolbring, "'Culture of Peace' from an Ability and Disability Studies Lens," in *Expanding Peace Ecology: Peace, Security, Sustainability, Equity and Gender; Perspectives of IPRA's Ecology and Peace Commission*, ed. Ursula Spring, Oswald Spring, Hans-Guenter Brauch, and Keith Tidball (New York: Springer, 2013), 193.

6 Francis Galton, *Inquiries into Human Faculty and Its Development* (London: Macmillan, 1883); also in Galton, *Hereditary Genius: An Inquiry into Its Laws and Consequences* (London: Macmillan, 1869); 30; Galton, "Eugenics: Its Definition, Scope, and Aims," *American Journal of Sociology* 10, no. 1 (1904): 1–25.

7 Rudolf Kraemer, *Kritik der Eugenik: Vom Standpunkt des Betroffenen* (Berlin: Reichsdeutscher Blindenverband, 1933).

8 Douglas C. Baynton, *Defectives in the Land: Disability and Immigration in the Age of Eugenics* (Chicago: University of Chicago Press, 2016).

9 Carol Poore, "Recovering Disability Rights in Weimar Germany," *Radical History Review* 4, no. 1 (2006): 38–58.

10 Gregor Wolbring, "The Politics of Ableism," *Development* 51, no. 2 (2008): 252–58.

11 Gregor Wolbring, "Why NBIC? Why Human Performance Enhancement?," *Innovation: The European Journal of Social Science Research* 21, no. 1 (2008): 25–40.

12 Catrine Clay and Michael Leapman, *Master Race: The Lebensborn Experiment in Nazi Germany* (London: Hodder & Stoughton, 1995).

13 Gregor Wolbring and Lucy Diep, "The Discussions around Precision Genetic Engineering: Role of and Impact on Disabled People," *Laws* 5, no. 3 (2016): 1–23.

14 Derrick Thomas, "Geneticist Defends Sterilization in Era before the Pill," *Calgary Herald*, June 29, 1995, A14.

15 See, for example, in James Scott Thompson and Margaret Wilson Thompson, *Genetics in Medicine* (Philadelphia: WB Sauders Company, 1966), 260; Elaine Hutton and Margaret Wilson Thompson, "Carrier Detection and Genetic Counselling in Duchenne Muscular Dystrophy: A Follow-up Study," *Canadian Medical Association Journal* 115, no. 8 (1976): 749–52, esp. 751.

16 Mary Ziegler, "Eugenic Feminism: Mental Hygiene, the Women's Movement, and the Campaign for Eugenic Legal Reform, 1900–1935," *Harvard Journal of Law and Gender* 31, no. 2 (2008): 211–35.

17 Elasah Drogin, *Margaret Saenger. Gruenderin der modernen Gesellschaft* (Abtsteinach, Germany: Aktion Leben, 2000).

18 David Paul Nord, "A Republican Literature: A Study of Magazine Reading and Readers in Late Eighteenth-Century New York," *American Quarterly* 40, no. 1 (1988): 42–64.

19 Anna S. Burns, "Beard v. Banks: Restricted Reading, Rehabilitation, and Prisoners' First Amendment Rights," *Journal of Law and Policy* 15, no. 12 (2007): 1225–70; Neil Weinstock Netanel, "Copyright and a Democratic Civil Society," *Yale Law Journal* 106, no. 2 (1996): 283–387.

20 Bernard I. Weiner, "The Democratic Exchange of Reading and Writing: Americanization and Periodical Publication, 1750–1810," *Christ Church Library Newsletter* 7, no. 1 (2011): 102–13, esp. 102; Weiner, "The Americanization and Periodical Publication, 1750–1810," *Cercles* 19, no. 2 (2009): 102–13; Weinstock, "Copyright and a Democratic Civil Society," 283-387.

21 Lawrence M. Wallack, *Mass Media and Health Promotion: The Promise, the Problem, the Challenge* (Berkeley: School of Public Health, University of California, 1989); Wallack, "Mass Media and Health Promotion: Promise, Problem, and Challenge," in *Mass Communication and Public Health: Complexities and Conflicts*, ed. Charles Atkins and Lawrence Wallack (Newbury Park, CA: Sage, 1990), 43–57.

22 *Convention on the Rights of Persons with Disabilities*, New York, December 13, 2006, *United Nations Treaty Series*, vol. 2515, p. 3, https://treaties.un.org/

pages/ViewDetails.aspx?src=TREATY&mtdsg_no=IV-15&chapter=4; United Nations Office of the High Commissioner for Human Rights, "Monitoring the Convention on the Rights of Persons with Disabilities Guidance for Human Rights Monitors" (Professional Training Series No. 17, New York and Geneva, 2017), http://www.ohchr.org/Documents/Publications/Disabilities_training_17EN.pdf.

23 See Lori Lyon and Rick Houser, "Nurse Educator Attitudes toward People with Disabilities," *Nursing Education Perspectives* 39, no. 3 (2018): 151–55; Beth A. Marks, "Jumping through Hoops and Walking on Egg Shells or Discrimination, Hazing, and Abuse of Students with Disabilities?," *Journal of Nursing Education* 39, no. 5 (2000): 205–10; and Eamonn Slevin and David Sines, "Attitudes of Nurses in a General Hospital towards People with Learning Disabilities: Influences of Contact, and Graduate-Non-Graduate Status, A Comparative Study," *Journal of Advanced Nursing* 24, no. 6 (1996): 1116–26.

24 Alison Bashford, "Epilogue: Where Did Eugenics Go?," in *The Oxford Handbook of the History of Eugenics*, ed. Alison Bashford and Philippa Levine (Oxford: Oxford University Press, 2010), 539–58.

CONCLUSION

1 Carolyn Strange and Jennifer A. Stephen, "Eugenics in Canada: A Checkered History, 1850s–1990s," in *The Oxford Handbook of the History of Eugenics*, ed. Alison Bashford and Philippa Levine (Oxford: Oxford University Press, 2010), 523–38; Edward Shorter, *A History of Psychiatry: From the Era of the Asylum to the Age of Prozac* (New York: John Wiley & Sons, 1997), 218–24; Mark Adams, *The Wellborn Science: Eugenics in Germany, France, Brazil, and Russia* (Oxford: Oxford University Press, 1990), 3–7.

2 See also Sally Ledger and Scott McCracken, *Cultural Politics at the Fin de Siècle* (Oxford: Oxford University Press, 2003).

3 José Brunner, "Psychiatry, Psychoanalysis and Politics during the First World War," *Journal of the History of the Behavioral Sciences* 27, no. 4 (1991): 352–65. On the relationship of health care and policy reforms in the wider context of increasing industrialization in modern Western societies in the early 1900s, see, for example, Joachim Radkau, "The Neurasthenic Experience in Imperial Germany: Expeditions into Patient Records and Side-Looks upon General History," in *Cultures of Neurasthenia: From Beard to the First World War*, ed. Marijke Gijswijt-Hofstra and Roy Porter (Amsterdam: Rodopi, 2001), 199–217.

4 On increasing social clashes in the spheres of gender and class during the 1920s and early 1930s, see Paul Weindling, *Health, Race and German Politics between National Unification and Nazism, 1870–1945* (Cambridge: Cambridge University Press, 1989), 61–105.

5 Volker Roelcke, "Funding the Scientific Foundations of Race Policies: Ernst Ruedin and the Impact of Career Resources on Psychiatric Genetics, ca. 1910–1945," in *Man, Medicine, and the State: The Human Body as an Object of Government Sponsored Medical Research in the 20th Century*, ed. Wolfgang U. Eckart (Stuttgart: Franz Steiner, 2006), 73–87.

6 Volker Roelcke, "Psychiatry in Munich and Yale, ca. 1920–1935: Mutual Perceptions and Relations, and the Case of Eugen Kahn (1887–1973)," in *International Relations in Psychiatry: Britain, America, and Germany to World War II*, ed. Volker Roelcke, Paul Weindling, and Louise Westwood (Rochester, NY: University of Rochester Press, 2010), 156–78.

7 Philipp Blom, *The Vertigo Years: Europe, 1900–1914* (New York: Basic Books, 2008).

8 See, for example, Ian Dowbiggin, *The Sterilization Movement and Global Fertility in the Twentieth Century* (Oxford: Oxford University Press, 2008), 1–16; and Erika Dyck, *Facing Eugenics: Reproduction, Sterilization, and the Politics of Choice* (Toronto: University of Toronto Press, 2013), 143–68.

9 Joseph W. Easton and Robert Weil, *Culture and Mental Disorders: A Comparative Study of the Hutterites and Other Populations* (Glencoe, IL: Free Press, 1955).

10 See Paul Weindling, ed., *Healthcare in Private and Public from the Early Modern Period to 2000* (London: Routledge, 2014).

11. Frank W. Stahnisch, *A New Field in Mind: A History of Interdisciplinarity in the Early Brain Sciences* (Montréal and Kingston: McGill-Queen's University Press, 2020), 131–200.

12 Frank W. Stahnisch, "The Early Eugenics Movement and Emerging Professional Psychiatry: Conceptual Transfers and Personal Relationships between Germany and North America, 1880s to 1930s," *Canadian Bulletin of Medical History* 31, no. 1 (2014): 17–40; Frank W. Stahnisch and Fred Weizmann, eds., "Eugenics and Psychiatry—Analyzing the Origin, Application, and Perception of Early Forced Sterilization Programs from a Medical History Viewpoint," in *ISHN and Cheiron*, ed. University of Calgary (Calgary, AB: University of Calgary, 2011); accessed on August 27, 2014, www.ucalgary.ca/ISHN_Cheiron/node/39.

13 Karen Stote, *An Act of Genocide: Colonialism and the Sterilization of Aboriginal Women* (Halifax and Winnipeg: Fernwood, 2015); Stote, "An Act of Genocide:

Eugenics, Indian Policy and the Sterilization of Aboriginal Women in Canada" (PhD diss., University of New Brunswick, 2012).

14 See Douglas Francis, R., Robert Jones, and Donald B. Smith, *Origins: Canadian History to Confederation* (Toronto: Harcourt Brace Canada, 2004); and, Douglas Francis, R., Robert Jones, and Donald B. Smith, *Destinies: Canadian History since Confederation* (Toronto: Harcourt Brace Canada, 2007), 173; as well as Rankin K. Hay, *Neurosurgery and Neurological Science in Manitoba, 1884–1984* (Winnipeg: Schacht, 2003), 3.

15 Warren Elofson, *Frontier Cattle Ranching in the Land and Times of Charlie Russell* (Montréal and Kingston: McGill-Queen's University Press, 2004), 42–62.

16 See the Eugenics Archives website, http://eugenicsarchive.ca.

17 Frank W. Stahnisch, "The Early Eugenics Movement and Emerging Professional Psychiatry: Conceptual Transfers and Personal Relationships between Germany and North America, 1880s to 1930s," *Canadian Bulletin of Medical History* 31, no. 1 (2014): 17–40.

18 See Angus McLaren, *Our Own Master Race: Eugenics in Canada, 1885–1945* (Toronto: McClelland & Stewart, 1990), 15–18; Dyck, *Facing Eugenics*; Erna Kurbegović, "The Influence of the Manitoba Mental Hygiene Survey, 1918," *Western Humanities Review* 69, no. 3 (2016): 298–323.

19 Strange and Stephen, "Eugenics in Canada."

20 See, for example, David Gibson, "Involuntary Sterilization of the Mentally Retarded: A Western Canadian Phenomenon," *Canadian Psychiatric Association Journal* 19, no. 1 (1974): 59–63; and Neal Ross Holtan, "The Eitels and Their Hospital," *Minnesota Medicine* 36 (2003): 52–54.

21 Paul Lerner, *Hysterical Men: War, Psychiatry, and the Politics of Trauma in Germany, 1890–1930* (Ithaca, NY: Cornell University Press), 36-39.

22 Joachim Radkau, *Das Zeitalter der Nervositaet. Deutschland zwischen Bismarck und Hitler* (Munich: Fink Verlag, 1998), 9–15; Axel Karenberg, "Klinische Neurologie in Deutschland bis zum Ersten Weltkrieg—die Begruender des Faches und der Fachgesellschaft," in *100 Jahre Deutsche Gesellschaft fuer Neurologie*, ed. Detlef Koempf (Berlin: Deutsche Gesellschaft fuer Neurologie, 2007), 20–29.

23 Heinz-Peter Schmiedebach, "The Public's View of Neurasthenia in Germany—Looking for a New Rhythm of Life," in Gijswijt-Hofstra and Porter, *Cultures of Neurasthenia*, 219–38; Wolfgang U. Eckart, "'Die wachsende Nervositaet unserer Zeit'—Medizin und Kultur im Fin de siècle am Beispiel der Modekrankheit Neurasthenie," in *Psychiatrie um die Jahrhundertwende*, ed. Fritz Reimer (Heilbronn, Germany: Weinsberger Kolloquium, 1994), 9–38; Hans Georg Hofer, "War Neurosis and Viennese Psychiatry in World

War One," in *Uncovered Fields: Perspectives in First World War Studies*, ed. Jenny Macleod and Pierre Purseigle (Amsterdam: Amsterdam University Press, 2004), 243–60.

24 Johannes Hendrikus Burgers, "Max Nordau, Madison Grant, and Racialized Theories of Ideology," *Journal of the History of Ideas* 72, no. 1 (2011): 119–40.

25 See, for example, Volker Roelcke, "Electrified Nerves, Degenerated Bodies: Medical Discourses in Neurasthenia in Germany, ca. 1990–1914," in Gijswijt-Hofstra and Porter, *Cultures of Neurasthenia*, 177–97; William H. Tucker, *The Funding of Scientific Racism: Wickliffe Draper and the Pioneer Fund* (Urbana: University of Illinois Press, 2002), 32–47.

26 Roelcke, "Electrified Nerves."

27 Joan Sangster, *Dreams of Equality: Women on the Canadian Left, 1920–1950* (Toronto: McClelland & Stewart, 1989).

28 On the issue of eugenics-oriented public health, eugenic, and immigration policies in Nazi Germany, see the excellent study by Andreas Strippel, *NS-Volkstumspolitik und die Neuordnung Europas. Rassenpolitische Selektion der Einwandererzentralstelle des Chefs der Sicherheitspolizei und des SD (1939–1945)* (Paderborn, Germany: Ferdinand Schoeningh Verlag, 2011), 105–93; on those policies' implications for the disciplines of psychiatry and neurology, see Paul Weindling, *John W. Thompson: Psychiatrist in the Shadow of the Holocaust* (Rochester, NY: University of Rochester Press, 2010), 3–10.

29 Diane B. Paul, John Stenhouse, and Hamish G. Spencer, "Introduction: Eugenics as a Transnational Subject: The British Dominions," in *Eugenics at the Edges of Empire: New Zealand, Australia, Canada and South Africa*, ed. Diane B. Paul, Hamish G. Spencer, and John Stenhouse (Cham, NY: Palgrave Macmillan, 2017), 1–19.

30 See Weindling, *Health, Race and German Politics*, 155–69.

31 Stefan Kuehl, *The Nazi Connection: Eugenics, American Racism, and German National Socialism* (New York: Oxford University Press, 1994), 53–64.

32 Renate Rissom, *Fritz Lenz und die Rassenhygiene* (Husum, Germany: Matthiesen Verlag, 1983), 83–97. Often these exchanges included the German émigré biologist Leo Loeb (1869–1959), with whom Charles B. Davenport corresponded regarding funding for German brain psychiatry, on behalf of the Carnegie Institution of Washington and the Rockefeller Foundation in New York. Furthermore, Loeb, who had close contacts among eugenic researchers on both sides of the Atlantic, had advisory-member status on genetic issues at the Eugenics Records Office in Cold Spring Harbor. See, for example, correspondence from Leo Loeb with the Eugenics Record Office in Cold Spring Harbor, 1942–43, FC0002, correspondence C–Ha, box 2, folder: Leo Loeb, Leo Loeb fonds, Archives and Rare Books Division of the Becker

Library, Washington University School of Medicine, St. Louis, Missouri, United States.

33 Fritz Lenz, "Eugenics in Germany," *Journal of Heredity* 15, no. 2 (1924): 223.

34 See also Jonathan Harwood, *Styles of Scientific Thought: The German Genetic Community, 1900–1933* (Chicago: University of Chicago Press, 1993), 138–80.

35 Rissom, *Fritz Lenz.*

36 Fritz Lenz, *Menschliche Auslese und Rassenhygiene (Eugenik)* (Munich: Lehmann, 1921).

37 See also Véronique Mottier, "Eugenics and the State: Policy-Making in Comparative Perspective," in Bashford and Levine, *Oxford Handbook of the History of Eugenics*, 134–53; and Véronique Mottier and Natalia Gerodetti, "Eugenics and Social-Democracy: Or, How the Left Tried to Eliminate the 'Weeds' from Its National Gardens," *New Formations* 60, no. 1 (2006–7): 35–49.

38 Alfred Hoche, ed., *Handbuch der gerichtlichen Psychiatrie*, 3rd ed., comp. Gustav Aschaffenburg (Berlin: Springer, 1934).

39 Anne Harrington, *Reenchanted Science: Holism in German Culture from Wilhelm II to Hitler* (Princeton, NJ: Princeton University Press, 1996), 178–96.

40 Paul Eden, *Socialism and Eugenics* (Manchester: National Labour Press, 1911).

41 Robert N. Proctor, *Racial Hygiene: Medicine under the Nazis* (Cambridge: Harvard University Press, 1980), 145–48.

42 Kuehl, *Nazi Connection*, 20.

43. Stahnisch, *A New Field in Mind*, 183–186.

44 Hans-Peter Kroener, *Von der Rassenhygiene zur Humangenetik* (Stuttgart: Gustav Fischer, 1998), 16–39.

45 Kroener, *Von der Rassenhygiene*, 28–29.

46 Matthias M. Weber, *Ernst Ruedin: Eine kritische Biographie* (Berlin: Springer, 1993), 114–56; Roelcke, "Programm und Praxis der psychiatrischen Genetik an der Deutschen Forschungsanstalt fuer Psychiatrie unter Ernst Ruedin: Zum Verhaeltnis von Wissenschaft, Politik und Rasse-Begriff vor und nach 1933." *Medizinhistorisches Journal* 37, no. 1 (2002): 21–55.

47 Erwin Ruedin to His Excellency Herrn Staatsminister Schmidt-Ott, January 16, 1930, America's Great Depression Portfolio, 45–46, Historisches Archiv des Max-Planck-Instituts fuer Psychiatrie, Rockefeller Archive Center, International Finance Corporation (in alliance with the Rockefeller Foundation, Kaiser Wilhelm Institute for Brain Research, Berlin-Buch (hereafter KWIBR).

48 "Your Excellency have shown in your invitation from Nov-3 [1930] that the anthropological research endeavours in the German 'population' shall be put on a much broader basis. [. . .] However, this branch of *Volkskunde* also needs to be supplemented with human–biological and human–medical

science, as well as with studies in animals and plants. These complementary studies are important because they can give insights into the undisturbed developments of race, when only the appropriate objects are correctly chosen.... From the drosophila fly we can harvest 25 generations in only one year! ... And when regular and constant hereditary factors were studied in the past, it was found that not all hereditary modes applied to human reproduction, making it necessary to conduct new animal experiments again. It is particularly my collaborator N[icolai]. Timoféeff-Ressovsky [1900–81] who has developed this important field of study and who began to elucidate the inconstantly manifest hereditary factors in (neurological) disease." Oskar Vogt to Deutsche Forschungsgemeinschaft president Friedrich Schmidt-Ott, December 2, 1930, America's Great Depression Portfolio, 64–65, Historisches Archiv des Max-Planck-Instituts fuer Psychiatrie, RAC, International Finance Corporation, KWIBR; translation and italics by author.

49 Typescript of historical précis Geheimnisse des Gehirns. Weg und Werk des Hirnforscherehepaars Cécile and Oskar Vogt by institute assistant Thea Luers, ca. 1950, 148pp., 31–4, KWI for Brain Research fonds, Historical Archive of the Max Planck Society, Berlin, Germany.

50 As an indication of the magnitude of these exchanges, there were two hundred North Americans at the DFA alone. Kraepelin himself spoke of the educational value of "his institute" in only the highest forms of praise in 1920: "I am pleased that I could help to bring this work [the creation of the DFA for Psychiatry] into existence, as the necessity for such research [an interdisciplinary exploration of the various perspectives in brain psychiatry] has probably not been more obvious at any other time in our history. We hope that the intended further development of this haven of German science will help to reconstruct our national integrity effectively." Kraepelin, *Memoirs*, 190.

51 Frank W. Stahnisch, "Flexible Antworten—Offene Fragen: Zu den Foerderungsstrategien der Rockefellerstiftung fuer die deutsche Hirnforschung im Nationalsozialismus," *Journal fuer Neurologie, Neurochirurgie und Psychiatrie* 12, no. 2 (2011): 56–58.

52 Weber, *Ernst Ruedin*, 53–92.

53 Letter by Alan Gregg to clinical psychiatrist and epidemiologist Roy Grinker (1900–93), Chicago, November 8, 1935, Alan Gregg (Germany) fonds, Rockefeller Foundation, series 106, Rockefeller Archive Center, Sleepy Hollow, New York, United States; see also Cornelius Borck, "Mediating Philanthropy in Changing Political Circumstances: The Rockefeller Foundation's Funding for Brain Research in Germany, 1930–1950,"

Rockefeller Archive Center Research Reports, April 2001, http://www.rockarch.org/publications/resrep/borck.pdf.

54 See Theodore M. Brown, "Friendship and Philanthropy: Henry Severest, Alan Gregg and the Rockefeller Foundation," in *Making Medical History: The Life and Time of Henry E. Sigerist*, ed. Elizabeth Fee and Theodore M. Brown (Baltimore: Johns Hopkins University Press, 1997), 288–311.

55 Denyse Baillargeon, *Babies for the Nation: The Medicalization of Motherhood in Québec, 1910–1970* (Waterloo, ON: Wilfred Laurier University Press, 2009).

56 Rhodri Hayward, "Germany and the Making of 'English' Psychiatry," in Roelcke, Weindling, and Westwood, *International Relations in Psychiatry*, 67–90.

57 Ernst Klee, *Auschwitz, die NS Medizin und ihre Opfer* (Frankfurt am Main: S. Fischer, 1997), 434–36.

58 This has been shown by recent scholarship both for the United States since 1900 and for Germany after 1905. Kuehl, *Nazi Connection*, 27–63.

59 Weindling, *Health, Race and German Politics*, 305–98.

60 Proctor, *Racial Hygiene*, 5.

61 Proctor, *Racial Hygiene*, 1.

62 Garland-Thomson, Rosemarie, "The Case for Conserving Disability," *Journal of Bioethical Inquiry* 9, no. 3 (2012): 339.

63 Erika Dyck and Alex Deighton, *Managing Madness: Weyburn Mental Hospital and the Transformation of Psychiatric Care in Canada* (Winnipeg: University of Manitoba Press, 2017). See also the explicit comparison of neighbouring provinces Alberta and Saskatchewan in Karolina Kowalewski and Yasmin Mayne, "The Translation of Eugenic Ideology into Public Health Policy: The Case of Alberta and Saskatchewan," in *The Proceedings of the 18th Annual History of Medicine Days Conference*, ed. Lisa Peterman, Kerry Sun, and Frank W. Stahnisch (Newcastle upon Tyne: Cambridge Scholars Publishing, 2012), 53–74.

64 Robert Lampard, *Alberta's Medical History: Young and Lusty and Full of Life* (Red Deer, AB: Friesens, 2008), 212.

65 See Volker Roelcke, "Die Etablierung der psychiatrischen Genetik in Deutschland, Grossbritannien und den USA, ca. 1910–1960. Zur untrennbaren Geschichte von Eugenik und Humangenetik," *Acta Historica Leopoldina* 48, no. 2 (2007): 173–90; and Peter Hoff and Matthias M. Weber, "Sozialdarwinismus und die Psychiatrie im Nationalsozialismus," *Der Nervenarzt* 11, no. 10 (2002): 1017–18.

66. Ilana Loewy, "The Strength of Loose Concepts: Boundary Concepts, Federative Experimental Strategies and Disciplinary Growth: The Case of Immunology," *History of Science* 30, no. 4 (1992): 371–439.

67 Adams, *Wellborn Science*, 6.

68 Kuehl, *Nazi Connection*, 6–20.

69 Philip R. Reilly, "Eugenics and Involuntary Sterilization: 1907–2015," *Annual Review of Genomics and Human Genetics* 16, no. 3 (2015): 351–68.

BIBLIOGRAPHY

PRIMARY SOURCES

Alexander, Leo. *Public Mental Health Practices in Germany: Sterilization and Execution of Patients Suffering from Nervous or Mental Disease.* Combined Intelligence Operations Services, Item No. 24, File No. XXVIII-60, Aug. 1945, 1–173.

———. "Medical Science under Dictatorship," *Lancet* 241, no. 2 (1949): 39–47.

Altenburg, Edgar. *Genetics*. New York: Henry Holt, 1945.

Alzheimer, Alois. "Ist die Einrichtung einer psychiatrischen Abteilung im Reichsgesundheitsamt erstrebenswert?" *Zeitschrift fuer die gesamte Neurologie und Psychiatrie* 6, no. 2 (1911): 242–46.

Anastasi, Anne. *Differential Psychology*. 3rd ed. New York: Macmillan, 1958.

———. *Psychological Testing*. New York: Macmillan, 1954.

Australia. Parliament. Senate. Community Affairs References Committee. *Involuntary or Coerced Sterilisation of People with Disabilities in Australia*. Canberra, July 2013. http://www.aph.gov.au/Parliamentary_Business/Committees/Senate/Community_Affairs/Involuntary_Sterilisation/First_Report.

Babcock, Ernest Brown. *Genetics in Relation to Agriculture*. New York: McGraw-Hill, 1918.

Bach, M[ichelle] I[rmgard]. "Interview with Kurt Goldstein (June, 1959) in NYC." In *Auszug des Geistes. Bericht ueber eine Sendereihe*, edited by Lutz Besch, 93–114. Bremen, Germany: B. C. Hege, 1962.

Baragar, Charles A., George A. Davidson, William J. McAlister, and David L. McCulloch. "Sexual Sterilization: Four Years Experience in Alberta." *American Journal of Psychiatry* 91 (1935): 897–923.

Barritt, Robert. *History of United Farm Women* (unpublished manuscript, 1934), M1749, File 45, Glenbow Archives, Calgary.

Bell, Leslie. "Nurses and Their Attitude towards Sex." *Canadian Nurse* 24, no. 10 (1928): 524–28.

Binding, Karl, and Alfred Hoche. *Die Freigabe der Vernichtung lebensunwerten Lebens: Ihr Mass und ihre Form*. Leipzig: Verlag von Felix Meiner, 1920.

Binet, Alfred. *Modern Ideas about Children* (1909), translated by Suzanne Heisler. 1975; Albi, France: Les Presses de l'Atelier Graphique Saint-Jean, 1984.

Binet, Alfred, and Théodore Simon. *The Development of Intelligence in Children (The Binet-Simon Scale)*, translated by Elizabeth S. Kite. Vineland, NJ: The Training School at Vineland, 1916.

Blair, William. *Mental Health in Alberta: A Report on the Alberta Mental Health Study, 1968*. Vol. 1. Edmonton: Human Resources Research and Development Executive Council, Government of Alberta, 1969.

Bow, Malcolm, and Francis Cook. *The History of the Department of Public Health of Alberta*. Edmonton: Canadian Public Health Association, 1935.

Bruce, Herbert Alexander. "Sterilization of the Feebleminded." *Canadian Medical Association Journal* 29, no. 3 (1933): 260–63.

Bumke, Oswald. *Ueber Nervoese Entartung*. Berlin: Julius Springer, 1912.

Canadian National Committee for Mental Hygiene. *Manitoba Survey*. Winnipeg: October 1918.

Cashman, Tony. *Heritage of Service: The History of Nursing in Alberta*. Edmonton: Alberta Association of Registered Nurses, 1966.

Cattell, Raymond Bernard. "The Fate of National Intelligence: Test of a Thirteen-Year Prediction." *Eugenics Review* 42, no. 3 (1950): 136–48.

———. "Is National Intelligence Declining?" *Eugenics Review* 28, no. 1 (1936–37): 181–203.

Caunt, Thomas. "Some Facts Concerning Mental Diseases." *University of Manitoba Medical Journal* 3/4, no. 2 (1931–33): 119–21.

Chase, Allan. *The Legacy of Malthus: The Social Costs of the New Scientific Racism*. New York: Knopf, 1977.

Clarke, Stanley Charles Tremayne, Verner Nyberg, and Walter Worth. *Technical Report on Edmonton Grade III Achievement 1956–1977 Comparisons*. Edmonton: Alberta Advisory Committee on Educational Studies, 1978.

Crow, Lester, and Alice Crow. *Educational Psychology*. New York: American Book Co., 1948.

Darwin, Charles. *On the Origin of Species by Means of Natural Selection, Or the Preservation of Favoured Races in the Struggle for Life*. London: J. Murray, 1859.

Davenport, Charles. *Heredity in Relation to Eugenics*. New York: H. Holt, 1911.

D'Eschambault, Antoine. *Eugenical Sterilization*. Winnipeg: Canadian Publishers, 1937.

"Developments in the Law: The Law of Marriage and Family." *Harvard Law Review* 7 (2003): 1996–2122.

Douglas, Tommy. *The Making of a Socialist: The Recollections of T. C. Douglas*, edited by Lewis Thomas. Edmonton: University of Alberta Press, 1984.

———. "The Problems of the Subnormal Family." MA thesis, McMaster University, 1933.

Du Maurier, George. *English Society*. New York: Harper and Brothers, 1897.

Easton, Joseph, and Robert Weil. *Culture and Mental Disorders: A Comparative Study of the Hutterites and other Populations*. Glencoe, IL: Free Press, 1955.

Eden, Paul. *Socialism and Eugenics*. Manchester: National Labour Press, 1911.

Edinger, Ludwig. *The Anatomy of the Central Nervous System of Man and of Vertebrates in General*, translated by Winfield Hall, Philo Leon Holland, and Edward Halton. Philadelphia: F. A. Davis, 1899.

Erb, Wilhelm. *Ueber die wachsende Nervositaet unserer Zeit. Akademische Rede zum Geburtsfeste des hoechstseligen Grossherzogs Karl Friedrich am 22. November 1893 beim Vortrage des Jahresberichts und der Verkuendigung der akademischen Preise gehalten* ... Heidelberg: Universitaetsreden, 1893.

Fairfield, Lettilia. *The Case against Sterilization*. Pamphlet. London, ON: Catholic Truth Society, 1934.

Falconer, Douglas. *Introduction to Quantitative Genetics*. Edinburgh: Oliver and Boyd, 1960.

Farrar, Clarence. "Editorial." *Canadian Public Health Journal* 22, no. 1 (1931): 92–93.

Forel, Auguste. *Hygiene der Nerven und des Geistes im Gesunden und kranken Zustande*. Stuttgart: E. Moritz, 1905.

Fraser, F. Clarke. "Medical Genetics in Pediatrics." *Journal of Pediatrics* 44, no. 1 (1954): 85–103.

———. "The Use of Genetics in Clinical Medicince," *McGill Medical Journal* 18, no. 1 (1949): 176–81.

Freud, Sigmund. *Vorlesungen zur Einfuehrung in die Psychoanalyse und Neue Folge* (1916/17) [Vol. 1 of the series: Collected works of Sigmund Freud (*Studienausgabe*), edited by Mitscherlich, Alexander, Angela Richards, and James Stratchey]. Frankfurt am Main: S. Fischer, 1989.

Frohmader, Carolyn. *Dehumanised: The Forced Sterilisation of Women and Girls with Disabilities in Australia*. Women with Disabilities Australia (WWDA) submission to the Senate Inquiry into the Involuntary or Coerced Sterilisation of People with Disabilities in Australia. Rosny Park, Tasmania, March 2013. http://wwda.org.au/wp-content/uploads/2013/12/WWDA_Sub_SenateInquiry_Sterilisation_March2013.pdf.

Fuller, John, and Robert Thompson. *Behavior Genetics*. New York: Wiley, 1960.

Galton, Francis. *English Men of Science: Their Nature and Nurture*. London: Macmillan, 1874.

———. *Essays in Eugenics*, edited by Eugenics Education Society. London: Eugenics Education Society, 1909.

———. "Eugenics: Its Definition, Scope, and Aims." *American Journal of Sociology* 10, no. 1 (1904): 1–25.

———. *Hereditary Genius: An Inquiry into Its Laws and Consequences*. London: Macmillan, 1869.

———. *Inquiries into Human Faculty and Its Development*. London: Macmillan, 1883.

———. "The Possible Improvement of the Human Breed under the Existing Conditions of Law and Sentiment (1905)." In *Essays in Eugenics*, edited by Eugenics Education Society, 1–34. London: Eugenics Education Society, 1909.

Gardner, Howard. "Who Owns Intelligence?" *Atlantic Monthly*, February 1999, 67–76.

Gates, Arthur I., Arthur Thomas Jersild, Thomas R. M. McConnell, and Robert C. Challman. *Educational Psychology*. New York: Macmillan, 1948.

Gibson, David. "Involuntary Sterilization of the Mentally Retarded: A Western Canadian Phenomenon." *Canadian Psychiatric Association Journal* 19, no. 1 (1974): 59–63.

Goddard, Henry. *The Kallikak Family: A Study in the Heredity of Feeble-Mindedness*. New York: Macmillan, 1913.

Goldstein, Kurt. *Der Aufbau des Organismus: Einfuehrung in die Biologie unter besonderer Beruecksichtigung der Erfahrungen am kranken Menschen*, edited by Hoffmann, Thomas, and Frank W. Stahnisch, 2nd ed. Munich: Wilhelm Fink, 2014.

———. *Der Aufbau des Organismus: Einfuehrung in die Biologie unter besonderer Berueck-sichtigung der Erfahrungen am Kranken Menschen*. The Hague: M. Nijhoff, 1934.

———. *Die Behandlung, Fuersorge und Begutachtung der Hirnverletzten: Zugleich ein Beitrag zur Verwendung psychologischer Methoden in der Klinik*. Leipzig: F. C. W. Vogel, 1919.

———. *Human Nature in the Light of Psychopathology*. Cambridge, MA: Harvard University Press, 1940.

———. *Language and Language Disturbances: Aphasic Symptom Complexes and Their Significance for Medicine and Theory of Language*. New York: Grune & Stratton, 1948.

———. "Die Neuroregulation. Referat." *Verhandlungen der Deutschen Gesellschaft fuer Innere Medizin* 43, no. 1 (1931): 9–13.

———. "Notes on the Development of my Concepts." In *Selected Papers/Ausgewaehlte Schriften*, edited by Aron Gurwitsch, Else M. Goldstein-Haudek,

and William E. Haudek, 1–12. The Hague, The Netherl.: Martinus Nijhoff, 1971.
———. "Das psychophysische Problem in seiner Bedeutung fuer aerztliches Handeln." *Therapie der Gegenwart* 72, no. 1 (1931): 1–11.
———. *Ueber Rassenhygiene*. Berlin: Springer, 1913.
———. *Selected Papers/Ausgewaehlte Schriften*, edited by Aron Gurwitsch, Else M. Goldstein-Haudek, and William E. Haudek. The Hague, The Netherl.: Martinus Nijhoff, 1971.
Government of Alberta. *Annual Reports of Public Health (Province of Alberta; Edmonton)*. Edmonton: J. W. Jeffrey, King's Printer, 1955.
Government of Alberta. *Department of Education: Fiftieth Annual Report*. Edmonton: Department of Education, 1958.
Government of Alberta. *A Survey of Alberta's Health*. Health Survey Committee. Edmonton: Department of Public Health, 1950.
Griesinger, Wilhelm. *Mental Pathology and Therapeutics*. London: New Sydenham Society, 1867.
Gruber, Max, and Emil Kraepelin. *Wandtafeln zur Alkoholfrage. Erlaeuterungen nebst den 10 verkleinerten Tafeln in mehrfachem Farbendruck*. Munich: Lehmann, 1911.
Haldane, John Burdon Sanderson. *Heredity and Politics*. London: Allen & Unwin, 1938.
Hayward, Rhodri. "Germany and the Making of 'English' Psychiatry." In *International Relations in Psychiatry: Britain, Germany, and the United States to World War II*, edited by Volker Roelcke, Paul J. Weindling, and Louise Westwood, 67–90. Rochester, NY: University of Rochester Press, 2010.
Hincks, Clarence. *Mental Hygiene Survey of the Province of Alberta*. Ottawa: Canadian National Committee for Mental Hygiene, 1921.
———. "Survey of the Province of Manitoba." *Canadian Journal of Mental Hygiene* 1/2, no. 1 (1919–20): 77–82.
Hitler, Adolf. *Mein Kampf*. Munich: Franz Eher, 1925.
Hoche, Alfred, *Die Grenzen der geistigen Gesundheit*. Halle, Germany: Marhold, 1903.
———. "Konstitutionelle Psychopathien." In *Lehrbuch der Psychiatrie*, edited by Ernst Schultze, Alfred Hoche, Alexander Westphal, Rolf Wallenberg, Otto Binswanger, and Ernst Siemerling, 290–321. Jena, Germany: Gustav Fischer, 1926.
———, ed. *Handbuch der gerichtlichen Psychiatrie*. 3rd ed. Compiled by Gustav Aschaffenburg. Berlin: Springer, 1934.
Hoche, Alfred, and August Finger. *Zur Frage der Zeugnisfaehigkeit geistig abnormer Personen*. Halle, Germany: Marhold, 1904.

Hogben, Lancelot. *Nature and Nurture*. London: Williams & Norgate, 1933.

Hutton, Elaine, and Margaret Wilson Thompson. "Carrier Detection and Genetic Counselling in Duchenne Muscular Dystrophy: A Follow-up Study." *Canadian Medical Association Journal* 115, no. 8 (1976): 749–52.

James, William. *Pragmatism: A New Name for Some Old Ways of Thinking*. New York: Longmans, Green and Company, 1907.

Johnson, Corey. "Female Inmates Sterilized in California Prisons without Approval." Reveal. Center for Investigative Reporting, July 7, 2013. https://www.revealnews.org/article/female-inmates-sterilized-in-california-prisons-without-approval/.

Jones, Harold. "The Environment and Mental Development." In *Manual of Child Psychology*, edited by Leonard Carmichael, 631–96. New York: Wiley, 1954.

Jung, Richard. "Ueber eine Nachuntersuchung des Falles Schn. von Goldstein und Gelb." *Psychiatrie, Neurologie und medizinische Psychologie* 1, no. 3 (1949): 353–62.

Kallmann, Franz Josef. *The Genetics of Schizophrenia: A Study of Heredity and Reproduction in the Families of 1,087 Schizophrenics*. New York: J. J. Augustin, 1938.

Kraemer, Rudolf. *Kritik der Eugenik: Vom Standpunkt des Betroffenen*. Berlin: Reichsdeutscher Blindenverband, 1933.

Kraepelin, Emil. *Memoirs* (1920), translated by Cheryl Wooding-Deane. Berlin: Springer, 1987.

———. "Psychiatric Observations on Contemporary Issues" (1919), translated by Eric J. Engstrom. *History of Psychiatry* 3, no. 2 (1992): 256–69.

———. *Psychiatry: A Textbook for Students and Physicians* (1899), translated by Jacques M. Quen. Canton, MA: Science History Publications, 1990.

———. "Zur Entartungsfrage." *Zentralblatt fuer Neurologie und Psychiatrie*, n. s., 31, no. 7 (1908): 745–51.

Lenz, Fritz. "Eugenics in Germany." *Journal of Heredity* 15, no. 2 (1924): 223–31.

———. *Menschliche Auslese und Rassenhygiene (Eugenik)*. Munich: Lehmann, 1921.

Lewy, Frederic Henry. "Historical Introduction: The Basal Ganglia and Their Diseases." In *The Diseases of the Basal Ganglia*, edited by Research Publication of the Association for Research in Nervous and Mental Disease, 1–20. Baltimore: Johns Hopkins University Press, 1942.

Lindeburgh, Marion. "The Educational Objective of Public Health Nursing." *Canadian Public Health Journal* 23, no. 3 (1932): 327–30.

———. "Why Canada Is Healthier . . . ." *Canadian Public Health Journal* 30, no. 1 (1939): 11.

Lush, Jay Lawrence. *Animal Breeding Plans*. Ames: Iowa State College Press, 1945.

Lyon, Lori, and Rick Houser. "Nurse Educator Attitudes toward People with Disabilities." *Nursing Education Perspectives* 39, no. 3 (2018): 151–55.
MacEachran, John. "Crime and Punishment: Address to the United Farm Women's Association of Alberta." Reprint. *Press Bulletin*, May 6, 1932, 1–4.
———. "Criminals Are Not Reformed by Brutality or Inhumanity." *Mental Health* 7 (1932): 9–14.
———. "A Dream of Olympus," typescript of a paper presented to the Faculty Club at the University of Alberta, Edmonton, October 23, 1932, John MacEachran fonds, acc. no. 71-217, University of Alberta Archives, Research & Collections Resource Facility, Edmonton.
———. Interview by C. Roger Myers. 1970. Canadian Psychological Association fonds, MG 28 I 161, 25–17, Library and Archives Canada.
———. "John Watson." In *Some Great Men of Queen's*, edited by Robert Charles Wallace, 22–50. Toronto: Ryerson University, 1941.
———. *An Outline of Modern Philosophy*, typescript, Edmonton, n. d. Edmonton: University of Alberta Archives, n.d., John MacEachran fonds, acc. no. 1.79, University of Alberta Archives, Research & Collections Resource Facility, Edmonton.
———. "A Philosopher Looks at Mental Hygiene." *Mental Hygiene* 16 (1932): 101–19.
———. *Pragmatismus: Inaugural-dissertation zur Erlangung der Doktorwuerde der hohen philosophischen Fakultaet*. Leipzig: Druck von G. Kreysing, 1910.
———. "Twenty-Five Years of Philosophical Speculation." In *These Twenty-Five Years: A Symposium*, edited by William Hardy Alexander, Edmund Kemper Broadus, Francis John Lewis, and John M. MacEachran, 79–113. Toronto: Macmillan, 1933.
MacKinnon, Wayne. "Wide-Awake." *Canadian Nurse* 6, no. 5 (1925): 247–48.
MacLean, K. Randall, and Ethel T. Kibblewirthe. "Sexual Sterilization in Alberta." *Canadian Public Health Journal* 28, no. 5 (1937): 587–590.
MacMurchy, Helen. *Sterilization? Birth Control? A Book for Family Welfare and Safety*. Toronto: Macmillan, 1934.
Marks, Beth. "Jumping through Hoops and Walking on Egg Shells or Discrimination, Hazing, and Abuse of Students with Disabilities?" *Journal of Nursing Education* 39, no. 5 (2000): 205–10.
McVicker-Hunt, Joseph. *Intelligence and Experience*. New York: Ronald Press, 1961.
Mendel, Gregor. "Versuche ueber Pflanzenhybriden." *Verhandlungen des naturforschenden Vereines in Bruenn* 4, no. 1 (1866): 3–47.
Menzies, Edward. "Sterilization of the Feebleminded." *Canadian Medical Association Journal* 29, no. 6 (1933): 657–59.

Miller, Jordan, Nicola Fairbrother, and Rob Wilson, dirs. *Surviving Eugenics*. Vancouver: Moving Images Distribution, 2015. DVD. http://eugenicsarchive.ca/film/.

Millman, Mary. "Special Classes as a Factor in Health." *Canadian Public Health Journal* 21, no. 3 (1930): 355–57.

Morel, Bénédict Augustin. *Traité des dégénérescences physiques, et intellectuelles et morales de l'espèce humaine et de ces causes qui produisent ces variétiés maladives*. 2 vols. Paris: Baillière, 1857–58.

Morgan, Thomas Huxley. "The Mechanism and Laws of Heredity." In *The Foundations of Experimental Psychology*, edited by Carl Murchison, 1–44. Worcester, MA: Clark University Press, 1929.

Muir, Leilani. *A Whisper Past: Childless after Eugenic Sterilization in Alberta*. Victoria, BC: Friesen Press, 2014.

Muller, Henry J. "The Dominance of Economics over Eugenics." In *A Decade of Progress in Eugenics: Scientific Papers of the Third International Congress of Eugenics*, 142–44. Baltimore: William & Wilkins, 1933.

Myerson, Abraham, James B. Ayer, Tracy J. Putnam, Clyde E. Keeler, and Leo Alexander. *Eugenical Sterilization: A Reorientation of the Problem*. Committee of the American Neurological Association for the Investigation of Eugenical Sterilization. 30 USAR/JAG War Crimes Records Regarding Medical Experiments. New York: Macmillan, 1936.

National Academy of Sciences, *International Summit on Human Gene Editing: A Global Discussion–Meeting in Brief, December 1–3, 2015*, 6–7. Washington, DC: National Academy of Sciences of the United States of America, 2016. https://www.ncbi.nlm.nih.gov/books/NBK343651/.

Odell, Elizabeth. "Eliminating the Unfit from the School of Nursing." *Canadian Nurse* 11, no. 12 (1929): 723–24.

Oppenheim, Hermann. *Die traumatischen Neurosen nach den in der Nervenklinik der Charité in den letzten 5 Jahren gesammelten Beobachtungen*. Berlin: Hirschwald, 1889.

Peck, David. "The Conversion of Progressive Matrices and Mill Hill Vocabulary Raw Scores into Deviation IQ's." *Clinical Psychology* 26, no. 1 (1970): 67–70.

Penrose, Lionel. *The Biology of Mental Defect*. London: Sidgwick and Jackson, 1949.

Pius XI. *Casti connubii*. Encyclical letter, December 31, 1930. Vatican website. https://w2.vatican.va/content/pius-xi/en/encyclicals/documents/hf_p-xi_enc_19301231_casti-connubii.html.

Plato. *Charmides*. Trans. by W. R. M. Lamb. Loeb Classical Library 12. Cambridge, MA: Harvard University Press, 1927.

Ploetz, Alfred. *Grundlinien einer Rassenhygiene*. Vol. 1. Berlin: Prognos, 1895.

Plumptre, Adelaide. "Caught Napping." *Canadian Nurse* 6, no. 1 (1925): 5–8.

Pocock, Hilda. "Eugenics Propaganda." *Eugenics Review* 30, no. 1 (1938): 77.

Public Health Nursing Division. *Public Health Nursing in Manitoba, 1916–1936*. Winnipeg: Department of Public Health and Welfare, 1936.

Puplampu, Korbla. "Knowledge, Power, and Social Policy: John M. MacEachran and Alberta's 1928 Sexual Sterilization Act." *Alberta Journal of Educational Research* 54, no. 1 (2008): 129–46.

Reed, Sheldon. *Counseling in Medical Genetics*. Philadelphia: Saunders, 1955.

"Reports of Societies." *British Medical Journal* 3868 (February 23, 1935): 378.

Riese, Walter. "Kurt Goldstein: The Man and His Work." In *The Reach of Mind: Essays in Memory of Kurt Goldstein*, edited by Marianne L. Simmel, 17–29. New York: Springer, 1968.

Ruedin, Ernst. "Die Bedeutung der Eugenik und Genetik fuer die Psychische Hygiene." *Zeitschrift fuer psychische Hygiene* 3, no. 1 (1930): 133–47.

———. "Ueber den Zusammenhang zwischen Geisteskrankheit und Kultur." *Archiv fuer Rassen- und Gesellschaftsbiologie* 7, no. 1 (1910): 722–48.

———. *Zur Vererbung und Neuentstehung der Dementia Praecox*. Berlin: Springer Verlag, 1916.

Schumann, Horst. *Zur Frage der Jodresorption und der therapeutischen Wirkung sogenannter Jodbaeder*. Halle, Germany: Hallische Nachrichten, 1933.

Skodak, Marie, and Harold Skeels. "A Final Follow-Up Study of One Hundred Adopted Children." *Journal of Genetic Psychology* 75, no. 1 (1949): 85–125.

Slevin, Eamonn, and David Sines. "Attitudes of Nurses in a General Hospital towards People with Learning Disabilities: Influences of Contact, and Graduate-Non-Graduate Status, A Comparative Study." *Journal of Advanced Nursing* 24, no. 6 (1996): 1116–26.

Smith, Douglas A. "Development of the Department of Psychology, University of Alberta: 1909–1963," typescript, 1975, UAA-2006-163, Department of Psychology collection, University of Alberta Archives, Research & Collections Resource Facility, Edmonton.

Statistics Canada. *Canada Year Book*. Ottawa: Government of Canada, 1929–47.

Sternberg, Robert. "How Intelligent Is Intelligence Testing?" *Scientific American* 9, no. 1 (1999): 12–7.

Stevens, Amory C. "Perfect Men and Women." *Blue Grass Blade* 15 (November 18, 1906): 1.

Stoddard, George. *The Meaning of Intelligence*. New York: Macmillan, 1945.

Terman, Lewis. *The Measurement of Intelligence*. Boston: Houghton Mifflin, 1916.

Terman, Lewis, and Maud Merrill. *Measuring Intelligence: A Guide to the Administration of the New Revised Stanford-Binet Tests of Intelligence*. Boston: Houghton Mifflin, 1937.

———. *Stanford-Binet Intelligence Scale: Manual for the Third Revision Form L-M.* Boston: Houghton Mifflin, 1960.

Teuber, Hans-Lukas. "Kurt Goldstein's Role in the Development of Neuropsychology." *Neuropsychologia* 4, no. 4 (1966): 299–310.

Thompson, James Scott, and Margaret Wilson Thompson. *Genetics in Medicine.* Philadelphia: Saunders, 1966.

"A True Story." *Canadian Nurse* 11, no. 10 (1929): 629.

Tuddenham, Read. "Soldier Intelligence in World Wars I and II." *American Psychologist* 3, no. 1 (1948): 54–6.

Unkauf, Byron. "The Sterilization of the Mental Defective." *University of Manitoba Medical Journal* 5/6, no. 1 (1933–35): 46–9.

Von Monakow, Constantin, and Raoul Mourge. "Introduction biologique à l'étude de la neurologie et de la psychopathologie." *Zeitschrift fuer Psychologie* 115, no. 4 (1928): 403–10.

Von Verschuer, Otmar. "Alfred Ploetz." *Der Erbarzt* 8, no. 6 (1940): 69–72.

Wallace, Russell. "The Quality of the Human Stock." *Canadian Medical Association Journal* 31, no. 4 (1934): 427–30.

Wechsler, David. *The Measurement of Adult Intelligence.* 3rd ed. Baltimore: Williams & Wilkins, 1944.

———. *The Measurement of Adult Intelligence.* 4th ed. Baltimore: Williams & Wilkins, 1958.

Woodsworth, James S. *Strangers within our Gates: Or, Coming Canadians.* 1909. Reprint, Toronto: University of Toronto Press, 1972.

Wundt, Wilhelm. *Grundzuege der physiologischen Psychologie.* 3 vols. Leipzig: W. Engelmann, 1859–62.

SECONDARY SOURCES

Abrams, Kerry, and Kent Piacenti. "Immigration's Family Values." *Virginia Law Journal* 100, no. 7 (2014): 629–709.

Ackerknecht, Erwin. *A Short History of Psychiatry.* New York: Hafner, 1968.

Adams, Mark. *The Wellborn Science: Eugenics in Germany, France, Brazil, and Russia.* Oxford: Oxford University Press, 1990.

Allen, Garland. "Eugenics and Modern Biology: Critiques of Eugenics, 1910–1945." *Annals of Human Genetics* 75, no. 3 (2011): 314–25.

———. "The Ideology of Elimination: American and German Eugenics, 1900–1945." In *Medicine and Medical Ethics in Nazi Germany: Origins, Practices, Legacies,* edited by Francis Nicosia and Jonathan Huener, 13–39. New York: Berghahn Books, 2002.

Aly, Goetz, ed. *Aktion T4 1939–1945. Die "Euthanasie–Zentrale" in der Tiergartenstrasse*. Berlin: Edition Hentrich, 1987.

Annau, Catherine. "Eager Eugenicists: A Reappraisal of the Birth Control Society of Hamilton." *Histoire Sociale / Social History* 27, no. 53 (1994): 111–33.

AODA Alliance. *Report on the Enforcement of the Accessibility for Ontarians with Disabilities Act*. Ottawa: AODA Alliance, 2018.

ARCH Disability Law Centre. "A Brief History of Disability Rights in Canada." Unpublished PowerPoint presentation, ARCH Disability Law Centre, Toronto, October 21, 2013. http://www.archdisabilitylaw.ca/sites/all/files/history%20of%20disability%20rights%20-%20pp_0.ppt.

Arendt, Hannah. *Eichmann in Jerusalem: A Report on the Banality of Evil*. New York: Penguin, 1963.

Armour, Leslie, and Elizabeth Trott. *The Faces of Reason: An Essay on Philosophy and Culture in English Canada, 1850–1959*. Waterloo, ON: Wilfrid Laurier University Press, 1981.

Artibise, Alan. *Winnipeg: A Social History of Urban Growth, 1874–1914*. Montréal and Kingston: McGill-Queen's University Press, 1975.

Asch, Adrienne. "Disability Equality and Prenatal Testing: Contradictory or Compatible?" *Florida State University Law Review* 30 (2003): 315–42.

———. "Why I Haven't Changed My Mind about Prenatal Diagnosis: Reflections and Reminders." In *Prenatal Testing and Disability Rights*, edited by Erik Parens and Adrienne Asch, 234–58. Washington, DC: Georgetown University Press, 2000.

Ash, Mitchell. *Gestalt Psychology in German Culture, 1890–1967: Holism and the Quest for Objectivity*. Cambridge: Cambridge University Press, 1995.

———. "Scientific Changes in Germany 1933, 1945, 1990: Towards a Comparison." *Minerva* 37, no. 3 (1999): 329–54.

Avery, Donald. *Reluctant Host: Canada's Response to Immigrant Workers, 1896–1994*. Toronto: McClelland & Stewart, 1995.

Aylward, Glen, and Terry Stancin. "Measurement and Psychometric Considerations." *Developmental-Behavioural Pediatrics* 1, no. 1 (2008): 123–201.

Bacchi, Carol Lee. *Liberation Deferred? The Ideas of the English-Canadian Suffragists 1877–1918*. Toronto: University of Toronto Press, 1983.

———. "Race Regeneration and Social Purity: A Study of the Social Attitudes of Canada's English-Speaking Suffragists." In *Readings in Canadian History: Post-Confederation*, edited by Douglas Francis and Donald Smith, 460–74. Toronto: Holt, Rinehart and Winston, 1986.

Baillargeon, Denyse. *Babies for the Nation: The Medicalization of Motherhood in Québec, 1910–1970*. Waterloo, ON: Wilfred Laurier University Press, 2009.

Baker, Graham. "Eugenics and Migration: A Case Study of Salvation Army Literature about Canada and Britain, c.1890–1930." *Canadian Bulletin of Medical History* 31, no. 1 (2014): 77–98.

Ball, Natalie. "Le Vann, Leonard J." Eugenics Archives, n.d. http://eugenicsarchive.ca/database/documents/512fa4b134c5399e2c00000d.

———. "Galton, Sir Francis." Eugenics Archives, n. d. http://eugenicsarchive.ca/database/documents/518c1ed54d7d6e0000000002.

———. "MacEachran, John." Eugenics Archives, n.d. http://eugenicsarchive.ca/database/documents/512fa14834c5399e2c000006.

Barker, Matthew J., and Robert A. Wilson. "Well-Being, Disability, and Choosing Children." *Mind* 128, no. 510 (2019): 305–28.

Barrett, Deborah, and Charles Kurzman. "Globalizing Social Movement Theory: The Case of Eugenics." *Theory and Society* 33, no. 5 (2004): 487–527.

Bashford, Alison. "Epilogue: Where Did Eugenics Go?" In Bashford and Levine, *Oxford Handbook of the History of Eugenics*, 539–58.

Bashford, Alison, and Philippa Levine, eds. *The Oxford Handbook of the History of Eugenics*. Oxford: Oxford University Press, 2010.

Baumann, Stefanie Michaela. *Menschenversuche und Wiedergutmachung*. Munich: Oldenbourg, 2009.

Baumann, Ulrich. *Der Prozess: Adolf Eichmann von Gericht*. Berlin: Gedenk- und Bildungsstaette Haus der Wannsee-Konferenz, 2011.

Bayertz, Kurt, Juergen Kroll, and Peter Weingart. *Rasse, Blut und Gene. Geschichte der Eugenik und Rassenhygiene in Deutschland*. Frankfurt am Main: Suhrkamp, 1988.

Baynton, Douglas. *Defectives in the Land: Disability and Immigration in the Age of Eugenics*. Chicago: University of Chicago Press, 2016.

Becker, Peter Emil. *Zur Geschichte der Rassenhygiene. Wege ins Dritte Reich*. Stuttgart: Thieme, 1988.

Begos, Kevin, Danielle Deaver, John Railey, and Scott Sexton. *Against Their Will: North Carolina's Sterilization Program and the Campaign for Reparations*. Apalachicola, FL: Gray Oak Books, 2012.

Bell, Leslie. "Nurses and Their Attitude towards Sex." *Canadian Nurse* 24, no. 10 (1928): 524–28.

Belz, Wolfram. "Kurt Goldstein (1878–1965)—Lebens- und zeitgeschichtliche Hintergruende." In Danzer, *Vom Konkreten zum Abstrakten*, 11–70.

Bender, Daniel. *American Abyss: Savagery and Civilization in the Age of Industry*. Ithaca, NY: Cornell University Press, 2009.

Benedict, Susan. "The Medicalization of Murder: The 'Euthanasia' Programs." In *Nurses and Midwives in Nazi Germany: The "Euthanasia Programs,"* edited by Susan Benedict and Linda Shields, 71–104. London: Routledge, 2014.

Benjamin, Ludy, Maureen Durkin, Michelle Link, Marilyn Vestal, and Jill Acord. "Wundt's American Doctoral Students." *American Psychologist* 47, no. 2 (1992): 123–31.

Ben-Yishay, Yehuda, and Leonard Diller. "Kurt Goldstein's Holistic Ideas—An Alternative, or Complementary, Approach to the Management of Traumatically Brain-Injured Individuals." *US Neurology* 4, no. 1 (2008): 79–80.

Benzenhoefer, Udo, and Gerald Kreft. "Bemerkungen zur Frankfurter Zeit (1917–1933) des juedischen Neurologen und Psychiaters Walther Riese." *Schriftenreihe der Deutschen Gesellschaft fuer Geschichte der Nervenheilkunde* 3, no. 1 (1997): 31–40.

Bilson, Geoffrey. "'Muscles and Health': Health and the Canadian Immigrant." In *Health, Disease and Medicine*, edited by Charles Roland, 398–411. Toronto: University of Toronto Press, 1984.

Black, Edwin. *War against the Weak: Eugenics and America's Campaign to Create a Master Race.* New York: Dialog, 2007.

Bland, Lucy, and Lesley Hall. "Eugenics in Britain: The View from the Metropole." In Bashford and Levine, *Oxford Handbook of the History of Eugenics*, 213–27.

Blom, Philipp. *The Vertigo Years: Europe, 1900–1914*. New York: Basic Books, 2008.

Borck, Cornelius. "Mediating Philanthropy in Changing Political Circumstances: The Rockefeller Foundation's Funding for Brain Research in Germany, 1930–1950." Rockefeller Archive Center Research Reports, April 2001, https://www.issuelab.org/resources/27901/27901.pdf.

Boschma, Geertje. "A Family Point of View: Negotiating Asylum Care in Alberta, 1905–1930." *Canadian Bulletin of Medical History* 25, no. 2 (2008): 367–89.

Bowler, Peter. *Evolution: The History of an Idea*. Berkeley: University of California Press, 2003.

———. *The Mendelian Revolution: The Emergence of Hereditarian Concepts in Modern Science and Society.* Baltimore: John's Hopkins University Press, 1989.

Boyer, Yvonne, and Judith Bartlett. "External Review: Tubal Ligation in the Saskatoon Health Region: The Lived Experience of Aboriginal Women." Unpublished paper, Saskatoon, July 27, 2017. https://www.saskatoonhealthregion.ca/DocumentsInternal/Tubal_Ligation_intheSaskatoonHealthRegion_the_Lived_Experience_of_Aboriginal_Women_BoyerandBartlett_July_22_2017.pdf.

Bozeman, John. "Eugenics and the Clergy in the Early Twentieth Century United States." *Journal of American Culture* 27, no. 4 (2004): 422–30.

Bramadat, Ina, and Marion Saydak. "Nursing on the Canadian Prairies, 1900–1930: Effects of Immigration." *Nursing History Review* 1, no. 1 (1993): 105–17.

Bridges, Robert, and Neil Bradbury. "Cystic Fibrosis, Cystic Fibrosis Transmembrane Conductance Regulator and Drugs: Insights from Cellular Trafficking." *Handbook of Experimental Pharmacology* 103, no. 1 (2018): 1–41.

Brilliant, Mark. *The Color of America Has Changed: How Racial Diversity Shaped Civil Rights Reform in California, 1941–1978*. Oxford: Oxford University Press, 2010.

"The British Medical Association and the Prevention of Mental Deficiency." *Mental Welfare* 6 (1925): 11–3.

Broberg, Gunnar, and Nils Roll-Hansen, eds. *Eugenics and the Welfare State: Norway, Sweden, Denmark, and Finland*. East Lansing: Michigan State University Press, 2005.

Brown, Theodore. "Friendship and Philanthropy: Henry Sigerist, Alan Gregg and the Rockefeller Foundation." In Fee and Brown, *Making Medical History*, 288–312.

Brunner, José. "Psychiatry, Psychoanalysis and Politics during the First World War." *Journal of the History of the Behavioural Sciences* 27, no. 4 (1991): 352–65.

Burgers, Johannes Henderikus. "Max Nordau, Madison Grant, and Racialized Theories of Ideology." *Journal of the History of Ideas* 72, no. 1 (2011): 119–40.

Burns, Anna. "Beard v. Banks: Restricted Reading, Rehabilitation, and Prisoners' First Amendment Rights." *Journal of Law and Policy* 15, no. 12 (2007): 1225–70.

Cairney, Richard. "'Democracy Was Never Intended for Degenerates': Alberta's Flirtation with Eugenics Comes Back to Haunt It." *Canadian Medical Association Journal* 155, no. 7 (1997): 789.

Canguilhem, George. *The Normal and the Pathological*, translated by Carolyn R. Fawcett. New York: Zone Books, 1989.

Carlson, Elof Axel. "The Indiana Origins of Sterilization." In *A Century of Eugenics in America*, edited by Paul Lombardo, 18–20. Bloomington: Indiana University Press, 2010.

Carr, Ian, and Robert Beamish. *Manitoba Medicine: A Brief History*. Winnipeg: University of Manitoba Press, 1999.

Cashman, Tony. *Heritage of Service: The History of Nursing in Alberta*. Edmonton: Alberta Association of Registered Nurses, 1966.

Caulfield, Timothy, and Gerald Robertson. "Eugenic Policies in Alberta: From the Systematic to the Systemic?" *Alberta Law Review* 35, no. 1 (1996): 59–79.

Chapman, Terry. "Early Eugenics Movement in Western Canada." *Alberta History* 25, no. 1 (1977): 9–17.

Charlton, James. *Nothing about Us without Us: Disability Oppression and Empowerment*. Berkeley: University of California Press, 1998.

Chase, Allan. *The Legacy of Malthus: The Social Costs of the New Scientific Racism*. New York: Knopf, 1977.

Christian, Timothy and Burke Barker. "The Mentally Ill and Human Rights in Alberta: Study of the Alberta Sexual Sterilization Act." Honours thesis, University of Alberta, 1974.

———. *The Mentally Ill and Human Rights in Alberta: A Study of the Alberta Sexual Sterilization Act*. Edmonton, AB: University of Alberta with the Assistance of Professor Burke Barker of the Faculty of Law, 1973.

Churchill, Frederick B. "Regeneration, 1885–1901." In *A History of Regeneration Research: Milestones in the Evolution of a Science*, edited by Charles Dinsmore, 113–32. Cambridge: Cambridge University Press, 1991.

Cina, Stephen, and Joshua Perper. *When Doctors Kill: Who, Why, and How*. New York: Copernicus Books, 2010.

Clark, Christopher. *The Sleepwalkers: How Europe Went to War in 1914*. New York: Penguin, 2013.

Clarke, C. K. "Immigration Restriction, and Canadian Psychiatry, 1890–1925." *Canadian Historical Review* 76, no. 4 (1995): 598–627.

Clarke, Ian. "Public Provisions for the Mentally Ill in Alberta, 1907–1936." Master's thesis, University of Calgary, 1973.

Clarke, Stanley Charles Tremayne, Verner Nyberg, and Walter Worth. *Technical Report on Edmonton Grade III Achievement 1956–1977 Comparisons*. Edmonton: Alberta Advisory Committee on Educational Studies, 1978.

Clay, Catrine, and Michael Leapman. *Master Race: The Lebensborn Experiment in Nazi Germany*. London: Hodder & Stoughton, 1995.

Coburn, Judy. "I See and Am Silent: A Short History of Nursing in Ontario." In *Health and Canadian Society: Sociological Perspectives*, edited by Janice Acton, Penny Goldsmith, and Bonnie Shepherd, 127–63. Toronto: Fitzhenry & Whiteside, 1981.

Convention on the Rights of Persons with Disabilities. New York, December 13, 2006. *United Nations Treaty Series*, vol. 2515, p. 3. https://treaties.un.org/pages/ViewDetails.aspx?src=TREATY&mtdsg_no=IV-15&chapter=4.

Cornwell, John. *Hitler's Scientists: Science, War, and the Devil's Pact*. New York: Viking, 2003.

Cottebrune, Anne. "Die Deutsche Forschungsgemeinschaft, der NS-Staat und die Foerderung rassenhygienischer Forschung: 'Steuerbare' Forschung durch Gleichschaltung einer Selbstverwaltungsorganisation?" In *Zwischen Erziehung und Vernichtung. Zigeunerforschung und Zigeunerpolitik des 20. Jahrhunderts*, edited by Michael Zimmermann, 354–78. Stuttgart: Franz Steiner, 2007.

Coull, William. *A Normative Survey of Reading Achievement of Alberta Children in Relation to Intelligence, Sex, Bilingualism, and Grade Placement*. MEd thesis, University of Alberta, 1957.

Crouthamel, Jason. "Invisible Traumas: Psychological Wounds, World War I and German Society, 1914–1945." PhD diss., Indiana University, 2001.

Czarnowski, Gabriele. "'Die restlose Beherrschung dieser Materie.' Beziehungen zwischen Zwangssterilisation und gynaekologischer Sterilitaetsforschung im Nationalsozialismus." *Zeitschrift fuer Sexualforschung* 14, no. 2 (2001): 226–46.

———. "Nationalsozialistische Frauenpolitik und Medizin: zum Zusammenhang von Zwangssterilisation und Sterilitaetsforschung am Beispiel des Koenigsberger Universitaetsgynaekologen Felix von Mikulicz-Radecki." In *Frauen und Faschismus in Europa. Der faschistische Koerper*, edited by Leonore Siegele-Wenschkewitz and Gerda Stuchlik, 90–113. Pfaffenweiler, Germany: Centaurus, 1990.

Czech, Herwig. *Erfassung, Selektion und "Ausmerze": Das Wiener Gesundheitsamt und die Umsetzung der nationalsozialistischen "Erbgesundheitspolitik" 1938 bis 1945*. Vienna: Deuticke, 2003.

Dantonio, Patricia. "Histories of Nursing: The Power and the Possibilities." *Nursing Outlook* 58, no. 2 (2010): 207–13.

Danzer, Gerhard, ed. *Vom Konkreten zum Abstrakten. Leben und Werk Kurt Goldsteins (1878–1965)*. Frankfurt am Main: Mabuse Verlag, 2006.

Dauvergne, Catherine. "International Human Rights in Canadian Immigration Law—The Case of the Immigration and Refugee Board of Canada." *Indiana Journal of Global Legal Studies* 19 (2012): 305–26.

Davis, Lennard. *Enforcing Normalcy: Disability, Deafness, and the Body*. New York: Verso, 1995.

Deichmann, Ute. *Biologists under Hitler*. Cambridge, MA: Harvard University Press, 1996.

Deighton, Alex. "The Nature of Eugenic Thought and Limits of Eugenic Practice in Interwar Saskatchewan." In *Eugenics at Edges of Empire: New Zealand, Australia, Canada and South Africa*, edited by Diane B. Paul, Hamish G. Spencer, and John Stenhouse, 63–84. New York, NY: Palgrave Macmillan, 2018.

———. "Saskatchewan." Eugenics Archives, March 26, 2015. http://eugenicsarchive.ca/discover/world/551482b25eff8d344d000001.

Deutsch, Nathaniel. *Inventing America's "Worst" Family; Eugenics, Islam and the Fall and Rise of The Tribe of Ishmael*. Berkeley: University of California Press, 2009.

Devereux, Cecily. *Growing a Race: Nellie L. McClung and the Fiction of Eugenic Feminism*. Montréal and Kingston: McGill-Queen's University Press, 2006.

Devlin, Bernard, Michael Daniels, and Kathryn Roeder. "The Heritability of IQ." *Nature* 388, no. 4 (1997): 468–70.

Diamond, Solomon. "Buckle, Wundt, and Psychology's Use of History." *Isis* 75, no. 1 (1984): 143–52.

Dietrich, Donald J. "Catholic Eugenics in Germany, 1920–1945: Hermann Muckermann, and Joseph Mayer." *Journal of Church and State* 34, no. 3 (1992): 575–600.

———. "Catholic Theologians in Hitler's Reich: Adaptation and Critique." *Journal of Church and State* 29, no. 1 (1987): 19–45.

Dooley, Chris. "'They Gave Their Care, but We Gave Loving Care': Defining and Defending Boundaries of Skill and Craft in the Nursing Service of a Manitoba Mental Hospital during the Great Depression." *Canadian Bulletin of Medical History* 21, no. 2 (2004): 229–51.

Dowbiggin, Ian Robert. *Keeping America Sane: Psychiatry and Eugenics in the United States and Canada, 1880–1940*. Ithaca, NY: Cornell University Press, 2003.

———. "'Keeping This Young Country Sane': Charles Kirk Clarke, Immigration Restriction, and Canadian Psychiatry, 1890–1925." *Canadian Historical Review* 76, no. 4 (1995): 598–627.

———. *The Quest for Mental Health: A Tale of Science, Medicine, Scandal, Sorrow, and Mass Society.* Cambridge: Cambridge University Press, 2011.

———. *The Sterilization Movement and Global Fertility in the Twentieth Century.* Oxford: Oxford University Press, 2008.

Drogin, Elasah. *Margaret Saenger. Gruenderin der modernen Gesellschaft.* Abtsteinach, Germany: Aktion Leben, 2000.

Duffin, Jacalyn. "The Guru and the Godfather: Henry Sigerist, Hugh MacLean, and the Politics of Health Care Reform in 1940s Canada." *Canadian Bulletin of Medical History* 9, no. 2 (1992): 191–218.

Dupras, André. "Public Attitudes towards the Sterilization of Handicapped People." In *Sterilization and Mental Handicap: Proceedings of a Symposium Sponsored by the National Institute on Mental Retardation and the Ontario Association for the Mentally Retarded*, edited by Mental Institute on Mental Retardation, Ontario Association for the Mentally Retarded, 65–153. Downsview, ON: National Institute on Mental Retardation, 1980.

Dyck, Erika. *Facing Eugenics: Reproduction, Sterilization, and the Politics of Choice.* Toronto: University of Toronto Press, 2013.

———, ed. "The History of Eugenics Revisited." Special issue, *Canadian Bulletin of Medical History* 31, no. 1 (2014).

———. "Sterilization and Birth Control in the Shadow of Eugenics: Married, Middle-Class Women in Alberta, 1930–1960s." *Canadian Bulletin of Medical History* 31, no. 1 (2014): 165–88.

Dyck, Erika, and Alex Deighton. *Managing Madness: Weyburn Mental Hospital and the Transformation of Psychiatric Care in Canada*. Winnipeg: University of Manitoba Press, 2017.

Dyrbye, Amy, and Caroline Lyster. "Alberta Repeals the Sexual Sterilization Act." Eugenics Archives, n. d. http://eugenicsarchive.ca/discover/timeline/517310e2eed5c60000000032.

Ebbinghaus, Angelika, and Heidrun Kaupen-Haas. *Heilen und Vernichten im Mustergau Hamburg. Bevoelkerungs- und Gesundheitspolitik im Dritten Reich*. Marburg, Germany: Konkret Verlag, 1984.

Eckart, Wolfgang. "'Die wachsende Nervositaet unserer Zeit'—Medizin und Kultur im Fin de Siècle am Beispiel der Modekrankheit Neurasthenie." In *Psychiatrie um die Jahrhundertwende*, edited by Fritz Reimer, 9–38. Heilbronn, Germany: Weinsberger Kolloquium, 1994.

Eckart, Wolfgang, and Christoph Gradmann, eds. *Die Medizin und der Erste Weltkrieg*. Pfaffenweiler, Germany: Centaurus, 1996.

Efron, John. *Medicine and the German Jews: A History*. New Haven: Yale University Press, 2001.

Ehrenstroem, Paul. "Eugenics and Public Health: Legal Sterilization of Mentally Ill in the Vaud Canton (Switzerland)." *History and Philosophy of the Life Sciences* 15, no. 2 (1993): 205–27.

Eldergill, Anselm. *Mental Health Review Tribunal: Law and Practice*. London, Dublin, and Hong Kong: Sweet & Maxwell, 1997.

Eliadis, Pearl. *Speaking Out on Human Rights: Debating Canada's Human Rights System*. Montréal and Kingston: McGill-Queen's University Press, 2014.

Elofson, Warren. *Frontier Cattle Ranching in the Land and Times of Charlie Russell*. Montréal and Kingston: McGill-Queen's University Press, 2004.

Engstrom, Eric. *Clinical Psychiatry in Imperial Germany: A History of Psychiatric Practice*. Ithaca, NY: Cornell University Press, 2003.

Fangerau, Heiner, and Irmgard Mueller. "Das Standardwerk der Rassenhygiene von Erwin Baur, Eugen Fischer und Fritz Lenz im Urteil der Psychiatrie und Neurologie 1921–1940." *Der Nervenarzt* 73, no. 10 (2002): 1039–46.

Farrar, Clarence. "Editorial." *Canadian Public Health Journal* 22, no. 1 (1931): 92–93.

Fay, Terence. *A History of Canadian Catholics: Gallicanism, Romanism, and Canadianism*. Montréal and Kingston: McGill-Queen's University Press, 2002.

Fee, Elizabeth, and Theodore Brown, eds. *Making Medical History: The Life and Time of Henry E. Sigerist*. Baltimore: Johns Hopkins University Press, 1997.

Felder, Bjorn, and Paul Weindling, eds. *Baltic Eugenics: Bio-Politics, Race and Nation in Interwar Estonia, Latvia, and Lithuania 1918–1940*. Amsterdam: Rodopi, 2013.

Finkel, Alvin. *Social Policy and Practice in Canada*. Waterloo, ON: Wilfrid Laurier University Press, 2006.

Flynn, John. "Massive IQ Gains in 14 Nations: What IQ Tests Really Measure." *Psychological Bulletin* 101, no. 2 (1987): 171–91.

Foulkes, Richard. "British Columbia Mental Health Services: Historical Perspective to 1961." *Canadian Medical Association Journal* 85, no. 6 (1961): 649–55.

Francis, Douglas, Robert Jones, and Donald Smith. *Destinies: Canadian History since Confederation*. Toronto: Harcourt Brace Canada, 2007.

———. *Origins: Canadian History to Confederation*. Toronto: Harcourt Brace Canada, 2004.

Friedlander, Henry. *Origins of Nazi Genocide: From Euthanasia to the Final Solution*. Chapel Hill: University of North Carolina, 1995.

Friesen, Gerald. *The Canadian Prairies: A History*. Toronto: University of Toronto Press, 1987.

Frost, Mary. "Sterilization in Alberta: A Summary of the Cases Presented to the Eugenics Board for the Province of Alberta from 1929 to 1941." Master's thesis, University of Alberta, 1942.

Gairdner, Douglas. "Reading for Pleasure: History Opened My Eyes!" *British Medical Journal* 284, no. 11 (1982): 1105–6.

Garland-Thomson, Rosemarie. "The Case for Conserving Disability." *Journal of Bioethical Inquiry* 9, no. 3 (2012): 339–55.

Gauvreau, Michael, and Olivier Hubert, eds. *The Churches and Social Order in Nineteenth and Twentieth Century Canada*. Montréal and Kingston: McGill-Queen's University Press, 2006.

Gerrens, Uwe. *Medizinisches Ethos und theologische Kritik. Karl und Dietrich Bonhoeffer in der Auseinandersetzung um Zwangssterilisation und 'Euthanasie' im Nationalsozialismus*. Munich: Oldenbourg, 1996.

Gerwarth, Robert. *Hitler's Hangman: The Life of Heydrich*. New Haven: Yale University Press, 2011.

Gibbons, Sheila. "'Our Power to Remodel Civilization': The Development of Eugenic Feminism in Alberta, 1909–1921." *Canadian Bulletin of Medical History* 31, no. 1 (2014): 99–122.

Gibson, David. "Involuntary Sterilization of the Mentally Retarded: A Western Canadian Phenomenon." *Canadian Psychiatric Association Journal* 19, no. 1 (1974): 59–63.

Gidney, Robert Douglas, and Wyn Millar. *How Schools Worked: Public Education in English Canada, 1900–1940*. Montréal and Kingston: McGill-Queen's University Press, 2012.

———. "The Salaries of Teachers in English Canada, 1900–1940: A Reappraisal." *Historical Studies in Education* 22, no. 1 (2010): 1–38.

Gijswijt-Hofstra, Marijke, and Roy Porter, eds. *Cultures of Neurasthenia: From Beard to the First World War*. Amsterdam: Rodopi, 2001.

Goldstein, Gerald. "Contributions of Kurt Goldstein to Neuropsychology." *Clinical Neuropsychology* 4, no. 1 (1990): 3–17.

Goodenough, Florence. "The Measurement of Mental Growth in Childhood." In *Manual of Child Psychology*, edited by Leonard Carmichael, 459–91. New York: Wiley, 1954.

Goodley, Dan. "Dis/entangling Critical Disability Studies." *Disability & Society* 28, no. 6 (2012): 631–44.

Gottlieb, Gilbert, Douglas Wahlsten, and Robert Lickliter. "The Significance of Biology for Human Development: A Developmental Psychobiological Systems View." In *Handbook of Child Psychology*. Vol. 1, *Theoretical Models of Human Development*, edited by Richard Lerner, 233–73. 5th ed. New York: Wiley, 1997.

Gould, Stephen. *The Mismeasure of Man*. Rev. ed. New York: Norton, 1996.

Grekul, Jana. "The Social Construction of the Feebleminded Threat: Implementation of the Sexual Sterilization Act in Alberta, 1929–1972." PhD diss., University of Alberta, 2002.

———. "Sterilization in Alberta, 1928–1972: Gender Matters." *Canadian Review of Sociology* 45, no. 3 (2008): 247–66.

———. "A Well-Oiled Machine: Alberta's Eugenics Program, 1928–1972." *Alberta History* 59, no. 1 (2011): 16–23.

Grekul, Jana, Harvey Krahn, and David Odynak. "Sterilizing the 'Feeble-Minded': Eugenics in Alberta, Canada, 1929–1972." *Journal of Historical Sociology* 17, no. 4 (2004): 358–84.

Grob, Gerald. *Mental Illness and American Society, 1875–1940*. Princeton: Princeton University Press, 1983.

Hafner, Karl Heinz, and Rolf Winau. "'Die Freigabe der Vernichtung lebensunwerten Lebens': Eine Untersuchung zu der Schrift von Karl Binding und Alfred Hoche." *Medizinhistorisches Journal* 9, no. 2 (1974): 227–54.

Hagner, Michael. *Homo cerebralis. Der Wandel vom Seelenorgan zum Gehirn*. Frankfurt am Main: Insel, 2000.

Haines, Michael, and Richard Steckel, eds. *A Population History of North America*. Cambridge: Cambridge University Press, 2000.

Hammerstein, Notker. *Die Deutsche Forschungsgemeinschaft in der Zeit der Weimarer Repu-blik und im Dritten Reich; Wissenschaftspolitik in Republik und Diktatur*. Munich: C. H. Beck, 2000.

Hansen, Randall, and Desmond King. *Sterilized by the State: Eugenics, Race, and the Population Scare in Twentieth-Century North America*. New York: Cambridge University Press, 2013.

Harrington, Anne. "Kurt Goldstein's Neurology of Healing and Wholeness: A Weimar Story." In *Greater Than the Parts: Holism in Biomedicine, 1920–1950*, edited by George Weisz and Christopher Lawrence, 24–45. New York: Oxford University Press, 1998.

———. *Reenchanted Science: Holism in German Culture from Wilhelm II to Hitler*. Princeton: Princeton University Press, 1996.

Harris-Zsovan, Jane. *Eugenics and the Firewall: Why Alberta's UFA/Social Credit Legacy Matters to 21st Century Canadians.* Winnipeg: J. Gordon Shillingford, 2010.

Harwood, Jonathan. *Styles of Scientific Thought: The German Genetics Community, 1900–1933*. Chicago: University of Chicago Press, 1993.

Hasian, Marouf Arif. *The Rhetoric of Eugenics in Anglo-American Thought*. Atlanta: University of Georgia Press, 1996.

Hau, Michael. *The Cult of Health and Beauty in Germany: A Social History, 1890–1930*. Chicago: Chicago University Press, 2003.

Hauss, Gisela, and Beatrice Ziegler. "Sterilisationen bei Armen und Unmuendigen. Eine Untersuchung der Vormundschaftspraxis in den Staedten St. Gallen und Bern." In *Wie nationalsozialsozialistisch ist die Eugenik?/What is National Socialist about Eugenics?*, edited by Regina Wecker, Sabine Braunschweig, Gabriela Imboden, Bernhard Kuechenhoff, and Hans Jakob Ritter, 75–91. Vienna, Cologne, and Weimar, Germany: Internationale Debatten zur Geschichte der Eugenik im 20. Jahrhundert/International Debates on the History of Eugenics in the 20th Century, 2009.

Hay, Rankin. *Neurosurgery and Neurological Science in Manitoba, 1884–1944*. Winnipeg: Schadt, 2003.

Hayword, Rhodri. "Germany and the Making of 'English' Psychiatry." In *International Relations in Psychiatry*, edited by Volker Roelcke and Paul J. Weindling, 67–90. London: Westwood, 2010.

Heller, Geneviève, Gilles Jeanmonod, and Jacques Gasser, eds. *Rejetées, rebelles, mal adaptées: Débats sur l'eugénisme—Pratiques de la stérilisation non volontaire en Suisse romande au XXe siècle*. Geneva: Georg Editeur, 2012.

Hill, Mavis, and Norman Williams. *Auschwitz in England: A Record of a Libel Action*. London: Ballantine, 1966.

Hobsbawm, Eric. *The Age of Extremes: The Short Twentieth Century, 1914–1991*. London: Michel Joseph, 1994.

Hofer, Hans-Georg. "War Neurosis and Viennese Psychiatry in World War One." In *Uncovered Fields: Perspectives in First World War Studies*, edited by Jenny Macleod and Pierre Purseigle, 243–60. Amsterdam: Amsterdam University Press, 2004.

Hoff, Peter, and Matthias Weber. "Sozialdarwinismus und die Psychiatrie im Nationalsozialismus." *Der Nervenarzt* 11, no. 10 (2002): 1017–18.

Holtan, Neal Ross. "The Eitels and Their Hospital." *Minnesota Medicine* 36 (2003): 52–54.

Huonker, Thomas. *Anstaltseinweisungen, Kindswegnahmen, Eheverbote, Sterilisationen, Kastrationen. Fuersorge, Zwangsmassnahmen, "Eugenik" und Psychiatrie in Zuerich zwischen 1890 und 1970*. Zurich: Orell Fuessli Verlag, 2003.

Inglis, Jan, and John Inglis, eds. *Davenport's Dream: 21st Century Reflections on Heredity and Eugenics*. Cold Spring Harbor, NY: Cold Spring Laboratory Press, 2008.

Jacques, Carol. *Unifarm: A Story of Conflict and Change*. Calgary: University of Calgary Press, 2001.

Jennekens, Frans. "A Short History of the Notion of Neurodegenerative Disease." *Journal of the History of the Neurosciences* 23, no. 1 (2014): 85–94.

Johns, Walter. *A History of the University of Alberta, 1908–1969*. Edmonton: University of Alberta Press, 1981.

Joseph, Jay, and Norbert Wetzel. "Ernst Ruedin: Hitler's Racial Hygiene Mastermind." *Journal of the History of Biology* 46, no. 1 (2013): 1–30.

Kahane, David, David Sharp, and Martin Tweedale. "Report of the MacEachran Subcommittee." Department of Philosophy, University of Alberta, April 1998. https://cloudfront.ualberta.ca/-/media/arts/departments-institutes-and-centres/philosophy/maceachran_report.pdf

Kaler, Amy. *Baby Trouble in the Last Best West: Making New People in Alberta, 1905–1939*. Toronto: University of Toronto Press, 2017.

Karenberg, Axel. "Klinische Neurologie in Deutschland bis zum Ersten Weltkrieg—die Begruender des Faches und der Fachgesellschaft." In *100 Jahre Deutsche Gesellschaft fuer Neurologie*, edited by Detlef Koempf, 20–29. Berlin: Deutsche Gesellschaft fuer Neurologie, 2007.

Kater, Michael. *Doctors under Hitler.* Chapel Hill: University of North Carolina Press, 1989.

———. "Hitler's Early Doctors: Nazi Physicians in Pre-Depression Germany." *Journal of Modern History* 95, no. 1 (1987): 25–52.

———. *The Nazi Party: A Social Profile of Members and Leaders, 1919–1945*. Cambridge: Cambridge University Press, 1983.

Keith, Ellen. "'Human Wreckage from Foreign Lands': A Study of the Ethnic Victims of the Alberta Sterilization Act." *Constellations* 2, no. 2 (2011): 81–89.

Kelley, Ninette, and Michael Trebilcock. *The Making of the Mosaic: A History of Canadian Immigration Policy*. Toronto: University of Toronto Press, 1998.

Kendle, John. *John Bracken: A Political Biography*. Toronto: University of Toronto Press, 1979.

Kersten, Luke. "Alberta Passes Sexual Sterilization Act." Eugenics Archives, n.d. http://eugenicsarchives.ca/discover/timeline/5172e81ceed5c6000000001d.

Kevles, Daniel. *In the Name of Eugenics*. Cambridge, MA: Harvard University Press, 1995.

Kidd, Bruce. "Canadian Opposition to the 1936 Olympics in Germany." *Sport in Society* 16, no. 4 (2013): 425–38.

Kirkebaek, Birgit. "Da de andssvage blev farlige" [When the Mentally Deficient Became Dangerous]. PhD diss., Forlaget Socpol, Copenhagen, Denmark, 1993.

Klausen, Susanne. "Rethinking Reproduction: New Approaches to the History of Sexuality, Gender, the Family, and Reproductive Control." *Journal of Contemporary History* 44, no. 1 (2009): 117–27.

Klee, Ernst. *Auschwitz, die NS-Medizin und ihre Opfer*. Frankfurt am Main: S. Fischer, 1997.

Kline, Wendy. *Building a Better Race: Gender, Sexuality and Eugenics from the Turn of the Century to the Baby Boom*. Berkeley: University of California Press, 2001.

———. "Eugenics in the United States." In Bashford and Levine, *Oxford Handbook of the History of Eugenics*, 511–22.

———. "Sterilization." Eugenics Archives, September 14, 2013. http://eugenicsarchive.ca/discover/encyclopedia/5233e4e35c2ec500000000e0.

Kloocke, Ruth, Heinz-Peter Schmiedebach, and Stefan Priebe. "Psychological Injury in the Two World Wars: Changing Concepts and Terms in German Psychiatry." *History of Psychiatry* 16, no. 1 (2005): 43–60.

Knowles, Valerie. *Strangers at Our Gates: Canadian Immigration and Immigration Policy, 1540–1990*. Toronto: Dundurn Press, 1992.

Koester, Elizabeth. "An Evil Hitherto Unchecked: Eugenics and the 1917 Ontario Royal Commission on the Care and Control of the Mentally Defective and Feebleminded." *Canadian Bulletin of Medical History* 33, no. 1 (2016): 59–81.

Kolb, Stephan, Paul Weindling, Volker Roelcke, and Horst Seithe. "Apologising for Nazi Medicine: A Constructive Starting Point." *Lancet* 380, no. 7 (2012): 722–23.

Kowalewski, Karolina, and Yasmin Mayne. "The Translation of Eugenic Ideology into Public Health Policy: The Case of Alberta and Saskatchewan." In *The Proceedings of the 18th Annual History of Medicine Days Conference 2009*, edited by Lisa Peterman, Kerry Sun, and Frank W. Stahnisch, 53–74. Newcastle upon Tyne: Cambridge Scholars Publishing, 2012.

Kroener, Hans-Peter. *Von der Rassenhygiene zur Humangenetik*. Stuttgart: Gustav Fischer, 1998.

Kuehl, Stefan. *The Nazi Connection: Eugenics, American Racism, and German National Socialism*. Oxford: Oxford University Press, 2001. [First published in 1997, Frankfurt am Main: Campus Verlag.]

Kuetemeyer, Michael, and Ulrich Schultz. "Kurt Goldstein (1878–1965): Begruender einer psychosomatischen Neurologie?" In *Nicht misshandeln. Das Krankenhaus Moabit, 1920–1933. Ein Zentrum juedischer Aerzte in Berlin, 1933-1945. Verfolgung, Widerstand, Zerstoerung*, edited by Christian Pross and Rolf Winau, 133–39. Berlin: Edition Hentrich, 1984.

Kurbegović, Erna. "Eugenics in Comparative Perspective: Explaining Manitoba and Alberta's Divergence on Eugenics Policy, 1910s to the 1930s." PhD diss., University of Calgary, 2019.

———. "The Influence of the Manitoba Mental Hygiene Survey, 1918." *Western Humanities Review* 69, no. 3 (2016): 298–323.

Kutschera, Ulrich, and Niklas Karl Ulrich. "The Modern Theory of Biological Evolution: An Expanded Synthesis." *Naturwissenschaften* 91, no. 2 (2004): 255–76.

Lamb, Susan. "'The Most-Important Professorship in the English-Speaking Domain': Adolph Meyer and the Beginnings of Clinical Psychiatry in the United States." *Journal of Nervous and Mental Diseases* 200, no. 12 (2012): 1061–66.

———. "Pathologist of the Mind: Adolf Meyer, Psychobiology and the Phipps Psychiatric Clinic at the Johns Hopkins Hospital, 1908–1917." PhD diss., Johns Hopkins University, 2010.

Lampard, Robert. *Alberta's Medical History: Young and Lusty and Full of Life.* Red Deer, AB: Friesens, 2008.

Lang, Hans-Joachim. *Die Frauen von Blok 10: Medizinische Versuche in Auschwitz.* Hamburg: Hoffmann and Campe Verlag, 2011.

Lanzoni, Susan. "Diagnosing Modernity: Mania and Authenticity in the Existential Genre." *Configurations* 12, no. 2 (2004): 107–31.

Larson, Edward. *Sex, Race, and Science: Eugenics in the Deep South*. Baltimore: Johns Hopkins University Press, 1995.

Lawrence, Christopher, and George Weisz, eds. *Greater Than the Parts: Holism in Biomedicine, 1920–1950*. New York: Oxford University Press, 1998.

Leahey, Thomas Hardy. *A History of Modern Psychology*. Upper Saddle River, NJ: Prentice Hall, 2001.

Ledger, Sally, and Scott McCracken. *Cultural Politics at the Fin de Siècle*. Oxford: Oxford University Press, 2003.

Leist, Anton. *Auguste Forel. Eugenik und Erinnerungskultur*. Zurich: Hochschulverlag, 2006.

Leon, Sharon, "'Hopelessly Entangled in Nordic Pre-suppositions': Catholic Participation in the American Eugenics Society in the 1920s." *Journal of the History of Medicine and Allied Sciences* 59, no. 1 (2004): 3–49.

———. *An Image of God: The Catholic Struggle with Eugenics*. Chicago: University of Chicago Press, 2013.

Leonard, Thomas. "American Economic Reform in the Progressive Era: Its Foundational Beliefs and Their Relation to Eugenics." *History of Political Economy* 41, no. 1 (2009): 109–41.

Lepicard, Etienne. "Eugenics and Roman Catholicism An Encyclical Letter in Context: *Casti connubii*, December 31, 1930." *Science in Context* 11, no. 3–4 (1998): 527–44.

Lepofsky, David. "The Long, Arduous Road to a Barrier-Free Ontario for People with Disabilities: The History of the Ontarians with Disabilities Act—The First Chapter," *National Journal of Constitutional Law* 15 (2004): 125–33.

Lerner, Paul. *Hysterical Men: War, Psychiatry, and the Politics of Trauma in Germany, 1890–1930*. Ithaca, NY: Cornell University Press.

Levine, Philippa, and Alison Bashford. "Introduction: Eugenics and the Modern World." In Bashford and Levine, *Oxford Handbook of the History of Eugenics*, 4–56.

Ley, Astrid. *Zwangssterilisation und Aerzteschaft. Hintergruende und Ziele aerztlichen Handelns 1934–1945*. Frankfurt am Main: Campus, 2004.

Leys, Ruth, and Rand Evans, eds. *Defining American Psychology: The Correspondence between Adolf Meyer and Edward Bradford Titchener*. Baltimore: Johns Hopkins University Press, 1990.

Lifton, Robert. *The Nazi Doctors*. New York: Basic Books, 1986.

Lilienthal, Georg. "Patientinnen und Patienten aus brandenburgischen Heil- und Pflegeanstalten als Opfer der NS-'Euthanasie'-Verbrechen in Hadamar." In *Brandenburgische Heil- und Pflegeanstalten in der NS-Zeit*, edited by Christina Huebener and Martin Heinze, 303–18. Berlin: Bebra Wissenschaftsverlag, 2002.

Loewenau, Aleksandra. "The Failure of the West German Judicial System in Serving Justice: The Case of Dr. Horst Schumann." *Wiener Klinische Wochenschrift* 18, no. 3 (2018):169–172.

———. "The Impact of Nazi Medical Experiments on Polish Inmates at Dachau, Auschwitz and Ravensbrueck." PhD diss., Oxford Brookes University, 2012.

Loewy, Ilana. "The Strength of Loose Concepts: Boundary Concepts, Federative Experimental Strategies and Disciplinary Growth: The Case of Immunology." *History of Science* 30, no. 4 (1992): 371–439.

Lombardo, Paul, ed. *A Century of Eugenics in America: From the Indiana Experiment to the Human Genome Era*. Bloomington: Indiana University Press, 2011.

———. "Eugenics Bibliography." Buck v Bell Documents 96, Georgia State University College of Law, 2009.

———. *Three Generations, No Imbeciles: Eugenics, the Supreme Court, and Buck v. Bell.* Baltimore: Johns Hopkins University Press, 2008.

Lorenz, Maren. "Proto-Eugenic Thought and Breeding Utopias in the United States before 1870." *Bulletin of the German Historical Institute* 43, no. 1 (2008): 67–90.

Luedecke, Andreas. *Der 'Fall Saller' und die Rassenhygiene. Eine Goettinger Fallstudie zu den Widerspruechen sozialbiologischer Ideologiebildung*. Marburg, Germany: Tectum Verlag, 1995.

Lunbeck, Elizabeth. *The Psychiatric Persuasion: Knowledge, Gender, and Power in Modern America*. Princeton: Princeton University Press 1995.

MacLean, Randall, and Ethel Kibblewhite. "Sexual Sterilization in Alberta." *Canadian Public Health Journal* 28, no. 5 (1937): 587–90.

MacLennan, David. "Beyond the Asylum: Professionalization and the Mental Hygiene Movement in Canada, 1914–1928." *Canadian Bulletin of Medical History* 4, no. 1 (1987): 7–23.

Maggs, Christopher. "A History of Nursing: A History of Caring?" *Journal of Advanced Nursing* 22, no. 6 (1996): 630–35.

Malacrida, Claudia. *A Special Hell: Institutional Life in Alberta's Eugenic Years*. Toronto: University of Toronto Press, 2015.

Mansell, Diana, and Judith Hibberd. "'We Picked the Wrong One to Sterilise': The Role of Nursing in the Eugenics Movement in Alberta, 1920–1940." *International History of Nursing Journal* 3, no. 4 (1998): 4–11.

Marshall, Dominique. *The Social Origins of the Welfare State: Quebec Families, Compulsory Education, and Family Allowances, 1940–1955*. Waterloo, ON: Wilfrid Laurier University Press, 2006.

Mattila, Markku. *Kansamme parhaaksi: Rotuhygienia Suomessa vuoden 1935 sterilointilakiin asti*. Helsinki: Biblioteca Historica, 1999.

McLaren, Angus. *Our Own Master Race: Eugenics in Canada, 1885–1945*. Toronto: McClelland & Stewart, 1990.

———. *Reproduction by Design: Sex, Robots, Trees, and Test-Tube Babies in Interwar Britain*. Chicago: University of Chicago Press, 2012.

McLaren, Angus, and Arlene Tigar McLaren. *The Bedroom and the State: The Changing Practices and Politics of Contraception and Abortion in Canada, 1880–1980*. Toronto: McClelland & Stewart, 1997.

McWhirter, Kennedy, and Jan Weijer. "The Alberta Sterilization Act: A Genetic Critique." *University of Toronto Law Journal* 19, no. 3 (1969): 424–31.

Mendes, Errol, and Beaulac, Stéfane, eds. *Charte canadienne des droits et libertés / Canadian Charter of Rights and Freedoms*. 5th ed. Markham, ON: LexisNexis Canada.

Millman, Mary. "Special Classes as a Factor in Health." *Canadian Public Health Journal* 21, no. 3 (1930): 355–57.

Mitchinson, Wendy. *The Nature of Their Bodies: Women and Their Doctors in Victorian Canada*. Toronto: University of Toronto Press, 1991.

Moran, James, and David Wright, eds. *Mental Health and Canadian Society*. Montréal and Kingston: McGill-Queen's University Press, 2008.

Moss, Erin, Henderikus Stam, and Diane Kattevilder. "From Suffrage to Sterilization: Eugenics and the Women's Movement in 20th Century Alberta." *Canadian Psychology* 54, no. 1 (2013): 105–14.

Mottier, Véronique. "Eugenics and the State: Policy-Making in Comparative Perspective." In Bashford and Levine, *Oxford Handbook of the History of Eugenics*, 134–53.

Mottier, Véronique, and Natalia Gerodetti. "Eugenics and Social-Democracy: Or, How the Left Tried to Eliminate the 'Weeds' from Its National Gardens." *New Formations* 60, no. 1 (2006–7): 35–49.

Mottier, Véronique, and Laura von Mandach, eds. *Pflege, Stigmatisierung und Eugenik: Integration und Ausschluss in Medizin, Psychiatrie und Sozialhilfe*. Zurich: Seismo, 2007.

Muir, Leilani. *A Whisper Past: Childless after Eugenic Sterilization in Alberta*. Victoria, BC: Friesen Press, 2014.

Mundt, Christoph, Gerrit Hohendorf, and Maike Rotzoll, eds. *Psychiatrische Forschung und NS-Euthanasie, Beitraege zu einer Gedenkveranstaltung an der Psychiatrischen Universitaetsklinik Heidelberg*. Heidelberg: University of Heidelberg, 2001.

Myskiw, Mary. "The Influence of the Alberta Association of Registered Nurses on Health Care Policy from 1916 to 1950." MA thesis, University of Alberta, 1992.

Nelson, Thomas. "John A. [*sic*] MacEachran." *Western Psychologist* 3 (1972): 51–62.

———. "Psychology at Alberta." In *History of Academic Psychology in Canada*, edited by Mary Wright and Roger Myers, 192–219. Toronto: C. J. Hogrefe, 1982.

Neumaerker, Klaus, and Andreas Joachim Bartsch. "Karl Kleist (1879–1960)—A Pioneer of Neuropsychiatry." *History of Psychiatry* 14, no. 4 (2003): 411–58.

Nicosia, Francis R. and Jonathan Huener, eds. *Medicine and Medical Ethics in Nazi Germany: Origins, Practices, Legacies*. New York: Basic Books, 2002.

Nind, Naomi. "Solving an 'Appalling' Problem: Social Reformers and the Campaign for the Alberta Sexual Sterilization Act, 1928." *Alberta Law Review* 38, no. 4 (2000): 536–62.

Noppeney, Uta. "Kurt Goldstein—A Philosophical Scientist." *Journal of the History of the Neurosciences* 10, no. 1 (2001): 67–78.

Nord, David Paul. "A Republican Literature: A Study of Magazine Reading and Readers in Late Eighteenth-Century New York." *American Quarterly* 40, no. 1 (1988): 42–64.

Normandin, Sebastian. "Eugenics, McGill and the Catholic Church in Montréal and Québec, 1890–1942." *Canadian Bulletin of Medical History* 15, no. 1 (1998): 59–86.

O'Brien, Gerald. *Framing the Moron: The Social Construction of Feeble-Mindedness in the American Eugenic Era*. Manchester: Manchester University Press, 2013.

Oliveria, Amanda. "The Coming and Going of Eugenics in Alberta: A Discarded History, 1928 to 1972." MA thesis, Lakehead University, 2016.

Olson, Thomas. "Laying Claim to Caring: Nursing and the Language of Training, 1915–1917." *Nursing Outlook* 41, no. 2 (1993): 68–72.

Owram, Doug. *Born at the Right Time: A History of the Baby-Boom Generation.* Toronto: University of Toronto Press, 1999.

Palmer, Howard. *Patterns of Prejudice: A History of Nativism in Alberta*. Toronto: McClelland & Stewart, 1982.

Palmer, Howard, and Tamara Palmer. *Alberta: A New History*. Edmonton: Hurtig, 1990.

Park, Deborah. "From the Case Files: Reconstructing a History of Involuntary Sterilization." *Disability & Society* 13, no. 3 (1998): 317–42.

Pascoe, Peggy. *What Comes Naturally: Miscegenation Law and the Making of Race in America*. Oxford: Oxford University Press, 2009.

Paul, Diane. *Controlling Human Heredity, 1865 to the Present*. Atlantic Highlands, NJ: Humanities Press, 1995.

Paul, Diane, John Stenhouse, and Hamish Spencer. "Introduction: Eugenics as a Transnational Subject: The British Dominions." In *Eugenics at the Edges of Empire: New Zealand, Australia, Canada and South Africa*, edited by Diane Paul, Hamish Spencer, and John Stenhouse, 1–19. New York, NY: Palgrave Macmillan, 2017.

Peck, David. "The Conversion of Progressive Matrices and Mill Hill Vocabulary Raw Scores into Deviation IQ's." *Clinical Psychology* 26, no. 1 (1970): 67–70.

Penrose, Lionel. *The Biology of Mental Defect*. London: Sidgwick and Jackson, 1949.

Pernick, Martin. "Eugenics and Public Health in American History." *American Journal of Public Health* 87, no. 11 (1997): 1767–72.

Peukert, Detlev. *The Weimar Republic: The Crisis of Classical Modernity*, translated by Richard Deveson. New York: Hill and Wang, 1989.

Plaenkers, Thomas, ed. *Psychoanalyze in Frankfurt am Main. Zerstoerte Anfaenge. Wiederannaehrung. Entwicklungen*. Tuebingen, Germany: Niemeyer, 1996.

Poore, Carol. "Recovering Disability Rights in Weimar Germany." *Radical History Review* 4, no. 1 (2006): 38–58.

Poston, Kathleen, and David Eidelberg. "Network Biomarkers for the Diagnosis and Treatment of Movement Disorders." *Neurobiological Diseases* 35, no. 1 (2009): 141–47.

Pow, Stephen, and Frank W. Stahnisch. "Kurt Goldstein (1878–1965)—Pioneer in Neurology." *Journal of Neurology* 261, no. 10 (2014): 1049–50.

Pressman, Jack. *Last Resort: Psychosurgery and the Limits of Medicine*. Cambridge: Cambridge University Press, 1998.

Proctor, Robert. *Racial Hygiene: Medicine under the Nazis*. Cambridge, MA: Harvard University Press, 1988.

Promitzer, Christian, Sevasti Trubeta, and Marius Turda. *Health, Hygiene, and Eugenics in Southeastern Europe to 1945*. Budapest: Central European University Press, 2010.

Puplampu, Korblu. "Knowledge, Power, and Social Policy: John M. MacEachran and Alberta's 1928 Sexual Sterilization Act." *Alberta Journal of Educational Research* 54, no. 1 (2008): 126–46.

Radford, John, and Deborah Park. "A Convenient Means of Riddance: Institutionalization of People Diagnosed as Mental Defective in Ontario, 1876–1934." *Health and Canadian Society* 1, no. 3 (1993): 369–92.

Radkau, Joachim. *Das Zeitalter der Nervositaet. Deutschland zwischen Bismarck und Hitler*. Munich: Fink Verlag, 1998.

———. "The Neurasthenic Experience in Imperial Germany: Expeditions into Patient Records and Side-Looks upon General History." In Gijswijt-Hofstra and Porter, *Cultures of Neurasthenia*, 199–217.

Rainer, John. "Franz Kallmann's Views on Eugenics." *American Journal of Psychiatry* 146, no. 12 (1989): 1361–62.

Rashed, Mohammed Abouelleil. "In Defense of Madness: The Problem of Disability." *Journal of Medicine and Philosophy* 44, no. 2 (2019): 150–74.

Refvik, Kurt. *History of the Brandon Mental Health Centre, 1891–1991*. Brandon, Manitoba Historical Museum, 1991.

Reid, Thomas James. "A Survey of the Language Achievement of Alberta School Children in Relation to Bilingualism, Sex, and Intelligence." MEd thesis, University of Alberta, 1954.

Reilly, Philip. "Eugenics and Involuntary Sterilization: 1907–2015." *Annual Review of Genomics and Human Genetics* 16, no. 3 (2015): 351–68.

Rennie, Bradford. *The Rise of Agrarian Democracy: The United Farmers and Farm Women of Alberta, 1909–1921*. Toronto: University of Toronto Press, 2000.

"Reports of Societies." *British Medical Journal* 3868 (February 23, 1935): 378.

Revie, Linda. "More Than Just Boots! The Eugenic and Commercial Concerns behind A. R. Kaufman's Birth Controlling Activities." *Canadian Bulletin of Medical History* 23, no. 1 (2006): 119–43.

Richardson, Angelique. *Love and Eugenics in the Late Nineteenth Century: Rational Reproduction and the New Woman*. Oxford: Oxford University Press, 2003.

Richardson, Sharon. "Political Women, Professional Nurses and the Creation of Alberta's District Nursing Service, 1919–1925." *Nursing History Review* 6, no. 1 (1998): 25–50.

Richardson, Theresa. *The Century of the Child: The Mental Hygiene Movement and Social Policy in the United States and Canada*. New York: State University of New York Press, 1989.

Ringer, Fritz. *The Decline of the German Mandarins: The German Academic Community, 1890–1933*. Cambridge, MA: Harvard University Press, 1969.

Rissom, Renate. *Fritz Lenz und die Rassenhygiene*. Husum, Germany: Matthiesen Verlag, 1983.

Ritter, Hans Jakob. *Psychiatrie und Eugenik. Zur Auspraegung eugenischer Denk- und Handlungsmuster in der schweizerischen Psychiatrie 1850–1950*. Zurich: Chronos Verlag, 2009.

Roberts, Barbara. *Whence They Came: Deportation from Canada, 1900–1935*. Ottawa: University of Ottawa Press, 1988.

Rodgers, Daniel. *Atlantic Crossings: Social Politics in a Progressive Age*. Cambridge, MA: Belknap Press of Harvard University Press, 1998.

Roelcke, Volker. "Die Etablierung der psychiatrischen Genetik in Deutschland, Grossbritannien und den USA, ca. 1910–1960. Zur untrennbaren Geschichte von Eugenik und Humangenetik," *Acta Historica Leopoldina* 48, no. 2 (2007): 173–90.

———. "Electrified Nerves, Degenerated Bodies: Medical Discourses in Neurasthenia in Germany, ca. 1990–1914." In Gijswijt-Hofstra and Porter, *Cultures of Neurasthenia*, 177–97.

———. "Funding the Scientific Foundations of Race Policies: Ernst Ruedin and the Impact of Career Resources on Psychiatric Genetics, ca. 1910–1945." In *Man, Medicine, and the State: The Human Body as an Object of Government Sponsored Medical Research in the 20th Century*, edited by Wolfgang Eckart, 73–87. Stuttgart: Franz Steiner, 2006.

———."Programm und Praxis der psychiatrischen Genetik an der Deutschen Forschungsanstalt fuer Psychiatrie unter Ernst Ruedin: Zum Verhaeltnis von Wissenschaft, Politik und Rasse-Begriff vor und nach 1933." *Medizinhistorisches Journal* 37, no. 1 (2002): 21–55.

———. "Psychiatric Research and Science Policy in Germany: The History of the Deutsche Forschungsanstalt fuer Psychiatrie." *History of Psychiatry* 11, no. 2 (2000): 235–58.

———. "Psychiatry in Munich and Yale, ca. 1920–1935: Mutual Perceptions and Relations, and the Case of Eugen Kahn (1887–1973)," in *International Relations in Psychiatry: Britain, America, and Germany to World War II*, edited by Volker Roelcke, Paul Weindling, and Louise Westwood, 156–78. Rochester, NY: University of Rochester Press, 2010.

———. "Von Emil Kraepelin zu Ernst Ruedin: Die Deutsche Forschungsanstalt fuer Psychiatrie 1917–1945." *Schriftenreihe der Deutschen Gesellschaft fuer Psychiatrie* 2, no. 4 (1997): 419–35.

Roige, Aida. "Intelligence and IQ Testing." Eugenics Archives, April 29, 2014. http://eugenicsarchive.ca/database/documents/535eecb77095aa000000023a.

Roland, Charles. *Clarence Meredith Hincks: Mental Health Crusader*. Toronto: Oxford University Press, 1990.

Rose, Nikolas S.. *The Psychological Complex: Psychology, Politics and Society in England, 1869–1939*. London: Routledge, 1985.

Rosen, Christine. *Preaching Eugenics: Religious Leaders and the American Eugenics Movement*. Oxford: Oxford University Press, 2004.

Ross, Sheila. "'For God and Canada': The Early Years of the Catholic Women's League in Alberta." *Historical Studies* 62, no. 1 (1996): 89–108.

Ross-Kerr, Janet. *Prepared to Care*. Edmonton: University of Alberta Press, 1998.

Rotzoll, Maike, Gerrit Hohendorf, Petra Fuchs, Paul Richter, Christoph Mundt, and Wolfgang Eckart, eds. *Die nationalsozialistische "Euthanasie" – Aktion "T4" und ihre Opfer: Geschichte und ethische Konsequenzen fuer die Gegenwart*. Paderborn: Ferdinand Schoeningh, 2010.

Rotzoll, Maike, Volker Roelcke, and Gerritt Hohendorf. "Carl Schneiders 'Forschungsabteilung' an der Heidelberger Psychiatrischen Universitaetsklinik 1943/44." *Heidelberger Jahrbuch zur Geschichte der Stadt* 16, no. 1 (2012): 113–22.

Rubab, Arim. *A Profile of Persons with Disabilities among Canadians aged 15 Years or Older* (Ottawa, ON: Statistics Canada, 2012). http://www.statcan.gc.ca/pub/89-654-x/89-654-x2015001-eng.pdf.

Russell, Guel. "Eugenics: A Paradigm for the Future?" In *The Proceedings of the 22nd Annual History of Medicine Days Conference at the University of Calgary, Alberta*, Canada, edited by Aleksandra Loewenau, William Pratt, and Frank W. Stahnisch, 114–48. Newcastle upon Tyne: Cambridge Scholars Publishing, 2013.

Samson, Amy. "Eugenics in the Community: Gendered Professions and Eugenic Sterilization in Alberta, 1928–1972." *Canadian Bulletin of Medical History* 31, no. 1 (2014): 143 63.

———. "Eugenics in the Community: United Farm Women of Alberta, Public Health Nursing, Teaching, Social Work, and Sexual Sterilization in Alberta, 1928–1972." PhD diss., University of Saskatchewan, 2014.

Sangster, Joan. *Dreams of Equality: Women on the Canadian Left, 1920–1950*. Toronto: McClelland & Stewart, 1989.

Saxton, Marsha. "Why Members of the Disability Community Oppose Prenatal Diagnoses and Selective Abortion." In *Prenatal Testing and Disability Rights*, edited by Erik Parens and Adrienne Asch, 147–64. Washington, DC: Georgetown University Press, 2000.

Schilter, Thomas. "Psychiatrieverbrechen im Dritten Reich: Die Karriere Horst Schumanns." *NTM* 6, no. 1 (1998): 42–51.

Schoek, Ellen. *I Was There: A Century of Stories about the University of Alberta, 1906–2006*. Edmonton: University of Alberta Press, 2006.

Schmiedebach, Heinz-Peter. "The Public's View of Neurasthenia in Germany—Looking for a New Rhythm of Life." In Gijswijt-Hofstra and Porter, *Cultures of Neurasthenia*, 219–38.

Schmuhl, Hans-Walther. *Hirnforschung und Krankenmord. Das Kaiser-Wilhelm-Institut fuer Hirnforschung 1937–1945*. Berlin: Max-Planck-Gesellschaft, 2000.

Schmuhl, Hans-Walther, and Volker Roelcke, eds. *"Heroische Therapien": Die deutsche Psychiatrie im internationalen Vergleich, 1918–1945*. Goettingen: Wallstein Verlag, 2013.

Schneider, William. *Rockefeller Philanthropy and Modern Biomedicine: International Initiatives from World War I to the Cold War*. Bloomington: Indiana University Press, 2002.

———. "Toward the Improvement of the Human Race: The History of Eugenics in France." *Journal of Modern History* 54, no. 2 (1982): 268–91.

Schoen, Johanna. *Choice and Coercion: Birth Control, Sterilization, and Abortion in Public Health and Welfare*. Chapel Hill: University of North Carolina Press, 2005.

Schoenemann, Peter. "On Models and Muddles of Heritability." *Genetica* 99, no. 1 (1997): 97–108.

Schwelb, Egon. *Human Rights and the International Community*. Chicago: University of Chicago Press, 1964.

Scull, Andrew. *Madness in Civilization: A Cultural History of Insanity*. Princeton: Princeton University Press, 2015.

Sealy, Patricia, and Paul Whitehead. "Forty Years of Deinstitutionalization of Psychiatric Services in Canada: An Empirical Assessment." *Canadian Journal of Psychiatry* 49, no. 4 (2004): 249–57.

Seidelman, William. "The Legacy of Academic Medicine and Human Exploitation in the Third Reich." *Perspectives in Biology and Medicine* 43, no. 3 (2000): 325–34.

———. "Medical Selection: Auschwitz Antecedents and Effluent." *Holocaust and Genocide Studies* 4, no. 4 (1989): 437–48.

Shermer, Michael. *The Moral Arc*. New York: Henry Holt, 2015.

Shevell, Michael. "A Canadian Paradox: Tommy Douglas and Eugenics." *Canadian Journal of Neurological Sciences* 39, no. 1 (2012): 35–39.

———. "Neurosciences in the Third Reich: From Ivory Tower to Death Camps." *Canadian Journal for Neurological Sciences* 26, no. 2 (1999): 132–38.

Shorter, Edward. *A History of Psychiatry: From the Era of the Asylum to the Age of Prozac*. New York: John Wiley & Sons, 1997.

Sieg, Ulrich. *Geist und Gewalt. Deutsche Philosophen zwischen Kaiserreich und Nationalsozialismus*. Munich: Carl Hanser, 2013.

Simmel, Marianne. "Kurt Goldstein 1878–1965." In *The Reach of Mind: Essays in Memory of Kurt Goldstein*, edited by Marianne Simmel, 2–11. New York: Springer, 1968.

———, ed. *The Reach of Mind: Essays in Memory of Kurt Goldstein*. New York: Springer, 1968

Simunek, Marek. "Making Infertile (Unfruchtbarmachung)/Sterilisations in the Reich District of Sudetenland during the Nazi Occupation, 1938–45: Overview." *Specialni pedagogika* 24, no. 1 (2014): 24–40.

Soltan, Hubert, ed. *Medical Genetics in Canada: Evolution of a Hybrid Discipline: Essays on the Early History*. London: University of Western Ontario, 1992.

Spring, Claudia. *Zwischen Krieg und Euthanasie. Zwangssterilisation in Wien*. Vienna: Boehlau, 2009.

Springer, Sean. "Eugenics in Ontario: Reconsidering Catholicism, the Culture of Government, and Post War Eugenics in the Canadian Historiography." MA thesis, Trent University, 2012.

Stahnisch, Frank W. "'Der Rosenthal'sche Versuch' oder: Ueber den Ort produktiver Forschung—Zur Exkursion des physiologischen Experimentallabors von Isidor Rosenthal (1836–1915) von der Stadt aufs Land." *Sudhoffs Archiv. Zeitschrift fuer Wissenschaftsgeschichte* 94, no. 1 (2010): 1–30.

———. "The Early Eugenics Movement and Emerging Professional Psychiatry: Conceptual Transfers and Personal Relationships between Germany and North America, 1880s to 1930s." *Canadian Bulletin of Medical History* 31, no. 1 (2014): 17–40.

———. "Eugenics and Psychiatry—Analyzing the Origin, Application and Perception of Early Forced Sterilization Programs from a Medical History Viewpoint." *Journal of the History of the Neurosciences* 21, no. 1 (2012): 97–98.

———. "Flexible Antworten—Offene Fragen: Zu den Foerderungsstrategien der Rockefellerstiftung fuer die deutsche Hirnforschung im Nationalsozialismus." *Journal fuer Neurologie, Neurochirurgie und Psychiatrie* 12, no. 2 (2011): 56–62.

———. "German-Speaking Émigré Neuroscientists in North America after 1933: Critical Reflections on Emigration-Induced Scientific Change." *Oesterreichische Zeitschrift fuer Geschichtswissenschaften (Vienna)* 21, no. 1 (2010): 36–68.

———. "Griesinger, Wilhelm (1817–1869)." In *Dictionary of Medical Biography*, edited by William F. Bynum and Helen Bynum, vol. 2, 582–83. London: Greenwood, 2007.

———. "Ludwig Edinger (1855–1918)—Pioneer in Neurology." *Journal of Neurology* 255, no. 1 (2008): 147–48.

———. *A New Field in Mind: A History of Interdisciplinarity in the Early Brain Sciences*. Montréal and Kingston: McGill-Queen's University Press, 2020.

———. "Psychiatrie und Hirnforschung: Zu den interstitiellen Uebergaengen des staedtischen Wissenschaftsraums im Labor der Berliner Metropole—Oskar und Cécile Vogt, Korbinian Brodmann, Kurt Goldstein." In *Psychiater und Zeitgeist. Zur Geschichte der Psychiatrie in Berlin*, edited by Hanfried Helmchen, 76–93. Berlin: Pabst Science Publisher, 2008.

———. "Von der Kriegsneurologie zur Psychotherapie—Kurt Goldstein (1878–1965) und die fruehen Ansaetze der Gruppenanalyse." *Gruppenpsychotherapie und Gruppendynamik* 50, no. 2 (2014): 146–65.

Stahnisch, Frank W., and Thomas Hoffmann. "Kurt Goldstein and the Neurology of Movement during the Interwar Years—Physiological Experimentation, Clinical Psychology and Early Rehabilitation." In *Was bewegt uns? Menschen im Spannungsfeld zwischen Mobilitaet und Beschleunigung*, edited by Christian Hoffstadt, Franz Peschke, and Andreas Schulz-Buchta, 283–311. Bochum, Germany: Projektverlag, 2010.

Stahnisch, Frank W., and Fred Weizmann. "Eugenics and Psychiatry—Analyzing the Origin, Application, and Perception of Early Forced Sterilization Programs from a Medical History Viewpoint." In *ISHN and Cheiron*, edited by University of Calgary, 97–8. Calgary: University of Calgary, 2011. https://www.ucalgary.ca/ISHN_Cheiron/node/39.

Stepan, Nancy Leys. *"The Hour of Eugenics": Race, Gender, and Nation in Latin America*. Ithaca, NY: Cornell University Press, 1991.

Steppe, Hilde. "Historical Research in Nursing." *13th Meeting of the Workgroup of European Nurse Researchers for National Representatives, September 1990*. Berlin Department of Historical Care Research of the German Society for Nursing Science, 1992.

Stern, Alexandra Minna. *Telling Genes: The Story of Genetic Counseling in America*. Baltimore: Johns Hopkins University Press, 2012.

———. *Eugenic Nation: Faults and Frontiers of Better Breeding in Modern America.* Berkeley: University of California Press, 2005.

———. "Improving Hoosiers: Indiana and the Wide Scope of American Eugenics." *Indiana Magazine of History* 106, no. 2 (2010): 219–23.

———. "'We Cannot Make a Silk Purse Out of a Sow's Ear': Eugenics in the Hoosier Heartland." *Indiana Magazine of History* 103, no. 1 (2007): 3–38.

Stewart, Ian. "Commandeering Time: The Ideological Status of Time in the Social Darwinism of Herbert Spencer." *Australian Journal of Politics and History* 57, no. 4 (2011): 389–402.

Stote, Karen. *An Act of Genocide: Colonialism and the Sterilization of Aboriginal Women.* Halifax and Winnipeg: Fernwood, 2015.

———. "An Act of Genocide: Eugenics, Indian Policy and the Sterilization of Aboriginal Women in Canada." PhD diss., University of New Brunswick, 2012.

———. "The Coercive Sterilization of Aboriginal Women in Canada." *American Culture and Research Journal* 36, no. 3 (2012): 117–50.

Strachan, Tom, and Andrew Read. *Human Molecular Genetics.* Philadelphia and London: Garland Science, 2010.

Strange, Carolyn, and Jennifer Stephen, "Eugenics in Canada: A Checkered History, 1850s–1990s." In Bashford and Levine, *Oxford Handbook of the History of Eugenics*, 523–38.

Strippel, Andreas. *NS-Volkstumspolitik und die Neuordnung Europas. Rassenpolitische Selektion der Einwandererzentralstelle des Chefs der Sicherheitspolizei und des SD (1939–1945).* Paderborn, Germany: Ferdinand Schoeningh Verlag, 2011.

Sturtevant, Alfred. *A History of Genetics.* New York: Harper & Row, 1965.

Tabery, James. "Genetics." Eugenics Archives, April 29, 2014. http://eugenicsarchive.ca/discover/encyclopedia/535eec197095aa000000022c.

Taylor, Georgina. "Ground for Common Action: Violet McNaughton's Agrarian Feminism and the Origins of the Farm Women's Movement in Canada." PhD diss., Carleton University, 1997.

Tekin, Serife, and Robyn Bluhm, eds. *The Bloomsbury Companion to Philosophy of Psychiatry.* London: Bloomsbury, 2019.

Teuber, Hans-Lukas. "Kurt Goldstein's Role in the Development of Neuropsychology." *Neuropsychologia* 4, no. 4 (1966): 299–310.

Tolman, Charles. *John Watson of Queen's.* Unpublished manuscript, Kingston, ON, 1999.

Torrance, Kelley. "The Sterilization of History." *Alberta Report* 24, no. 47 (1997): 32–33.

Torrey, Fuller, and Robert Yolken. "Psychiatric Genocide: Nazi Attempts to Eradicate Schizophrenia." *Schizophrenia Bulletin* 36, no. 1 (2010): 26–32.

Tremblay, Mary. "Lieutenant John Counsell and the Development of Medical Rehabilitation and Disability Policy in Canada." In *Disabled Veterans in History*, edited by David A. Gerber, 322–46. Ann Arbor: University of Michigan Press, 2012.

Tucker, William. *The Funding of Scientific Racism: Wickliffe Draper and the Pioneer Fund*. Urbana: University of Illinois Press, 2002.

Turda, Marius. *Modernism and Eugenics*. London: Palgrave Macmillan, 2010.

Turda, Marius, and Paul Weindling, eds. *Blood and Homeland: Eugenics and Racial Nationalism in Central and Southeast Europe, 1900–1940*. Budapest: Central European University Press, 2006.

Ulrich, Robert. "Kurt Goldstein." In *The Reach of Mind: Essays in Memory of Kurt Goldstein*, edited by Marianne Simmel, 13–15. New York: Springer, 1968.

United Nations Office of the High Commissioner for Human Rights. "Monitoring the Convention on the Rights of Persons with Disabilities: Guidance for Human Rights Monitors." Professional Training Series No. 17, New York and Geneva, 2010. http://www.ohchr.org/Documents/Publications/Disabilities_training_17EN.pdf.

Unkauf, Byron. "The Sterilization of the Mental Defective." *University of Manitoba Medical Journal* 5/6, no. 1 (1933–35): 46.

Uris, Leon. *Exodus*. Garden City, NY: Doubleday, 1958.

Valverde, Mariana. *The Age of Light, Soap and Water: Moral Reform in English Canada, 1885–1925*. Toronto: University of Toronto Press, 2008.

Van Rahden, Till. *Jews and Other Germans: Civil Society, Religious Diversity, and Urban Politics in Breslau, 1860–1925*. Madison: University of Wisconsin Press, 2008.

Volkov, Sulamit. "Jewish Scientists in Imperial Germany (Parts I and II)." *Aleph: Historical Studies in Science and Judaism* 1, no. 1 (2001): 1–36.

Von Schwerin, Alexander. *Experimentalisierung des Menschen: Der Genetiker Hans Nachtsheim und die Erbpathologie, 1920–1945*. Goettingen: Wallstein, 2000.

Wahlsten, Douglas. "The Eugenics of John M. MacEachran Warrants Revocation of Honours." *History and Philosophy of Psychology Bulletin* 10, no. 1 (1998): 22–25.

———. *Genes, Brain Function, and Behaviour: What Genes Do, How They Malfunction, and Ways to Repair Damage*. London, UK: Elsevier, 2019.

———. "The Hunt for Gene Effects Pertinent to Behavioral Traits and Psychiatric Disorders: From Mouse to Human," *Developmental Psychobiology* 54, no. 5 (2013): 475–92.

———. "The Intelligence of Heritability." *Canadian Psychology* 35, no. 2 (1994): 244–58.

———. "Leilani Muir versus the Philosopher King: Eugenics on Trial in Alberta." *Genetica* 99, no. 1 (1997): 185–98.

———. "The Malleability of Intelligence Is Not Constrained by Heritability." In *Intelligence, Genes, and Success: Scientists Respond to the Bell Curve*, edited by Bernie Devlin, Stephen E. Fienberg, Daniel P. Resnick, and Kathryn Roeder, 71–87. New York: Copernicus, 1974.

———. *Report on Eugenic Sterilization in Alberta from 1950 to 1968* (June 15, 1999). Edmonton, AB: Department of Psychology, University of Alberta, 1999.

———. "Single-Gene Influences on Brain and Behaviour." *Annual Review of Psychology* 50, no. 6 (1999): 599–624.

———. "The Theory of Biological Intelligence: History and a Critical Appraisal." In *The General Factor of Intelligence: How General Is It?*, edited by Robert Sternberg and Elena Grigorenko, 245–77. Mahwah, NJ: Erlbaum, 2002.

Wallack, Lawrence. "Mass Media and Health Promotion: Promise, Problem, and Challenge." In *Mass Communication and Public Health: Complexities and Conflicts*, edited by Charles Atkins and Lawrence Wallack, 43–57. Newbury Park, CA: Sage, 1990.

———. *Mass Media and Health Promotion: The Promise, the Problem, the Challenge*. Berkeley: School of Public Health, University of California, 1989.

Washington, Natalia. "Contextualism as a Solution to Paternalism in Psychiatric Practice." *Philosophy, Psychiatry, & Psychology* 25, no. 4 (2018): 235–43.

———. "Culturally Unbound: Cross-Cultural Cognitive Diversity and the Science of Psychopathology." *Philosophy, Psychiatry, & Psychology* 23, no. 2 (2016): 165–79.

Weber, Matthias. "Die Deutsche Forschungsanstalt fuer Psychiatrie." In *75 Jahre Max-Planck-Institut fuer Psychiatrie*, edited by Max-Planck-Gesellschaft, 11–33. Munich: Max-Planck-Gesellschaft, 1992.

———. "Ernst Ruedin, 1874–1952: A German Psychiatrist and Geneticist." *American Journal of Medical Genetics* 26, no. 4 (2007): 323–31.

———. *Ernst Ruedin: Eine kritische Biographie*. Berlin: Springer, 1993.

———. "Harnack-Prinzip oder Fuehrerprinzip? Erbbiologie unter Ernst Ruedin an der Deutschen Forschungsanstalt fuer Psychiatrie (Kaiser-Wilhelm-Institut) in Muenchen." In *Die Kaiser-Wilhelm-Max-Planck-Gesellschaft und ihre Institute*, edited by Bernhard vom Brocke and Hubert Laitko, 409–22. Berlin: de Gruyter, 1996.

Weikart, Richard. "Darwinism and Death: Devaluing Human Life in Germany 1859–1920." *Journal of the History of Ideas* 63, no. 3 (2002): 323–44.

———. "The Origins of Social Darwinism in Germany, 1859–1895." *Journal of the History of Ideas* 54, no. 3 (1993): 469–88.

Weinberger, Ruth Jolanda. *Fertility Experiments in Auschwitz-Birkenau: The Perpetrators and Their Victims*. Saarbruecken, Germany: Suedwestdeutscher Verlag fuer Hochschulschriften, 2009.

Weindling, Paul. "Entschaedigung der Sterilisierungs- und Euthanasie-Opfer nach 1945." In *Toedliche Medizin im Nationalsozialismus. Von der Rassenhygiene zum Massenmord*, edited by Klaus-Dietmar Henke, 31–46. Cologne: Boehlau, 2008.

———. "From International to Zonal Trials: The Origins of the Nuremberg Medical Trial." *Holocaust Genocide Studies* 14, no. 3 (2000): 367–89.

———, ed. *Healthcare in Private and Public from the Early Modern Period to 2000*. London: Routledge, 2014.

———. *Health, Race and German Politics between National Unification and Nazism, 1870–1945*. Cambridge: Cambridge University Press, 1989.

———. "International Eugenics: Swedish Sterilization in Context." *Scandinavian Journal of History* 24, no. 1 (1999): 179–97.

———. *John W. Thompson: Psychiatrist in the Shadow of the Holocaust*. Rochester, NY: University of Rochester Press, 2010.

———. *Nazi Medicine and the Nuremberg Trials: From Medical War Crimes to Informed Consent*. Basingstoke: Palgrave Macmillan, 2004.

———. "Sonstige Personenschaeden—die Entschaedigungspraxis der Stiftung, Erinnerung, Verantwortung und Zukunft." In *Die Entschaedigung von NS-Zwangsarbeit am Anfang des 21. Jahrhunderts*, edited by Constantin Goschler, 197–225. Vol. 2. Goettingen: Wallstein Verlag, 2012.

———. *Victims and Survivors of Nazi Human Experiments: Science and Suffering in the Holocaust*. London: Bloomsbury, 2014.

Weiner, Bernard I. "The Americanization and Periodical Publication, 1750–1810." *Cercles* 19, no. 2 (2009): 102–13.

———. "The Democratic Exchange of Reading and Writing: Americanization and Periodical Publication, 1750–1810." *Christ Church Library Newsletter* 7, no. 1 (2011): 102–13.

Weingart, Peter. "Eugenics—Medical or Social Science?" *Science in Context* 8, no. 2 (1995): 197–207.

Weinstock Netanel, Neil. "Copyright and a Democratic Civil Society." *Yale Law Journal* 106, no. 2 (1996): 283–387.

Weiss, Sheila Faith. "The Race Hygiene Movement in Germany." *Osiris*, 2nd ser., 3, no. 1 (1987): 193–236.

Weiss, Sheila Faith, Mark Adams, and Garland Allen. "Human Heredity and Politics: A Comparative Institutional Study of the Eugenics Record Office at Cold Spring Harbor (United States), the Kaiser Wilhelm Institute for Anthropology, Human Heredity and Eugenics (Germany) and the Maxim Gorky Medical Genetics Institute (USSR)." *Osiris* 20, no. 1 (2005): 232–62.

Weitz, Eric. *Weimar Germany: Promise and Tragedy*. Princeton: Princeton University Press, 2007.

White, Anne. "The Calgary Local Council of Women: Traditional Female Christianity in Action (1895–1897 and 1912–1933)." *Canadian Society of Church History, Historical Papers* 7, no. 1 (1998): 67–87.

Whorton, James. "The Solitary Vice: The Superstition that Masturbation Could Cause Mental Illness." *Western Journal of Medicine* 175, no. 1 (2001): 66–68.

Wilson, Robert. "Contemporary Forms of Eugenics." *eLS Wiley Online*, September 15, 2017. https://doi.org/10.1002/9780470015902.a0027075.

———. *The Eugenic Mind Project*. Cambridge, MA: MIT Press, 2018.

———. "Eugenics Never Went Away." *Aeon Magazine*, June 5, 2018. https://aeon.co/essays/eugenics-today-where-eugenic-sterilisation-continues-now.

———. "Eugenic Thinking." *Philosophy, Theory, and Practice in Biology* 10, no. 12 (2018): 1–8.

———. "Eugenic Traits." Eugenics Archives, April 28, 2014. http://eugenicsarchive.ca/database/documents/535eeb757095aa0000000221.

———. "Psychology." Eugenics Archives, December 1, 2014. http://eugenicsarchive.ca/database/documents/547ce966d7dacd0147000002.

———. "The Role of Oral History in Surviving a Eugenic Past." In *Beyond Testimony and Trauma: Oral History in the Aftermath of Mass Violence*, edited by Steven High, 119–38. Vancouver: University of British Columbia Press, 2015.

Wilson, Robert, and Joshua St. Pierre. "Eugenics and Disability." In *Rethinking Disability: World Perspectives in Culture and Society*, edited by Patrick Devlieger, Beatriz Miranda-Galarza, Steven E. Brown, and Megan Strickfaden, 93–112. Antwerp: Garant, 2016.

Winau, Rolf. "Menschenzuechtung—Utopien und ethische Bewertung." In *Machbarkeitsphantasien*, edited by Alfred Schaefer and Michael Wimmer, 55–65. Berlin: Reimer Verlag, 2002.

Wittmann, Rebecca Elizabeth. *Beyond Justice: The Auschwitz Trial*. Cambridge, MA: Harvard University Press, 2005.

———. "The Wheels of Justice Turn Slowly: The Pretrial Investigations of the Frankfurt Auschwitz Trial 1963–65." *Central European History* 3, no. 3 (2002): 345–78.

Woerster, Peter. "Archive im Koenigsberger Gebiet nach 1945." *Zeitschrift fuer Ostmitteleuropaforschung* 39, no. 1 (1990): 85–92.

Wojak, Irmtrud. *Fritz Bauer 1903–1968: Eine Biographie*. Munich: C. H. Beck, 2013.

Wolbring, Gregor. "Ability Privilege: A Needed Addition to Privilege Studies." *Journal for Critical Animal Studies* 12, no. 1 (2014): 118–41.

———. "'Culture of Peace' from an Ability and Disability Studies Lens." In *Expanding Peace Ecology: Peace, Security, Sustainability, Equity and Gender; Perspectives of IPRA's Ecology and Peace Commission*, edited by Ursula Spring,

Oswald Spring, Hans-Guenter Brauch, and Keith Tidball, 183–99. New York: Springer, 2013.

———. "Expanding Ableism: Taking Down the Ghettoization of Impact of Disability Studies Scholars." *Societies* 2, no. 1 (2012): 75–83.

———. "The Politics of Ableism." *Development* 51, no. 2 (2008): 252–58.

———, ed. "What Sorts of People Should There Be?" Special issue, *International Journal of Disability, Community, and Rehabilitation* 12, no. 2 (2013).

———. "Why NBIC? Why Human Performance Enhancement?" *Innovation: The European Journal of Social Science Research* 21, no. 1 (2008): 25–40.

Wolbring, Gregor, and Lucy Diep. "The Discussions around Precision Genetic Engineering: Role of and Impact on Disabled People." *Laws* 5, no. 3 (2016): 1–23.

Ziegler, Mary. "Eugenic Feminism: Mental Hygiene, the Women's Movement, and the Campaign for Eugenic Legal Reform, 1900–1935." *Harvard Journal of Law and Gender* 31, no. 2 (2008): 211–35.

Zimmerman, David. "'Narrow Minded People': Canadian Universities and the Academic Refugee Crises, 1933–1941." *Canadian Historical Review* 88, no. 3 (2007): 291–315.

Zuerner, Peter. "Von der Hirnanatomie zur Eugenik. Die Suche nach den biologischen Ursachen der Geisteskrankheiten. Eine Untersuchung am Beispiel des Werkes von August Forel (1848–1931)." MD diss., University of Mainz, 1983.

NEWS SOURCES

"Against Sterilization." *New York Times*, January 26, 1936.

Amiel, Barbara. "Sweden's Shameful Eugenics Policies." *Maclean's*, September 8, 1997, 13.

Begos, Kevin. "The American Eugenics Movement after World War II (Part 1 of 3)." *Indy Week*, May 18, 2011. https://indyweek.com/news/american-eugenics-movement-world-war-ii-part-1-3/.

"Bill Sponsored by Hoey in Legislature Meeting Opposition." *Winnipeg Free Press*, February 23, 1933.

Blue Grass Blade. "Editorial." November 18, 1906.

Buckingham Law Post. "Editorial." December 9, 1935.

Buckingham Law Post. "Editorial." March 12, 1927.

Calgary Herald. "Immigration to Canada Has Fallen Off Greatly." September 11, 1930.

"Capping the Cost of Atrocity: Survivor of Nazi Experiments Says $8,000 Isn't Enough." *New York Times*, November 13, 2003.
"Child Quality Not Quantity." *Toronto Daily Star*, April 14, 1910.
"Class-Action Lawyer Told of 2 Coerced Sterilizations of Indigenous Women in Manitoba." *CBC News*, November 14, 2018. https://www.cbc.ca/news/canada/manitoba/manitoba-indigenous-women-forced-sterilization-lawsuit-1.4904421.
"Close Divorce Doors If Any Children." *New York Times*, January 30, 1908.
Davenport, Eugene. "To Weed Out Human Race." *Washington Post*, January 30, 1909.
Dolphin, Ric. "Honours Shelved for Professor Linked to Eugenics." *Edmonton Journal*, October 17, 1997.
Edmonton Bulletin. "Editorial." April 1, 1937.
Edmonton Bulletin. "Editorial." March 20, 1927.
Edmonton Journal. "Editorial." June 29, 1996
Edmonton Journal. "Editorial." March 1, 1996.
"Eugenics Head Takes Prof. Larkin to Task." *San Francisco Call*, September 15, 1907.
"Fight against Sterilization Is to Be Resumed." *Winnipeg Free Press*, April 21, 1933.
"First Eugenic Baby Born in England." *Day Book*, October 29, 1913.
Foulkes, Imogen. "The Trauma of Switzerland's Morality Detentions." *BBC News*, September 14, 2010. http://www.bbc.co.uk/news/mobile/world-europe-11295538.
Hudson, John C. "The School System of Chicago." *Chicago Daily Tribune*, July 17, 1905, 14.
"Immigration Activities Will Be Curbed." *Edmonton Journal*, March 7, 1929.
"Improve Human Race." *Washington Post*, October 28, 1906.
"Improved Quality of Humans Sought." *Los Angeles Times*, October 31, 1906.
James, Susan Donaldson. "Baby Sent to Foster Care for 57 Days Because Parents Are Blind." *ABC News*, July 28, 2010. http://abcnews.go.com/Health/missouri-takes-baby-blind-parents/story?id=11263491.
Keller, Albert Galloway. "Folk Ways and Eugenics." *New York Times*, August 14, 1908.
Kirkup, Kristy: "Examine 'Monstrous' Allegations of Forced Sterilization of Indigenous Women: NDP." *CBC News*, January 8, 2019. https://www.cbc.ca/news/politics/sterilization-indigenous-allegations-forced-1.4911837.
"Lovemaking." *Boston Daily Globe*, September 2, 1906.
"Manitoba Legislature Condemns Sterilization of Mental Defectives." *Catholic Register*, March 20, 1933.

Martin, Sandra. "Ralph Klein, 70: The Man Who Ruled Alberta." *Globe and Mail*, March 29, 2013. https://www.theglobeandmail.com/news/national/ralph-klein-70-the-man-who-ruled-alberta/article10569210/.

McQuigge, Michelle. "What Will Canada's New Accessibility Law in 2018 Look Like?" *Toronto Star*, December 29, 2017.

———. "Federal Government Passes Canada's First National Accessibility Legislation." *National Post*, May 30, 2019.

"Mental Deficiency Measure Effective in Province since June 1." *Winnipeg Free Press*, June 7, 1933.

Montréal Gazette. "Editorial." February 7, 1934.

"Nazis Bar Jews from Citizenship." *Calgary Daily Herald*, September 16, 1935.

"New Defectives Bill Passes Law Amendments Body." *Winnipeg Free Press*, February 23, 1933.

"New Laws Persecute German Jews." *Calgary Daily Herald*, September 16, 1935.

"A Perfect Race of Men." *New York Times*, September 27, 1908.

Pringle, Heather. "Alberta Barren." *Saturday Night*, June 1997, 35.

"Quest of a Standard." *New-York Daily Tribune*, April 25, 1909.

"Rosebery on Eugenics." *New York Times*, July 5, 1908.

Sadava, M., and T. Arnold. "Sterilization Victim Receives Personal Apology from Klein." *Edmonton Journal*, February 20, 1997, A4.

"Scandals over Sterilization." *Maclean's*, September 8, 1997, 42.

Schmidt, John. "Agricultural Alberta." *Calgary Herald*, March 27, 1931, 61.

Schultz, Eric. "Blind Independence Couple Gets Newborn Back after 57 Days." KSHB Kansas City, July 21, 2010.

"Science to Make Men and Women Better." *Washington Post*, May 18, 1906.

"Selective Environment." *New York Times*, October 2, 1905.

Spitzka, Edward C. "Health First and Matrimony Afterward." *San Francisco Call*, May 18, 1913.

"Sterilization." *Northwest Review*, March 4, 1933.

"Sterilization Bill Passes Third Reading." *Edmonton Bulletin*, March 7, 1928,

"Sterilization Board Given Wide Powers." *Calgary Daily Herald*, April 1, 1937.

"Sterilization Clause Passed by Committee." *Winnipeg Tribune*, April 22, 1933

"Sterilization Forced upon Her." *Washington Post*, January 7, 1936.

"Sterilization Proposals Are Killed by House." *Winnipeg Tribune*, May 4, 1933.

Thomas, Derrick. "Geneticist Defends Sterilization in Era before the Pill." *Calgary Herald*, June 29, 1995, A14.

Torrance, Kelley. "The Sterilization of History." *Alberta Report* 24, no. 47 (1997): 32–33.

von Windmann, Antje. "Ein Stigma, lebenslang." *Der Spiegel*, September 1, 2014.

Watkins, John Elfreth. "Quest of Superman." *Evening Star*, November 10, 1906.

"Whither Germany?" Editorial. *Edmonton Journal*, July 16, 1933.
"Whom Would You Choose as Father." *Washington Times*, July 29, 1912.
Winnipeg Tribune. "Editorial." May 4, 1933.
Winnipeg Tribune. "Editorial." March 21, 1933.
Winnipeg Tribune. "Editorial." March 11, 1933.
Winnipeg Tribune. "Editorial." March 8, 1933.
"Woman Is Saved from Sterilization." *Washington Post*, January 23, 1936.
Wright, Teresa. "After 40 Years, Federal Government Removes Barriers to Disabled Immigrants." *National Post*, April 16, 2018.

CASES AND STATUTES

Accessibility for Ontarians with Disabilities Act, 2005, S.O. 2005, c. 11.
An Act Respecting Immigration and Immigrants, S.C. 1869, 32–33 Vic., c. 10.
Americans with Disabilities Act of 1990, 42 U.S.C., s. 12101.
Buck v. Bell, 274 U.S. 200 (1927).
Canadian Charter of Rights and Freedoms, s. 8, Part 1 of the Constitution Act, 1982, being Schedule B to the Canada Act 1982 (UK), 1982, c 11.
Canadian Human Rights Act, R.S.C. 1985, c. H-6.
Eldridge v. British Columbia (Attorney General) (1997), 3 S.C.R. 624.
Grosjean v. American Press Co., Inc., 297 U.S. 233 (1936).
Immigration and Refugee Protection Act, S.C. 2001, c 27.
Mental Defectives Act, R.S.A. 1955, c. 199 (Alberta).
Mental Defectives Act, R.S.S. 1930, c. 196 (Saskatchewan).
Mental Deficiency Act, S.M. 1933, c. 24 (Manitoba).
Muir v. Alberta (1996), 132 D.L.R. (4th) 695.
Ontarians with Disabilities Act, 2001, S.O. 2001, c. 32.
Sexual Sterilization Act, S.A. 1928, c. 37 (Alberta).
Sexual Sterilization Act Amendment Act, S.A. 1937, c. 47 (Alberta).
Sexual Sterilization Act Amendment Act, S.A. 1942, c. 194 (Alberta).
Sexual Sterilization Act, R.S.A. 1955, c. 194 (Alberta).
Sexual Sterilization Repeal Act, S.A. 1972, c. 87 (Alberta).
Vriend v. Alberta (1998), 1 S.C.R. 493.

ARCHIVAL SOURCES AND LIBRARY COLLECTIONS

Austria

Collection of Autographs, History of Medicine Library. Institute for the History of Medicine. Josephinum: Collections of the Medical University of Vienna.

Canada

Canadian Psychological Association fonds. MG 28 I 161, accession no. 1986-0317. Library and Archives Canada, Ottawa.

Canadian Society for the Protection of Science and Learning. File. RG95-1. Box 540. Library and Archives Canada, Ottawa.

Collection on Immigration to Canada. Bibliothèque et Archives nationales du Québec, Montréal.

Convention minutes 1925–1932, United Farm Women of Alberta Collection. Official minutes of the UFWA board and annual conventions, 1915–49. Series 4, Micro/ufa. M-1749-44. United Farmers of Alberta fonds. Glenbow Archives, Calgary.

Department of Physiology and Pharmacology Collection, 1933, UAA-2012-044, University of Alberta Archives, Research & Collections Resource Facility, Edmonton.

Department of Psychology Collection, 1975, UAA-2006-163, University of Alberta Archives, Research & Collections Resource Facility, Edmonton.

Department of Public Health Fond. Accession no. 86.36, files RPC 85/230, 1935 (1919–2018). Provincial Archives of Alberta, Edmonton.

Department of Public Health, Province of Alberta, Annual Report of the Bureau of Vital Statistics, Ottawa, ON: Annual Report, Department of Public Health, 1959. Accession no. 86.36, files 11-5-Z 517. Provincial Archives of Alberta, Edmonton.

Eugenics Board Minutes, 1949 (1933–37). GR0008.0004F. Provincial Archives of Alberta, Edmonton.

Eugenics Board Minutes Collection, Eugenics Board Minutes series, 1939–41, no. GR0008.0004F, "Transcript Excerpts from the Examination for Discovery." Provincial Archives of Alberta, Edmonton.

Glenbow Library and Archives. "Immigration Report." United Farm Women of Alberta, Fifteenth Annual Convention, 1929. M1749, File 44. Glenbow Western Research Centre, Archives and Special Collections, Taylor Family Digital Library, University of Calgary, Calgary, AB.

Government of Alberta, Annual Report of the Department of Public Health, Edmonton, AB: Government of Alberta, 1955 Accession no. 86.36, files 16-5-Z 517. Provincial Archives of Alberta, Edmonton.

Government of Alberta. Health Survey Committee. *A Survey of Alberta's Health*. Edmonton: Department of Public Health, 1950 Accession no. 86.36, files 30-5-Z 517. Provincial Archives of Alberta, Edmonton.

Journals of the Legislative Assembly of Manitoba: Nineteenth Legislative Assembly. Manitoba Legislative Library Collection, Winnipeg, 1933.

MacEachran, John Malcolm Fonds. Accession no. 71–217. University of Alberta Archives, Edmonton.
Mackie Family History of Neuroscience Collection. Health Sciences Library. University of Calgary, AB.
Mathers, Alvin T. "Report on the Prevention of Mental Disorders." 1925. G541. Provincial Archives of Manitoba, Winnipeg.
Special Collections and Journal Collections; McGill University, Redpath Library, Montréal. Sessional Papers. Select Standing Committee on Law Amendments re: Mental Deficiency. G8250 (1933).
Sterilization Bill. 1933. Premier's Office Files. G601. EC 0016, accession no. GR1661. Provincial Archives of Manitoba, Winnipeg.
United Farmers of Alberta. Official minutes and reports of the UFA annual conventions, 1910–49. Series 2, Micro/ufa. United Farmers of Alberta fonds. Glenbow Archives, Calgary.
University of Alberta. Course calendars: 1917–24, 1950–51, 1955–56, 1960–61, 1965–66, University of Alberta Archives, Research & Collections Resource Facility, Edmonton.

Germany

Berichte ueber die Prozesse gegen Rudolf Hoess und Erhard Milch (Menschenversuche). B 126, 61085. Bundesarchiv Berlin.
Deutsche Forschungsanstalt fuer Psychiatrie Collections. External Historical Archive of the Max Planck Institute for Psychiatry, Munich.
Deutsche Forschungsgemeinschaft (DFG) Collection. R 73. Praesidium Minutes Collection. Bundesarchiv Koblenz.
Edinger Commission Collection and Medical Faculty Collection. University Library Johann Christian Senckenberg. Frankfurt am Main University Archives of the Johann Wolfgang University of Frankfurt.
Kaiser Wilhelm Society Collection. Div. I, Rep. IA. Archives of the Max Planck Society, Berlin.
Landesarchiv Schwerin, Mecklenburg-Vorpommern: ZAST K 153 70/47 Bd. 1, 3.
Library of the Max Planck Institute for the History of Science, Berlin.
Ludwig Edinger Institute Collections. Institute for the History and Ethics of Medicine. Johann Wolfgang Goethe University, Frankfurt am Main.
Medical Faculty Collections and Human Resources Files. University Archives. Humboldt University of Berlin.

Switzerland

Main Library. University of Zurich.

Monakow, Constantin von. Correspondence. Archives. Museum for the History of Medicine. University of Zurich.
Plight of Survivors of Concentration Camps Weis Note. SOA 407/02, 1951. United Nations Office at Geneva.

United Kingdom

Correspondence from Ludwig Guttmann, 1938–1939, PP/GUT/A.1/3, box.1, 6, Wellcome Library of the History of Medicine, London, United Kingdom.

United States

Alan Gregg Collection; German Displaced Scholars; Germany; Kaiser Wilhelm Society in Germany; Rockefeller Collection and Funding Program for Psychosomatics. Rockefeller Foundation, series 1.1, record group 717A, box 1.1/2, box, box 9, box 10, box 11, box 12; series 106, RAC, RF 1.1, KWI for Psychiatry, Germany, Rockefeller Archive Center, Sleepy Hollow, NY.
Center for the History of Medicine. Francis A. Countway Library of Medicine. Harvard Medical School, Boston.
Faculty of Medicine, Central Administration, and Archival Collections on the American
Academy of Neurology. RG01C-15:2, Department of Neurology and Psychiatry, Series 2. Bernard Becker Medical Library Archives. Washington University School of Medicine, St. Louis, MO.
Goldstein, Kurt. Papers, 1900–1965. MS#0498. Rare Book & Manuscript Library. Columbia University, New York.
Judge Advocate General, records of the office of the. RG153, 153.13.1 Records relating to World War II war crimes, incl. persons and places file (dossier files) 1944–49. National Archives and Record Administration, Washington DC.
National Library of Medicine: Collection of the Annual Research Reports of the Intramural Program and Extramural Program of the National Institutes of Health, 1948–60; National Institutes of Health, Bethesda, MD.
Office of NIH History. National Institutes of Health, Bethesda, MD.
Oskar Diethelm Library. DeWitt Wallace Institute for the History of Psychiatry. Weill Cornell Medical College. Cornell University, New York.

CONTRIBUTORS

Ashley Barlow is a clinical psychologist with Alberta Health Services in Edmonton. She received her PhD in clinical psychology with a specialization in forensics from the University of Saskatchewan, where her dissertation investigated media representations of intimate partner homicide. Ashley has a variety of research interests relating to media and the representation of pertinent psychological issues, including bullying and public perceptions of criminality. She currently works primarily with adolescents who are experiencing a variety of substance abuse, mental health, and legal issues. Ashley is also an adjunct professor in the University of Alberta's Educational Psychology Department. Her publications include (with Mary E. Oliver) "Public Attitudes toward Sex Offenders and their Relationship to Personality Traits and Demographic Characteristics" (*Behavioural Sciences & the Law*, 2010).

Mikkel Dack is an assistant professor in modern European history at Rowan University in New Jersey. He received his PhD in German history at the University of Calgary and his MA in history at the University of Waterloo, with study periods at the Free University of Berlin and the Helmut Schmidt University in Hamburg, Germany. His major research interests are in transatlantic and German cultural and psychosocial history, with a particular emphasis on German–North American relations—including the history of the Nazi sport movement in the 1930s. Several of his publications in peer-reviewed history journals and books are concerned with the postwar Allied occupation of Germany and the German response to programs of denazification, including "Crimes Committed by Soviet Soldiers against German Civilians, 1944–1945: A Historiographical Analysis" (*Journal of Military and Strategic Studies*, 2008).

Erna Kurbegović received her PhD from the Department of History at the University of Calgary. She has also worked as a research assistant in the multicentre research project Living Archives on Eugenics in Western

Canada, which was funded through a grant from the Social Sciences and Humanities Research Council of Canada's Community-University Research Alliance (SSHRC-CURA). She is interested in twentieth-century history of Canadian medicine, the history of eugenics, and the history of public health. She has published "Eugenics in Canada: A Historiographical Survey" (*Acta Historiae Medicinae, Stomatologie, Pharmaciae, Medicinae Veterinariae*, 2016); and "The Influence of the Manitoba Mental Hygiene Survey, 1918" (*Western Humanities Review*, 2015).

Diana Mansell is a retired nursing professor at the University of Calgary, where she had been teaching the history of nursing in the Faculty of Nursing for many decades. In the past, she has also been affiliated with the Hannah Institute for the History of Nursing in Ontario. She has published *Forging the Future: A History of Nursing in Canada* (2003) and "'We picked the wrong one to sterilise': The Role of Nursing in the Eugenics Movement in Alberta, 1920–1940" (*International History of Nursing Journal*, 1998). Her research interests include leadership in Canadian nursing, and she coordinated the work for an edited collection titled *Bedside and Community: 50 Years of Contributions to the Health of Albertans from the University of Calgary* (2020).

Guel A. Russell is a full professor of history of medicine in the Department of Humanities in Medicine at Texas A&M University's Health Science Center. A specialist in the history of neurophysiology, vision neuroscience, and pre-modern history of medicine, her teaching provides a historical perspective on the health sciences, clinical practice, and the rise of bioethics and integrates the history of cognitive neuroscience and the visual arts to help promote observational, critical, and perceptual skills of future physicians. She has been on the editorial board of *The Stanford Encyclopedia of Philosophy*, the executive board of the International Society for the History of Neuroscience, and vice-president of the International Union of the History of Science and Philosophy.

Celeste Tường Vy Sharpe is the interim director of academic technology at Carleton College in Northfield, Minnesota. She received her PhD in history from George Mason University for a digital dissertation project "They Need You! Disability, Visual Culture, and the Poster Child, 1945–1980," and has published in the digital humanities, history, pedagogy, and the scholarship of teaching and learning. Previously, she worked at the Roy Rosenzweig Center for History and New Media on a number of education and public history projects and was a Penn Pre-doctoral Fellow for Excellence through Diversity at the University of Pennsylvania in Philadelphia.

Frank W. Stahnisch is a full professor in the Department of History and the Department of Community Health Sciences, as well as an adjunct professor in the Department of Classics and Religion, at the University of Calgary, and he has been a visiting professor at the Centre for the History of Science, Technology and Medicine at the University of California at Berkeley. He holds the Alberta Medical Foundation/Hannah Professorship in the History of Medicine and Health Care at the University of Calgary and is the author of *A New Field in Mind* (2020), *Medicine, Life and Function* (2012), and *Ideas in Action* (2003). He co-edited *Medizin, Geschichte und Geschlecht* (with Florian Steger; 2005), *Albert Neissers "Stereoscopischer Medicinischer Atlas"* (with Ulrich Schoenherr and Antonio Bergua; 2006), *Bild und Gestalt* (with Heijko Bauer; 2007), *Ludwik Fleck—Denkstile und Tatsachen* (with Sylwia Werner and Claus Zittel; 2011), *Kurt Goldstein—Der Aufbau des Organismus* (with Thomas Hoffmann; 2014), and *Trading Zones and Boundary Concepts in the History of Medicine and Medical Humanities* (with Dorothy Porter, 2015).

Henderikus J. Stam is a full professor in the Department of Psychology and an adjunct professor in the Department of History at the University of Calgary. He was the founding editor of the bimonthly journal *Theory & Psychology*, which he edited for its first twenty-six years. He has published widely on the foundational and historical problems of twentieth-century psychology, including papers on the history of melancholia, the history of hypnosis, the history of psychosurgery, and the history of animal research in psychology. He is the co-author (with Erin Moss and Diane Kattevilder) of "From Suffrage to Sterilization: Eugenics and the Women's Movement in 20th Century Alberta" (*Canadian Psychology*, 2013). He is a fellow of the American and Canadian Psychological Associations; a founding member and former president of the International Society for Theoretical Psychology; and former president of Division 24 of the APA (Society for Theoretical and Philosophical Psychology), as well as Division 26 (Society for the History of Psychology). In 2015, he was honoured with the American Psychological Foundation's Joseph Gittler Award for his contributions to the philosophy of psychology.

Douglas Wahlsten is an emeritus professor of psychology in the Faculty of Science and adjunct professor in the Division of Neuroscience, Faculty of Medicine, at the University of Alberta in Edmonton. He has taught psychology and behavioural neuroscience at the University of Alberta for over three decades. He has studied individual differences in brain structure and behaviour, specializing in genetic experimentation and statistical analysis of data. His publications include *Genes, Brain, Function, and Behaviour* (2019), "The Hunt for Gene Effects Pertinent to Behavioural Traits and Psychiatric Disorders: From Mouse to Human" (*Developmental Psychobiology*, 2012), "The Eugenics of John M. MacEachran Warrant Revocation of Honours" (*History of Psychology and Philosophy Bulletin*, 1999), "Leilani Muir versus the Philosopher King: Eugenics on Trial in Alberta" (*Genetica*, 1997), and "Race, Evolution and Behaviour" (*Canadian Journal of Sociology*, 1995).

Paul J. Weindling is the Wellcome Trust Research Professor in the History of Medicine at Oxford Brookes University in England. His research focuses on the history of eugenics, public health organization, and human experimentation. From 1999 to 2004 he was a member of the Max-Planck-Gesellschaft's President's Committee for the History of the Kaiser-Wilhelm-Gesellschaft under National Socialism. He further served on the advisory boards of the British Arts and Humanities Research Council projects on German-Jewish refugees and on the history of the Robert Koch-Institute. He is currently on the advisory board of the German Society for Psychiatry project on psychiatrists in Nazi Germany and a member of the project on the history of the German Foundation for Memory, Responsibility and the Future. He has advised the Deutsche Forschungsgemeinschaft (DFG), the Centre national de la recherche scientifique (CNRS), the Swiss Research Council, and other national funding agencies. He edited *Victims and Survivors of Nazi Human Experiments: Science and Suffering in the Holocaust* (2014) and is the author of *John W. Thompson: Psychiatrist in the Shadow of the Holocaust* (2010), *Nazi Medicine and the Nuremberg Trials: From Medical War Crimes to Informed Consent* (2004), and *Epidemics and Genocide in Eastern Europe, 1890–1945* (2000).

Robert A. Wilson is a full professor in the Department of Philosophy at University of Western Australia in Perth, Australia, and has been a faculty member in the Department of Philosophy at the University of Alberta for twenty-five years. He has also been the project director and principal investigator of the SSHRC-CURA project "Living Archives on Eugenics in Western Canada." His research interests include philosophy of mind and cognitive science, philosophy of biology, and philosophy of science. He is the co-author (with Andy Clark) of "How to Situate Cognition: Letting Nature Take Its Course," in *The Cambridge Handbook of Situated Cognition* (ed. M. Aydede and P. Robbins; 2009). His work has been honoured with a Fellowship of the Royal Society of Canada. He recently published *The Eugenics Mind Project* (2018).

Gregor Wolbring is an associate professor in the Community Health Sciences Department at the University of Calgary. His research interests include ability and ableism, disability studies, social, ethical, legal, economic, and cultural issues surrounding science and technology, and human rights issues. He is the author of *Ability Privilege: A Needed Addition to Privilege Studies* (2014), has edited "What Sorts of People Should there Be?" (*Journal of Disability, Community, and Rehabilitation*, 2013), and has published widely in numerous journals, including *Nature*, *Neuroethics*, *Nanoethics*, *Review of Disability Studies*, *Disability Studies Quarterly*, *International Journal of Social Robotics*, *Canadian Journal of Public Health*, and *Journal of Personalized Medicine*. His work has been honoured with multiple teaching awards from the University of Calgary and, in 2013, a Queen Elizabeth II Diamond Jubilee Medal. In 2017, he was awarded the CDSA-ACEI Tanis Doe Award for Canadian Disability Study and Culture from the Canadian Disabilities Studies Association.

Marc Workman participated in the Living Archives on Eugenics in Western Canada project as a research assistant while working on a PhD in the Department of Philosophy at the University of Alberta. A long-time disability rights activist, he has spent the last ten years volunteering for disability organizations including the Alliance for Equality of Blind Canadians, the Council of Canadians with Disabilities, and Barrier Free Canada. Professionally, Marc has held senior roles within the Canadian National Institute for the Blind, and he currently works as an executive advisor for the Government of Alberta. Additionally, he regularly guest lectures on disability-related topics at MacEwan University and the University of Alberta. He has published the "Report on the Inaugural Conference for Living Archives on Eugenics in Western Canada" (2010) and reviewed Jonathan Glover's *Choosing Children: Genes, Disability, and Design* for *Ethics — An International Journal of Social, Political, and Legal Philosophy*, 2007.

INDEX

Photographs indicated by page numbers in italics.